Schizophrenia as a Human Process

By HARRY STACK SULLIVAN, M.D.

Conceptions of Modern Psychiatry
The Interpersonal Theory of Psychiatry
The Psychiatric Interview
Clinical Studies in Psychiatry
Schizophrenia as a Human Process

Prepared under the auspices of
THE WILLIAM ALANSON WHITE PSYCHIATRIC FOUNDATION
COMMITTEE ON PUBLICATION OF SULLIVAN'S WRITINGS
Mabel Blake Cohen, M.D.   Dexter M. Bullard, M.D.
David McK. Rioch, M.D.   Otto Allen Will, M.D.

sapiens, and the species-identity of all the people with whom we are primarily concerned,— be they genius or imbecile, "saint" or "fiend incarnate", friend or foe, "sane" or "insane" x

This was presented in an approach to a theorem: Everyone ~~[crossed out]~~ and anyone ~~[crossed out]~~, is much more simply human than otherwise, more like everyone else than different, ~~from another person~~ and the data of interpersonal phenomena which may be ~~[crossed out]~~ derived in participant observation with him are relevant

Species Identity Theorem

This is a leaf from one of Sullivan's notebooks, dated about 1944. The clinical background for this "Species Identity Theorem"—formulated later as the "one-genus postulate"—is largely found in the papers presented in this book.

HARRY STACK SULLIVAN, M.D.

Schizophrenia as a Human Process

With Introduction and Commentaries
by HELEN SWICK PERRY

W·W·NORTON & COMPANY·INC·*New York*

COPYRIGHT © 1962 BY THE WILLIAM ALANSON WHITE
PSYCHIATRIC FOUNDATION

FIRST EDITION

LIBRARY OF CONGRESS CATALOG CARD NO. 61-11349

All Rights Reserved
Published simultaneously in the Dominion of Canada
by George J. McLeod Limited, Toronto

PRINTED IN THE UNITED STATES OF AMERICA
FOR THE PUBLISHERS BY THE VAIL-BALLOU PRESS, INC.
1 2 3 4 5 6 7 8 9

Contents

Preface

Plan of book.—This book covers all the major articles that Sullivan wrote from the beginning of his writing career (1924) through 1935, either through the articles themselves or in the Commentaries. From 1935 until the time of his death, there are a few other articles that deal centrally with the subject of schizophrenia, and the names of these articles are given below:

1. "The Language of Schizophrenia," in *Language and Thought in Schizophrenia: Collected Papers;* edited by J. S. Kasanin, M.D. (Berkeley and Los Angeles: Univ. of Calif. Press, 1944; pp. 4–15).

2. "Therapeutic Investigations in Schizophrenia," *Psychiatry* (1947) 10:121–125. This is an introductory statement to a series of three papers on schizophrenia, written by Herbert Staveren, Sarah S. Tower, and Robert A. Cohen; Sullivan had acted as their consultant on schizophrenic cases.

3. "Notes on Investigation, Therapy, and Education in Psychiatry and Their Relations to Schizophrenia," *Psychiatry* (1947) 10:271–280.

In addition, Sullivan's previously published books contain significant discussions of his later thinking on the schizophrenic process. In particular, chapters 19, 20, and 21 of *The Interpersonal Theory of Psychiatry* may be usefully read as an extension of this book; see also Lectures III, IV, and V of *Conceptions of Modern Psychiatry*, and the index entries for Schizophrenia in *Clinical Studies in Psychiatry* and *The Psychiatric Interview* (all published by Norton).

Acknowledgements.—My chief consultant at all stages of this book has been my husband, Stewart E. Perry. I should also like to mention my continuing debt to Patrick Mullahy who for over fifteen years has been the real expert on Sullivan's ideas and who continues to bring fresh insights to Sullivan's work whenever I talk to him. This is the first of the books published since Sullivan's death that does not carry the name of Mary Gavell as my collaborator; although geographic distance has made it impossible for us to collaborate intensively on this particular book, she has continued to lend official and unofficial aid, and her current and past staff on the journal *Psychiatry*—Gloria H. Parloff, Benita S. Harris, and Genevieve A. Highland—have participated in various ways in the preparation of this book. The tasks of bookmaking that could not be carried on long distance have been performed for me by various people living in this area who have cheerfully mobilized their energies for emergency proofing, typing, pasting, and so on; I would like to mention particularly Sandra Rudnick, who has followed the book through a three-year period and substantially assisted in the proofing; also Mrs. Lonavene Mc-Gaughey, Margaret Hamwey, and Mrs. Erica Gerschenkron have ably assisted me at various stages.

In tracing out the historical development of Sullivan and his ideas, I have been heavily dependent on the help of librarians. I would like to mention particularly the staff of the Widener Library, the Law Library, and the Medical Library of Harvard University; and Mrs. Loretta F. Smith, Librarian at the Massachusetts Mental Health Center. In addition Mrs. Elisabeth A. Dexter and Lewis A. Dexter made it possible for me to use the Boston Athenaeum, where I found certain books unobtainable in other libraries in the area. Some monographs, which were not easily available at any library, were generously loaned me by Mr. James I. Sullivan and Professor Gordon W. Allport from their private collections. In the gathering of informal information on Sullivan's intellectual and personal biography as background for this book, I am grateful for the cooperation of Mr. J. Ruthwin Evans, Professor Harold D. Lasswell, William V. Silverberg, M.D., Mrs. Edward Nash, and others.

On behalf of the William Alanson White Psychiatric Foundation, I wish to make grateful acknowledgement to the following publishers:

The *American Journal of Psychiatry*, published by the American Psychiatric Association, for permission to publish "Schizophrenia: Its Conservative and Malignant Features"; "Peculiarity of Thought in Schizophrenia"; "The Onset of Schizophrenia";

"Tentative Criteria of Malignancy in Schizophrenia"; "Research in Schizophrenia"; "Socio-Psychiatric Research: Its Implications for the Schizophrenia Problem and for Mental Hygiene"; "The Modified Psychoanalytic Treatment of Schizophrenia"; and "Psychiatric Training as a Prerequisite to Psychoanalytic Practice."

The Johns Hopkins Press, for permission to publish "Schizophrenic Individuals as a Source of Data for Comparative Investigation of Personality," from *Proceedings, Second Colloquium on Personality Investigation;* Baltimore: The Johns Hopkins Press, 1930.

MD Publications, Inc., for permission to publish "Environmental Factors and Course Under Treatment of Schizophrenia," from the *Medical Journal and Record.*

The Macmillan Company, for "Mental Disorders," from the *Encyclopaedia of the Social Sciences,* volume 10, copyright 1933 by The Macmillan Company and used with their permission.

The Psychiatric Quarterly, for permission to publish "The Common Field of Research and Clinical Psychiatry."

Routledge & Kegan Paul Ltd. of London, for permission to publish "Archaic Sexual Culture and Schizophrenia," from *Sexual Reform Congress: Proceedings of the Third Congress of the World League for Sexual Reform,* edited by Norman Haire.

The Williams and Wilkins Company, for permission to publish "The Relation of Onset to Outcome in Schizophrenia," from *Schizophrenia [Dementia Praecox]: An Investigation of the Most Recent Advances* (1931).

Full bibliographic information on each of these articles will be found at the beginning of each selection in this book.

H.S.P.

Introduction

AMONGST clinicians, Sullivan is probably best known for his early work with schizophrenics at the Sheppard and Enoch Pratt Hospital in Towson, Maryland. Yet this fame has been largely legendary, since the only full record of this work is found scattered through various professional journals and monographs published more than twenty-five years ago and in an unpublished book written in the thirties, *Personal Psychopathology*. In this present book of selected papers, I have tried to reconstruct this work by bringing together what I consider to be the most crucial of these papers.

In part, the fact that these papers on schizophrenia were not brought together by Sullivan reflects his reluctance to set schizophrenia apart from living itself; in part, also, he came to feel, increasingly in the last ten years of his life, that the main implication of his work was in the field of social psychology—in the wide spectrum of preventive measures within the society itself. Remedial attempts, he felt, could lessen the incidence of schizophrenia in young adolescents. I have tried to keep to the spirit of this thinking in selecting the title of the book, for Sullivan put schizophrenic process into the human perspective.

Since participant observation was a central tool in Sullivan's approach to the patient, it seems appropriate at this juncture to introduce two central biographical givens in this man's approach to mental order and disorder. I am indebted to a cultural anthropologist, Mark Zborowski, for alerting me to the importance of the first given: One of the significant differences between Freud's and Sullivan's approach to mental illness is implicit in their differences in cultural background. Freud came from a middle-class Viennese, Jewish background; Sullivan came from a Catholic, Irish-American family. Freud had the orientation of the typical middle-class neurotic of his day and time. Sullivan had first-hand information on the peculiarly isolating experience of a young

Irish Catholic boy, son of an immigrant father, growing up in a farming area where all the other families were Protestant and mostly old Yankee. Freud's thinking reflects a Talmudic background, scholarly, thoughtful, and deep; Sullivan's thinking is almost Joycean in its intricate processes, rich and varied, occasionally almost poetic, but difficult and complex. It seems to me that this biographical given for each of these men clarifies the contribution of each. It is academic to set their thinking in opposition: They came out of different societies; and out of his own experience, each posed the problem and sought some solution. In this selection from the early writings, it becomes clear that Sullivan began his work with the findings of Freud; although he moved far away from Freud's thinking in many areas, he never saw himself as being in opposition to Freud.

The second biographical given, which derives mainly from the first, concerns Sullivan's exposure to psychological trauma in his growing-up years. Out of his own cultural experience, he early came to see that the young person growing up in a new and conflictful society was exposed to stresses that were of a substantially different ilk from those undergone in the older, European community. The gifted adolescent who was, for whatever reason, deprived of the good things of life in this new country, this 'democracy,' often found himself forced to make a choice between a life of crime and mental disorder. The exposure to the danger of a schizophrenic break in the early years was a ubiquitous one, Sullivan postulated; most people rode through such an acute break in adolescence, without any clear awareness on their part, or the part of others, that such a danger had existed; but the strains were there, the danger was omnipresent, the catastrophes were monumental and on the increase. Sullivan has made many references, in his published and unpublished writings and in his communcations with colleagues and friends, to his personal knowledge of this kind of stress in his own growing-up years. An interesting sidelight on the kinds of stresses that a child experiences in a community in which he is an outsider is found in Sullivan's report that he did not speak with an Irish brogue until after his own encounter with adolescent turmoil; he had successfully spoken the language of his peers, school children in central New

York State, until—through an experience of reintegration—he
accepted the reality of his beginnings; thereafter, he lapsed into the
Irish brogue on occasions throughout the rest of his life.[1] I, myself, have had occasion in the last year and a half to study the
saliency of Sullivan's approach to schizophrenic process in the
adolescent. In the course of participating in a study of adolescents
on the adult wards of a mental hospital, I have come to know
rather well over forty adolescents, many of them clearly evi-
dencing schizophrenic process. Since this patient population comes
from all the varied subcultures and classes of any large Eastern
city in the United States, I have had occasion to experience in a
participant way many of the same anxieties and insecurities that
Sullivan reported on thirty years ago; needless to say, I have also
relived some of my own growing-up experience. It becomes increasingly clear to me that our culture and institutions are still
largely at sea as to how the differences in values and customs in
our diversified society can be translated into a productive experience for the adolescent, rather than a devastating and disorienting
experience in hiding the fact that one is somehow 'different' in
a shameful way. In essence, we seemed to have fashioned a society
in which there is a mythical, ideal American—an ideal painfully
removed from the possible achievement of most of us. As Sullivan
notes, most of us have but the "peace and quiet of fresh thistle-
down on a windy day."

The question is often asked, Did Sullivan himself have any
analytic experience? As an additional and pertinent biographical
datum, I would like to note here Sullivan's formal training as I
know it: His first analytic experience consisted of about 75 hours
with a Chicago analyst [2] in the winter of 1916–1917; needless to
say, there was not much analytic training going on in the United
States generally at that time. In 1930, he began his formal analytic
training in New York City, with Clara Thompson, M.D., who
had herself trained with Sandor Ferenczi in Europe. I have included, at the beginning of this book, Clara Thompson's biographical evaluation of Sullivan, written at the time of his death;

---

[1] I am indebted to William V. Silverberg, M.D., for a clarification of this
phenomenon in Sullivan's speech.
[2] The identity of this analyst is not certainly known.

part of its importance is found, of course, in the fact of this relationship between them.

There are, of course, other biographical givens. In 1922, for instance, Sullivan came under the intimate tutelage of William Alanson White, M.D., the superintendent of St. Elizabeths Hospital in Washington. White was one of the early proponents of the new dynamic psychiatry of Freud, but this was tempered with an important knowledgeability of the current stirrings in American social psychology. Many personal encounters with American social psychologists were made possible for Sullivan by the good offices of White and Smith Ely Jelliffe, M.D., both of whom were important figures in Sullivan's early intellectual development. I have included in the commentaries and in the next section of this introduction, any of the pertinent memorabilia of Sullivan's intellectual development that have come to my attention in the course of work on this book.

The Philosophy of the Ward at Sheppard-Pratt

In the years from 1923 to 1930, Sullivan was an Assistant Physician and then Director of Clinical Research at Sheppard-Pratt. During the latter part of his stay at the Hospital, he designed and established a receiving ward for male schizophrenics. A good deal of legend, often without basis in fact, exists about this ward and Sullivan's work at Sheppard. This first came to my attention about a year and a half ago when various psychiatric residents in the mental hospital where I am currently employed expressed great interest in this ward at Sheppard. My own answers were often vague and ill-formed; I had certain general impressions, but few facts. These questions have prodded me into an attempt to reconstruct those years and the philosophy of that ward. I, myself, did not know Sullivan until 1946, three years before his death, so that I have been largely dependent on collateral information, although certain personal conversations with Sullivan and a multitude of impressions about him—gained in part from listening to his voice, on recordings, for almost a decade since his death—have added all kinds of fringe impressions to this account. Most of the information may be found scattered among his published and unpublished papers—some of it is included in the papers in this book. But Sullivan spoke of his own role at Sheppard in a rather diffident way, so that it is not always easy to get any feel for the situation. Of crucial importance to me in recapturing the quality of Sullivan in action at Sheppard have been two long conversations I have had with Mr. J. Ruthwin Evans, who worked with Sullivan at Sheppard, chiefly in connection with the hydrotherapy department. Mr. Ray Pope, too, who also worked on Sullivan's ward at Sheppard, talked with me some years ago about the Sheppard ward; unfortunately, I did not make notes of these conversations, and Mr. Pope is now dead. Two other people I have talked with, both now dead, knew Sullivan in those early years, Clara Thompson, M.D., and Mr. Donald Reeve, his printer at The Lord Baltimore Press and lifelong friend. Their insights have been valuable to me, and I can only regret that I did not interview them more formally on certain crucial information that they were in possession of, while I still had the opportunity.

Sullivan went to Sheppard in 1923 as an Assistant Physician. In 1925, he was made Director of Clinical Research there, and he remained in that post until June, 1930. Actually, he was Associate Professor of Psychiatry at the University of Maryland School of Medicine for the same period as he was in research at Sheppard; and he continued to lecture at that school until 1933, probably retaining some significant informal contact with Sheppard until about the same time, although he had established himself in private practice in New York City in 1931.

Sometime near the end of the period that Sullivan was formally connected with Sheppard, probably for the last twelve months, Sullivan established a special receiving service at Sheppard. The social structure of the ward was drawn to his specifications, but it was based on certain changes he had already partially incorporated on other wards at Sheppard. This special ward, consisting of six beds (three beds in each of two rooms separated from each other by intercommunicating sitting-rooms and a corridor), was housed in a relatively new building which was separated from the other buildings. There were several wards in this building (75 beds in all), and Sullivan's influence on the other wards was probably also considerable. But the one ward was run by Sullivan in such a way that it was uniquely cut off from various usual hierarchical structures that exist in any hospital. The freedom with which Sullivan was allowed to run this ward was quite remarkable; Sullivan gave the credit for this freedom to the superintendent, Ross McClure Chapman, M.D., who undoubtedly displayed a great deal of courage in allowing the independent functioning of this ward. In the first place, the ward was entirely removed from the supervision of the Nursing Service; in fact, no woman was ever allowed on this ward. There were six attendants (plus various relief personnel), working in two 12-hour shifts. The day shift was composed of four attendants; the night of two. These attendants were hand-picked by Sullivan from the hospital at large; some of them may even have been hired directly by him. Although they were low in the hierarchy, as all attendants were and still are in mental hospitals, these attendants were trained in an intensive way by Sullivan to become full-fledged assistants. Their pay was low, but they came to have high morale and to operate in a truly professional manner. At least two of them underwent personal analysis; and probably all of them had more than passing opportunity to have some benefit from analytic procedures.

During the same period that Sullivan had this special ward, he maintained a private residence near the hospital grounds. This house became the informal setting for the discussion of the day's work (or the night's work) of the attendants. The house was open at all times to the attendants for talk and for frequent meals. Thus Sullivan formally established what has existed informally for many years as an adjunct to the mental hospital—a bar or a lunchroom near a mental hospital, whether private or state, where the lower-echelon staff have their own 'staff conferences,' somewhat more rough-and-ready than the psychoanalytically oriented staff conferences of doctors within the hospital, but rich in the data of living on the wards with the patient. There was one difference in the after-work meetings of Sheppard, however; Sullivan, the psychiatrist, was often an important participant in these informal and continuing sessions. (Before he acquired the house, the sessions with attendants took place in other settings, including a private clubhouse.)

In elevating the attendant to this important position in the social system, Sullivan used the principle of *"similia similibus curantur."* He came to feel that those attendants who were successful with schizophrenics were people who were potentially schizophrenic patients with good prognosis. This principle was certainly related to Sullivan's feeling that some of his skill with schizophrenics came importantly from his own early encounter with schizophrenic process.

Sullivan's reasons for eliminating the registered nurse from contact with the patient stemmed in part from certain important theoretical considerations which continue to merit attention in terms of the present-day hierarchy in the hospital. To expect a patient who had suffered humiliation in his family and the world at large to find a cure in an institution riddled with outworn codes of hierarchical values seemed nonsensical to Sullivan. In addition, Sullivan's ward was composed of male schizophrenics. On a male ward, the registered female nurse may become the prototype of the high-status female in an inferior male society—a condition which is still all too evident on a male ward in almost any state hospital, where the high-status doctor seldom appears. In addition, of course, the profession of nursing, as one of the oldest professions for women, has certain inherent superordinate-subordinate standards that may militate against the establishment of what Sullivan thought necessary—a sympathetic personal environment for the patient. The ingrained nursing attitude, as Sullivan has described it, of "my Profession, right or wrong, but always my Profession" was so strong that "only by a personal personality upheaval is she [the nurse] apt to come again to that intuitive grasp of personal totalities that was once her property in common with all preadolescents." It should be remembered that Sullivan's criticisms applied to the female nurse on a male ward; certainly there is important data now available that the female nurse-therapist has an important contribution to make, at least with female patients.[3]

In addition, and perhaps more importantly than any other factor, Sullivan found the training in the medical professions per

[3] See, for instance, Gwen E. Tudor (Will), "A Sociopsychiatric Nursing Approach to Intervention in a Problem of Mutual Withdrawal on a Mental Hospital Ward," *Psychiatry* (1952) 15:193–217.

se—including nursing—somewhat handicapping for the field of psychiatry. In 1929, he reported on the difficulty of the medical training for psychiatric training, in part, as follows:

> There come to me physicians seeking insight into problems of the mind. They come to me as well trained physicians and therefore with an acquired inability to understand anything that I say to them. I don't believe that if they stayed with me from now on until Gabriel blows his hornpipes that they will acquire much notion of what I am talking about—or privately give a damn. They are already educated, they have a degree of Doctor of Medicine, and they have a whole system of ideas that takes its origin from certain misunderstandings about physical chemistry—on things which they probably don't realize are physico-chemical subjects—and they are pretty well organized.[4]

The above statement was made to a group of social scientists in which Sullivan was one of the few medical men present. I would suggest, as an aside, that he had more irritation with the scotoma of medical and nursing training than with any particular carriers of that culture.

Additionally, there is the biographical fact that Sullivan's first significant experience in training others was in terms of the attendants at Sheppard. It is often rewarding to teach the uninitiated, those low on the totem pole. That Sullivan found this an eminently rewarding experience is reported in various places in these papers and in others not included here. Retrospectively Sullivan referred to these attendants at Sheppard as "the most satisfactory employees that I have ever been able to make contact with."

From the beginning of his work with attendants, Sullivan began the practice of having one of his assistants (for the attendants became operationally trained assistants) in the room with him when he talked to the patient. Although this was not an absolute requirement, Sullivan often found it reassuring to the patient. In the first paper in this book, Sullivan reports: "The careful use of questions addressed to the patient, and to a trained assistant in the hearing of the patient, has been found effective in stimulating perception, analysis, and resynthesis of psychotic content." It

---

[4] *Proceedings*, Second Colloquium, cited in the book proper.

was of course, incidentally, an excellent way to rapidly train his assistants in his own approach to patients—a fact that undoubtedly contributed to the consensus between all three of them, the doctor, the attendant, and the patient—as to the therapeutic process.

Mr. Evans, who was centrally involved in the hydrotherapy work, has reported to me that occasionally he would be assigned to the task of escorting a particular patient into Sullivan's office and would remain there through the interview. More than once, a patient would become agitated in the course of the interview and might even slap Sullivan. The assistant was not allowed to move in on the patient in such a situation; Sullivan would remain completely unruffled to all outward appearances, often asking the patient in a quiet and understanding way, "Well, do you feel better now?" The only time that Sullivan would become extremely agitated with one of the attendants would be in the event that the attendant would strike the patient as a reaction to the patient's assaultive behavior. He impressed upon his employees the fact that the patient was apt to strike someone with whom he wished to make significant contact. On at least one occasion, Sullivan told a valued employee that he felt like striking this employee because the employee had, in a moment of considerable provocation, hit back at a patient. At the same time, Sullivan did not tolerate violence on the patient's part. "If there is violence," he said, "it is to be discouraged, *unemotionally*, and in the expressed interest of the general or special good. If, as is often the case, violence arises from panic, the situation must be dealt with by the physician." [5] It should be borne in mind that Sullivan had a ward of schizophrenic patients and that he did not tolerate on the ward the typical mischievous behavior of certain manic illness; contrary to most clinicians, Sullivan did not think that a manic patient livened up a ward of schizophrenics in any constructive fashion—a notion still held by many personnel in mental hospitals.

In general, Sullivan spoke out for a homogeneous ward—of

[5] In this section of the introduction, all quotations are from "The Modified Psychoanalytic Treatment of Schizophrenia," which is included in this book.

one sex, one general age, and so on. "The procedure of treatment begins with removing the patient from the situation in which he is developing difficulty," Sullivan notes, "to a situation in which he is encouraged to renew efforts at adjustment with others. This might well be elsewhere than to an institution dealing with a cross-section of the psychotic population; certainly, it should not be a large ward of mental patients of all sorts and ages." Although women patients are in general more comfortable with men therapists, and male patients more comfortable with females, Sullivan pointed out that the goal is not exclusively to make the patient comfortable. With the same sex, patients are not as comfortable, "but they are correspondingly more successful in achieving actual rather than fantastic results."

In particular, Sullivan stressed to his assistants the importance of the first 24 hours of any patient on a ward. He discouraged the practice, still prevalent on the wards that I have been familiar with, of all staff attempting to catch an early glimpse of the new patient. Since Sullivan's ward finally came to be separated from the rest of the hospital, this procedure for respecting the new patient's privacy was easier to carry out than in most hospital settings. At the same time, the assistants were encouraged to spend a great deal of time with the new patient in a close and reassuring way and to be very much aware of everything that happened to him. This data from the first 24 hours was carefully noted and might well be considered as crucial throughout the patient's stay. This is of course centrally tied in with Sullivan's dictum that the first hour of any analytic procedure is an important one, that the psychiatrist has then an opportunity to see the patient in the particular and unique situation of meeting for the first time a person who is both a stranger and an expert—the doctor; this significant opportunity cannot happen again during the course of a long and detailed inquiry. In a hospital setting, of course, the data of initial encounter comprises 24 hours, in which the patient makes his first encounter with the spectrum of daily living in a new setting—an institution. Therefore the data for study is more complex and in many ways more rewarding. It was this kind of thinking that led Sullivan to impress on his assistants that the life of the patient on the ward was in many ways more crucial to the patient's progress than the single hour a day usually spent with the doctor. In some cases, Sullivan recommended that the attendant, or trained assistant, be largely left with the care of the patient: "If . . . the patient seems obviously to increase in comfort without professional attention after the introduction to care, the physician can profitably await developments. A considerable proportion of these patients proceed in this really human environment to the degree of social recovery that permits analysis, without much contact with the supervising physician."

But the time spent with the doctor was also subjected to careful investigation. At Sheppard, Sullivan installed a microphone on his desk, concealed by an ornamental piece, so that his conversations with the patient could be recorded. At the time of the establishment of the special ward, this material was sound-tracked down to another floor where recordings were made by Sullivan's secretary. Even before the establishment of the special ward, however, Sullivan had transcriptions made of conversations with patients and collected various kinds of documents from the patients (see, for instance, "Peculiarity of Thought in Schizophrenia" in this book). This is probably one of the early instances of verbatim records being made of interviews with schizophrenic patients. Sullivan might term the thought of the schizophrenic "peculiar," but *thought* it was; by his work, schizophrenic thinking moved forever out of the simple "word salad" class.

It is impossible to discuss the ward at Sheppard without pausing briefly to consider the nature of the society created between patients and personnel; this is a subject on which there has been a good deal of idle and pseudopsychoanalytic speculation. It has, for instance, been termed a "homosexual society." In terms of Sullivan's later theory on developmental eras, the milieu of the ward was modeled on the *preadolescent society* in order to provide the schizophrenic patient with what Sullivan thought was the crucial experience needed for recovery. Undoubtedly Sullivan's belief in the importance of the preadolescent era as a prelude for more mature living had its origins in his own life pattern; he felt himself crippled by his isolation from boys his own age while he was growing up. This belief based on personal experience was strengthened by the clinical experience at Sheppard in which he felt patients responded to the positive ingredients found in a therapeutically controlled preadolescent society. At the same time, it is important to know that the ward was run in a completely professional manner; the assistants were encouraged to form a meaningful relationship with the patient, but no sexually entangling relationship between patients and hospital personnel was countenanced. One of the personnel connected with that ward has informed me that, after years of subsequent experience in mental hospitals, he could report that the personnel of Sullivan's ward had a degree of integrity and awareness in this area that is seldom found on mental-hospital wards.

I do not mean to imply by this that homosexuality was avoided as a subject for discussion on the ward. As a matter of fact, one of the therapeutic tools in general use on the ward was often a pre-designed discussion between two attendants about some experience they had had in growing up which paralleled the possible experience of the patient; sometimes this would be a homosexual experience. In one of the papers here presented, Sullivan reports a rapid social recovery in a very difficult patient which was effected by such a discussion; two attendants said in the patient's hearing that a particular kind of unpleasant experience had happened to them; they said "in passing that it was too bad that so many people who had that sort of experience didn't seem able to think about anything else, and so never discovered that there was a much better way of handling things." This is an undoubted reference to some form of homosexual encounter which the patient had considered infrahuman.[6]

Throughout the articles in this book, Sullivan calls for some kind of sexual reform in cultural attitudes transmitted to the young, as a way of avoiding the tragic waste in the form of schizophrenic breaks (or criminal careers) among the promising of each new generation. He tackled the problem from various angles, including, for instance, an important look at the work of Edward Kempf with infrahuman primates (cited in the Commentary on "Peculiarity of Thought in Schizophrenia") from which Sullivan obviously derived certain hypotheses for viewing sexual behavior and worries in the young human. That this area

[6] See "Socio-Psychiatric Research" in this book.

of life remains one that society continues to "selectively inat-tend" can be amply documented by anyone who is familiar with the adolescents still incarcerated in our public institutions, whether state hospitals or prisons; there seems to be little consensual vali-dation among either professional or custodial staff and/or the family as to how the sex interests and behavior of young adoles-cents in the institution are to be viewed or handled. In Sullivan's case material, it occupies a position of focal attention on an observational rather than a theoretical level. This central focus is undoubtedly derived, in large part, from Sullivan's participant observation of the ongoing social process on the ward at Shep-pard.

An Overview of Sullivan's Intellectual Biography

When I first set out upon the work of going through Sullivan's published papers, I looked upon it as the least challenging of the tasks that I had undertaken on the posthumous papers. It has proved to be anything but that. Now that I near the end of the task, I find myself wondering how I can adequately communicate to the reader the excitement I have felt as I have attempted in some small part to find the tracings, the beginnings of Sullivan's ideas in the books that he read; yet at the same time, neither space nor my own knowledge is sufficient to do other than suggest to the reader—mainly in the Commentaries—some of the rewards to be found in his own journey through the writings of Sullivan's intellectual companions. What is needed, in essence, is a study of the scientific mind at work that parallels in its imagination and its scope John Livingston Lowes' study of Coleridge's poems in *The Road to Xanadu*.[7] Lowes' study shows that words and phrases from Coleridge's reading are retained in the creative well until they are fragmented and changed; when they emerge, they are used like bits of colored glass worn by the sea to color the poet's own observation in a new and transmuted effect. Sullivan synthesized his readings and clinical observations in some com-parable process.

Most of Sullivan's sources are reported in his own writings,

[7] John Livingston Lowes, *The Road to Xanadu: A Study in the Ways of the Imagination;* New York: Vintage Books, 1959.

particularly in the early papers, some of which are represented in this book. As time went on, Sullivan cited fewer and fewer of his sources. Since his later work (particularly the posthumous books) is much better known, a widespread criticism has emerged that Sullivan acted as if he were not basically indebted to certain thinkers, notably, for instance, Freud, Meyer, Cooley, and so on. Nothing could be further from the truth. In the early papers, not all of which are given here, Sullivan painstakingly traced his own areas of agreement and disagreement with a wide variety of thinkers. His reading was extensive, intensive, and catholic, and continued throughout his lifetime. As early as 1929, for instance, he reported on 113 books in an annotated bibliography for the *Proceedings* of the Second Colloquium on Personality Investigation (cited later in the book); these range from *The Polish Peasant in Europe and America* by William I. Thomas and Florian Znaniecki (New York: Knopf, 1927) to *Lectures on Conditioned Reflexes* by Ivan P. Pavlov (New York: International Publishers, 1928); and from the Gifford Lectures for 1927 by the Plumian Professor of Astronomy at the University of Cambridge (A. S. Eddington, *The Nature of the Physical World;* New York: Macmillan, 1929) to the *Sexual Life of Savages* by Bronislaw Malinowski (New York: Harcourt, Brace, 1927). When one adds to these titles, the writings referred to in the early papers, and the books reviewed by him in professional journals for the same period, there is clear evidence that Sullivan spent great hunks of time in reading and studying during the years at Sheppard.

When one begins systematically to go back over Sullivan's readings—whether Charles Cooley or Alfred Korzybski, George Herbert Mead or Edward Kempf—one finds Sullivan everywhere; or, to state it more accurately, one finds these men's concepts and words—as well as many others—everywhere in Sullivan. To suppose that Sullivan's contribution and thinking, however, was simply a composite of many men would be to miss the process of creation; for each of many thinkers supplied ideas and concepts, words and phrases which went through a transformation in the sea of Sullivan's clinical observation and knowledge. An amusing example of this is found in *The Interpersonal Theory of Psychiatry* (pp. 329 ff.), where Sullivan obviously has unintentionally wedded the characters in Mark Twain's story of *The Mysterious Stranger* with some actual clinical experience in an inexplicable way; yet the end result "makes sense."

At some level, Sullivan's final contribution was as American as Mark Twain. Once the son of Irish immigrants had explored the important European intellectual forebears, had become 'correct' in his learning of the great sources for his chosen task in psychiatry, he came to be at home in the intellectual atmosphere of America. Much of his divergence from formal psychoanalytic concepts in the direction of American social psychology was brought about by the fact that he came to feel intellectually comfortable with the phrases and words of Edward Sapir, Charles Cooley, Ruth Benedict, and others. The emphasis among these thinkers was on the sturdy development of the mainstreams of American thought; all of them had participantly observed the American scene. Whatever a scientist might observe in Europe, these people were not to be swept away from making their own observations, phrasing their own discoveries. Their intellectual leanings were literary, but it was the literature of simple observation found in the plain living and high thinking of the Concord, Massachusetts, group—Bronson Alcott, Thoreau, and Emerson. Such an intellectual heritage was directly and obviously Cooley's, as evidenced in his writings, and much of Cooley's unpretentiousness of insight and observation made sense to Sullivan in terms of his approach to the observation of patients. Whatever intellectual pretensions Sullivan might evidence at times in his theoretical discourses—which gradually simplified over the years—his *observation* of people from the beginning was within the framework of a democratic society. There was an acceptance of the basic dignity of mankind, which could only flourish in a new society. In discussing the qualifications of professional personnel for working with schizophrenics, Sullivan noted, as he did elsewhere, the importance of the living experience of the therapist in terms of the task: ". . . sadly enough, those to whom life has brought but a pleasant flood of trifling problems without any spectacular disturbances, who have grown up in quiet backwashes far from the industrial revolution, within the tinted half-lights of the passing times—these are afield in undertaking the schizophrenia problem." [8]

There was a restlessness about Sullivan, a drive toward the pragmatic, which is curiously American. There must be some solution for the problems that beset the young, for the old problems of war and peace that continually plague mankind. He sought a solution in many ways. Something had to work; one must make "current remedial attempts." This pragmatic approach found certain symbolic expression in his recurring interest in mechanical things—in finding better and better ways to record what went on in the psychiatric interview, for instance; in the end, he was as skillful with devising electronics equipment as he was in ferreting out the simple and workable way to turn the patient in a new and more hopeful direction.

This restless energy found strong and sympathetic encouragement among social scientists within the compass of the years at Sheppard. Sullivan's first important collaboration with social scientists probably took place at the First Colloquium on Personality Investigation, held in December, 1928. This was a meeting between psychiatrists and social scientists, held under the auspices of the American Psychiatric Association; William Alanson White as Chairman and Sullivan as Secretary were important figures at this meeting. A Second Colloquium took place a year later, and part of these *Proceedings* are reproduced later in the book. The *Proceedings* of these Colloquia are even today exciting documents and rich with hypotheses not yet explored. Edward Sapir, W. I. Thomas, Gordon W. Allport, Harold Lasswell, Sheldon Glueck, L. K. Frank, Arnold Gesell, David Levy—these are but a few of the people who significantly participated in these conferences. The papers and the informal discussion have about them the feel of action research—the desire to find ways for remedial action from informed hunches; at the same time, there is great emphasis on the necessity for the systematic collection of data, with Sapir noting that the "life history must be the document *par excellence* which interests us. . . ."

Since the one-genus postulate, as mentioned in the Frontispiece,

[8] See "The Modified Psychoanalytic Treatment of Schizophrenia," in this book.

is centrally important to the thinking of this book, I will make some brief reference to its historical antecedents—not in terms of its long philosophical history but to its somewhat immediate genealogy for Sullivan. Implicit in this postulate is the moving away from the old dichotomies between love and hate, between aggression and passivity, between good and bad, and so on. In the description of the Sheppard ward given earlier, I have noted Sullivan's clinical interpretation of the schizophrenic's assaultiveness toward a particular attendant as related to the patient's need for closeness with that same person. But this is somewhat more complicated with Sullivan than the simple explanation that the schizophrenic fears closeness. In quality it belongs to the thinking of Cooley: "[For the social, imaginative being as distinguished from simple, animal tendencies], hostility ceases to be a simple emotion due to a simple stimulus, and breaks up into innumerable hostile sentiments associated with highly imaginative personal ideas. In this mentally higher form it may be regarded as hostile sympathy, or a hostile comment on sympathy. That is to say, we enter by sympathy or personal imagination into the state of mind of others, or think we do, and if the thoughts we find there are injurious to or uncongenial with the ideas we are already cherishing, we feel a movement of anger." [9] Later on in the same passage, Cooley cites Thoreau: " 'you cannot receive a shock unless you have an electric affinity for that which shocks you,' and . . . 'He who receives an injury is to some extent an accomplice of the wrong-doer.' "

The focus here is the interpersonal situation, and the participants—regardless of their outward strife—have a basic understanding, because they belong to humanity. They interact humanly on the basis of their commonality, regardless of the nature of the interaction. With the assaultive patient, then, this "movement of anger" may find direct expression, particularly against the person for whom he feels a surge of sympathy—which, again, arises from both participants.

[9] Charles H. Cooley, *Human Nature and the Social Order;* Glencoe, Ill.: The Free Press, 1956; p. 266 ff. The Thoreau quotation is from *A Week on the Concord and Merrimack Rivers,* Boston, Houghton, Mifflin, revised 1883; pp. 303, 328.

I do not mean to imply by this that Sullivan's attitude towards the patient's antipathy was an intellectual conviction derived from Cooley or that it was any simple philosophy of turning the other cheek; it was rather Sullivan's conviction that the schizophrenic was a human being and that an observant person could participantly understand him; at some stage this conviction met Cooley's mind, found support for the conceptualization, and fused the whole into a working hypothesis eventuating in the one-genus postulate. Later on, in the same chapter as cited above, Cooley makes a statement that has more than a passing similarity to Sullivan's postulate: "It is the tendency of modern life, by educating the imagination and rendering all sorts of people conceivable, to discredit the sweeping conclusions of impulsive thought—as, for instance, that all who commit violence or theft are hateful ill-doers, and nothing more—and to make us feel the fundamental likeness of human nature wherever found" (p. 283). Without laboring the point, I would like to note that this kind of thinking and expression has its roots deep in American democratic ideals, and that these same ideals, in part through the work of Bronson Alcott, for instance, interpenetrated and affected, for example, the thinking of John Dewey—who from another direction also offered intellectual affinity for Sullivan's viewpoint. In some such complex and intricate network, Sullivan found great support among American thinkers for many of his formulations and contributions in psychiatry. In the Commentaries, I have attempted to suggest other avenues for further exploration.

A NOTE ON SULLIVAN'S PROSE STYLE

So many people have commented to me about Sullivan's prose style that I am moved to comment on it myself. Some people think that the style is peculiarly difficult, or even practically incomprehensible. Other people have indicated that the posthumous books were too heavily edited, or not edited enough. I offer no particular apology for what was done with the posthumous papers; in general, Mary Gavell and I struggled through the sentences to the point where we believed that we understood what Sullivan was saying and that we could, striving to keep drastic changes in content to an absolute minimum, translate for the reader into relatively parsable sentences. Through the years, and through thousands of Sullivan's sentences, off tape and on, I have finally come to feel in large measure devoted to his prose style. Certainly he was obscure at times; he had private grudges; many of his caustic allusions are bitter when understood, but are so obscure that they are often lost. Such sentences tend to lessen clarity from time to time.

But in the most intricate of his thinking, he is up against the inadequacy of the language itself for expressing other than the most simple of cause and effect relationships; the copulative verb, for instance, is in many instances tantamount to an inaccuracy in terms of scientific expression. Tolstoy has commented brilliantly on the search for simple cause and effect, innate in human nature:

The combination of phenomena is beyond the grasp of the human intellect. But the impulse to seek causes is innate in the soul of man. And the human intellect, with no inkling of the immense variety and complexity of circumstances conditioning a phenomenon, any one of which may be separately conceived of as the cause of it, snatches at the first and most easily understood approximation, and says here is the cause.[10]

This is a search that Sullivan attempted to discourage. He thought in terms of multiple feedbacks in any situation; it was impossible to weight all these processes, for what one saw in behavior was the end result, what he termed the "vector." In order to express the simultaneity of these processes, he often was forced to use complex sentences, with many different subordinate clauses in which he attempted to avoid weighting in terms of relative importance; also he employed "etc." in the same way that Korzybski did to indicate the open-endedness of most such simultaneous antecedents for any given result. He was obviously directly affected by Korzybski's writing early in his career; but the intellectual conviction seemed to have antedated his formal knowledge of Korzybski.

[10] Leo Tolstoy, *War and Peace;* Modern Library edition by Random House, Inc.; p. 928. I am indebted to a physical scientist, William G. Schlecht for calling this to my attention in connection with a similar point made by Edward M. Schrock in *Quality Control and Statistical Methods* [New York: Reinhold Publishing Corp., 1957], who cited the same passage from Tolstoy.

Some of the finenesses of Sullivan's style I have 'edited out' in these published papers, as well as in the earlier books. In this way, I have somewhat vulgarized his style, which has considerable meaning from a philosophical point of view. He was an innovator in scientific writing in many ways, rather than a murderer of the King's English. As an English major long ago, in undergraduate school, I might take exception to the particular way in which he tried to correct some of the inadequacies in the language; but I am at the same time in awe of his grasp of language and of the skill with which he selected out certain words, many of which he borrowed, of course, such as Storch's "uncanny"— giving it a quality in terms of schizophrenic-like experience that is unerringly correct, in my estimation. He could never be accused of constructing a sloppy sentence; nor did he ever forget his point, although the intervening digression, particularly on records, might run to a page in length, when transcribed; the transcriber might have difficulty in remembering and linking up the thought; but Sullivan had kept his finger on the point where the digression occurred; and eventually, he returned to the exact spot. A friend once remarked to me that Sullivan's sentences often have the quality of cut diamonds; one reads them, finds them exciting, and fully understandable; but perhaps a year later, one looks at the same sentence and finds that the light has fallen on another facet which did not appear in the earlier light; and in many sentences this quality of finding new facets seems to go on indefinitely. I have discovered that this is true, even in the posthumous volumes, where I may have tampered with part of the wording and so felt, at the time, quite in command of the thought; later I would discover that I had somehow missed some facet of the sentence (which by luck had magically survived my pencil)— a discovery which has often been unnerving to me, when I have realized that I had operated without a complete X-ray. In many ways, I find Sullivan's prose Joycean in this respect; and in my own thinking I relate it to the Irish mind. Both Joyce and Sullivan took off from Freud in different directions, but with a common cultural bias.

Lowes has written of the poet's creative process in *The Road to Xanadu.* But he inevitably links it to creative process, wherever it is found in the human search, including as an example the field of science. He notes that the moment of creative achievement in science, too, is reached by "accumulating masses of facts which [point] to a momentous conclusion. But they [point] through a maze of baffling inconsistencies." Sullivan's careful recording of schizophrenic thought and communication in the twenties, his intensive reading of the thinking of many workers in many fields, his participant observation of his own life in relation to patients he found in mental hospitals, all carry the quality of the restless search through baffling inconsistencies towards a theory of schizophrenia: " . . . it is of the utmost moment to more than poetry," Lowes writes, "that instead of regarding the imagination as a bright but ineffectual faculty with which in some esoteric fashion poets and their kind are specially endowed, we recognize the essential oneness of its function and its ways with all the creative endeavours through which human brains, with dogged persistence, strive to discover and realize order in a chaotic world." In some such fashion, Sullivan became, first, the Recording Angel for the schizophrenic process in the mental hospital; and having realized some measure of hope in that chaotic world set out in later studies to find some path for order in the vastly troubled ways of the larger world.

H.S.P.

18 Louisburg Square
Boston, Massachusetts
July 5, 1961

Harry Stack Sullivan, the Man †

by CLARA THOMPSON *

WE HAVE met here tonight to honor the memory of a man who has left a sense of loss in all our lives. For many the grief is at the loss of a teacher; for others the regret is that a thinker of such wisdom and perceptiveness is gone; some will miss the intuitive sensitiveness of a great therapist; and for all of us there is sadness at the loss of a friend.

Harry Stack Sullivan was a lonely person from his earliest childhood. He was the only surviving child of a poor Irish farmer in upstate New York. All the other children died in infancy. The mother, who thought she had married beneath her, was a complaining semi-invalid with chronic resentment at the humble family situation. She gave the young boy little warmth. In fact, he said she was not interested in knowing the boy who was her son, but used him as a dummy on which to hang her illusions. He always had the feeling if he could only reach his father there would be understanding, and that indeed finally occurred after he had reached adult life. But in his childhood his father was a shy withdrawn person whose occasional words of approval the boy treasured. The close friends of his childhood were the livestock on the farm. With them he felt comfortable and less lonely. There were no companions, and when he finally went to school he felt out of place, not knowing how to be a part of the group. This is the early background of a man who for years has tried to understand the lonely ones. And out of this search has developed thinking of great importance to us all.

There was also a mystical sentimental side to Harry. His

† Reprinted from *Psychiatry* (1949) 12:435-437.

[* This is the text of an address given by Dr. Clara Thompson at memorial services for Sullivan on February 11, 1949, following his death in Paris on January 14, 1949. A more formal biographical statement on Sullivan's life will be found in the yearbook of *Current Biography* for 1942 (New York: H. W. Wilson, Co.). H.S.P.]

mother, full of the feeling of the superiority of her family over his father's, used to tell the young boy tales of the past. One story especially fascinated him: one of his ancestors was the West Wind depicted as a horse which ran towards the sunrise to meet the future. I could never be quite sure that Harry with his senti- mental, humorous Irish mind did not partly believe this. At any rate his feeling for horses was a very strong one and he adopted the horse as a kind of symbol for himself.

Although this poor farm boy had a long journey to go, some- thing in him would not rest. He early showed a talent for and in- terest in physics. He finally got to medical school where his pov- erty and his feeling of not knowing how to belong kept him still isolated from his contemporaries. As an outcome of World War I he found himself a liaison officer at St. Elizabeths Hospital where he came under the influence and encouragement of William Alan- son White. Dr. White's interest in him had a profound effect on his life, and he always gladly acknowledged this indebtedness. It was at about this time that Harry became interested in schizo- phrenia.

It was a few years later, when he first went to Sheppard Pratt Hospital in about 1923, that our friendship began. The origin of the friendship was characteristic of him. I was presenting my first scientific paper at a meeting at the Phipps Clinic which Harry was attending. In addition to the qualms of a beginner, I had been having an afternoon rise in temperature for about a week and I must have looked very ill. My paper was about schizophrenic suicidal attempts. Harry later told me that he was not only im- pressed by my interest in schizophrenia but by the fact that I looked very ill from which he concluded: This woman must be schizophrenic, I must know her. And so an attack of typhoid fever is responsible for one of the richest friendships in my life, a friend- ship which has persisted with unswerving loyalty over twenty- five years.

Our mutual interest in patients was a very strong bond between us. We early discovered that we both had the same kind of feeling for patients, a genuine liking and respect. His ideas about patients always seemed to make sense to me, and I absorbed them intui- tively and almost unconsciously. I soon learned that this man, who in public could tear a bad paper to bits with his scathing sarcasm, had another side—a gentle, warm, friendly one. This was the side he showed his patients. Anyone who has seen him talking with a disturbed catatonic can know that he has seen the real Harry without pretense or defenses. There was nothing maudlin about his tenderness—it rather conveyed a feeling of deep understanding.

The quality of his friendship showed the same genuineness and tolerance so characteristic of his relation to patients. He was slow in making friends. He tested them for a long time: Were they over-competitive or neurotically ambitious? Did they have jealous natures? Were they opportunistic? For these characteristics he had no tolerance. Once a person had passed the test he could count on Harry for absolute loyalty. No matter what your mistakes— and he might point them out to you privately—before the world he was on your side. I once had reason to be grateful for this loyalty in a situation where a lesser man might have been concerned at the possible jeopardy to his own status by defending me. I believe that self-interest never had any weight with him when loyalty to a friend was the issue. In all crises he was at hand.

In looking out for his own personal affairs Harry was strangely impractical. His head was in the clouds and his feet were often not on the earth. Perhaps this was to be expected from a descendant of the West Wind. For a hard-headed scientist this man had much poetry in his nature. He loved music. Perhaps it was a combination of this side of him with his scientific investigativeness which led him to discoveries of the meaning of various qualities in the human voice.

He was brought up as a Catholic and although his thinking took him far from formal religious beliefs, he retained a great fondness for the beauty and dignity of the Catholic ritual. He was deeply religious in the sense of believing in the positive qualities of man. He had a characteristic phrase when parting from a friend— "Gods keep you." This phrase always seemed to me to roll back a curtain and one got a glimpse of the Irish lad with the tradition of pagan gods. One could have no doubt that he meant, May the good forces in your world protect you.

His belief that a way could be found to bring lasting peace to the world was a fire within him which sustained his frail body in the last physically ill years of his life. Several times in the last few years he outwitted death in a way that seemed like a miracle. He wanted to live and he lived productively. He will go on living with us and through us who have known him. He died the death of a hero in the midst of carrying on the work dearest to his heart. Truly we have known a man of great stature.

Schizophrenia as a Human Process

1

Commentary

SULLIVAN was 32 years old when he presented his first two papers at scientific meetings in 1924; he had been at Sheppard for a year. The two papers were written simultaneously and were designed to be a unit. One of them, "The Oral Complex," [1] which was presented at the 1924 meeting of the American Psychoanalytic Association, has been omitted from this book. It represents Sullivan's first attempt at a developmental theory; any modifications that he made in the existing psychoanalytic theory attempted, however, to be "in strict conformity to the delineation of Professor Freud," as he notes. Historically speaking, this paper contains a fascinating preformulation of many of Sullivan's later developmental theories, such as the nipple-in-lips configuration of early infancy, which is a relatively central concept for infancy in his final theoretical formulation.[2] At the same time, many of the central preoccupations of the paper represent an early and somewhat unsuccessful attempt to fit his observations of schizophrenia into the then existing psychoanalytic theory; and the paper has been omitted because of such considerations, including that of space.

The other paper, "Schizophrenia: Its Conservative and Malignant Features," which was presented at the 1924 meeting of the American Psychopathological Association, is the first article in this book. It shows, of course, some of the same preoccupations as "The Oral Complex," particularly in some of the footnotes. But the last half

---

[1] "The Oral Complex," *Psychoanalytic Rev.* (1925) 12:31–38.
[2] See *The Interpersonal Theory of Psychiatry*, the index entry for Nursing.

3

of the paper reports specifically on his clinical work with schizophrenic patients at Sheppard, including work at St. Elizabeths Hospital in Washington, D.C., in the year before he came to Sheppard.

The use of the word "conservative" in the title represents a sharp moving away from the poles of "benign" and "malignant," then current constructs in approaching dementia praecox, and part of the general medical tradition. Sullivan has not used "conservative" to mean a lack of change, but rather to describe the act of salvaging something out of potential disaster. He indicates that the first incidence of psychosis (after puberty) must be considered to have as its purpose some conservation of personality. Even with some loss of so-called superior traits, "the psychosis [in those who made some social recovery] was none the less conservative, for it made subsequent social life possible and thereby preserved an individual who had not been equal to the demands of the social integration [previous to his illness]." Already Sullivan reports that the group of catatonic dementia praecox is one in which therapeutic endeavor is consistently encouraging and then goes on to say that *almost all initial schizophrenic psychoses should be considered of this category* [italics mine]."

In the first half of the paper, Sullivan is concerned with changing certain stereotypes about schizophrenia and with placing schizophrenia as a process within the framework of 'normal' prototypes for thinking, expanding Freudian terms and concepts in such a way as to encompass this approach. In particular, Sullivan has coined the Freudian-like term "preconcept" (which he later abandoned) to designate structures of thought arising from experience prior to birth to explain some of the phenomena found in the schizophrenic process. Footnotes 2 and 4 expound the theoretical considerations for this approach (which he then developed in a more leisured way in "The Oral Complex"). Much of this thinking came to be subsumed in Sullivan's later theory under what he called the *prototaxic mode of experience*.[3] Closely related to the idea of "preconcept" is Sullivan's use of the term "uncanny" which was borrowed from Storch and appears first in "The Oral Complex." The prototype for the uncanny is found in the early experience of life, before there is any significant consensually valid communication by language or signs.

[3] See *The Interpersonal Theory of Psychiatry*, index entry for same.

In the earlier papers, Sullivan develops the idea that this experience goes back to the period before birth—the preconcepts; but in the later theory, he lumps together the experience of the early organism before there is language, without attempting to discriminate between the experience before and after birth. Such diffuse experience belongs to the "uncanny" and emerges when the 'normal' or disturbed person is 'out of touch' (in dreams, for instance), or threatened by the emergence of acute anxiety or panic.

To those interested in tracing out Freud's influence on Sullivan, this paper clearly illustrates that Sullivan's approach was in the beginning centrally influenced by Freud. He is reporting in this paper on his first seven years of work after he left medical school, which included work in the Army, at a Public Health Institute, and as a Veterans Bureau Liaison Officer at St. Elizabeths Hospital; this work obviously represented a patient population considerably different from the patients seen by Freud. Sullivan in this paper clearly tries to modify at a conservative pace Freud's theories in order to make them workable for his own observations; he has not dumped the theories overboard, nor has he rebelled against them in the traditional mode of youth. He thinks that free association in its usual form must be modified for acute and subacute states of schizophrenia, but he attempts to hold on to the "death-evil preconcept," stating in the early part of the paper that this particular preconcept arises from the inception of labor just before birth. Later, of course, he abandoned entirely Freud's death instinct.[4]

Already there is clear indication that Sullivan has begun the process of synthesizing knowledge and terms from many different disciplines. For instance, his use of the term "vector," which he retained throughout his writing, comes from physics, although he notes that he is using it in a "purely expository" way (see footnote 3). Shand's "self-love" is closely related to Sullivan's self-esteem, as he later developed it. McDougall's concept of "I" and "me" is later elaborated and combined with the theory of reflected appraisals of the self as conceptualized by Cooley and Mead, the whole being expanded to include Sullivan's own contribution of good-me, bad-me, and not-me.

The boldness of the paper can only be seen, of course, against the backdrop of the then current attitudes toward the so-called dementia

[4] See, for instance, *Conceptions of Modern Psychiatry*, p. 98 *n.*

praecoxes. The use of the word *mind* in the early part of the paper to discuss schizophrenia represents an elevation of the process. He also makes a strong bid for other workers in the field to *personally observe* schizophrenic content and behavior rather than depending on outworn clichés about dementia praecox.

Schizophrenia: Its Conservative and Malignant Features

A PRELIMINARY COMMUNICATION †

SCHIZOPHRENIA as a clinical entity continues to occupy an uncertain position. In particular, the matter of prognosis swings between the two poles of an absolute pessimism shown by some followers of Kraepelin, and a rather humble optimism reflected in several schools of research. The general tendency of the former is to divert from the so-called "praecox" group such cases as recover. For this purpose such conceptions as the benign stupor of Hoch,* and nonpraecox catatonia, among others, have been added to our clinical labels. . . . The following is an attempt to show in concise form a little of the promising side of the matter.

Research workers in this field have the concrete problems of science before them; they must collate and classify their data, seeking always the *fundamentum divisionis*. That success is at the end of a long path is indubitable; the length of the path has certainly been demonstrated in the past 40 years. Striking—peculiarly so in retrospect—is the frequency with which the workers have passed early from the science to the philosophy of schizophrenia. The attractiveness of philosophy in this most difficult of all the

† Reprinted from *Amer. J. Psychiatry* (1924–25) 81:77–91. Read at the fourteenth annual meeting of the American Psychopathological Association, Philadelphia, June 7, 1924.

[* August Hoch, *Benign Stupors: A Study of a New Manic-Depressive Reaction Type;* New York: Macmillan, 1921.]

7

fields of human endeavor arises from much the same things that have evolved in rational psychology as distinguished from empirical psychology. Rational or metaphysical psychology consists in the interpretations of mental facts and phenomena in terms of meaning, purpose, and value. Empirical or scientific psychology, on the other hand, is occupied solely with the discovery of causal relations. The field of study being *mind*, any major tendency of scientific thought to pass over to philosophy must reside in the nature of mind itself. What seems to be the principal feature of mind which stimulates this generally unwitting transition? Now that the enthusiasm for quasi-scientific obscurantism is failing with the collapse of materialism in the joint fields of physics and biology, it seems reasonably safe to express, as an answer to the question, the obvious fact of *teleology* as a characteristic of things mental. As McDougall has put it, "Purposive activity is the most fundamental category of psychology." The element of purpose, which biologists are beginning to invoke in the explanation of vital facts, expends the abstraction principle of science, and enters into the realm of means and ends, of meanings and contexts. In attacking the problem of understanding and treatment of schizophrenia, the element of motivation seems logically fundamental to all others. As Dr. William A. White has said, "We must understand what the patient is trying to do." If the element of purpose and means is eliminated, there results sterile brain physiology, psychologization, and that type of hypothesis so well criticized by Henri Bergson, when he wrote of the theory of memory, "Hence the strange hypothesis of recollections stored in the brain, which are supposed to become conscious as though by a miracle, and bring us back to the past by a process that is left unexplained." Bertrand Russell in his *Analysis of Mind*,* remarks, "The response of an organism to a given stimulus is very often dependent upon the past history of the organism, and not merely upon the stimulus and the *hitherto discoverable* present state of the organism." This represents the epilogue of the stimulus-response psychology. The hitherto undiscovered present state of the organism, including its past history, is the basic phenomenal explanation which we subsume in the term mind.

[* Bertrand Russell, *The Analysis of Mind;* New York: Macmillan, 1921.]

The observation, experimental deflection, analysis, and classification of the thinking and behavior phenomena of a small but especially suitable group of schizophrenics, a few epileptics, and some of those suffering milder disorders, have provided the data from which the notions here to be presented have their origin. It is the hope that a number of those fortunately located for such research may escape the restraint of neurological explanations, dualist bugbears, and anthropomorphic reifications, to the end that they engage in that intimate personal observation of schizophrenic content and behavior which may eventuate in views which do not expend the universe, and do offer at least a promise in the preventive field.

The epistemology of this work derives from critical realism; the foundations are pluralist; and the final implications will, perhaps, prove to be objective social idealism. Besides the uniform conceptual basis of science, three particular conceptions have been accepted or developed for the interpretation of data. The first is the postulate of the unconscious, the great contribution of Professor Freud.[1] The second is the teleological vitalist hypothesis which has been subsumed in Nunn's concept of hormic energy,[*] intimately related to Jung's concept of libido. The third is a genetic hypothesis of mental structure and functions: it implies a vital sequence of experience (itself purely subjective, even if with objective reference), the related parts of which are structuralized into preconcepts,[2] complexes, and sentiments (partly

[1] This concept, the history of which includes Leibnitz, Schopenhauer, Helmholtz, V. Hartmann, Herbart, Sir William Hamilton, Charcot, Ribot, Janet, M. Prince, and finally Freud and Jung, has been the grounds for perennial controversy. As usual, the contestants have fought over terms, not facts. Bernard Hart has given the most comprehensive exposition not only of the concept itself, but of its necessity. As he has shown, the unconscious is a "non-phenomenal conceptual construction designed to explain the facts of phenomenal consciousness." J[ared] S[parks] Moore has reviewed the situation in Chapter VIII of *The Foundations of Psychology* (Princeton University Press, 1921), which should be read by those disinclined to accept the concept.

[* This "teleological vitalist hypothesis" was abandoned by Sullivan later. See "Peculiarity of Thought in Schizophrenia," footnote 2. The concept was one set forth by T. Percy Nunn, physicist-philosopher. H.S.P.]

[2] Discontinuous events of intrauterine life which (a) follow in time the functional evolution of the fœtal sense organs, and (b) are of such nature as to give rise to sense impressions, make up the material from which comes

accessible to awareness).

The mental functions are derivative vectors [3] of the primordial or libidinal energy, the relative directions of which (goals) are determined by experience configurations—archaic preconcepts, and the group of complexes and sentiments. Of the structures of the mind there are several of great importance. As a basis are the group of cosmos, time, organic-oral, organic-urethral, organic-striped-muscle, and the death-evil preconcepts.[4] Secondar-

---

the first experience. Experience is used here in the sense of the ultimate psychical "unit." It is purely subjective in fact, regardless of its known or unknown objective relation. "Thought," "percept," "sensation," "image," or what-not, all are terms for particular forms of experience. Experience is not fragmentary but an unbroken discrete sequence. The totality is related to the "pure memory" concept of Bergson. Various relationships of the parts of the sequence lead to functional affinity and synergy which we imply in speaking of a mental structure. The term, *preconcept*, is used to designate such structures as arise from experience prior to birth, as these structures function in the form of a dynamism amounting to affinity for related postnatal experience, and determine the formation of primal complexes of experiences—the governing unconscious structures fundamental in the personality.

The analysis of clinical data, correlated to known biological events, leads to the identification of the following major events of intrauterine life: (1) The cœnæsthesis—structuralized in what we term the *cosmos preconcept*, the "Gestalt" of mind; (2) the excretion of amniotic fluid, structuralized in the *urethral preconcept*, the ultimate basis of "genital localization" of sexual sensations; (3) the intrauterine activity of the mouth and appendages, the *oral preconcept*, of profound significance (*vide*, "The Oral Complex"); (4) the *kinaesthetic preconcept*, from striped-muscle activity in utero; (5) the beats of the circulation-pressure rhythm of fœtal and maternal circulations, structuralized as the *time preconcept*, the "Gestalt" of scientific (causal) and philosophical (logical and teleological) thinking—once objective reference has been developed.

[3] Mental function, a kinetic matter, must be clearly distinguished from mental structure, a potential affair. The term "vector" is adapted from physics, as a purely expository term, meaning that in an energy diagram the activity of an innate or acquired tendency may be represented by a geometric line. The genetic viewpoint implies the evolution of new vectors (new tendencies) from the primordial root, wholly as a result of the vital experience and the structures of it which result from the joint interaction of the hormic energy and the inhering nature of the experience.

[4] The term *death-evil preconcept* is applied to the structuralization of the experience arising from the inception of labor. This represents the interruption of a totality of satisfactory conditions, and the first experience of "unlust." As such, it is the "Gestalt" of subsequent pleasure—in this relationship it gives rise to what has been conceptualized by Freud as the pleasure principle. The *structure of the pleasure principle* is, then, a sec-

ily, there is the relational preconcept designated the pleasure principle. Of the postnatal structures, the first is the oral complex,[5] the subject of a recent communication, the kinæsthetic, the urethral, the anal, and other complexes. Of the major systems of complexes, by far the most important so far as influence is concerned is that group making up the Ego and *"Das Es"* of Freud. To this is applied the term, sentiment of self-regard.[6] This third basic postulate accentuates the contention that the gamut of behavior and thinking, usual or unusual, "normal" or psychotic, can be explained very largely on the basis of the individual's experience. It must await detailed treatment elsewhere.

Schizophrenia, in the light of clinical observations, is not to be regarded as a primary disease such as that which one may visualize when mentioning dementia praecox. There is no profit from

ondary structure, the first in which primary psychic entities relate to form a structure. *Functionally*, however, the pleasure principle shows as a primal vector the direction or goal of which is the avoidance of all unlust. It is this latter aspect which has occupied Freud.

[5] The oral complex is the profoundly unconscious structuralization which has its origin in the first natal activity of breathing, then in suckling, etc. Its importance in character formation, on the one hand, and in the interpretation of normal and abnormal psychology, on the other, has been neglected.

[6] Of this sentiment (mental structure, part of which is readily accessible to awareness), A. F. Shand has written: "In all normal individuals, then, there is a love of something to give some order and unity to their lives; and the system which is found generally pre-eminent is the great principle of self-love or the self-regarding sentiment, analogous to the chief bodily systems in respect of the number of subsidiary systems which it is capable of containing . . . and joined to this self-love in subtle and intimate ways . . . are a variety of disinterested sentiments. . . . . There is finally a system of unique importance . . . which is known as 'respect for conscience.' . . . Two other sentiments closely connected with one another belong to this same class: Self-respect, and respect for others." McDougall, in his *Outline of Psychology*, [New York: Scribners, c. 1923] has discussed this sentiment and its extension, very capably. As he expresses it: "This is the most important of all the sentiments, by reason both of its strength and the frequency and far-reaching nature of its operations . . . . the word, 'I' or 'me' grows richer in meaning, as he [the child] builds up a system of belief about his own nature. . . . This object 'me' thus becomes represented in the structure of the mind by a system of dispositions of extraordinary extent and complexity, a system also which is associated with a multitude of past events and objects, . . . and the conative dispositions of the system, being brought into play so frequently, by every social contact, whether actual or imagined, become delicately responsive in an extraordinary degree, as well as very strong through much exercise. . . ."

pondering on an organic substratum which cannot now, or in the next many years, be demonstrated in the patient who comes for treatment. Karl Wilmanns has expressed the fact of the anatomo-physiological dilemma when he said, "Many things indicate that the situation is still very complicated." Professor Adolf Meyer's dynamic view-point, and the work to which it supplied impetus, has proven vastly more cogent to the life problems of the patient.

Jaspers has come close to the crux of the situation in his study of transitory schizophrenic episodes. It was his conclusion that even the most brief of these leads to permanent change in the personality. (Bornstein and Wilmanns do not agree with this, for some unfathomable reason.)

The important conclusion reached in the investigations from which this paper proceeds, designates schizophrenia as a series of major mental events always attended by material changes in personality, but in itself implying nothing of deterioration or dementia. The disorder is one in which the total experience of the individual is reorganized; there is a great eruption of primitive functions—of thinking in complex-images, to use Lévy-Bruhl's excellent expression; and there is an at least temporarily profound alteration of the egoistic structures, the sentiment of self-regard. It is a disorder which is determined by the previous experience of the individual—regardless of whether it is excited by emotional experience (psychic traumata), by the toxæmia of acute disease, by cranial trauma, or by alcoholic intoxication.[7] That there is hereditary predisposition to the schizophrenic dissociation is fairly certain, just as it is possible that this hereditary predisposition to such a collapse of mental organization is coupled

[7] This deviation from the classical formulation seems necessary. The effects of a mental disorder, immediate and remote, are the subject for psychiatric deliberation—not the over-fine delineation of "clinical entities." Schizophrenic content and behavior is seen, for instance, in a proportion of the alcoholic psychoses; these disorders, however completely "normal" the thinking and behavior after recovery may seem, leave clear traces in the personality. Any attempt to clear away their evil consequences must take exactly that form which is found to be applicable to "major" schizophrenia. The idea of restricting the term schizophrenia to disorders of unknown exciting cause is dogmatic. From all this, it seems to follow that our position is but the acceptance of the simplest hypothesis explaining the facts.

with demonstrable physical peculiarities, such as those engaging the attention of Kretschmer. But it is not the outbreak of schizophrenic content and behavior which bears upon the individual prognosis: it is the dynamics of the several regressions which seems to be of final importance in determining recovery, chronicity, or a dementing course. The emphasis here is put upon the fact that schizophrenia has to be recognized as a mental process, regardless of anything other than the individual's behavior and thinking during the disorder. When this is done, and study is made of the actual content and of the details of behavior, the phenomena of value in determining unfavorable factors can be collected and classified.

Schizophrenia as a disorder of mind shows as disordered behavior and thinking. The characteristics by which it is distinguished have not been worked out with precison. Bleuler's formulation, for example, is unsatisfactory alike in its basis in the old idea-association psychology and in its contradictory, if not actually incoherent, propositions. Berg's concept, too, is deemed inconsistent. Gruhle has come fairly close in his conclusion that the malady is basically a disturbance of motives. American and British conceptions, which have been reviewed so far, show either defect of psychological basis, or the imputation of primary rôle to factors either too vague for clinical application, or too indefinite for the differentiation of the disorder. The tentative conclusions from our work are that the primary disorder in this illness is one of mental structure; and then shows as Gruhle's disorder of motivation, in turn reflected in the thought content and in the purposive activity—behavior. The mental structure is disassociated in such fashion that the disintegrated portions regress in function to earlier levels of mental ontology, without parallelism in individual depth of regression. This disparity of depths seems the essence of that which is schizophrenia, as distinguished from other mental disorders. Judging from our clinical material and from the splendid monograph of Dr. Alfred Storch,* the depths of regression in this disorder greatly exceed that in other forms of mental upset; this, too, may

[* Storch's work is cited more specifically by Sullivan in the next paper in this book. H.S.P.]

be found to be an essential feature. That there is any necessity for accepting the notion of phyletic regression of mind structure is not proven. The phenomenology does not seem to expend that subsumed in the ontogenetic psychology already mentioned.

The conservative features of schizophrenic dissociation have not been emphasized [in the literature]. It is but natural that a condition assumed to be uniformly destructive should be looked upon as completely malignant. Yet clinical experience points definitely to the contrary. In the past seven years, there have been seen and studied a group of brief schizophrenic illnesses which recovered with definite favorable change of personality.* The majority of these had been diagnosed by staff conferences of various hospitals, as dementia praecox. In a large number there had been markedly psychopathic traits in the childhood of the patient. Ungovernable temper tantrums, destructiveness, malicious behavior, emotional instabilities of high degree, excessive sensitiveness, extreme self-consciousness, and severe neuroses are among the defective reaction-types pictured in the histories. The postpsychotic personality in these cases showed the disappearance or mitigation of defect and a greater adaptability or a greater self-satisfaction such that the stress incident to ordinary life was much nearer the usual. An improvement from seclusive, self-contained, or pent-up attitude with lack of the ability to use available outlets for the expression of distressing content, to one in which the patient was relatively open and able frankly to discuss some of his life problems, was generally observed. Even in the group who came out of their psychosis with a decidedly paranoid adjustment to reality, there had been a change from an obviously ineffectual adaptation to one in which the social contacts of the individual caused him much less profound discomfort; emotional introversion and brooding gave way to the less individually destructive projection of discomfort and hate. None of these cases is an instance of emotional or intellectual deterioration such that the personality was reduced below the average of those similarly situated in the social fabric. That each represented a loss of some "superior traits" may be true, but the

[* Sullivan is here referring to his clinical experience at St. Elizabeths Hospital as well as at Sheppard. H.S.P.]

psychosis was none the less conservative, for it made subsequent social life possible and thereby preserved an individual who had not been equal to the demands of the social integration. Relapse into psychosis has been observed in a group, some of whom had undoubtedly improved in social adaptability as a result of the initial disorder. The subsequent psychosis has not always proven to be more severe than the former. In one case, in particular, the subsequent mental disorder was peculiarly mild, and the conservative features of the process so clear-cut that it will be reported in detail elsewhere. In this connection, it must be obvious to anyone, that the social milieu to which the patient has to return, has a great deal to do with his future. If the conservative reorganization of complexes and sentiments, which appears to underlie a goodly share of the early schizophrenic phenomenology, leads the patient to the foreconscious belief that he can circumvent or rise above environmental handicaps, and if this belief is the presenting feature of a comprehensive mental integration, his recovery proceeds. If no such reconstruction is accomplished, the patient does not recover. If such a reintegration is made solely on the basis of the particularly favorable institutional environment, with repression of hopeless features of the social situation awaiting him outside, a recovery of a tenuous and unstable kind may be accomplished—the prospect being for prompt relapse. Relapse, which would appear to be more ominous than the first psychosis, if only because of increased discouragement, is not invariably so: in a very few cases, it has seemed as if the patient went into the second illness with fewer problems than into the first, and showed a profiting by the former experience in terms of a prompter and more comprehensive recovery. The degree of "insight" which the patient brings from his psychosis is quite generally accepted as having an important relation to the stability of recovery. Insight, however, is never perfect, and there are a large proportion of recovered or arrested schizophrenics who have achieved a reasonably unified personality, fairly adapted to the social integration, without any ability for the conscious formulation and expression which we generally seek as evidence of insight.

Wherein the factors of good are contained in the frequently

destructive process has been the principal subject of study. From the start, evidence has been abundant to the effect that, while most schizophrenic dissociations are initially persecutory in coloring, and in many cases explanatory grandiose notions make their appearance, it is only the individual who develops somewhat logical beliefs in persecution, with or without grandiose notions, that comes under the unfavorable rubrics of the paranoid group. Of this section the paraphrenic of Kraepelin is typical. The point here is that *illogical* or bizarre persecutory beliefs show in subsequent developments not as an adjustment to reality, but as events of psychical reorganization as transient as the notions themselves. The beliefs which are rather *consistent, logically*— once a small group of false premises have been accepted—are to be viewed as unsuccessful outcome of the psychosis, and are an unfavorable omen.

Again from the outset of the study, before the content and behavior of such cases had received much attention, it appeared that the case showing silliness as the prevailing affect, and with this much manneristic activity, did not progress but deteriorated. Acting upon the theory of Kempf, that the hebephrenic was to be regarded as one in whom interests were prevailingly anal, fecal, urinal and sodomistic, and the cravings "would rather remain infantile than strive for the responsibilities of maturity," I made an attempt to determine which of a group of patients diagnosed as hebephrenic dementia praecox fitted this description. It became evident that there was in fact at least two types of content in the general clinical group of hebephrenics. There was one (which is accepted as hebephrenic) in which fecal, anal, and urinary interests dominate the personality. In these, the mannerisms were of great interest. So far, it has seemed that the hostile egoistic desires stirred in opposition to the perverse infantile cravings were the motivation of the mannerisms. This is a tentative conclusion. The appearance of a mannerism, as well as the time of its repetition, the exaggeration of its manifestations, and the available content before its appearance and subsequent to an occasional disappearance, has led to the rather startling surmise that the mannerism is a regression to almost purely physiological existence of a mental content, the distinguishing nature of which was its conflict with the perverse adaptation. As such the hebephrenic mannerism may be a bridge from conversion phenomena to tics, on the one hand, and to epileptiform seizures, on the other. Further development of this subject will be undertaken in a study of epileptic phenomena. The point here is that the group of individuals who lose egoistic strivings and develop mannerisms—this situation being concomitant with frank excretory interests—is of very poor prognosis. Silliness is not a criterion, probably being the affect of perverse infantile behavior in contempt of external disapproval.

The other class of patient found in the clinical group of hebephrenics was made up of diverse "deteriorating" schizophrenics in which conflict with the antisocial desires and with the content antagonistic to more adult egoistic satisfaction had not disappeared. As such, the prognostic criteria seemed more favorable. Attempts at treatment led to the conclusion that the deterioration features were due to splitting of the sentiment of self-regard in somewhat the fashion seen in multiple personality, so that in these schizophrenics there are a variety of partial goals of the mental life, instead of an integrated ego dominating or striving to dominate the innate and derivative tendencies. It is in this group that many of the "paranoid praecox" cases come to rest, for a time, on their course into dementia.

Finally, there were the group where therapeutic endeavor was consistently encouraging. The rough clinical label of this group is, of course, catatonic dementia praecox. (*Passim,* almost all initial schizophrenic psychoses should be considered of this category.) The individual whose struggles in personality reorganization takes this form is primarily distinguishable as one in whom there is neither recourse to comprehensive projection of his problems upon his colleagues, nor such a form of multiple splitting of the ego as that mentioned above in discussing the second hebephrenic group. Also, in contradiction to the pure hebephrenic, his psychosis does not represent a satisfactory adjustment with loss of egoistic strivings and with perverse (antibiological) pleasure-taking. Because his problems are not solved in these socially destructive fashions, the severe conflict remains unabated, and the purely schizophrenic dissociation becomes greater in the catatonic than elsewhere. The regressive processes go deeper in the mental structures; and the functions appearing in content and behavior become lower and lower in the scale of psychologic ontogenesis. Thus it is here that we see that really marvelous demonstration (by regression) of the intra-uterine mind—the prenatal attitude, sometimes with makeshift uterine environment (tightly enwrapping blanket, darkness, wetness, etc.). Here we see the unmistakable evidence of prenatal experience. The certain experimental proof of ontogenic psychology is provided by the startlingly prompt recovery to accessibility and subsequent health which has been observed, occasionally, to follow upon a fortunately well-timed interpretation of the behavior.

It is imperative to note, at this point, that there is vastly more of harm than good to be accomplished by unstudied interpretations of schizophrenic phenomena, in general. The theoretical consideration which has prompted such objective interpretation in the regressive prenatal state is also a reflection from the ontogenic viewpoint—viz., that the patient, having reverted to the beginning of mind, nothing further of regression could occur, and that, therefore, the vital impulse might safely be directed from without to the end of retracing the genetic pathway to adulthood, with the assistance of such experience as could be directed objectively after study of the patient and his pre-psychotic environment. Lest this be misunderstood, it is emphasized that interpretations and other suggestions thrust upon the patient without close regard to the life situation from which the psychosis resulted, and painstaking study of indices to the actual conflicts which necessitated the upheaval, in themselves represent a destructive dilettantism which jeopardize any success which might otherwise result from the psychosis; and thus tend to determine an unfavorable outcome. Observations are plentiful which suggest that the catatonic is frequently the victim of psychological homicide unwittingly perpetrated by attendant, nurse, or the psychiatrist who forgets that his duty is to understand and assist, not to tinker and amuse himself. The pernicious effects of misguided relatives and friends need not be emphasized, being evidenced *ad nauseam*, everywhere.

To resume the theme of the catatonic phenomena and their

conservative features, one may refer to cogent statements encountered elsewhere. Jung, in his *Psychology of Dementia Praecox*,* stated as his conclusion that a dreamer acting his dreams would show the behavior of dementia praecox. While his statement was far too inclusive, it relates directly to catatonic schizophrenia, and requires for its application to the latter group of behavior phenomena, the proviso, only, that such behavior is of a *genetically more primitive nature* than ever appears in a remembered dream. In this connection, reference to pavor nocturnus may be interpolated, with correlation on the one hand to infantile fear reactions, and on the other to anamnestic significance. J. B. Watson, in particular, emphasized the ease with which the primitive fear response could be elicited by trifling environmental changes occurring as the infant was falling asleep. This, as has been mentioned elsewhere, is due to ecphorization of the death-evil preconcept by experience which is related to the preliminaries of birth in that it, too, represents a disturbance of the make-shift resumption of intrauterine "pleasure" which is constituted by infantile sleep. The future implication of night terrors in childhood is thus seen to reside in its demonstrating an adaptation to reality so poor that the dream-handling of the child's life-problems is unsuccessful to such a degree that the death-evil preconcept is ecphoriated with the felt emotion of terror. That grave regressive phenomena are apt to occur later in the life of such an individual is the direct conclusion from the genetic viewpoint, for here we have early experience the integration of which is clearly unsatisfactory. A digression into the dynamics which determine an ultimate schizophrenia, an epilepsy, or another disorder, seems unwarranted. The cogent point is that the content of the night terror is never conceptual or perceptual; the victim can give nothing to explain the fear; the content is of that inaccessible character typical of prenatal and early infantile psychisms; and just such nonconceptual, nonperceptual, ultrainfantile content is the analogue in dream of the content expressed in typical catatonic schizophrenia. This is the proviso in the application of Jung's dream parallel to catatonic behavior.

[* See C. G. Jung, *The Psychology of Dementia Praecox;* New York: Journal of Nervous and Mental Disease Publishing Co., 1929. Sullivan is obviously referring to an earlier edition, perhaps the original German.]

* * *

To conclude this preliminary and necessarily fragmentary presentation, the conservative aspect of catatonic states in particular, and of early schizophrenia in general, are to be identified as *attempts by regression* to genetically older thought processes—to infantile or even prenatal mental functions—*successfully to reintegrate masses of life experience* which had failed of structuralization into a functional unity, and finally lead by that very lack of structuralization to multiple dissociations in the field of relationship of the individual not only to external reality, including the social milieu, but to his personal reality.

Just as the primitive thinking in more normal sleep solves many a problem, and, in the remembered dream, brings up for assistance many an unsolved problem with which we now feel able to deal, so do these primitive processes in schizophrenia, so far as they can be comprehended by another mind (and turned to some purpose in reorganizing experience which had not been integrated), offer a field for direct therapeutic activity and a promise which removes this disorder from the category of unmitigated evil.

While it is not intended that this paper shall relate directly to the therapy of schizophrenia—it being the desire merely to insure a measure of new interest, so that these patients will cease to be regarded by so many as *a priori* inexplicable and hopeless—a word may be said of clinical applications of the theory. Far more than any single action of the physician, it is his general attitude towards the patient that determines his value. Primitive sympathy phenomena, such as, in fact, unduly the psychoanalytic "transference mechanism," are of prime importance in relieving the introversion of mental life of the patient, to such effect that his experiences can be brought more and more into objective relations, with increasing adaptation of his personality to reality, and increment in the biological utilization of the hormic energy. The schizophrenic appreciates all too definitely the attitude of the physician regarding the life situation presented by the patient. Solipsism, excursions into phantasmagorical "collective" and "racial" unconscious, or even the "purely scientific" attitude which eliminates the element of purpose and reduces the individual to organismic cravings in pitched battle—all these views bring to the patient much the same destructive influences to which he was previously subjected in the world, in the guise of naive materialism, absolute determinism, patristic theism, or the multiform complex-determined quasi-idealism. Primitive processes of thought make up too much of the physician's thinking for him to settle easily into the interpretation of the more primitive processes of the patient, until he shall have developed insight— at least to the extent of dissolving the factitious good-evil antithesis which seems to be our universal heritage from the old Persian dualism that has come to us among the trappings of Christianity. An approach to psychopathological problems which is not critically realistic seems to negative anything more controlled than unconsciously directed suggestion. In dealing with suggestion, the limitations of the agent are certainly the limits of effect possible in the patient; for, no matter how extensive and benevolently efficacious the patient's ideal of the physician may be, the more purely projected features are not effective in the face of actual contact; and the schizophrenic who objectifies his interests in an illusory fellow whose limitations break through to the distress of the sufferer will naturally retreat again into more profound psychosis.

It has seemed that there were two courses open for therapy of this disorder. Of course, some incipient and early states can be analyzed directly, as was demonstrated by Hoch some years back. In acute and subacute states, however, the application of the discoveries of psychoanalysis have to be divorced from the method of free-association in its usual form. The careful use of questions addressed to the patient, and to a trained assistant in the hearing of the patient, has been found effective in stimulating perception, analysis, and resynthesis of psychotic content. In other cases, recourse is to be had to primitive forms of thought exchange, and utilization made of symbols, allegories, and even rituals, for the induction in the disorganized individual of therapeutic experience assimilable at the levels of regression to which he has reverted. These therapeutic attempts have proven, so far, anything but economical of effort. Their results, while far too incomplete to justify any extensive program (or even discussion), suggest that this may be the proper direction for groping towards the clinical desiderata.

It is hoped that many others will return to this field of work; for even if the individual patient is not deemed worth the effort, the profit in the field of mental hygiene which will result from the comprehensive understanding of this mental disorder is of unparalleled importance; and the prophylaxis it would make possible justifies a wealth of intensive work.

2

Commentary

THE NEXT paper is included, in spite of its length—and in preference to several shorter papers—because (1) it includes a relatively complete survey of Sullivan's thinking at the time and its relation to other workers in several related fields, and (2) it contains the most extensive case material to be found in any of the published or unpublished writings.

In spite of the length of the case material, there is clear indication that what is reported here is only a fraction of the data that Sullivan had assembled on each of the six cases here included.[1] During the years at Sheppard, Sullivan assembled comparable data on 250 patients. Three of the cases reported on in this paper went on to social recovery (Cases 1, 3, and 6), and the other three showed unfortunate outcome (Cases 2, 4, and 5). Throughout his work, Sullivan religiously attempted to report on failures.

Sullivan introduces the case material by noting: "We shall attempt to escape 'great theoretic difficulty' by avoiding the assertion that they are cases of schizophrenia, as three of them patched up 'recovery.'" It is obvious from the title of the paper and from the case material itself that Sullivan considers these cases as showing primarily schizophrenic process; but he is here making somewhat sarcastic reference to the medical dictum current at that time: *If the patient recovers, then he couldn't have been schizophrenic: he was obviously misdiagnosed.*

The title of the paper is notable. From now on, Sullivan is talking about *thought* in schizophrenia and relating it to the content of

[1] Four additional cases are briefly mentioned—P.J., S.D., C.C., and Y.C.

adolescent or adult thought; he has moved it out of the primitive-archaic category, which was a popular concept at that time. Whatever its "primitive" characteristic, schizophrenic thought had certain clear connections with experience of the developmental eras through which the person had passed; its "peculiarity" could not completely camouflage its meaning, once the therapist had some clue to the patient's experience. And schizophrenic thought was a human process: "Schizophrenic thinking shows in its symbols and processes nothing exterior to the gamut of ordinary thinking, including therein that of revery and of dreams."

Although the paper focuses on the thinking of the schizophrenic, there is already clear indication that the content of the patient's thought is not considered important for the purpose of diagnosis: "It does not make one bit of difference, per se, whether a patient be labeled manic-depressive, hypothyroid, or sexually neurasthenic; the life situation is what distinguishes him completely from any other patient and places him almost entirely beyond useful statistical inquiry." Again he notes that ". . . it is the life situation of the patient that determines the prognosis." This early abandonment of statistical inquiry for determining prognosis is an important decision; Sullivan retained, however, a natural bent toward the systematic collection and analysis of data.

The use of multiple kinds of data-collection is illustrated in this paper: various personal documents from the patient; data from the nurses and attendants on the ward (this was before the establishment of his special ward); verbatim transcripts of the patient-doctor interactions; case history material, some of it obtained from collateral informants in the family and among friends; data from word association tests; and so on. For the convenience of the reader, Sullivan's questioning of the patients in the case material has been italicized; an examination of it will show certain characteristic procedures, such as the use of the expletive *"Continue!"* to keep the patient sternly moving along what Sullivan considered an important line of inquiry.

There is clear evidence in this paper, explicitly in the literature section (see footnote 5) and implicitly in the case material, that Sullivan has adopted certain assumptions made by Edward Kempf and has used them in analyzing the content of the communication of his young patients. In this connection, the Conclusion of Kempf's paper should be studied; it reads, in part: "In the infrahuman primates as well as in the genus *Homo*, homosexual interests predominate and normally precede heterosexual interests until the adult stage is well established. Homosexual interests occur in both sexes but are more common in the male. . . . The transfer of the affective cravings from a homosexual type of object to a heterosexual object is a very delicate biological procedure and one that must not be inhibited by fear" (see p. 153 of Kempf's article, as cited).

Peculiarity of Thought
in Schizophrenia †

IN HIS "Comparative Method in Psychiatry," Dr. William A. White * has expressed his belief that more of general value can come to psychiatry from the study of schizophrenia than from preoccupation with any other of the mental disorders: an extension of this remark to the field of psychology does not seem unwarranted.

Under these circumstances, the relative neglect of the schizophrenic in favor of the manic-depressive is not only to be regretted, but, if possible, to be rectified.

The difficulty in communication with the victims of the graver psychosis—the distance by which they seem removed from our normal mental processes—seems to be the chief handicap in the way of general interest in these patients. Besides this *real* factor, there is a vicious element that has entered into our clinical activities in the guise of diagnosing zeal and taxonomic enthusiasm. While there need be no complaint at the occasional designation of new subentities in the alleged manic-depressive psychosis, there is a remote effect of this procedure which is thoroughly bad.

† Reprinted from *Amer. J. Psychiatry* (1925–26) 82:21–86. Presented in abstract at the fifteenth annual meeting of the American Psychopathological Association, Washington, D.C., May 7, 1925, and at the eighty-first annual meeting of the American Psychiatric Association, Richmond, May 13, 1925.

[* Address delivered before the Chicago Neurological Society at Chicago on April 17, 1924. Digested in *Arch. Neurol. and Psychiat.* (1924) 12:123–125.]

The ancient predisposition is to expect from the manic-depressive an, at worst, tardy "recovery"; this expectation extends by the illusion of confluence to the new subentity. As a result, by unwitting complacency, one gets to feel that he need not exercise himself unduly in therapeutic effort for these patients, as the desired end is guaranteed by the manic-depressive alliance.

As we have attempted to show, it is the life situation of the patient that determines the prognosis. What he has derived from his forebears, his life experience, and that which befalls him during his illness—these, correlated with the situation which confronts or seems to confront him in the event of his recovery—these, and these only, are the determining factors which make in their biological summation, for benignity or malignancy of the situation. That he is of that type of personality which permits him to make use of the catatonic reaction, plus the necessity, determines his catatonic psychosis. Others of the given factors determine what that is extraneous or eccentric shall appear during or after the psychosis. The biological situation—largely psychobiological, of course—determines the ability to struggle successfully with the unimaginable schizophrenic perplexity and accounts for a final resolution and post-psychotic adaptation, or a final collapse of critique and a more dangerous form of schizophrenic phenomenology. Again, the development of serious anxiety states into recovery, chronicity, or into graver disorders—this, too, is a dynamic situation in which the above-mentioned factors exhaust the bases. It does not make one bit of difference, per se, whether a patient be labeled manic-depressive, hypothyroid, or sexually neurasthenic; the life situation is what distinguishes him completely from any other patient, and places him almost entirely beyond useful statistical inquiry.

These are no ex cathedra statements—they are the conclusions dictated by clinical data: "benign" stupors which proceeded into delapidation; "malignant" stupors with quite fair social readjustment; perplexity states which demonstrated MacCurdy's "*ipso facto*"; * schizophrenic perplexities which pulled themselves together; anxiety psychoses which showed no promising signs in

[* See John T. MacCurdy, *The Psychology of Emotion, Morbid and Normal;* New York: Harcourt, Brace, 1925.]

their course into delapidation; and, over and above all, schizo-phrenic psychoses which showed changing types or reactions to changing situations. And the reason that these conclusions have been dictated by the nature of the clinical data is to be found in the freedom of our study from either the necessity of dealing with large numbers of patients—perhaps under unfavorable asylum influences (such as appear to have existed to bring about the type of schizophrenia to which Bleuler seems generally to refer); or the urge to delimit something new in the way of a disease entity or syndrome to be torn from the dementia praecox of Kraepelin (as is, more or less of necessity, the case where one has to erect prognostic criteria for the guidance of a large group of more or less overworked physicians). Anything of value in our work comes from the intimate and detailed study of partic-ular individuals suffering disturbances of the mental or symboliz-ing activity—study which has been limited in its direction and intensity by our personal limitations, only (excepting always the interfering relative).

The immediate concern of this paper is that very difficulty in communication, in exchanging intelligence, which confronts us when we approach the schizophrenic. With no prejudice to the tripartite character of mental items,[1] one cannot but appreciate that it is by cognitive characters that we achieve intelligibility in thought and in conversation; so, by attention to the cognitive *aspect* of mental activity in schizophrenia, one may perhaps learn to talk with the victims.

---

[1] Cognitive considerations must be dealt with before the conative and affective aspects of mental situations can be elucidated. At the same time, it is unduly easy to lose appreciation of the artificial abstraction by which we come to speak of cognition as if it were in itself some independent "faculty" of "the mind." Emphasis must be laid on the tripartite character: (1) the *affective* element—unique aspects, which, if slight, can be subsumed as pleasantness and unpleasantness, but which, if they are the accentuated aspect of the symbol situation, appear as the principal ingredient of what are called "the emotions"; (2) the more or less representative aspect, the *cognitive* element, unique but in genetic analysis, elaborations from elementary "items" of sentience; (3) the *conative* element, that aspect which when itself cognized, is referred to as "impulse," and which under-lies the phenomenon of *desire*. Since the "knowing" process stresses the cognitive aspects, a comprehensive reference to the genetic elementary matter is, so far, feasible on this side only.

Bleuler, in relating the situation to "some associational weakness," has provided us with a concept inutile alike for scientific or therapeutic application. For that matter, he is compelled to admit that "the schizophrenic associations have not yet been differentiated from the functional changes of mental trend in the dream and in distracted attention." Storch, Reiss,* and others have seen fit to stress the importance of those "primitive-archaic" characters of thought to which Dr. White made reference before the American Psychiatric Association last year. These features of thought, as long as they are used merely as a sort of reference frame for the accumulation of observational data, are of much interest. Unfortunately, as far as the concept of the archaic-primitive functions as an explanation of schizophrenia, it appears to the writer to expend the universe—to necessitate an excursion into realms, the atmosphere of which is not suited to the metabolism of many: witness, "Particularly is the revival of the primitive and archaic in the schizophrenic (especially in the catatonic condition) to be regarded as a situation in which mental and bodily processes at the various levels of the personality are displaced into a primitive plane" (Storch speaking before the Deutschen psychiatrisches Verein, 1924). It will be necessary for at least three people to agree on the nature and meaning of regression before much can be made of this "displacement" into primitive "planes."

Bleuler, in addition to his devotion to the cause of psychological "associationism," has given some measure of prominence to the terminology and notions of Semon.** The sort of bull in the china shop which comes to mind as a parallel to a schizophrenic disturbance among the stored up engrams, is, of course, more amusing than useful. Mnemic causation—the doctrine that Semon developed in such a masterly fashion, in effect that a part of an original situation, recurring, may reactivate a connected "impression" or engram-complex of the former total situation—is, even if none too fully established, none the less a principle meriting

[* See, for instance, Alfred Storch, *The Primitive Archaic Forms of Inner Experiences and Thought in Schizophrenia: A Genetic and Clinical Study of Schizophrenia;* tr. by Clara Willard; N.Y. & Washington, Nervous & Mental Disease Publ. Co., 1924. See, also, E. Reiss, "Über schizophrene Denkstörung," *Zeitschr. f. d. ges. Neurol. u Psychiat.* (1922) 78:479–487.]

[* * See Richard Semon, *The Mneme;* New York: Macmillan, 1921.]

careful investigation. It does not diminish the fallacy of the old psychological doctrine, however, any more than it saves from error one who, like Rignano,* chooses to designate as "affective tendencies," the presenting dynamic features of great mental systems of those very "materials" which the alleged tendencies allegedly control. It would seem quite evident that mnemic causation, or for that matter, the whole mneme hypothesis, valuable or otherwise as it may finally prove to be, is no especially promising basis for speculations as to the causation or therapy of schizophrenia.

To render explicit the foundations on which our contemplation of thinking is based, we shall begin with the statement of Prof. Adolf Meyer ** to the effect that all mental reactions are to be regarded as a particular type of biological reaction, their characteristic being found in their occurrence with a *system of symbolization*. In his presidential address to the Neurological Association, 1922, Meyer set forth the position of neuro-psychiatry in the universe of knowledge, in a manner both enlightening and stimulating to the student who seeks to avoid mysticism and cant. Having shown the cosmos as a vast problem of "systematic formulation and practical control," he referred to the fundamental position of the facts and methods of physics and chemistry in this cosmos. "But," he continues, "the masses or entities which we meet are specifically integrated. From a certain level of complexity, they show more or less individuation [*e. g.*, the crystal], and constitute finally what we call biological units." In this scale of increasing complexity, there comes the animal types and finally, those which have developed a definite nervous system, with "literal organization of reflex processes." In this latter group, there has occurred another specialization and systematization of function, "that of symbol activity, and what we, in ourselves, know and describe as integration in more or less of consciousness." This last specialization, which he emphasizes as not only an organization of structure, but "specifically of function," one that we individually experience in the guise of "more or less '*conscious*'

[* This is probably a reference to the work of Eugenio Rignano. See, for instance, *Biological Memory*, tr. by E. W. MacBride; New York: Harcourt, Brace, 1926.]

[* * *Psychol. Bull.* (1907) 4:170–179.]

activity," is made possible by the "use of symbols, or symbolization." As soon as this type of *integration with the help of meanings* is "involved in actions and reactions, we find a type of function or behavior which constitutes itself as 'function or behavior
of the individual.'" The "organism as a whole," the watchword
of psychological medicine, is thus found to have its origin in the
specialization of a type of activity, the essential characteristic of
which is its use of symbols "in the form of gestures, emotional
display, and language, and in their silent forms"—thought. These
symbols are built up "out of perceptive-cognitive-discriminative,
and affective and conative assets." Their use is perhaps most striking in its great economizing effect, which is seen in the ability to
use "on the same level, reality and fancy; past, present, and future;
one's own ideas, and those of others; in overt effective and expressive action," behavior, "or in the especially economizing form of
implicit symbolization," thought. This biological advance includes,
finally, the unique phenomenon from which we derive the notion
of the "individual in action as an agent or subject; . . . as the
'he' or 'she,' the 'you' or 'I' that we know as a biological individual and a social entity . . . . instead of acting as an ordinary
mechanical reflex-machine, the organism constitutes itself as a
subject. . . ." This accomplishment, to which he refers as "*sub-
ject-organization*"—that by which is created the "ego," for example—he sees as simply a "specifically integrated type of activity
of the cerebrally integrated organism." [2]

[2] This development represents in generally acceptable language, the matter that we had chosen to subsume in the hormic, teleological, evolutionary
hypothesis of the organism. Since the publication of our preliminary communication ["Schizophrenia: Its Conservative and Malignant Features"],
emphasis has been laid upon meanings of the term "vitalism" which tend to
discourage our further use of it. The concept of the "horme," Dr. Meyer
deems dispensable in the realm of psychology—or psychobiology, as he
prefers to designate it—none the less, in this particular subdivision of
knowledge, there seems to be little difference in the philosophical aspects
of our views. Dr. Meyer's is a philosophy of monistic implication which
seeks to replace the "sham unity in science . . . . by pluralist *consistency*;"
ours is a rigid pluralism based on objective or teleological idealism—including in it the conception of energies, physical and hormic. Leighton
[unidentified, perhaps Joseph A. Leighton] has expressed our notion of
unity in his statement that "with regard to the *relation of the individual to
the world whole*, the latter is to be interpreted in so far as it is a unity, as,
at its highest level, a dynamic and social unity."

From this viewpoint, it will be seen that any problem in psychopathology becomes a problem of symbol functioning, a matter of seeking to understand and interpret eccentric symbol performances. Perhaps a review of the progress to date in the elucidation of these symbol dysfunctions as seen in the nosological group "schizophrenia" or "parergastic reactions," may contribute to an understanding of the views presently to be presented.

Historically, we may extend to Jung the primus in this field. Working under the tremendous incentive he received in the Freudian formulations, he penetrated the forbidding exterior of schizophrenic symbolization and discovered that relationship with more normal phenomena which was a necessary preliminary to constructive investigation. Bleuler, working with him at the time, developed a "new" psychiatry for which we can properly give the greatest credit.[3]

In 1906, Dr. Meyer announced his "Dynamic Conception," which he presented in full in 1909.[*] On the former occasion, Dr. Brush [**] bespoke the hope that careful study of everything which entered into the life history of *individual cases* would provide the psychiatrist with means for carrying a number to recovery. One can look back at that three-year period which culminated in the assembly at Clark University, with Freud, Jung, and Ferenczi present, as the infancy of the psychopathology of schizophrenia. By 1917, the period of great

---

As to epistemology, certain questions of which fall within the province of psychopathology (as do representatives of almost all branches of knowledge), we can again quote: "We know reality, *not uncritically,* however. It is a fact that we do perceive, and it is a further fact that we can improve our perceptions by means of the organizing activity of thought." This is the "organization of function" of Meyer; the "structuralization of experience" in our language; the "organizing perceptual experience, . . . discovering the systematic and intelligible character of reality as an orderly whole of things-in-relation" of Leighton.

[3] Bleuler's handicap of a lifeless associationism, which could not be vivified by the mneme hypothesis, has been most unfortunate. His *Textbook* [Eugen Bleuler, *Textbook of Psychiatry;* tr. by A. A. Brill; N.Y.: Macmillan, 1924] continues to be a book of "asylum illnesses," sharing with the work of Kraepelin, the signal position as a compilation of observational data on the *developed* disorders, illustrated with specimens (occasionally of the "side-show" variety) collected after the abnormal reactions had become habitual and relatively immutable adjustments to reality. His "schizophrenias" (concerning which the above remarks are specially cogent) are more descriptive matters, still, than psychobiological reaction-types.

[* See, for instance, Adolf Meyer, "The Dynamic Interpretation of Dementia Praecox," *Amer. J. Psychol.* (1910) 21:285–403.]

[** This is probably Edward N. Brush, M.D., for many years an editor of the *American Journal of Psychiatry.*]

development was well begun. Meyer produced, that year, a statement which constituted the point of departure of the writer's research work,[4] and Kempf published the results of his observations on Rhesus monkeys, including the explicit statement of the sex factor in schizophrenic illnesses;[5] this being followed, in 1920, by his massive *Psychopathology* [St. Louis: Mosby] in which the genetic and dynamic aspects of the life-process of the individual came in, for the first time in a text-book, for a reasonable share of consideration.

Among the Europeans, Alfred Storch of Tübingen, in 1922, produced a masterpiece (now available in excellent translation), *The Primitive Archaic Forms of Inner Experience and Thought in Schizophrenia* (op. cit.); and, in 1923, a study (as yet unavailable in English) on "Planes of Consciousness and Realms of Reality." In so far as his work reflects a close attention to the mental situation of the patient, it is invaluable; his tendency to pass on to speculations about paleogenetic mental contents seems to the writer to be dangerous.

Mention should be made of the contributions of Dr. T. V. Moore to the theory and therapy of the disorder. In his concept of the "Psychotaxes" and "Parataxes" ["The Parataxes," *Psychoanalytic Rev.* (1921) 8:252–283], which is developed and extended in his *Dynamic Psychology* [Philadelphia: Lippincott, 1924], we find a healthy em-

---

[4] "The Approach to the Investigation of Dementia Præcox," *Chicago Medical Recorder* (1917) 39:441–445. The most significant text is as follows: "In such a matter, for instance, as the catatonic tendency, it may not by any means be excluded that the capacity to go into a catatonic reaction may be looked upon as a positive asset; *i. e.,* not as a product of 'disease,' but as a defense mechanism indicative of constitutional make-up. With a more adequate study of the mechanism it may easily be found that the forces at work in the reaction as such might be turned to the use of therapy, as undoubtedly nature 'intended' to do, rather than into a blind and crude use of automatic exclusion from the outside world. It therefore becomes obvious that the whole problem of suggestion and of automatisms should be taken up in all its ramifications."

[5] Edward J. Kempf, "The Social and Sexual Behavior of Infrahuman Primates, with Some Comparable Facts in Human Behavior," sixth annual meeting of The American Psychoanalytic Association [*Psychoanalytic Rev.* (1917) 4:127–154]. He writes of "the psychopathological mechanisms involved in these cases" which are "at present classified as dementia præcox types." "The two important principles that seem to underlie each case are (1) that the individual is the host of well-developed motives, generated at the phylogenetic level, to perform certain sexual acts which he is unable to dissociate or in many instances to even control without (2) intensively developing another series of motives (at the habit level) which seem to functionate at the levels of the personality of which he is conscious. They are organized unconsciously for the purpose of controlling or at least diverting the undesirable, otherwise unmodifiable sexual tendencies." In this connection, see our "Regression: A Consideration of Reversive Mental Processes."

phasis on the subpsychotic nature of incipient mental disorders—
if one may use such language to convey the idea that the incipient
patient is not an "asylum case." His "parataxis of recoil," he appreciates, is distinguishable in many cases, in outcome only, from schizophrenia. Of therapy in such incipient conditions, he writes, "In many
præcox reaction types such efforts will be crowned with surprising
success." This is decidedly the attitude to take towards all such cases.

Reference, also, should be made to the more purely psychoanalyt-
ical discussions of schizophrenia. Professor Freud, five years after
the Clark University meeting, brought out in "Zur Einfuhrung des
Narcissmus" ["On Narcissism: An Introduction;" Collected Papers
(1925) 4:30–59], the notion of the narcissistic situation to which the
schizophrenic psychosis was considered to owe its "inaccessibility,"
and, hence, to be incurable. In his "Das Unbewusste" ["The Unconscious," Collected Papers (1925) 4:98–136], there is some further reference to "dementia præcox" in which inability to transfer (very
dubious), withdrawal of interest from the outer world (not yet rig-
orously demonstrated), libidinal inflation of the ego (very far from
a pathognomonic symptom), and complete apathy, are described. Recently, Ferenczi has carried this view to such lengths that the patient
suffering a catatonic psychosis and demonstrating waxy flexibility is
seen to "permit anything to happen to his body, which has become
to him as immaterial as the outer world. His whole narcissism retreats
into the spiritual ego, which is, so to speak, a citadel which still holds
out, though outer and inner forts are lost."

MacCurdy, who has previously identified among the pathognomonic
symptoms of dementia præcox "the acceptance with pleasurable emotion of ideas essentially painful," and, as a fundamental process, the
patient's substantiating in his mind by perversions of bodily sensations,
of memory, and of perceptions, a central idea or dominant theme, has
now brought in his Psychology of the Emotions (op. cit.), a more
unsatisfactory attitude. In addition to the well-known elimination of
the "benign stupor," he demonstrates in 50 of 585 pages, the notions of
"perplexity states" which he adopts as a "manic-depressive type of
reaction" and thereby "obviates the necessity of fabricating 'mixed
conditions' as Kraepelin has done—an invention which involves serious
theoretic difficulties"(!). This is, of course, a development of the
Hoch-Kirby "distressed perplexity" reaction type, 1919. After com-
paring his gloomy glossary definition of "dementia præcox," his dogmatic statements under the heading of "perplexity states," and such
other references as he makes to schizophrenic psychoses, with actual
clinical data, one cannot but feel that, even in his views, "there is
a bit missing." An analysis of the remarks about the perplexity patient would require too long a quotation, or series of quotations: all
in all, there are a variety of fallacies, but the most entertaining is that
of the "shifting term"—"meaning" (of which term, Ogden and Rich-

ards find "no less than 16 groups of definitions") plays a number of tricks on him. [C. K. Ogden and I. A. Richards, *The Meaning of Meaning*; N.Y.: Harcourt, Brace, 1947 (revised edition)] Elsewhere, he expresses the notion that the grave psychosis is to be explained on the basis of a regression to a level at which *instinctively repressed* tendencies to incest and similar crimes, which are unbiological (whence the "instinctive" repression), become active. This repression he distinguishes from that which "reflects the normal or expedient attitude of the society in which accident places us." In so far as this is an effort to distinguish a particular type of conflict as peculiarly dangerous, it is beyond criticism; if homosexuality were included in the "instinctively repressed crimes," it would get him out of one difficulty, as it paved his way into another: all in all, however, the inconsistency of his various opinions about schizophrenia simply reflect his preoccupation with successful prophesy—a poor approach to our problem.

With this sketchy outline of some of the outstanding writings on the subject, we shall present, in the briefest of abstract, a few cases which have been of value in our efforts to elucidate the meaning of schizophrenic phenomena. We shall attempt to escape "great theoretic difficulty" by avoiding the assertion that they are cases of schizophrenia, as three of them patched up "recovery."

CASE I

E. K., æt. 19. The third of nine children (two dead). An older brother and sister living. Mother and father living, born abroad; the latter irregularly alcoholic, quiet, stubborn, much hen-pecked none the less. Patient an instrumental delivery, required resuscitation. Infancy average. He was the most stubborn, disobedient, and wilful of the generally mismanaged family. He was negativistic, very sensitive, but gentle and kind to younger children, and generous. He felt his parents cared for him less than for the other children. He entered school at six and progressed until 12, when he developed a mental disorder seen in retrospect to have been allied to the obsessional type. At this time, his parents and relatives regarded him as indolent, lazy, and without ambition. He quit school, after much truancy. From 13 to 16, he was a juvenile court problem; then (having been examined by a psychologist and found not defective) he was sent to a reform school. He was discharged after five months, on writ. Difficulties—in the shape of profound feelings of inferiority, blushing, feelings that "he looked guilty of anything" so that he was horribly upset if anything was lost or stolen, and great indecision—increased. At 18, he was definitely seclusive, decidedly overscrupulous, and at times showed compulsive behavior. This he to some extent overcame; he took a job with two minor criminals (bootleggers), attended a mixed party on Hallowe'en, at which he had much trouble with his thinking, and "would laugh frequently without cause." A few days later, the psychosis was obvious. He was received after a panic in which he walked the streets, believing himself pursued by all the automobiles of a city, that every third house was alight, that he was to be crucified or otherwise killed. He was found to be tense, scattered, rambling in conversation, troubled by constant "rotten" thoughts (pertaining to a desire to do fellatio), sometimes confused(?), things "had a blurred look like the world was coming to an end," misinterpreted occurrences about him, felt everyone thinks him an oral pervert, had many delusions of reference, and projections involving nearly everyone.

It was found that this patient had never solved a powerful but markedly ambivalent attachment to the mother. He had, similarly, persistent strong emotional attitudes towards the father and at times a very disquieting desire to submit to sexual advances which he fancied his father making to him (this with notions that his father was "queer"). At the age of eight, he was submitted to pederasty by his elder brother, towards whom he maintained a strong conscious affection. Thereafter, he maintained a perverse adaptation with active and passive pederasty, with companions of approximately his own age. His social difficulties became marked after one of his companions refused to reciprocate as the passive agent—and told some others of his use of the patient. He masturbated frequently, to the accompaniment of homosexual anal phantasies. *On an occasion when about 17,* he, having inserted a candle into the rectum "to increase satisfaction," as the orgasm approached, withdrew the candle and thrust it into his mouth. The orgasm, he remembers vividly, was very powerful. This recollection was strongly resisted. He had never repeated the procedure. Not long after this, he discovered that several of his mates in the pederasty were making successful heterosexual adjustments, as it appeared to him; he, on the other hand, could not do better than to go to decidedly low houses, and then achieved no satisfaction. One night, having deliberately arranged to spend the night with a public pervert, he drank and submitted to pederasty, as he had expected; about two hours after falling asleep—quite intoxicated—he awoke to find the penis on his lips. Completely sobered, he dressed and left the place. His difficulties in ordinary affairs increased rapidly thereafter. He next accompanied a colored pervert, submitted to pederasty, and was disturbed to discover that he thereafter entertained vague oral cravings. He had once spent a night with one who remarked on his liking for cunnilingus. Thoughts of the desirability of this perversion now began to trouble the patient. These latter facts were obtained after months of treatment. Shortly after his affair with the colored boy, while he was sleeping on the floor in the room occupied by one of his employers, he awakened to hear his room-mate saying "I'd like to make five dollars today." Without hesitation, and without cause of the ordinary kind, the patient misinterpreted this as indicative of his companion's belief that the patient was addicted to fellatio, a subject never discussed or suggested. He stumbled through some revealing recriminations to the astonishment and contempt of the other, and, by night was in panic.

This patient did not do really free associations for months; in the meanwhile, pathological swallowing, salivation, expectoration, as well as unconscious sublimatory efforts towards the perfection of his vocabulary, were in evidence. Finally, after attempting to compromise by accepting cunnilingus desires, he was the recipient of an homosexual advance from another patient—the conflict became acute —and he entered a profitable phase. Resistance became great again, as the childhood attitudes came to light. Negative transference in many guises was apparent. Again, contact with a cultured homosexual, who "took an interest in him"—discussing literature, women, his relations to the therapist, and so forth—started up the quiescent component, and the therapy proceeded, bringing up quite remarkable phantasies about his mother and her fondling of his younger brother's penis; and the process of readjustment of experience was again under way.

He is now in training for an occupation for which he has capacity. He is not "normal," but his cravings no longer disorder his thinking and behavior. Schizophrenic phenomena, projections, compensatory and decidedly pathological sublimatory activities are not in evidence.

This case is of especial interest in that it pertains to a catatonic dissociation on the basis of oral homosexual cravings which had twice "broken cover," only to be suppressed, but which, growing more indomitable, as less and less satisfaction was acquired by other means, were carried into full, if feebly disguised, awareness on the basis of *an unrelated remark*, made by a not particularly attractive roommate, *as the patient was arousing himself from sleep*. The autogenous nature of the situation, if one may so describe it, is neatly illustrated by the sobering effect of the actual oral advance which he had resisted, from the moment of awakening, some number of weeks earlier.

Limitations of space and lack of verbatim record prevent a discussion of the "cosmic drama" of punishment which the panic thoughts constituted. The peculiarities of thought under treatment soon reverted to the well known "mechanisms" of projection, etc.

CASE 2

V. H., æt. 24. The sixth of six children, the two eldest died in infancy; a brother and two sisters surviving, æt. 30, 28, and 26, respectively. Father died when patient was under five years of age. Mother living and well. Brother married, away from home. Younger sister married and away from home. Elder sister single, works in town, highly "neurotic." Father was quick-tempered, but in general a kindly and very religious man with many friends; he used some alcoholic liquor for years, but was never drunk. The mother has periods of gloominess, but no disabling depressions. She is described as easy-going, and not sociable. She is in such circumstances that she must work. Two of the maternal collaterals have had nervous or mental disorders. The patient's birth and infancy were the average; he was good-natured and happy, as a child. Shortly after the death of the father, he was sent to a neighboring city to an orphanage, in which he completed his grammar schooling, and from which he went to a parochial school with the intention of preparing for the priesthood. For two or three years there he did well. During this time, he was devout in religious matters. About the age of 16 to 17, his interest in such affairs dwindled; he was involved in a drinking party with some other pupils, and expelled. On his return to the home, the family was distressed to find that he was entirely indifferent to church matters. He then worked as delivery boy for about a year; then took a job as clerk, which he held until, æt. 21, he underwent a tonsillectomy. About a month later, acute nephritis developed. For this, he received several months of hospital care, later securing employment in the hospital, as an orderly—during convalescence. While so employed, in February, 1923, æt. 22, he returned to his home one morning (he worked at night) in a disheveled condition, perspiring freely, although in shirt sleeves, and laughing in an extraordinary fashion. He had left the home, the afternoon preceding, apparently normal. A physician was called, and he was put under medicinal treatment. For over a year, he was fairly quiet, spent much of his time in bed; smoked constantly, "heard voices," had periods during which he replied to questions with difficulty. He remained indoors; was secretive, suspicious, and often fearful. "Imagined people in New York could read his thoughts." By the fourteenth month from onset, he began going out to baseball games, etc., including frequent attendance at moving picture performances. By the eighteenth month, he again relapsed into seclusiveness, became restless at night, would not eat without much coaxing, was silly and slovenly. He did attend to his excretory function. He was admitted in the twenty-third month of his illness.

On admission, he showed markedly reduced interest, activity, and distractibility; he gave the impression of feeling sad, ill, and hopeless. He was relatively immobile during interviews, and tended to avoid the physician's gaze. His speech was toneless, never spontaneous, and often so muffled as to be unintelligible. Showed some manneristic activities, and a sly, rather than silly, laughter, without apparent reason; this connected with unobtainable hallucinatory content of "people talking in my head." Often showed absorption in this inner experience; frequently deliberately occupied himself with objects in his environment, to avoid thoughts suggested by questions. He was not wholly seclusive, playing pool with skill, interest, and apparent enjoyment. But he was in no sense companionable.

His replies, when obtained, showed no abnormal "progression of ideas," no neologisms and were relevant; but questions were often parried by stereotyped remarks. It seemed as if superficial associations to words, etc., were connected with inner experiences, resulting in the grinning and silliness. At times, he was mute for brief periods; this seemed more the result of dilapidation of volition than to the usual blocking. He was generally apathetic, but one could detect a slight but harmonious toning of his voice in keeping with the historic matter he was bringing up. One of his most striking manneristic activities—an inhalation, opening of the mouth, and sudden exhalation —seems directly an emotional expression, much distorted. In addition to this, he sighed frequently. He showed no flushing, perspiration, nor moisture of the eyes. The following is verbatim: * [Doctor: *Are you easily influenced?*] Patient: (sighs deeply): "To what? . . . can I be influenced easily? . . . (sighs deeply) influenced to do what . . . now? . . . like smoking or something like that? . . . Giving up smoking cigarettes . . . is a hard thing to do. [*Have you started a conversation with anyone, since you have been here?*] Started a conversation? . . . with anybody? . . . No . . . I don't speak much. [*Why?*] . . . Well, I don't care much about talking . . . [*Have you always been silent?*] No, I sort of . . . I have always been sort of quiet. [*Never spoken until spoken to?*] . . . (sighs deeply) Usually. [*What can you talk about most easily?*] Huh . . . talk about most easily? . . . sports and so forth. [*Are you ever angry?*] Sure; occasionally. [*At what?*] Oh, anything. I am subject to fits of anger, just like everyone else. [*What was the last occasion?*] I don't remember. I have not been angry for a long time . . . About six years. [*Have you felt like fighting anyone, lately?*] . . . Fighting anyone? Uh,

[* In the unpublished book, *Personal Psychopathology*, Sullivan reports that he has used dots (. . .) in the case material to indicate that matter has been excluded at this point; the asterisk (*) is used to indicate pauses in conversation. The quoted matter presented in part of the case material is not always in the exact order of its production; Sullivan sometimes rearranged it in the interest of clarity within a context.

Unfortunately, no such simple use of dots and asterisks can be traced throughout the case material. The reader will note that asterisks are used in, for instance, letters written by the patient, where there would obviously be no conversation pauses. They may indicate long deletions.

In this new compositing, we have in general followed the old system, although the meaning of the various numbers of dots and asterisks has been lost. In general, they probably represented the length of the omission, or the length of the pause in the original compositing. H.S.P.]

uh (*negation*). It has been a long time. [*How long since you last tried to assert yourself?*] . . . (sighs very deeply) Two years. I don't know what you mean by that. [*Do you like to have your own way, to make people give in to you?*] To make people give in . . . try to assert myself . . . What do you mean? I don't know, I don't know, I don't have anything like that . . . (sighs deeply). [*How long since you have felt an interest in another person?*] Huh, I don't know . . . I am not interested in any one, I don't care . . . [*Eh, really?*] I don't know, I don't think of anyone. (a quite explosive sigh) [*Why do you sigh so much?*] I don't know . . . habit, I guess . . . I don't know . . . it's just depression or something like that . . . I don't know; I am tired out . . . mentally depressed. [*By what?*] I don't know . . . I am all in; I don't rest, don't sleep, will wake up in the morning with face all puffy, mouth with bitter taste, I am half-awake all night. I don't dream much, I can't remember . . . I don't remember much, any way. [*Do you like to be with others?*] . . . (sighs) Not much, any more. I am too tired out most of the time, and feel rotten . . . Sometimes I do, in the evening, in the pool room, and we . . . bowling and so forth. [*Have you ever tried to please people?*] Please them? . . . Oh, it's hard to please people . . . No, I never try to please them . . . I don't try to please people. [*When did you give up the effort?*] I never did try . . ."

In earlier interviews, the following selected utterances were obtained: As to the incident of his illness (to which he first replies about the nephritis) he says, "About a year ago . . . nervousness . . . well, I had trembling, and so forth . . . trembly, that's all . . . and this talking in my head . . . came on suddenly." To an inquiry as to the cause of the mental trouble—"This has something to do with another cause . . . I think it has to do with hypnotism or mesmerism, or something." He has no person in mind as the source; earlier in his illness, he suspected everyone, but now has no idea of who exerts the influence. He showed some interference in discussing his brother and sisters and displaced the marriage from his younger to his elder sister. He says his brother visited them about a year ago. ". . . I was sick then, I was getting over the second attack of kidney trouble. [*But the mental trouble?*] Well, I have been sort of nervous for a long time. [*Then, the voices?*] No, doctor . . . about a year after. It has been about two years since I have seen him . . . he is married and lives down in the country . . . I've never been down there. [As to the married sister,] lives in the country, too (here he gulps) one child, married a little over a year, I am not sure. [Her husband?] I never knew him. She was married to a fellow down in the country. [Question] No, we didn't know it. She got married without letting us know. [Happy?] Suppose so. [*Have you ever thought of getting married?*] No, I have been too sick. [*Ever had a girl?*]" To this he shakes his head in negation. He then corrects his statement that it was his older sister that was married.

Following a discussion of his occupational history, he arrives at the event of the illness: [*When was the first that you heard one of these voices in the head?*] ". . . I remember all right . . . yes, doctor, I remember . . . it has been . . . about everything that happened in my life . . . pretty near . . . I was doing a lot of cussing and arguing and everything else. It was a hypnotism, and I got all mixed up in the head, and left and came home, and heard the voice, and got to talking and fussing and nervous and everything. [*Always things that you knew about?*] Yes, doctor. [*Pleasant or unpleasant?*] Both, mostly unpleasant."

The masturbation motif having been reached, he stated that he began this, by himself, when about 13, that about 7 years ago, he went to a doctor "about my troubles, and he told me to stop it, and to stop smoking, too . . . used to have sort of pains around my heart, and suffered dizzy spells, vertigo on the street, and things like that. I used to try to stop it . . . always fell again." As to heterosexual experiences—"No, doctor . . . I never tried any real life . . . I thought it was wrong; I didn't know what to do either, that's all." As to homosexual experiences, he hedged, at first.

At subsequent interviews, he related his illness to "I used to bother myself a good deal . . . used to masturbate a lot, and never tell anyone about it . . . some Peeping Tom, too, four times, at women . . ." He had two chums, at the orphanage. There, he was punished from time to time, mostly for lying and breaking things—including windows, which he broke "by accident." As to the spree after which he left school, "I just carried on, that is all . . . ashamed of myself. Just cussing and things like that." Asked why he seemed so indifferent now, he replied "I am an old man now (grins in a most natural fashion). I had an attack of nephritis, an enlarged scrotum . . . tonsillitis, also . . . that swelling that I had, it practically finished my genitals . . . maybe I used to do the habit too much." Asked if he referred to impotence, he replied, "That's it . . . I can do it . . . sure . . . but ain't much . . . little bit of semen." This came about two years ago: "While I was at the hospital I did it a great deal . . . should not have done it; and then I got weak . . . It doesn't worry me any; it's the condition I am in . . . I am weak and everything . . . nervous. Get dizzy and terrified like, and trembly. Scared of what was going to happen to me. Didn't know what was going to happen to me, and I left." He continued thereafter to talk of his life at the hospital, of much gambling, etc., and follows with, "Used to do a lot of day dreaming, you know . . . Talking to myself when nobody was around . . . Used to try to stop day dreaming and talking to myself." As to the content, nothing could be elicited: "Day dreaming . . . explaining things to people, you know, that's all I can remember."

The only marked emotion he showed during the 2 months 25 days under care was one week after admission, when he sent for a doctor. He was found in the toilet, sitting at stool, breathing hard, and seemingly in much distress. Asked what the trouble was, he said his "passage was coming out sidewise," but that he had been successful in expelling it, and felt all right. This incident he would not discuss, subsequently, with the writer.

On one occasion, when asked why he avoided gazing at the physician, he replied, ". . . I'm afraid of getting into more minds . . . I've got four or five talking in my head, already." The ability of another to talk in his head "depends on which is the stronger." It developed that he suffered from enuresis while in the orphanage, as a result of which he and others in that class were refused fluids before retiring. One of the older boys bribed him to submit to homosexual practices, in return for water. The details could not be obtained: the patient became decidedly too comfortable under treatment,* and was transferred at least temporarily to another institution.

The case is most interesting in the *apparently very great dilapidation*—obviously the great part of his thinking was divorced from reality, as had been the case for many months; yet the *mental examination* showed him to possess excellent "intellectual ability," and he was able, when discussing topics not too unpleasant (he showed no visible distress) to be relevant and coherent, and to proceed in logical series. Instead of obvious distress, *inner experiences*, probably of the nature of vulgar thoughts about himself and the physician, *and frankly purposive distraction by surrounding objects* were in evidence whenever he was led to thoroughly unpleasant topics. His detachment protected him from disturbing thoughts about those he was in contact with; his reaction to any approach could be seen to be colored by an (unexpressed) invariable apprehension of painful developments. This showed itself as a studiously maintained indifference, with which he would swiftly blot out any initial interest—which could be detected by the inflection of his first few words.

CASE 3

S. F., æt. 18 years. The eldest of three children, the other two, girls, 17 and 8, respectively. Father and mother living, both well. No antecedent mental disorders elicited. Birth, infancy, and childhood, of the patient average. At the age of 13, when in the seventh grade, he alleged he could not study, did not want to, and left school and went to work. In school, he had always had two or three chums; he got on well with his fellow employees, all of whom were much older

[* Sullivan is here referring to what is commonly termed hospitalitis, in which the patient obviously becomes somewhat too comfortable in the hospital and is unwilling to attempt life outside of the hospital. H.S.P.]

than he. He liked to ramble in the woods, was not much for games, but was a great reader of Bible stories, especially. In his work, he began earlier and worked later than was required; took a real interest in doing well. He showed no interest or embarrassment in the presence of the other sex. About two months ago, the family noticed that he was unwell: he admitted that he did not sleep. Soon, he gave up working, sat around the house, and would not do anything. He made noises to annoy the mother, and, on being reprimanded, did it the more. Observed for a week to determine if he was suffering "sleeping sickness"; a diagnosis of mental illness having been made, the father, upon advice, took him home. Things went worse, the patient becoming "stubborn, obstinate, indifferent, and showed no incentive to do anything nor to take any interest in what was going on." He would leave, if visitors came. The doctor finally advised hospitalization, and he was received by commitment; very unwilling, resentful, becoming mute after he found it inevitable.

On initial interview, it was observed that he glanced hastily at the physician, then looked away. He sat in fixed, rather tense, positions. His replies were at first monosyllabic, given in a choppy sort of way. At times, he smiled briefly in a fairly appropriate manner. He said that he had not been like other people for a long time, and that his peculiarities had become conspicuous during the last six or eight weeks. He felt he should go home and do the right thing, but realized that he did not know how to escape the handicaps that had developed. He felt that he had ruined himself by masturbation, which he started without example or advice, at about the age of 7. He felt that that practice had some etiological relation to constipation and other bowel disorders, and to vague pains in all parts of the body, which he has suffered in the past months. While he is very positive that he is "not like any one else," the only difference which he could state was in answer to a question as to whether he was able to take an interest in and to like others; to this, he replied with emphasis, "No, sir, I am not." He felt that he had been shy, unable to go out and join into things like other people. While once he had been an omnivorous reader, he had lost interest in that. He appreciated that he had been in deepening troubles since the age of 13, but was brought to admit that the mental disorder had become much worse subsequent to the disappearance of satisfaction (orgasm) on masturbation, several weeks since. He was not hopeful of a recovery of his sex feeling. Hetero- and homo-sexual experiences of any kind were denied. The patient stated definitely that he disliked girls and women.

While at first his replies were at times explosive, suggesting impending blocking, he improved in accessibility. He overcame his resistance to the extent of working out, superficially, his secret career as a drinker, and finally came to the point of airing his lone sexual intercourse—with a cow. This progress came after he had a mutinous, occasionally negativistic, tense, and indifferent period. He attempted to elope, and was assaultive and abusive on his apprehension; he was very unpleasant to his parents when they visited him. At times, he had frankly suicidal impulses, but never found the occasion for putting any into effect.

Having, one night, discovered an erection, he soon informed himself of the correctness of our opinion that his sex feelings would return. His transference developed to great lengths, thereafter. Improvement from a condition in which a diagnosis of early hebephrenia was considered, to a mischievous cooperation, was forthcoming. He became a source of much entertainment among the population for his imitations of the physician, made a transference "cure," and finally discussed his hallucinations, as he was leaving to take up a job. Because of his youth, and the gravity of the psychosis with which he had seemed to be involved, no pressure was exercised on him to discover the underlying factors. The loss of sex feeling preceded by a day or so, only, the occurrence of auditory hallucinosis; the voices disappeared with the re-discovery of the feelings. The employment in which he is being tried removes him from his principal problems, the parents and the next younger sister: the case is being followed as one in which the criteria of cure may be studied.

Before the last discussions, the patient wrote a series of his impressions, which may be worth inclusion: "Cause of my imaginations; when I was very young, further back in infancy than I can call back to mind, someone, an older person, made fun of or reprimanded me for something I had done which was wrong. This must have made me feel so bad that I became oversensitive of myself, and as I grew older I could see no good in myself. This may be the cause of my feeling so confused when I tried to be sociable with people, and made it appear to them that I didn't want to be, or that I was so ignorant I wasn't worth bothering with. If I had taken my troubles, as they were little then, to my father, he would easily have straightened them out for me before they grew into what they did grow into. There is nothing which I have done which is now a mystery to me. I know that had my mind been in a happy condition, I would not have done those things. I sometimes think that, although I have been for the best part of the past 12 years, always unhappy, I will for the rest of my life be a whole lot happier than I would have been if I had had a well mind all my life—because I think I can understand human nature a whole lot better on account of the unhappy condition I was in . . . I think people can sink down to the lowest of the low and that if they repent and see what they were, they can be made into respectable people again. . . ." Needless to say, this was leading up to the workout of the cow incident.

CASE 4

W. Q., æt. 23. The third of five children. An older brother, 28, a farmer; a sister, Eva, 27, a college graduate; and two younger brothers, one 22, a college student, the other, 19, in high school. The father, living and well. Mother died of carcinoma. No information as to antecedents and collaterals. Birth, infancy, and childhood, alleged to have been average. He was the most stubborn, selfish, and least religious of the children. Always irritable and easy to anger; rather revengeful. He never danced, nor was he very active in sports other than boxing and wrestling, which he discontinued after an injury to his shoulder, some three years ago. He entered college in his eighteenth year, and did well until, in his twentieth year, his mother died. Up to this time his elder sister was finishing college. Thereafter, he had some failures, and went in the third summer vacation, to a college in New York City, to make up the work. On his return, the family noted that he was irreligious. He should have graduated the next spring, but failed. He returned home to find that the father was contemplating marriage to the housekeeper, who had worked for them for twenty years past. The father, who probably was none too wise in the management of the children, refused to make a will, and the patient became decidedly troublesome about the situation. The elder sister, also, was engaged to be married the next spring. This, too, he opposed most bitterly. Finally, he settled down to a campaign of meanness to drive the woman away, apparently more with the idea of keeping the sister at home, than otherwise. While his elder brother, who had made all sorts of sacrifices for the family, urged him to go back to college, or to take some work away from home, the father encouraged him to remain. As it became evident that the sister's marriage would take place in spite of his open arguments against it and his campaign against the housekeeper, he gave vent to ideas that the family were trying to poison him, that he was being hypnotized, and that they wanted to get rid of him. He expressed many threats against them, but showed little or no inclination to carry them out.

When received into the hospital, he exhibited a continuous shallow smile, appeared quite confused, and made irrelevant remarks. When put to bed, he fell promptly asleep. When aroused, he refused to eat, showed vague suspiciousness of everyone. During the physical examination, his behavior was very odd; he showed much command negativism. In the next few days, he proceeded through periods of apprehensiveness, and noisy outbreaks, with active hallucinations, into a deep catatonic state. There was mutism, refusal of food (so that for a long period, he was artificially fed), rigidities, posturing, prolonged periods during which he insisted upon being nude, and times when he showed cerea flexibilitas. He was at times very noisy. In the second month in the hospital, he was very untidy, continually picking his face and body, and often smeared feces into the abrasions, so that he developed a number of infections. By the third month, there were evidences of beginning improvement, some feeble interest in events about him. In the fourth month, he began to speak; he was already taking some part in the occupational and recreation therapy. In the seventh month in hospital, he was seen by the writer. He was markedly blocked, amiable, frequently grinned spontaneously. He appreciated that he had been sick, but believed that he was then quite well, having recovered some time since. The only event he recalled of the early stages of his illness was the trip by motor to the hospital: he alleged that he was worried about nothing, intended to make the best of the situation; he supposed "going home" was about all he wanted. In the initial interview, he remarked that he had roomed at college with several fellows of whom he was fond, but that they were all through, now; that one of his brothers, the one of them he liked the best, was now in college.

A word-association test was done; the results cannot be summarized. A few will be listed without comment: *Trouble*—power of the will; *disgust*—exhaustion; *sacrifice*—(no response); *table*—herditionary (?); *to excite*—disgust; *passion*—subdued; *mouth*—vertebrate (with perseverated "men"); *habit*—force (with disturbance of next association); *emotion*—sexual; *sympathy*—exaggerate; *to remove*—possible; *emotion* (2nd time)—controlled; *day*—dreamers; *pump*—(1st) charry (possibly perseveration), (2nd) passion. There followed a few interviews in which nothing other than the recording of some expressed ideas was accomplished. His more vivid "memories" from his illness were, 1st, "being stuck somewhere in the back with a dagger—once only (explained as lumbar puncture); 2nd, being "embowled," his vital organs removed from the mouth downward, *in toto:* he had no idea as to the purpose of this, or what was done with the organs: he continued semi-conscious until they were returned, then he resumed eating; 3rd "a nigger who came in once and ate from the same dish"; 4th, people standing outside his room, talking all the time, day and night, about all the gods—seemed to be worshipping; it did not pertain to him, and he did not desire to take part in it. In subsequent interviews he related that the sun had seemed for a time to remain in his body; entered by his feet and leaving by the head; he felt a tingling which preceded its entry and a peculiar sensation during the period of its stay. The results of its presence in him were affected by what the "people outside said"—on one occasion "they called me the Baltimore *Sun*, and the sun was different that day. . . . Once a man with body and joints aglow came and went out and bound up all the hags and whores, and burned them . . . he was not me, but he was under my direction . . . I knew his name . . . he was the giant, a general; had charge of all the others, one was named Saul. I think they were all Sungods . . . All I did was to send them out to gather up the wickedness. Believe Saul became the [our own] sun. I was told that this [the accumulation of wickedness] would happen periodically." He had been told "by one of the men to write a Bible, . . . think they called this man a 'father' . . . one who came down and said something to me, but the 'sons,' who were outside, persuaded him I didn't; that I didn't want war between the 'fathers' and the 'sons' . . . There were 'nuns'; the 'fathers' could not agree with them . . . Every so many years a certain profession was to be extinct [Doctor: *Which ones?*] At one time, they was all to be extinct. [*In what order?*] Don't recall what order. . . . I think that meant we can't all be a success at one time, therefore one must be a failure at a certain period . . . After there was no war, the 'fathers' and 'sons' seem to have cooperated; and they told me, and I remember . . . that was they told me there was one profession to be extinct . . . period seemed to me to be every one thousand years . . . One extinct at present, don't know which one . . ." He believes that this happened some time after his arrival; probably the sun incident began before his viscera had been "returned." ". . . One time, men and women wanted to fight: I did not leave it happen, at that time I prevented it. Men proposed that men should be born from men, and women from women; but I proposed to leave it as it is . . . As I understand it now, they were to be hermaphrodites. There was to be war between them, and they were not to be marriage between the sexes . . . But I did not think it was practical . . . that they should continue men and women marriages, as it is . . . My opinion always has been that a man is a woman's protector . . . I think most happiness is generally by that relationship . . . I think the idea of that quarrel was from Adam and Eve . . . that was one of the causes of the war; . . . Eve's temptation of Adam . . . Also, feeling that women would control . . . all the government officers would be women . . . suffragism . . . It seemed that men could bear men, but don't recall method . . . I think now it [the peace between men and women] was probably accomplished by making women more fond of children . . ." In regard to the first luminous one: "He came up out of the ground and he gave a battle-cry, and all the others came up then . . . some came from the sky. (Then, rapidly) I think those from the sky pacified the world . . . and they told the others why it had happened; so that they would not fear . . . to teach men and women who were left, the after-effects of wickedness . . . I remember it took quite three days to clean up wickedness . . . Wickedness at that time seemed to be all women . . . I remember that there were to be no classes of criminals."

The next day, he said, "I remember I was asphyxiated with gas once, and they gave it to me often enough to keep me from regaining consciousness . . . Used to know when they gave it to me . . . Also they blew figures up to the ceiling . . . probably from the door; when the figures reached the ceiling, they remained as pictures . . . [*How were these figures gotten up?*] Some were dressed and some were nude . . . one figure a day . . . seems as though I was moved to another room later . . ." He went on to remark that at one time the "fathers" asked him to come with them, but the door was always closed, so he could not.

At one time, "they" had a radio attached to his bed, either the "fathers" or the "sons" told him so. He doesn't know "why they had it so, unless it was that they wanted to hear what I said." It develops that this was during the war between men and women. "Once they tried to throw me out of the window . . . but I didn't go out . . . Wanted to throw me into Hell. [Question] Don't know which group it was, they had my eyes bandaged. [*What do you think it means?*] . . . Think it probably represented temptation. It just occurs to me that they called it Hades, Chaos, and Hell at different times . . . that's odd . . . meant different groups of people, you know. For instance, now it is Hell and Harding, . . . Lloyd-George . . . no one's name is E . . . I went against my forefathers . . . I came of German, Dutch, and English . . . that was the reason for the original war between the fathers and the sons . . . There should be cooperation between sons and fathers. There is a tendency to have no connection with parents. [*How do you mean?*] I know a family who keep the grandfather almost in seclusion . . ."

Again, "I remember I could talk a different language, but I don't know what it was. It was probably—you remember the battle cry?— it was probably the first language ever spoken. Battle-cry was probably not more than three words . . . Latumbra . . . that was part of the battle-cry . . . just came to my mind, not certain it was a word from that language. . . . I remember the first time I saw heaven . . . at that time it was the purpose for the Elijah of the prophets to go forth nude and preach the gospel. Elijah was supposed to come from heaven to earth . . . I remember, he was to start in New York City. I think that was the time I learned that language. I was here and could see into Heaven. [*He was to go forth nude?*] At that time the people would not see him being nude, because of what he spoke: I remember the whole world was to see him come from heaven to earth, and that would be so great to them that they would not notice he was nude. [*Do you recall why he was to be nude?*] At that time I knew, I don't recall . . . it just seemed natural. Elijah was to appear first, as the Bible said, but it seemed God entered me first, an Elijah did not appear . . . [*What now?*] I recall one time the road I was in an automobile, all along the street was army men, and when I came to the city, the street was open, there were not any police there . . . at that time, I did not have any conception of what it . . . that was before I came here. If I was with some person, and bought something, they'd always give the money back . . . They've never told me, but I can see . . . As I see it now, I'd went to a certain place, the people would do the same—do business at the same place. [*Why was that?*] Represented God to them . . . at that time, did not realize . . . [*I don't understand.*] Since then I realized that I represented God . . . In college, usually around me was success . . . [*How was that?*] . . . room-mates (mutters). [*What is the purpose of all this?*] Since, I believe it happens once about every four thousand years . . . I remember people in New York called me God . . . on the street somewhere. One time it happened, I was on Broadway . . . I was just . . . a friend and myself were just walking—. don't recall his name . . . [*Someone of whom you were very fond?*] Yes." He then went on to say that he had known about 20 people there, supposed he had 4 or 5 intimate friends. "Met more different nationalities than I ever had before . . . probably most every nationality . . . two princes, one from Tokyo and one from Siam . . . knew them quite well. I recall that one time a man took me up in the arn and pointed out the people around as characters in the Bible." When questioned, he substitutes "ward" for "arn," saying that he does not think "he was anyone around here . . . that happened two or three months ago. . . . I remember, before I came here, they wanted war with Japan. I did not favor it. [*And that ended the matter?*] Yes."

"After my vitals return it took me a month to regain control . . . control of my excretions . . . I remember if they'd talk . . . or maybe, the smoking of a cigarette . . . would affect . . . would cause me to urinate. [*How was that?*] I don't know how . . . but I know different conversations at times did affect it." He would not recall anything as to the nature of the conversations, adding, "You see, it happened often. [*But you must have some notion about how it worked?*] They probably spoke something the time they urinated, and it affected me." Nothing further could be obtained. [*As to the cigarettes?*] "It seemed probable that they smoked when they urinated . . . I remember, if they'd light a cigarette or a pipe, it would cause me to urinate, but I don't recall why." Effort to secure more data in this connection led to definite attempt to avoid the subject: "I was just passing . . . [*Well?*] . . . I meant, I did not pass or form an opinion about it . . . [*Continue!*] . . . [*What are you thinking?*] I was just thinking of a chemical experiment . . . grape sugar . . . urine . . ."

With a keynote in the remark, "One time, I controlled the lightning (lowering his voice, as if in awe) . . . that was after I was here," the patient developed ideas that he controlled the weather, those about him, and so forth. A few more fragments, only, are worthy of note. "Wherever I went, if they wanted cold weather, it would be cold; and if they wanted warm, it would be warm: that was before I came here." "Recall if I'd leave one part of the country on account of weather, it would not be necessary, . . . just change it that way. [*How did you change the weather?*] Never paid any particular attention to climate; . . . the divine power." On a favorable occasion, an inquiry was made as to the "nuns"; the remarks were: "Remember once, was in the room and they were praying there . . . I think that was around just before the time there was war between men and women . . . the fathers controlled the nuns . . . I remember they were in the room all day . . . facing towards the bed . . . I remember they were men, who were fathers, and women . . . I remember they worshiped me as god of rain, as I recall . . . The thought just now entered me now whether the women who enter a convent benefit any person . . . inclined to think not . . . Remember one time, they questioned the influence of statuary . . . you know they are as a rule usually draped . . ."

As the patient seemed entirely resistant to any effort to dispel the factitious reality of his fancies, interviews were discontinued. He developed a syphilophobia, gradually became more suspicious, and finally a little expansive. By his thirteenth month under care, he was definitely paranoid, had tantrums of rage, projected all sorts of ideas, denied that he had been ill when he came here, saying "It was not long before I was, afterwards"; he believed that many plots were being formed against him, involving in them all the personnel with whom he had any contact. He was transferred to a state hospital, from which his family secured his parole, two months later. He then showed belief that he could influence others by wishing them to do things. He took an interest in things, however, worked, and read the newspapers, even was careful of his personal hygiene. He did not like to leave home, which, it being a small community, may have been quite natural. He took up the study of salesmanship in a night school in the neighboring city (in company with his elder brother). The father and this brother did not get on well, and the father criticized him to the patient. After about a month, the patient relapsed into acute psychosis, coming to breakfast trembling, perspiring, and blocked. He was hallucinated and accused the brother of ruining his name, etc. He had been sleeping in the same room with this brother: he now accused him of improper relations with a friend. He has continued in the state hospital since then.

CASE 5

I. O., æt. 36. The sixth of seven children. Of his more remote antecedents, nothing has been worked out, but both parents were mentally deranged. He was born on a farm, the family was quite poor, and not only was recreational opportunity of the simplest, but the school facilities were primitive. No one remains who was sufficiently acquainted with his early years to supply data. Most of what is known of his development came to light following his discharge from this hospital, as his wife, our informant during his stay here, was not of the immediate neighborhood of his home, and did not know him before his twenty-fourth year. He never discussed intimate details of his life with her; for that matter, he did not talk over his business, either. While she demonstrated a troublesome tendency to "cover up" the whole situation, there is no reason for supposing that he was other than an exemplary husband so far as affection, tenderness, and liberality as to money, etc., were concerned.

With but little school education, and with no previous family acquaintance with such work, he entered, at the age of 16 or 17, the employ of a large public utility company having extensive holdings in that territory. He did very well, showed many valuable traits, and rose to a high position in its field work. While his more intelligent associates regarded him as "always queer," and some of them knew that his family—excepting only himself—were "weak-minded," they noticed nothing particularly unusual until the end of April, 1924, near the end of his thirty-fifth year of age, and his eighteenth or nineteenth year with the company. He became seriously ill on the 14th of July. For some two months, he was unusually irritable, inclined to argue with his foremen, and showed some suspiciousness, thinking that they and his friends were working against him. About two weeks before the acute episode, he asked a visiting neighbor to bring her ouija board to the house. He developed a great interest in operating this, contrary to the wishes of his wife. He asked the board a number of questions pertaining to his personal affairs, his business, etc. The board "told" him that "they" were trying to get his job and "fire him," and that he was to be discharged on July 15th. He developed disordered sleep, seeming to his wife to be manipulating the board in his sleep. After about a week, he began to complain to his wife of stomach trouble, expressing a fear that he might be developing appendicitis. Two days before the acute episode, on the 12th of July, he went to the headquarters of his company and arranged a conference with the District Superintendent at a hotel. He expressed a complicated delusional system to the general effect that his immediate superior, a Catholic, had made a trip to the central office of the company, and there conspired with a high official, a Catholic, to oust him. In arguing in support of this system, he admitted certain irregular business transactions in which he himself had engaged, contrary to the interests of his company. His friend, to whom he was indebted for some of the progress he had made, pointed out the inherent improbabilities of many of his notions, but without success.

On July 14 he returned to his home about 3 p. m., went upstairs to his room, and was found there, standing in front of his desk, clutching it tightly with both hands. His eyes were closed, and he was tense and rigid. A physician was called; he found the pulse 114, and administered morphine, which brought it down. On the desk was a sheet of automatic script: "You are in great danger from heart trouble go up to see Dr. Yes I know you was I should have told you when you was sassing him so. Yes but you had a close call we are not there yet concentrate on the Blessed Jesus. Yes by all means." The physician, minister, and members of the family succeeded in getting him away from the desk at 1 a. m. He undressed, went to bed, and there lay rigid with his hands crossed on his chest, occasionally opening his eyes for a moment, the rest of the night.

Next morning, July 15, he arose, said he felt "all right," and apparently had no knowledge of what had transpired. He drank a cup of coffee and set out in his car, at breakneck speed. The neighbors failing to overtake him, the road was barricaded with a five-ton truck; into this, he drove at full speed, demolishing his car, but without discoverable injury. He was apprehended, handcuffed, and taken to the jail. There, he was stiff, uncommunicative, and would not eat.

On admission to the Sheppard and Enoch Pratt Hospital on July 16, he refused to talk; he wrote communications with one finger on the desk, so hastily that they were unintelligible: one was made out to be "Are any doctors here." On the trip, he had slept, as a result of narcotics, most of the time. On one occasion, only, he had been disturbed, but, finding himself handcuffed, and being reassured that he was en route to a hospital, he quieted down. He was mute, passive, slightly cooperative, and entirely negligent of bowels and bladder, besides requiring artificial feeding, for some time after admission. He would spend most of the daytime with eyes open, but always closed them on the approach of anyone. On occasion, he would insist on lying nude. On August 8, he rose during the night and closed the door of his room. On August 12, at noon feeding, he was somewhat resistive, coughed and sputtered, so that the nasal tube had to be reinserted. That afternoon, during a visit of his wife, he enticed her, by pursing his lips, to kiss him. As she leaned forward, he closed his arms about her with much force. Three attendants were required to release her. He resisted feeding again that evening. When his bed was changed at 11 p. m., he rose and walked about the room. At 12.10 a. m., he stealthily approached the night nurse from behind and attempted to choke him. He was put to bed after a great struggle; he lay quiet for a few minutes, then jumped from the bed and leaped against the window guard, striking it with his head, with force sufficient to break a heavy screen. He was restrained. He was removed from the rest-jacket on August 16, inert and passively cooperative as usual. On August 25, he for the first time varied from his stolid expression, smiling appropriately at something. On the 29th, he was again resistive to the feedings. On the evening of the 31st, he attempted to run out of his room. Next day, Sept. 1, he arose and dressed. He refused to speak, writing that he could not do so. He ate a good meal, and fed himself thereafter. One of his notes read, "Are you the Head Doctor? I am under the impression that you are the Head Doctor you was the one that received me in the reception Hall. [This after a reply in the negative.] Sir, my mouth is sore I want you look about it for me I cannot talk on this acount, I am well except this not much but I cannot articulate words." Asked if he would use a gargle, if it were prescribed, he wrote, "No I do not understand medicine, I wanted you because you are the Head Doctor and I want relief I am going home tomorrow. Did you send a tele-gram to my people to come and get me tomorrow morning." Prior to this, when writing notes asking for his clothing, he had included the remark "I was expecting the Head Doctor before this time can you tell me why He has not come." By night, he had begun speaking. He impressed the ward force as "very appreciative"; he said that he felt "fine except throat and mind is clear." He drank a notable amount of water. Next day, he was pleasant, quiet, cooperative, and spent his time reading and playing pool.

He was seen by the writer on Sept. 3. He expressed surprise at the passage of so much time since the beginning of his illness. He referred vaguely to an occasion when he was beaten; otherwise he had re-ceived excellent treatment, he said. Asked further about the beating, he went on to say that one night he had seen vaguely the figure of a man, in silhouette, in his doorway. It came to him "in some way" that he was to put the man out. His recollection is that he rose and attempted to do so, and "woke up" when he "was thrown on the floor." Thereafter, it came to him that if he did not get away then, he would be killed or very seriously injured, and that he should jump through the window, which he attempted. Having become pre-occupied with the notion of how to get away, he remained inert, thereafter, and it came to him that he should go through the door and down the hall, and in that way escape from the building. But he continued to ponder on that, feeling that he would not be able to do it, and was quiet awaiting his fate while being placed in restraint. When advised that he had attempted to choke the nurse that evening, he showed no emotion, but denied any recollection of it, saying that he really did not "come to" that night until he was on the floor the first time. He made polite expressions of regret.

His story of the onset of the illness was about as follows: He was in perfect health in every way, suffering no sleeplessness, suspiciousness, or anything else, including stomach trouble, until, while standing at his desk, some time or other, he had a very severe pain in the region of his heart, such that he thought he would die. He remembers standing there, clinging to the desk, until his legs grew weak and trembled, and he felt like falling; about that time, some doctor (he does not know which of several) came and gave him an injection in his left arm. He remembers nothing else, he alleged, until he awoke in the train en route here. When he regained consciousness on that occasion, his legs "were going like windmills," and he had twisted his forearm so that the handcuff had injured his left wrist. His left arm was "terribly sore and stiff." (Shortly after his reception, he developed a deep infection of that wrist, probably secondary to such trauma.) The deputies who accompanied him answered some of his questions, and encouraged him to go to bed. He recalls vaguely the arrival in Baltimore, and his being informed that he was to be taken to this hospital.

He admitted a great interest in spiritualism, for years past, but denies with great emphasis, any connection between it and his illness. He recalled that he had used an ouija board some little time ago, but would not discuss the matter. He denied, with vigour, the authenticity of the automatic script above referred to, which was exhibited to him. He then announced that the only thing on his mind was having his friends notified so that he could hurry home and investigate the whole matter. He emphasized that his friends had brought him here to avoid any publicity. Because of an undercurrent detected in these statements, he was advised that it had been by his wife's intervention that he had come to this rather than to the state hospital; his expression became hard, but he said nothing.

After a pause in the conversation, he expressed appreciation for the care he had received, and continued "But now they are coming for me tonight, and I want to have everything arranged to go without any delay." Asked as to whom "they" are, he replied, "Why, the deputies who brought me." Following an ensuing pause, he altered his tone and, with a stately gesture, charged the writer with full responsibility for seeing that he was ready to go when the men came for him. He refused to discuss the details of his illness, the events that might have brought it about, or his thoughts on the subject. He denied categorically and in detail any persecutory notions prior to the "heart attack." He refused to entertain the notion that any emotional stress preceded the illness.

In the next weeks, he was affable and agreeable to the physicians, but would not discuss his sickness. He refused to associate with other patients and would not go for walks outside. His wife grew to be terrified of him; he gibed her concerning her fear. She was requested to discontinue her visits. When seen in conference on Oct. 4, he was markedly grandiose, refused to answer questions, and finally said that he had not been treated fairly, and "there was no consideration shown me after I woke up . . . September first." Having cut himself off from contact with everyone and having a talent for penmanship, he now started the preparation of letters, very few of which were presented for mailing, the greater number being preserved among his effects and closely guarded. The quantity of his writings in the succeeding weeks was truly remarkable. He wrote what purported to be a battle hymn for his native state, and alleged music to accompany it. A little later, he started a series of neat drawings, working diagrams for an alleged steam automobile, this showing good drafting ability but more familiarity with gasoline than with steam motors.

The "Battle Song," mostly a wearying repetition and more than 800 words long, includes, in part: "We are too much engrossed with ourselves to heed the call to arms, We are too much interested in the things that do us harm. We are his children to him we owe all our Love, To him we owe our lives, And to him we are to pay for all our Sins. And when he calls us up above we will see him face to face, And when we see him, We will know him by his Grace . . . We do not fear a foreign foe. Or do we care to see, Our land so bright run red with blood. For him who is on high . . ." In a letter of transmittal, he asked a music house to send him a proof of this, saying that he would want a great many gramophone records made from it. In this letter, it becomes evident that he wishes to reassure them, saying that they will be in "no danger from prosecution as We will assume all responsibilities for issuing them. We are under no obligations to the pope at Rome . . . We owe allegiance to our Father in Heaven and our own Dear Government, which meets his approval to a greater extent than any other Government in the world yet there is some things He wishes us to do in order to keep our Government intact, one of those is to wrest from the pope at Rome the authority which he is now exorcising . . ." The peculiarities of these writings, which was at first taken as evidence of ignorance in the use of capital letters, and certain spelling, was later revealed as the result of instruction from his "Father in Heaven" who communicated with him continuously.

In a letter of Oct. 14, he, in part, said that his wife, he understood, had "circulated" information to the effect that he was a "hopeless case," which slander "she was just starting to try to create a sentiment to appease the peoples wrath against herself for her actions since I have been here which was for a purpose you will know about soon . . . I was given up as a Dead man here in fact I was dead to all intents and purposes but my Father in Heaven had important work for me to do so I was sent back and am glad that I was chosen for this work which is the greatest work any man has been allowed to do since Jesus Christ our Saviour was Crucified Nineteen Hundred and Thirty Seven years ago . . . You can state positively . . . that I have never had anything wrong with my brain here or elsewhere . . . I am ashamed that I have to acknowledge that I was enough fool to marry this woman [his wife] . . . she was here and stayed a long time with her Lover they even had the nerve to come to the Hospital here together. I seen them from a distance . . ." This letter, like all succeeding ones, contained much alleged information as to the daily life of the addressee, to impress upon her the supernatural nature of his information.

On Oct. 15, he wrote to a woman warning her that she was about to marry a married man. Next day, he "rescued" a woman in San Francisco from marriage to a married man, who had visited a "resort." By the 19th, another western woman was saved from a man *who had deserted a wife and children.* Under the same date, he wrote himself a soul-satisfying letter from "Miss Margaret Clark of Los Angeles," in which she thanks him for having rescued her from a "life of shame," which she was threatened with by marriage to a man with "a wife living and a little girl three years old needing his support." Needless to say, Miss Clark is a movie star.

Under date of Oct. 14, he wrote the first of a remarkable series, about 390 pages of script, which will be referred to as the "Sara correspondence." Two of these letters purport to come to him from another, one is the "copy," of transcendental origin, of a letter from God to Sara, and there are twelve envelopes of an unfinished letter from him to Sara. One "to" him is of 94 pages, and is unfinished! In his writings are eight "letters" addressed to him; twice, he refers to these as copies, supplied to him by his Heavenly Father, of letters which "they" would not deliver to him.

On Oct. 24, he wrote a fourteen page letter addressed to the General Manager of his company. This was not presented for mailing. In it, there occurs the following illuminating statements: "You are also aware of the fact that I was rather humiliated by the methods used after I was so sick that I was unable to help myself further" after his "Poisoning." He refers to "certain persons in the employ" of his company "who are to blame for me being brought to this place instead of being taken to the . . . Hospital in . . . where I should of been taken after I failed to get there by my own efforts." It is toward the city in which this hospital is located that he had started when his car was wrecked. ". . . You are aware that I was poisoned by order of the catholic hierarchy . . . I will relate with a full exactness the methods used to kill me after I was brought here . . . the inhuman methods used in order to take my Life. the first thing I was subjected to an injection of one fourth grain of 'Dentine' in my right leg above the knee that was sufficient to kill any man not under protection of the Fathers care . . . the second time . . . was ten days later . . . the second dose was of the same poison and was injected into me on the end of a temperature tube this contained one half grain and was a different form from the first was in a soluble form, the second was in a tablet form and was much more severe on account of the methods used. after another period of ten days I was further treated to an operation. As you have occasion to remember on account of the treatment I received on my journey here my wrists were wounded and badly swollen. in order to sure this time that I would die, they operated on the worst sore on my left wrist under the pretext of putting in a drain tube which was not needed. they performed this operation without applying any anthethetics whatever or even cocaining the flesh around the parts to be operated upon. naturally as I was unable to speak a word on account of the condition of my mouth and throat I stood for the operation without objecting volubly after the incision was in they proceeded to slip under the loose flesh a one grain tablet of the same poison. After ten days more and I still lived they decided that if I was to be dispatched some other method would have to be resorted to. they then proceeded to operate through my nose in order to reach my brain only the fact that my Father stood by my bedside saved me from a horrible death the probe was inserted the proper distance but it did not enter the brain by any means as my Father . . . this operation was also performed without the use of anthethetics or the parts being cocained. the pain in this case was also encruciating in the extreme. but as I stated before in this communication since I was unable to talk I did not object strenuously to the operation by saying so at least I bore the ordeal with as good a grace as possible since I was being talked to continuously by my Father who has been by my side continuously throughout the long persecution I was then left for a time in peace in order to die without any more noise than possible but I was not destined to die. so when this did not work it was necessary to try some other methods it was becoming a sore greviance to the people in whose hands I had been placed to be killed that I would not die. so I was to be further put to the test one night one of the henchmen came to my room with the intention of inserting another tablet with the temperature thermometer but as I was carrying all the poison that I was able to handle my Father told me to get up and put the man out of the room, which I proceeded to do even in my weakened condition but he was sport enough to call two more of the paid henchmen and the three after inflicting considerable punishment left me unconscious on the bed. when I woke up I was encased in a straight jacket which I was humiliated with for a period of two days and was relieved of it only then through the friendship of . . . It was necessary to feed me through a tube until I was able to throw off the poisons enough to try to eat. while I was still being fed by the tube method they put one fluid oz of the fluid poison as I named before in with the food into my stomach it was necessary for me to expel this dose quickly while I was vometing this up it was against the wishes of the henchmen so three of them attempted to hold me on my back in order to keep me from expelling this poison. I was able to expell this fluid by an extreme effort. but was subjected to extreme pain by reason of one of the men putting his whole weight on my sore wrist which was fulcrumed over the bed rail as a leverage this not only hurt the sore but it broke a piece off the wrist bone which was not set back in place. this was also a failure and the effort was growing on the nerves of the paid hench-men and as Mr. . . . who was a nurse in the ward and attended me daily was a good medium but innocent of any wrong intention was used by mixing up a paste for the purpose of cleaning my teeth I was able to exclude what little he was able to force between my shut teeth this was the last poison I was subjected to while in the bed and when I got up I was able to keep from the poison by watching what I was eating I was told by my Father what foods contained the poison that was offered me was one half grain of the same poison in a glass of water the second was three quarter grains of the same in some fish. the third was one grain of the same divided in two glasses of milk the fourth was one and one half grains of the same in two soft boiled eggs. the fifth was two grains of the same in two more glasses of milk the sixth was three grains put into some vegetables but I was told where it was each time so I was in a position to side-step the poisons. but it was not very satisfactory the way things were going since I had refused to go outside in the grounds with the patients since there was nothing the matter with my brain I did not mean to be humiliated by parading through the grounds under guard when I had made my position clear on this point, Mr. R. . . . who superintends the third ward decided that he would march me out by force . . . I am not in a good position here but in case it be comes necessary, I am ready to sell my Life for all I can collect for it which seems to be considerable since I now weigh one hundred and two and one half pounds . . ." [Should have been 202½ lbs.]

In the reply to this letter, which he prepared for himself, there occurs the following: "we were told you was a little boy and your Father was looking after your business while you was in jail . . ." There is also the interesting sentence, "Mrs. I. [the wife] had re-ported you in a general bad condition both physically and mentally I guess she was just stating her wishes in the matter." Needless to add, this allegation concerning the wife was quite unjustified; she attempted in every way to cover up and conceal his illness.

Of the remainder of his writings, a few excerpts only will be given, these to show a few of the major motifs. The first to be considered is the history of his sex life. This being autobiographic, there are many opportunities for speculation. "Sara . . . you made a mistake at the age of 18 years. You were at that time going with a boy by the name of I. O. who Loved you and started going with you with the avowed intention of marrying you . . . you broke down this Boys Faith in womanhood . . . you . . . wrote him a letter stating you was tired of going with him and wanted to quit . . . you quit him without explaining your reasons . . . you were aware of the fact that he was very sensitive in general and this is to be recom-mended in young people of both sexes as it shows they have an active brain . . . You knew some Boys were talking or rocking him because they were afraid of his cool nerve . . . you wanted to humiliate him in some way then you could make up with him. I [God] warned him in a dream that they were going to rock him . . . and he carried a gun for a long time for them . . . the boy you Loved and wanted after he was shot up or otherwise mutilated." He then refers to an occasion on which he kissed this girl in church, whereupon he saw "the hatred in your eyes as you raised to your feet after receiving the only Love kiss you have ever received in your life . . . you was willing to marry him in case you could succeed in humbling him . . . you had a whole lot of revenge by leaving him worry about what you was mad about and then to go with a widower . . . * * * When you was young and I [the patient] was too much in Love with you to know how to handle a bad naughty little Girl I was sure that I Loved you but I never thought you ever Loved me . . . young Girls do not like to marry bashful Boys . . . I would not have went with you long enough to have fallen in Love with you to the extent of ruining my whole Life . . . Sara . . . if you only knew what I suffered when I heard . . . that you was married to a man I was sure you did not Love you would pity me even now a great big man who only weighs 206½ lb and over six feet tall your little bashful Lover grew up into a good sized man . . . I am mad that you considered me a coward when you decided to humiliate me by having me rocked severely . . . They did go up into the woods to ambush me but . . . I was looking for this and had my revolver in my hand when I was walking slowly thru the woods, looking for my enemies, your good brave champions . . . If you only knew just how far you went to wreck me both physically and morally . . . those big brown eyes that have haunted my dreams ever since . . . * * * I was in mortal agony when I got a letter stating you was married to a man who was married before and had known the Loving embrace of a good little Girl and then immediately destroyed her by being a human beast which almost took your life for the first three months . . . do you wonder how I suffered when I knew you was in the arms of this Beast . . . and I was laying awake of nights crying myself to sleep because my little mate had deserted me for the man who had a farm already which I knew he had inherited and was much older than I was . . . * * I was not drinking to the extent of hurting me but did take the vile whiskey into my stomach but he or no other man ever seen me drunk [was drunk once], I mean to the extent of making me silly. one month after I got my death sentence from your Dear little mouth I quit drinking for all time, by making a solemn vow to . . . my Sister who Loved me and who I Love Dearly yet . . . * * the matter of being bad after women in general this was a dirty black lie. I never knew a womans embrase until I was married . . . for the last four years I have hardly known a womans Love. I was not in Love with this 'Demon' when I was married to her as you know but was marrying in order to have a Home and small children . . . Sara the fact that I was chosen for this important task [the repopulation of the world] does not show the World my people were foolish in general. I am ashamed to acknowledge that for reasons you will understand there was two 'Demons' born in our Family I almost lost my Life when a small Boy on account of one of these 'Demons' the other one was always my enemy although I have done everything possible to help her . . ." There is interspersed in these letters messages from deceased relatives; and at this point, the dead sister of "Sara" remarks the following, with reference to a "lie" told to the patient by another boy, concerning "Sara" "and him going to the church on . . . by themselves and engaging in sexual intercourse on the way home. Sara he [the patient] Loved you better for this this shows you how far he went to console himself . . . * * * * I was lied to about you and a certain woman in the mountains . . . that you parted an old man and his wife in the mountains . . . you was in bed with this bad old woman . . . [you are said to be] a good looking man who is bad after the old women . . . * * * *" In the pages that follow, he recites how he took the marriage vow with added solemnity, because of his disappointment in the Sara case; how he caused his wife but 15 minutes pain in 11 years of married life (this referring to the rupture of the hymen, one would judge from matter yet to be quoted); and then how he grew weak sexually, from attempts to satisfy his wife by "holding back."

As to his relation to God, the following excerpts may suffice. "God" in one of his letters states: "Jesus who died for you was sacrificed to save the other Children but at this time we do not have to sacrifice O . . . my other son [the patient]. I am in Love with him because he Loves me with his whole Heart Body and Soul . . . I have had to whip him for being disobedient already. he was wanting a ring he had when he went to the Enoch Pratt Asylum and when he got up he wanted this ring and because he thought a certain friend of his was responsible for him not getting it he wanted to punish him in a manner I did not like so we had a fight and he came out second best, * * *" [The patient, writing as himself] "my Father talks to me and we have a good time . . . * * you notice I am being talked to as I write I sometimes want to use capital letters when there is no importance attached to the name then my Father says to scratch that out Son we want it right. also when I shed tears when I think of what you and I missed my own Brave little Girl . . . he says now dont do that Please dont son you can do that later but not here be calm be calm." His "Father" assures him that he will restore various and sundry wives to the condition of virgin, for the patient's delectation. The "spirit" of Sara's mother "writes" her: "Sara you have never known this

Boy. we do. he is love itself, he measures one hundred and thirty two per cent on Love that is higher than anyone else in Heaven or on Earth except Jesus Christ who is one hundred and fifty six and as you know the Father is all Love and compassion . . . he is most Honored Boy in the whole big Earth today and is so modest he wont even think about it." Another "spirit" reports that the "Father" says of him, "you sass him and are fussy in your habits but he says he Loves you for it oh so well . . . you understand him so well he says that you hardly ever have to be brought to order at any time . . . we are very proud of him and that you are his little Boy who he Loves with such a passion . . . I L M . . . means I Love Me, a free Love Salute in Heaven."

There are many vituperations of his wife, the more vile being the "work" of "spirits" communicating with him: the rationale of this may be explained, along with something about the etiology of the stupor, by the following fragments. He refers to the "foul" deal he had, "caused by an old Love, which was supposed not to exist at this time or at the time we were married eleven years ago," in which he refers to a projected myth of an early love of his wife. One of his spooks writes as follows, "when we found out you was wounded for about the same way as all demons work on the genitel organs in order to stop the breeding of good children . . . 'Father' says you were never allowed the pleasure of sexual intercourse either . . . we know how you have have taking care of your own Dear Body in a good manner and your sexual strength 'Father' says is so much improved that you thought of curley head as soon as you woke up . . . I knew you was wounded in the left testicle . . . 'Father' says he was running a race with Satan and done this to keep me from being raped . . . * * * I would go through fire or untold agonies . . . to engage in sexual intercourse with you Father says we cant hurt you any at all we dont understand this as we are supposed to be the stronger as there is not so much semen excluded but he says you are being rebuilt so strong we three can Love you all we want to . . . you are to make up Happy three times apiece that same night he says you wont be hurt and we wont be very much fatigued he says further that you are to show us a new way . . ." As the major part of his script was devoted to the two purposes of (1) expressing hate of his male loves and (2) the upbuilding of an unlimited harem with the members of whom (mostly "remade" virgins) he was to have well nigh continuous coitus, we read such fragments, as the following, with double interest. Writing of a life long friend and the latter's wife, he states, to the wife, "you know I . . . Loved you and him both so well that I was afraid of myself." This wife had communicated earlier, "you told G. . . . that he and I ought to have a baby soon . . . he just literally raped me . . . what you said gave him courage to rape . . . he forced me always . . ." The patient, writing "to" her, then explained "I am so ashamed that I was the innocent cause of your being raped by that 'Demon' . . . I told G. . . . the 'Demon' wife raper . . . in nineteen hundred and thirteen when we were in Love with each other . . . * * I was in Love with Tom . . . but I hate him now most bitterly . . ." Then in a letter to Tom, the patient writes, "you came to S. . . . in nineteen hundred and nine at which time I fell in Love with you . . . dishonour which you participated in the City of . . . on the last day of June nineteen hundred and twenty four in which you were accompanied by your dishonorable companion Mr. G. . . . [above mentioned] you was in bed that night with prostitute Miss June . . . you G. . . . was in the arms of a prostitute of your own manufacture."

The "plan," which was vaguely discussed early in his writings, was finally revealed as the "repopulation of the world"; all the men who had had intercourse with women (a wife or otherwise) with a few, a very few, exceptions, were to die; the patient, with a little assistance, was to "marry for a brief period only" the women, all of whom were to be recreated virgins "in order to make him Happy," and was to impregnate them. At his most grandiose period, he started a list of the dates of impregnation of a few of them.

On Nov. 10, he became very talkative, expressing the notion, long developed in his writings, that he was the redeemer of the world. At 2 a. m., he rose, rushed into the ward office, and announced himself as the Messiah. That morning he was actively combative; he expressed great hate—at times becoming quite amazingly tense, and perspiring remarkably. In the course of a bitter interview, he said that he had often been in communication with heavenly spirits prior to his illness. His writings had not, at that time, come to hand. He was asked if his marital duties had had any connection with his illness: with tremendous vehemence, his color darkening almost to purple, he shouted "I have lived with a she-devil from Hell for eleven years, and she has broke me down." Later in the day, on the occasion of being given a urinal, he said to a nurse to whom he felt friendly, "That's where a woman ruined me when I was first married . . . I ruined myself by holding back . . . and she rewarded me by seeking the attentions of another man." He spoke of his three children, but said that his last had been "born a Demon," and would have to "be reborn"; that his "Father" had said that by being reborn, one "would get a new set of brains." The process of rebirth "would take about 4½ years." He reported that for the period of 42 days during which he was "unconscious here," he was not unconscious, but was having a death grapple with the Devil, as a result of which the Devil was bound. He did die while he was here. He recounted the following vision or dream that he had had, the occasion not being indicated: "Standing on a rocky ledge looking towards the East, with my wife, but it wasn't my wife, but my mother-in-law, and several small children; and a message was written in Jewish which I tried to comprehend." He deduced from it that he was to become a minister. "Above the light and the Hebrew characters was a code in English." He realized that he was to end it all this year, but he must continue to work out this message as it appeared to him. Later in the day, he reverted to his illness and said that for 42 days, he "wanted to die . . . could not talk."

From the 12th, he showed little of note; he made some overtures of peace to all concerned, including the Superintendent and the writer who were objects of his especial hatred. Being advised that he was to be transferred to a state hospital, he took to his bed again, claiming that he was resting for a long trip. He was received, Nov. 20, into the state institution, stuporous, passively resistant, and much as when he arrived here. During his first stay there, he refused food. He showed a change in that he would rise, when he believed himself unobserved, and rearrange the furniture, disorder the bed, or tear up his clothing. He finally lost so much weight that his wife sent him food twice daily; this, he would eat. On her visits, he was more apt than not to ignore her. She secured his parole on March 15, 124 days after reception there, about 270 days after the acute onset.

At home, he was potent for a few days; while his wife reviews his stay as a continuous improvement, the neighbors report much statuesque posing and erratic behavior with the children. He treated his former friends with complete indifference, ordered his elder brother not to approach him, and went about glowering at things in general. Usually, he walked on the street with his hands partly flexed, the fingers pointing towards his thighs. He sometimes stood for long periods in one spot on the street, oblivious of everyone. The community caused his return to the state hospital, where he is mean, uncooperative, and seemingly about to repeat his stupor reaction.

The noteworthy features of this case are too many and too poorly reflected in these occasional quotations. The entire voluminous script —with its peculiarities of capitalization, its shifting motifs, and the frequent grandiose flights—merits careful study. There are many fragments, such as the following, which shed light on his thought processes, but cannot be dealt with here, for considerations of space alone. Some time after his "awakening," he wrote the following—perhaps largely a retrograde falsification: "I was not unconscious when I was being taken from the jail and brought to the Depot I knew when I was put in the Coffin and laid on the railroad truck I knew when the firebox went over me and I smelt the burned tallow which was on the journels I was not in a good place when I was in jail I knew the Building rails were electrified . . ."

We have here the case of a man born of stock unusually heavily tainted.* Notwithstanding the apparent defect as shown in his psychotic productions, he did amazingly well in his early adult life. He did so well in fact, that he was the youngest of the several assistant superintendents of a large organization. The advancement which he secured was obtained on the basis of merit; that he was even then handicapped by an extensive superstitious system—belief and strong interest in spiritualism and telepathy—is even better evidence of his ability. With five older siblings, all defective or otherwise disordered, he experienced at the age of four, the birth of his younger sister. Later in life, she was the one of his surviving family for whom he had kindly feeling. In the winter of his fifteenth year, he was "converted" to religion. He then felt an inferiority, as he did not have the lurid experiences which came to the other youths and girls. His schooling was superficial and haphazard; he continued to have a great respect and affection for his last teacher (a man). In his seventeenth year, his eldest sister—whom he thoroughly disliked—died. At this time, he was deep in his dumb love affair with "Sara," who remained unaware of the depth of his feelings. She terminated this, the next year; it would have been easy for him to appreciate that the "weak-mindedness" of his family had much effect in rendering him undesirable. With her request that he discontinue his attentions to her, he became sleepless, depressed, and gave up drinking (which he had never carried to much excess). His mother died around this time. It is probable that he underwent a schizophrenic episode at that time —the "rocking" affair and the carrying of the gun for his feared assailants. In the first months of his twentieth year, "Sara" married. Three months later, owing to a steadily deepening mental disorder, his father was removed to a state hospital. One of his better friends married a girl whom he admired; shortly after, another of his boyhood friends married. Soon thereafter, there came to his neighborhood a young man of rather exceptional ability, and of that type of personality to which one would expect the patient to be attracted. Such was the case, and he developed a very strong attachment for "Tom." It may be mentioned that in his conversations with this friend, as with most of his life-long acquaintants, he revealed little indeed of his inner life, desires, beliefs, and difficulties. He had two cousins, boys, with whom he was on more confidential terms—much more intimate than with any member of his own family. He progressed in his twenty-second year to a material promotion. About that time, one of his two confidants left that part of the country under "a cloud," and his whereabouts continued to be unknown, thereafter, to the patient. In his twenty-third year, a sister "kept house"

[* This kind of etiology for schizophrenia was later abandoned by Sullivan, although he acknowledged heredity as a predisposing factor. The phrase "heavily tainted" is reminiscent of psychiatric literature of that period. H.S.P.]

for him; this girl was the next elder. Of her, he expressed no opinions in his writings. Shortly after his twenty-fourth birthday, she showed the initial symptoms of a rapidly developing schizophrenic illness. She became much disturbed and had to be removed, about a month later, to the state hospital. This, which drew new attention to the family heritage of mental trouble, is thought to have terminated another courtship of his. Whether that was the case or not, he left town for treatment in the Johns Hopkins Hospital, for "stomach trouble." (It is probable that he secured his admission under an assumed name; there is no record of such a name as his; yet, in his psychotic writings, he refers to the matter: "I was brought here poisoned and never have been insane in my Life regardless of the report that was brought to your institution by one of the Doctors from the Johns Hopkins Hospital. I was treated there but not for my brain those people will be humiliated soon about that untrue statement." This reference is purely autogenous; we did not then know of such treatment.)

He was promoted again to a position of some considerable responsibility. This required his living in a rather inaccessible part of the country. He took with him his remaining confidant. The next fall he married, after a brief courtship, "for a home and small children." Since he saw less of his friend G. at this time, his "love" for him grew stronger. He expressed, in those years, a great many notions about telepathy and about spookery. At this time, he grew very fond of another employee; and when the latter "accepted atheistic teachings," it occasioned in him a troubled state of mind which was still in evidence during his psychosis, ten years later. A son was born to him in his twenty-seventh year. This boy is now showing mental symptoms. Late in his twenty-eighth year, two events transpired which contributed important experiences: his boyhood confidant was killed while at work; and his sister (his former housekeeper) died in the state hospital. He began exerting pressure for a transfer, giving poor excuses. His foremen noted a marked tendency to procrastinate in the ordering of various pieces of work which were of the nature of emergencies. They took to doing the necessary tasks, without advising him.

The next year, a second son was born, and he was transferred to the still more responsible position in which he was at the time of the acute illness. Here he was in a situation where, at the start, he was more competent than his chief. He handled that well. In 1918, when he was in his thirtieth year, a daughter was born. By the end of that year, he had made the "discovery" of the earth's movement "in an easterly direction"—doubtless a psychotic experience, of a piece with so many schizophrenic astronomical observations. In the succeeding years, he covertly engaged in some financial transactions not in harmony with his company's policy, but to his own gain. His employees and associates did not notice any marked change in him during this period, but, from extrinsic evidence, and from the remarks in his writings, we are advised that he was suffering a marked diminution in *potentia coendi*.

On July 4, several days after he had shown clear symptoms of his illness, he met "Sara," at the town celebration. This was the first meeting in some years. It consisted in nothing more than greetings.†

Discussion of Cases

In the first of these cases, E.K., there is shown the impulses underlying schizophrenic panic. Had his attempt to project his oral cravings succeeded to the extent of abolishing his embarrassment and had it distorted consciousness of their autogenous character, we would have seen a paranoid state as a relatively permanent and irremediable condition. The earlier escape of these impulses, however—brief as they had been—were in the nature of experience which could not be reorganized into the paranoid attitude. The satisfaction by projection being imperfect and there being experience of very high value actually available in memory, a schizophrenic dissociation was necessitated if any self-esteem was to be preserved.

The panic situation which followed upon the failure of projection was, as usual, characterized by tremendous emotional features, relatively vague but typical cognitive items, and behavior initiated by a striving to escape man and the things of men. Since it is our present purpose to discuss the cognitive features only, the actual psychological significance of schizophrenic ("homosexual") panic need not delay us. What the patient can recall of his thoughts, at best, is not much. In the present case, suicidal thoughts—which started his evening, so that he sought an unfrequented street and prepared to swallow two bichloride tablets—were readily displaced. A passing automobile was distorted into something hostile, the passengers *wishing* him to take the poison. He then struggled against *their* wish to such effect that he dropped his poison and threw stones at the next auto-

[† At this juncture, Sullivan has circled back to the onset of the illness as reported early in the case history—the meeting with Sara. Apparently this meeting was a crucial factor in the onset of serious illness on July 14. H.S.P.]

mobile that passed. But the thought of *people* grew more and more terrible; he started to walk; automobiles *behind him* were now bearing terror towards him; as a car passed him without effect, it ceased to exist—it no longer affected his consciousness. By this means, it became evident to him that all the cars *followed* him, everywhere he went. He hurried, ran, halted in despair at times, cursed them, perhaps threw something at them. Houses, again of people, obsessed him. Some gave evidence of their active occupants; they showed lighted windows. These were much more terrible. They became the houses of his religious denomination— the symbol of the ideal society he had offended. The crucifixion motif now appeared. He was to be killed—killed in some ceremonial way . . . . that was why each *third* house was lighted and everyone followed him. . . . . He fled to the park . . . . at last he was alone, but still with terror. After crouching and lying behind bushes in a solitary spot for some hours, he grew calm enough to attempt flight to his *home* (in which he had not spent any time for weeks, and in which he was always in "hot water"); no sooner was he on the street car than people again obsessed him. He hurried to the front platform, but even the motorman showed that he *suspected* the patient of oral cravings!

It is not by any means necessary that these homosexual cravings shall be represented as such in full awareness. The source of initial panic in another patient, S.D., was no more fully cognized than thoughts to the general effect that nurses and doctors were watching him and driving him into masturbation, so that they might kill him. This chap had never masturbated in the usual fashion. He spent hours walking fashionable streets, maintaining an erection and securing orgasms by observing women's legs. He patched up a "transference cure" through the agency of a kindly young physician, without any insight; it was after this, when he attempted to resume work, that frank homosexual content made its appearance, and finally (after a truly heroic effort on his part) returned him to the hospital.

Neither is it necessary that the cravings shall have been unsatisfied. Another patient, C.C., had been a public pervert and had enjoyed thoroughly his homosexual practices. When, however, having been rather vilely imposed upon, he found himself confronted by a long prison term—and that for a charge "framed" upon him by a "father imago" to whom he had refused to submit —he grew unstable. On finding that his imprisonment did not secure him from further unsolicited advances, he developed an acute panic, quite typically schizophrenic.

That it is not from uncontrollable cravings, *per se*, but from the foreshadowed loss of esteem in the eyes of others which these uncontrollable cravings will bring about, is well illustrated by patient P.J., the only son in a family of ten, hating his father with a great hate, and already lonely and unhappy when he submitted to fellatio for the first time. Within two days, feeling but vaguely his own cravings, he attempted a religious sublimation which failed at once and gave place to rapidly developing and very severe panic.

Our second case [V.H.], unfortunately, does not show the genesis of the disorder. As such it becomes of little value for the schizophrenia theory. It is included for the light it sheds upon the thinking in "deteriorated præcox" conditions; this chap of the "deterioration type" of personality—giving evidences in plenty of being "all through"—gives a clear showing in the scant productions reported herein, of the profound disorder of conation and a rather impressive demonstration that thinking peculiarities, cognition, merely follows in the path of the distorted impulse-life. As a demonstration of the self-estimation of the patient, his remark anent heterosexual experience ("No, doctor, I never tried any *real* life") and the picture he reproduces of his prowess among others ("Day dreaming, explaining things to people") are classical. That his sexual potentia was completely tied up in the stable schizophrenic adaptation would follow from our experience with comparable cases; how well he expressed it. The protection by means of a fear of new minds "talking" in his head, the conscious excuse for his avoidance of interest in anyone, is no less teleological than most schizophrenic delusions.

The third case, S.F., shows how intimately the "cosmic drama" of punishment is related to the sex life. In this case, the flight motif, which determined his attempted elopement, was directed to getting "away" not only from other people, but from the family circle also. This is merely a little more developed attitude than the setting out for home of our first patient. Since the parents are more intimately entangled in the drama than are others, any initial flight to the home must give way sooner or later either to escape from them or to wonderfully distorted behavior with extensive cognitive peculiarities in dealing with the others. This particular patient [S.F.] may well have made his improvement by reorganizing his sentiment of self from the earlier Œdipus to a homosexual attitude. Certainly, with the growth of "transference," his distress on contact with his mother and sister diminished rapidly.

The fourth case, W.Q., shows how, with the failure of the unsocial purpose, the patient's guilt became acute and was dealt with by projection. We cannot demonstrate, in this case, the earlier experience which foredoomed the paranoid adjustment and necessitated the schizophrenic dissociation. In his "recollections" of his stupor content, there are several motifs quite clearly demonstrated. The "Œdipus situation," his childhood subject organization, contributing so heavily in the case, is revealed in almost pure allegory in the War of the Fathers and Sons; the intimate relations of the "Nuns" requires no stressing. In these productions, too, we see unusually clearly a cosmic expansion of the adolescent struggle for a solution of the sex problem: the destruction of "wickedness" (female), the attempt at a homosexual world, the altruistic attitude to woman followed so closely by fear of her, then a tentative consideration of the mother-son attitude.

Further on, W.Q. shows the apotheosis so ignobly executed by the fifth patient I.O. As the representative of God, much of his problem would undoubtedly be over. Unfortunately, reality clashed so badly with this that he was driven to identification—"I controlled the lightning." His previous experience (that is, the nature of his subject organization) being unsuited to this, and the cravings which had caused the upheaval being beyond his ability to resymbolize, he degenerated into a paranoid schizophrenic state with syphiliphobia as a barrier to interest in those about him. When the reality of his subordination was reimposed upon him by his transfer to the state hospital, he returned to a stuporous reaction. His experience from the first wave of this, together with the necessarily less considerate attitude of those among whom he found himself, led to a much less hostile and hateful attitude as he came out the second time.

The content pertaining to W.Q.'s gastro-intestinal and urinary apparatus is unusually simple in its formation. As has been discussed elsewhere ("see Erogenous Maturation"), the urination reaction must be accepted as a regressive form of orgasm. This patient's reaction by urinating when others smoked in his presence need not be regarded as by any means as mysterious as his evasive statement: "It seemed probable that they smoked when they urinated."

We are peculiarly estopped from data as to the genesis of the adolescent failure in the case of the fifth patient, I.O. It is thought that he suffered his first schizophrenic dissociation at seventeen or eighteen; it seems probable, also, that his later heterosexual adaptation was bolstered up by a great deal of homosexual sublimation. How much of a loss to him the death of his remaining confidant constituted is but a matter of speculation, but his expressions about spiritualism grew strikingly abundant thereafter, and continued so to the final break. That the first projections took the form of paranoid ideas about his superiors, and involved Catholics and so forth, is neither unusual nor contrary to the supposition that the difficulty resided in symbol situations most readily formulated in terms of sex. His production of the "Battle Hymn" directed against a "foreign power," the Pope, so soon after the passing of the stuporous adjustment, on the other hand, was most ominous and—if it had come to attention—would have justified an unfavorable prognosis at that time. For that matter, it seems increasingly evident that the appearance of content to the effect that a patient "was sick but is now well," immediately after a shift from a stuporous to an active adjustment, must be looked upon as a grave maneuver—one so poorly adapted to reality as to open the way for most massive falsifications and explanatory delusional rationalizations.

This patient's recollection of the stupor content are of two varieties—the sparse productions of the third of September interview, and the paranoid wealth of persecutory "data" later on. The latter cannot be accepted as authentic, *per se*, but they are none the less valuable as more indirect evidence. In his account of the first assault upon a nurse, he refers very clearly to a peculiar state of consciousness—he "woke up" when he was thrown down. The thinking he reproduced from the period immediately after this "awakening" is precisely like reproductions of experiences on awakening from nightmares and after disturbances following upon alcoholic over-indulgence. There is another point of interest in the third of September interview, the identity of the "they" who were coming to get him. One cannot but be impressed with the frequency of the schizophrenic attitude to the general effect that those particular persons who were immediately concerned in his physical admission to the hospital, rather than those concerned in a higher order of relationships (more significant relatives, social units, or even the medical staff as advisors) are the ones who can and should remove him.

Thoughts of death and related content were certainly present in the phase of stupor. His (subsequently elaborated) notion that he was removed from the jail to a coffin dates from the first thirty-six hours. The great motif of (death and) rebirth is exposed in unparalleled simplicity. That the symbols of sexual potency occur in such unbridled profusion in this case (this son of a zealous father, of a virtuous mother, among virtuous children, surrounded by that almost diabolical moral "virtue" which reminds us of what life under the Puritans might have been, whose fairly intimate boyhood friends make no single reference to sex, whose adulthood was filled with spook-doctrines and interest in the church and with most upright husbandhood and fatherhood, who, in fact, required the apotheosis to free him from criticism of his sexual desires—and all this without any possible "contamination" from anyone possessing psychoanalytic knowledge) this certainly gives a great deal of support to the hypothesis that sex symbolism is of unparalleled importance in the mental organization, and that its language—the activity of such symbols—can and does supply most of the deeper level of "psychic" life on which is erected by resymbolization (rationalization, compensation, substitution, evasive compromise, and, more fundamentally, by oral, kinæsthetic and other forms of primitive symbol activity) the basis of the "conscious" life of the individual. Throughout his writings, in all but the most absurd flights of grandeur, there is shown the surviving egoistic critique. When his flights have led him into statements which would lead to severe criticism by another, each time he drops the topic to plunge into the arms of his harem. Further comment on this must await treatment of the writings *in extenso*.

Behaviorists of the ultra school will be interested in his inability to "object" to his "encruciating" pain during the drainage of the wrist "since I was unable to talk." Perhaps they can explain the naming of the poison, "Dentine."

Peculiarly interesting is the sidelight thrown upon his attitude to himself in his statement that the wife had alleged him to be in poor physical and mental condition, thus "just stating her wishes in the matter." [6]

Finally it may be mentioned that, while he wrote of himself as the "Father's" Boy, and spoke to me of his having "come here an innocent boy," it was not until his second reception in the state hospital that he began to insist to those around him that he was a little boy.

To complete the presentation of clinical material, we shall recount in brief abstract the sixth case of the series, which clarifies many points. Here again, those who have expected an explanation of "crazy" productions will be required to use their imagination. The asylum patient is sufficiently exploited, for example, in Bleuler's *Textbook*; the incomprehensible is to be regarded as fragments of content which come to light after the patient has ceased his efforts at, and abandoned his hopes of, communicating with the environment. The case material in this paper is of an earlier period of psychosis.

This next patient was a case of schizophrenic perplexity, that state in which the most fertile clues to schizophrenic dissociation are to be found. In the final discussion, a few words will be said as to the productions of [Y. C.,] a "typical" but very early and well observed catatonic of unusual intelligence, so young that he had no great mass of adolescent experience to struggle with. As he was principally mute, his value in this study would be

[6] In explanation, it may be noted that the event when he "nearly lost" his life with one of his brothers refers to his saving a brother from drowning. The alleged immorality of his friends Tom and G— on "the last day of June" was mere phantasy.

solely as evidence for the generality of the thinking peculiarities we shall have illustrated.

CASE 6

G. H., æt. 24. The youngest of two boys. Both grandfathers died of some form of paralysis. Maternal grandmother died in mental illness. Mother a "nervous type," frequent headaches and "neuralgia," and decidedly oversolicitous as to patient. Father, a weak factor in the home life, otherwise without evidences of mental defect or disorder. The maternal collaterals include schizophrenic illnesses. The older brother has left home, probably as a result of the weaning effect of the military service; has married, recently, and is in business in a Southern city.

Gestation and delivery were average. Patient was thin infant and child, but not definitely malnourished. Severe pneumonia at 3. Walked and talked early. Control of sphincters about usual age. Generally happy, but given to explosive exhibitions of temper. Began school at 7, progressed each year until the second half of his third year in high school. He was then just past puberty (voice change), between 17 and 18 years of age. "He was very restless over his studies in the evenings. He worked fitfully and very frequently got up to go and get something to eat or to wander around the house." He quit school entirely for about three months in his fourth year, but then finished, graduating in his twentieth year. During this period, he had few recreations, and worked during the summer vacations. Up to this time, he had been much pampered by his mother; she says, "He always used to recite at Church so well. . . . His appetite was not so good, always had to cater to it. . . . He is an awfully sensitive boy. He never seemed to be real strong. He took life very seriously. . . . When he first started out, he found it an awful task to go and ask for a job. He always tired very quickly."

The patient's account of the beginning of his illness correctly relates it to the third year in high school. His brother, of whom he was very fond, with whom he had slept for years, enlisted the day war was proclaimed. The patient missed him very badly, and perhaps six months after this brother's departure, began to "get into a nervous condition, and my thoughts were getting more directed towards me . . . instead of towards other people . . . Felt I was stopped, and could not keep going . . . then, sort of losing consciousness, hazy one night; I was at home, became struck with that fear . . . couldn't swing all that was on my head, and swung off at a tangent; was really afraid that something terrible had happened . . . blamed myself for it . . . I have carried the fear from that night . . . fear of something . . . My feelings were off the track . . . Was fond of people before that, and fond of them afterwards, but dove into work . . . I kind of believe I [never] got over that night . . . Of course, it may be sensitiveness . . . my progress stopped . . . more like my clear vision stopped then . . . but I kept right on going."

After graduation, he decided that he should "see the world" and, contrary to the urgings of his mother, took a job as ordinary seaman. In France, he contracted a fever, was gravely ill on the return trip, and received little treatment other than mustard plasters applied by the Chinese cook. In the Marine Hospital, he was "delirious" for a long time. After treatment for three months, he returned home. His mother relates: "After his coming home, I noticed a different personality." He had anorexia and some insomnia. She did not let him go to work for another six months. On the trip, he had contracted the habit of cigarette smoking, had drunk a little, and had declined some heterosexual opportunities from fear of disease.

In his twenty-first year, a particularly unfortunate coincidence occurred. He played golf one day with a friend; standing too close, he was hit above the left eye. A few days later, while playing golf this time with a girl cousin, he struck her, accidentally, on the chin, loosening several teeth. He was greatly distressed by this, going home and weeping, walking about outside, muttering to himself. That evening, as he was about to go to his work, he read of the accidental electrocution of a fellow-workman of the day shift. He did not sleep well for a week, thereafter, and was much more quiet and uninterested than usual for a long time. He soon quit that job. The parents report that he was more irritable with them for some months.

Near the time of the twenty-second birthday, he began work for a company the manager of which was a rather curious individual —one who, for example, prided himself on the alleged fact that all his "boys are good boys and none of them are profane. They wouldn't even say 'damn.' " The patient's work was often such that he would become the center of a crowd of idlers interested in it. This was a "great strain," he said. He was most conscientious, worked harder than the others, and voiced his vague but acute ambitions. He was well liked but much "kidded," which he took in good part.

On Saturday, May 3, 1924, the boys were going on one of the manager's fishing parties. The patient refused to go. He seemed morose and showed a "violent hatred" of the manager. He was sent home the second next day. Concerning this episode, he said: "I collapsed . . . I was kind of lost. I felt my friends weren't close. I wanted to get out to get some excitement. They would make remarks about my personality, said I was a stick in the mud, that my mind was off on a tangent. Mr. G. [the manager] was always crabbing me. He is a rather effeminate person . . . I was trying to force myself; I didn't have the personality to keep up with the pace."

After resting at home from May 5 to Aug. 16, he resumed work.

As he was the most experienced of the gang, he was asked to take charge of it. He was very unwilling to do so. One Sunday, he attended a church where the sermon was from the text "To-day ye are dead and to-morrow ye shall live." That night, he rose suddenly, and dressed. He said to his room-mate that the preacher had said "I am dead to-day but to-morrow I shall live, so I am going to see him." By November 21, he felt he had not done enough to have earned his month's salary; he attempted to resign, and was given a year's leave. He wrote in his diary, at this time, "I have lost my grip . . . I have tried to treat everyone square, but I have lost my grip." With insomnia and other symptoms increasing, he was admitted to the Henry Phipps Psychiatric Institute on December 5. At that time, he was very bitter in his utterances against the manager, saying, in part, "I would like to get that son of a bitch. He has beat hell out of me." In a subsequent discussion, he added "He was kind of like an old woman * * * I guess I felt he kind of was getting too much control over me * * * kind of felt he was working a game on me * * *."

During his stay in that hospital, he did not show improvement. He was transferred to the Sheppard and Enoch Pratt Hospital on January 27, last. After discussing his life up to the time of his brother's enlistment, in our initial interview, he was asked if he had missed his brother. He replied, "Oh . . . He had his friends and went around with girls, too. I had friends, but . . . I could not keep up . . . They were a little ahead of me . . . Well, socially and . . . monetary reasons, too." Here he referred to a doctor with whom he had had some interviews, saying thereafter "I slept with my brother 'till the war * * * that homosexual feeling H— [the doctor] spoke of. I'd tell him . . . anything, and . . . it seemed I got worse and worse. All our actions and talks were tensions between us, you see. It was on the morning of the eclipse . . . I was relating it to myself . . . and the morning it came, I was wild, I thought I was dying or something. * * * I was supposed to be in hell, I guess . . . and they had a language there; I'd hear things . . . I couldn't smoke a cigarette or drink water * * * The whole thing was like going through a dream . . . I was two persons; one night, a man and a woman; and the next, two men. * * * Called all sorts of damnable things—dog, cock-sucker . . . everything that I had ever heard." Later in the discussion, he volunteered "Never had intercourse with a woman; never seen a naked woman: have fooled around when I was on the road"; the latter had occasioned two incidents of *ejaculatio præcox* some short time before his acute episode. He shied at any discussion of the homosexual goal, saying amiably but with tension, "Don't talk to me about those things, I will get all mixed up again . . . I think I know what ails me . . . my feelings have got swung around." Inquiry as to what he meant increased his discomfort.

During the first weeks of his stay, he spent much of his time watching the door and attempting to leave when others entered or went from his ward. His remarks anent this behavior throw light on the superficial order of rationalization with which the schizophrenic often cloaks profound motivations. "I'm more or less . . . ambitious, . . . and think more about getting out in the world and doing my share. I suppose you gain more by living than by sitting in a hospital. * * * I was thinking of my parents and wanting to be with them . . . that, and . . . then I felt I should have left . . . felt about well enough to leave, and I don't know why I didn't leave. * * * I don't feel that I can stand this . . . staying here. I feel I have the right to leave. * * * [Doctor: *Are you unhappy?*] (smiling) I certainly am . . . the fact of being here . . . I suppose I feel it my duty to be out and . . . * * * I don't care to stay here, and I can't find the way out . . . * * *."

A beginning of much promise having been made, his mother demanded his discharge. He left, against advice, on February 10, 1925. The mother brought him into contact with a so-called Christian Scientist. To the boy's credit, be it said that on being urged to pray with the "practitioner," he retorted that he did not need assistance in praying, put on his hat, and departed to a neighborhood hotel, where he spent the night. After some further efforts to establish a satisfactory attitude towards himself, he left home without notice and set out for F——, the southern city in which his brother was located. The account of his experiences, as he recalls them, appears below. He was returned to the hospital on March 15. As is so generally the case after premature removals, the patient was decidedly worse: he had developed the notion that he had married a girl, that she had followed him North, and that she was in the environs of the hospital, or at his home.

Rather than discuss the total situations of this patient throughout his course to social recovery, we shall give excerpts from his verbatim records (some 450 typewritten pages), these excerpts being illustrative of some major symbol activities, only. As additional evidence of inadequate, superficial formulations, the following may suffice. "I am feeling very well; I was talking with Dr. E— this morning, about going home, and he said to come up and see you. So here I am . . . So . . . [*So, what?*] I'm all . . . feeling fit . . . to go home. * * * I'm feeling . . . well . . . and felt that's the place . . . to go now. * * * I'm feeling well, doctor, and I feel that that's . . . accomplishment . . . Feeling so much better and then . . . go home with my people . . . 'Cause otherwise, just sit around here . . . and get no further. * * * [*Things indicate to you that patients come here, go to class three days, and leave?*] No indeed . . . I suppose they come here and stay 'till they are in shape to go to their homes and work . . . I certainly feel that I will do better by going home though. * * * I'm feeling a whole lot better and feel (sighs) that I'd feel a whole lot better being with my people . . . That's the reason I came up to put it up to you . . . to see if I couldn't go. * * * You can't do anything for me . . . in the way . . . of my going home! . . . I talked with Dr. Sullivan [Dr. E—] this morning, and he said to see you . . . I don't know what else to do . . . to . . . go home. * * Now that you feel well enough to go home, and you feel, too, you would be better with your people, and all . . . woy . . . certainly better . . . than staying around in the hospital . . . * * * * When you know that you desire to go home and feel better there . . . you certainly are not getting any better staying in a hospital. * * * When your interests are home and outside . . . woy, you're not advancing so much towards your life's happiness . . . by sitting in a hospital . . . * * * * * Is it your ideas around here that you should just ask to leave, and you should ask the attendant to let you out, and he'll open the door for you? . . . I came here and I've been under your care [13 days] and I tell you I feel much better and . . . I'll be taking a bigger step towards my happiness by leaving . . . and you seem to think that it's terrible, or something, that I have such ideas. [*Yes, I think it is terrible for one who can think so clearly to think so damn superficially!*] . . . Well, I don't! . . . I can't see why you should take it that way, doctor, when I tell you I'm feeling better and know I would be better by going home . . . I should think you could see some of those things . . . my way. * * * I came up to ask you in the right way . . . I've told you all my problems; will you let me go, doctor?" In a subsequent discussion of this preoccupation, he said; "I go along for a time, as I say, feel all right and . . . feeling very good and . . . I come out of . . . of . . . feel free-er and [of] fear or anything . . . and then I find myself sink back into the same hole again [thinking about "the girl," "going home," etc.]. * * * I reach a point where I'm feeling real good and away from all my troubles; and I reach a point where I feel if I could rush right out and home, I'd be all right, and I have to stay . . . and the restrictions . . . begin to down me, and I begin to think in those steps . . . Of course, these violations [restrictions] might be the same at home as here; it's all in yourself and your thinking, I suppose. [*You feel that the restrictions are responsible for your slipping back, eh?*] Somewhat, yes sir . . ." At a still later period, after being refused a peremptory demand "to be let out," he said "But I don't feel in the good condition now, that I did a little while ago. [*And what does that mean?*] . . . I suppose . . . that means . . . I ought to stay . . . longer . . . shouldn't go home. * * I've been feeling so good, all day, and my thoughts immediately turn to . . . being at home with my people and . . . [the girl] * * I was feeling well enough to . . . go home . . . and I think if I could have stayed in that condition . . . I could have impressed you so . . . but I didn't stay in that condition * * I was under the impression that when you have nerve enough to go out . . . and you're feeling just right . . . then they'd let you out, if you asked it. * * * [*It is dangerous to think that things will happen just because you want them to happen.*] . . . Believe they'll happen because you want them to happen . . . I don't think that that is a dangerous thought . . . Believe until they don't happen, and then, when they don't happen, I forget about it . . . If they don't happen, it's neither for the good or bad."

His recollections of the adventure of the southern trip are sufficiently formulated to give valuable data. The arrangement of the data is that in which they were produced by the patient in a series of interviews. "I got the boat and went down to Savannah. Tried to get a job in Savannah, and couldn't get a job there, didn't come across any in the papers . . . and . . . so . . . I started on to Fz—— . . . Didn't have any money . . . So I went to Fz—— to see my brother; he owed me a little money, and I was going there to get the money . . . My intentions were to go to Fz—— eventually, but to get a job and work before I saw them. But my money ran out, so I went up to Fz—— intending to call up my brother and . . . so I went to his wife's house, and his wife's father asked me to stay with them . . . They'd met me at the train. I went to bed there and felt so bad about it, and I got up and left . . . Didn't like the idea, and hiked around Georgia a bit . . . And before I left, I had a girl I liked . . . and I hiked around Georgia and I came back there, and my brother asked me to go to Fg——with him, and we went * * * So I went to Fg—— and started in working with him . . . His wife was along with him and . . . there was some girl there, and they introduced me to her, and we went out riding with them, and I think his wife wanted me to go around with her. But I didn't care for her, and I only saw her twice, and that's all I ever saw her after that. * * * But I had a hard time in Fg——, I'll tell you that, too. * * * Town seemed to be . . . Well, I don't know whether the . . . were kinda . . . against me, for . . . not going around with the other girl, I don't know . . . she was staying there at the house [the boarding house where his brother and wife lived as did also several young married couples. The patient took a room at the same place; he was thrown much with these young couples, at meals and in the evenings.] They had so many niggers walking around with different colored clothes, and all that . . . of course, I didn't take any interest in that kind of stuff, and . . . I was intending to go back to Fz——, and my father came down, and we all went to Fz——, and my brother declared he couldn't have me in his work, wasn't making any money, and I couldn't get my own money, and my father talked and talked, and we came up here. * * * The other girl came on the train with me, I'm pretty sure she was on the train . . . I know she was . . . She's the . . . my . . . wife, I suppose . . . as I was telling you

* * * * She came all the way from Baltimore; waiting as long as she has, I think she has shown as much favor as I have to her. * * * I didn't know whether they disliked me being there or not . . . You know, you get the feeling now and then that people think you are sponging on them; I had no intentions that way, I was trying to get a foothold on work. * * * He'd [the brother] made a success and I was coming down and kinda live on some of his success and be like him." Following the patient's return from his "hike," before he joined his brother, the brother's father-in-law had secured the patient a temporary job in a garage, for 4 days. Asked to give some facts for his belief that he had been married, he said, "Well, the fact of . . . the facts are hard to bring to light, I know . . . because I did not meet her so much . . . but at the same time . . . Well, I just feel it, that's all, and the fact that . . . was . . . Well, I was going to . . . work in this man's garage down there, and there was part of the machine . . . meaning this . . . a bolt out . . . different things came up . . . it was put in a vague light . . . but all the same, I understood it . . . I don't care so much about the facts or claims or anything . . . it's this feeling, I just know that it existed, and I can't be talked out of it, because I know it's true. * * * * * * My brother and his wife, and . . . this town of Fg——, where I was . . . Why should they seem to . . . know anything about me? . . . they all came around and seemed to . . . I had a pretty hard time in that town . . . I wanted to stay. Those people . . . talked to me through this . . . I don't know what you call it . . . Woy, talked through clothes and . . . automobiles, and . . . playing . . . niggers and everything else. * * * Can you tell me how or why any automobile should attract your mind, make you turn your head * * that attraction, different things * * license numbers, every license number seemed to mean something * * they meant, sort of time * * sort of line in my information about the girl . . . meeting the girl and things like that. But I can't understand; to my way of thinking, the whole town seemed to play me * *." It developed that the idea of his marriage did not reach clear awareness for some two weeks after he went to Fg—— and worked with his brother—in other words, not until the pressure of the environment of young married people had caused him great stress. " * * I wouldn't say it occurred to me quite suddenly . . . I'd thought of it Fz—— * *." He failed completely when asked to describe the woman. Somewhat later, he developed a change reflected in the following: "I told you I was married or something. It was a condition in my own mind. A sexual condition, I guess. I guess, being around my brother . . . had just been married, and I guess that was what put it in my mind. I guess some sexual condition . . . put a woman in your mind . . . I realize it was all out of order. It was my own condition that took that way of creating . . . sort of dream. * * * These feelings took an idea and centered that idea

in my own mind. I want to take back what I said about being married . . . I don't say those feelings . . . I have the feelings, but the idea . . . I was just off, that's all. * * * I know when I went South, I had intended to . . . go around with a woman, to give those feelings a release, you know . . . to take that away from your mind . . . Well, I didn't get a chance, and I suppose those feelings rose too high . . . sexual feelings went to my head, and sort of took the form of the idea I had a wife . . . * * I was in that stunned, dreamy, condition. * * My brother . . . had told me some time, that if I came south, we would get to going together. There were some girls at the house that we would get to going with. * *." After several relapses into this delusional system, he said "I didn't even know the girl . . . the one I have been talking about. * * * The color, brown, as I told you . . . sort of represents this . . . girl * * color, blue, it seems to me . . . the . . . color represents the other girl * * I went out with her a couple of times, and I had some imaginations about her. * * * When I left Fz— and was hiking it, and reached a town named Ej—. and was at the railroad station . . . and all these red lights around the station . . . and at that time I imagined it was for my purpose. Red torch light . . . and when I got off the train at the next town . . . a man across the street had one, and I had the notion that if I crossed that line, I would see red . . . and . . . white sand along the road . . . and when I looked across the fields, it looked like water, and I imagined I could see big boats there, . . . and the sand glowed red . . . I wonder if that was real or imaginary. * * * I'll tell you another instance of it. When I was down in Fg—, I . . . had a light on in my room, and I had a blue suit and this grey suit, lying on the chair . . . and as I turned the light out, and a big flash of red went over my blue suit. * * * * There was that girl . . . that I told you I went around with . . . and I had the blue suit on . . . and I forgot about her, I'd say, and I was thinking of this other girl that I've been talking about here . . . and I had the idea that the people of the town were talking because I had dropped the other girl; and when I turned the light out . . . I was thinking that that was some effect of it . . . There was a spring down near Fg—, called it 'Blue Spring,' and they talked, my brother's wife had talked to me . . . about a light down in the water, . . . and I had an idea that that Blue Spring represented the girl I had been going around with, and that Silver Springs represented the other one. * * And I was going out . . . there one night . . . going swimming in the spring . . . and I remember, some fellows and some girls were up on the bank, and I distinctly heard one of them say 'He isn't going to do it' . . . and that same night, I stayed around there 'till right late . . . and there was another machine out there, and nobody in it . . . and I had the idea it belonged to the other girl, and I even tried to start the machine. * * That same night, I saw something very . . . strange . . . it may have been only seeing it through my own eyes . . . I looked up at the sky, and saw a star that looked as if it went away in and then came way out, big . . . and a great big double cross, like the tuberculosis cross . . . appeared in the sky. It wasn't a flash; it stayed there while I was looking at it. * * * It just seemed like there was a terrible attachment to the girl . . . I had had feelings, when the idea came to me, like none I'd had before in my life * * * " At another interview, he opened the discussion by asking, "Are you a Mason?" He then recounted, somewhat incoherently, his initial contacts with the brother's father-in-law, Mr. R. "I went in a masonic hall one night down in Fz— . . . and . . . well, I was in there with this Mr. R. . . . I felt in some way there was some connection . . . I had asked my brother about; he said 'No indeed, it hadn't been anything' . . . I had always thought of it, but I never thought of it; just had it in mind . . . I was with this Mr. R. He took me in one night * * there's nothing to it. I just felt connected with the organization in some way, I always looked up to them in some way, thought a great deal of them. * * It changed me a good deal . . . since the day . . . the first day it started with Masons . . . when I went up to the masonic hall, there. * * As I say, I went up there with Mr. R., and I was very fond of him; he took me in there, and I worked for him; and I . . . sort of married him when I first went there; . . . went up in Mason's Hall, he did some things there, I sort of understood them . . . and I went to his home, and there's where I met this girl . . . I couldn't say I had seen her since . . . That night, I got to feeling bad about piling in there without money; I couldn't get out of the house, so I jumped out of the second story window (laughs); that's when I started hiking down the road. * * He's a wonderful man." [*And you think you moved your affection from him to this more or less fanciful girl?*] "Yes, sir. * * I never felt that way towards my brother; but I felt that way towards Mr. R. The whole thing started when I went up to the masonic hall. * * I sort of looked, or it was something sacred. * * * He was a pretty big man in Fz—. * * * * * * * * * "

We shall include but one more excerpt in this connection. "The first night I was there, I called her father . . . or called Mr. R. up . . . I thought I had met her before . . . That was the very first night I was ever there. * * I was met at the station by . . . four men, there . . . they were . . . four Masons . . . and went up to the masonic hall with them . . and . . went to his house and . . . This Mr. R.'s house. * * Right after I'd gone to bed, I suppose . . . I woke up and . . . called him upstairs, there, and asked him . . . her name. * * * * * * * I was interested in one girl . . . and down in Fg—, I was interested in the other one . . . for a little time there . . . I thought more of the one I had met in Fz—, and my feelings were . . . for the people down there in the South . . . Mr.

R. and those . . . * * * * "

There is a section of his productions which pertain to smoking, which is illuminating. "Does smoking cigarettes hurt you any? . . . that is, does it . . . I smoke when I'm nervous. * * Sometimes, it seems to have some meaning, or bearing . . . to smoke a cigarette after, for instance, in our talks here * * It seems to me, some of the ideas are . . . that smoking a cigarette . . . kinda relieves the ideas . . . of . . . * * kinda sends ideas up in smoke, as it were. * * Somebody said something about 'keeping himself alive on cigarettes,' I don't know who it was. * * Seems to . . . mean to . . . eliminate what you say . . . or . . . sort of that idea . . . * * it eliminates your actions . . . or . . . what you said . . . It seems to have some significance . . . and the significance . . . is sort of . . . the idea of . . . eliminating something. * * I was thinking that that sort of brings a change over you sometimes . . . a change in your feelings . . . * * * * Cigarette and smoke . . . * er, . . . small cigar or (laughs) . . . it's a destruction of some ideas, or something of that sort. * * Is it that when you haven't done right, or something, that a cigarette peps you up . . . so it seems to act both ways. * * * It is for the control of your own feelings . . . or to help your own life along . . . or to save your own self. * * * * Lamp . . . is . . . symbol of light . . . whether it is human light . . . or other light . . . and a . . . building is symbolic of . . . a human . . . building . . . or person . . . Well, you're smoking . . . you're burning . . . your building is burning down . . . * * Symbolizes a cigar . . . in my mind . . . it symbolizes . . . man . . . (deep sigh) . . . * * The cigar . . . is . . . cigar . . . Woy, it represents . . . man, and . . . form, or what?".

He gave an exceptionally clear discussion of urination in its schizophrenic correlations. The first occasion for this line of thought was a sudden impulse to urinate, during an interview. "Well, I don't quite understand . . . what it means to go in there . . . to pass urine. Well, it's your nature, I suppose, and . . . Well, for some reason or another, it's . . . it affects me very much . . . the . . . I don't know just how to explain . . . it affects me . . . well, just like . . . giving my . . . feelings away . . . to, say, . . . you, instead of . . . this girl. * * * I was thinking, I just told you . . . I felt like . . . I was . . . losing my soul . . . in this place. * * * * Well, that holds your feelings, sort of . . . and when you release of it . . . woy . . . it's sort of . . . pissing all of those feelings off . . . or it relieves your feeling. [*You are speaking of urinating?*] Uh-huh. [*But you can't consider stopping the practice of urinating!*] No, you can't . . . stop that, but . . . I suppose you can chose the right time, or something." Next evening, he referred to a distressing event; "Just a few minutes ago . . . what we were talking about . . . urinating, yesterday afternoon. * * I was . . . in there . . . shooting some pool, * *

I was in there shooting French . . . and . . . I . . . touches . . .
What's-his-name put the 3-ball in the pocket, and the 4-ball . . .
(deep sigh) . . . and a . . . I touched the 4-ball, and no more than
I did it, and I urinated some in my pants . . . And . . . I'd like to see
my girl . . . We . . . it was . . . If I understand it . . . in a
certain way . . . I . . . suppose it was more or less this . . . being
around here, and maybe I thought . . . Miss B. . . . I suppose she's
French . . . [the black-haired nurse in charge of his ward] . . . or
maybe the feelings . . . that everybody around here . . . I had sort
of been in contact with and . . . anyway, as soon as I touched the
4-ball, I couldn't hold my urine . . . And then, . . . after I had
urinated . . . I . . . I started to write a letter . . . to the . . . girl
I was talking about . . . I'd like to . . . go home . . . or see her
some other way . . . * * Number '4' . . . I suppose that was the
idea . . . to my mind, '4' is sort of . . . doctor's number, or something . . . As I told you, I touched the 4-ball and then urinated,
and then started writing this letter. * * * I didn't write . . . I took
it out and started to, but it was pitch dark in here, so I didn't
bother . . . [*Why didn't you turn on the light?*] . . . I never
thought about it . . . I just didn't feel like writing it, so much . . . as
I did lying there on the bed, for a while . . . * * * * It removes
the feelings that you've gathered up in contact with . . . * * * *
feelings that have been . . . sort of . . . nursed by everybody . . .
I'd say my feelings have sort of been nursed, by contact with everybody around here, and by urinating . . . woy, it sort of passes out." †

Theoretic Section

Thought, for our purpose, is organismic activity by the implicit
functioning of symbols, themselves abstracts from the "material"
of life—events. In the ontogenesis of a personality, we can see
cadres of these symbols, the fundamental differentia among the
individual members of which reside in the order of their abstraction from the experiential basis. The symbols of the lowest order,
those nearest to the experiential data, alike also those of higher
orders, are divisible into two categories; those which enter into
the mnemic series, and those which are transitional only. While
the inherent tendency of the organism is to the elaboration of the

[† A small part of this excerpt from the case material is included in
Conceptions of Modern Psychiatry where Sullivan uses it to illustrate the
"classical schizophrenic *spread of meaning*" and gives an interesting interpretation of what the patient means by this communication. (See p. 144 *ff.*
in Norton edition, 1953). H.S.P.]

symbol in those fashions so well discussed by Spearman,* there is none the less the peculiarity that in some cases, the ontogenetic steps are preserved and become memorial elements, while in by far the greater number of our innumerable symbol elaborations, the genetic steps fade completely so that, as the symbol grows, little or nothing of its evolutionary stages is preserved. We refer to the former type as primordial symbols, and to the latter, as sentience. For instance, those examples of lower order abstraction from multiple experiential data (which we have discussed in "The Oral Complex") even though they are removed further and further in the time-mnemic series from the functioning of the organism, as greater and greater numbers of *related* but more and more elaborated symbols appear, none the less retain potential activity and may make their appearance in certain special states, such as that of great weariness, profound revery, or in sleep, as well as in deep regressive processes. Of the other variety, of which the type is exemplified in the initial mental step in sensory awareness—unless the conative situation is especially "set" to preserve them—nothing of such a primitive order survives, and much practice in introspection is required before this "material" of the transfer from mere neurological processes to thought can be detected, unmixed with subsequent elaboration. One might surmise that any symbol which is unprecedented, which is not clearly a correlate of symbols at that time functionally available, persists in the time-mnemic series of the individual, and is more or less capable of recall and of function in its primitive state.

The growth of symbols from lower to higher orders of abstractness has been dealt with by Spearman. He shows that the processes concerned are those of finding *relations* and finding *correlates*. The three basic activities of this sort, as he has generalized them, consist of (I) the apprehension of experience, the events by which neurophysiological situations eventuate in primitive symbols; (II) the eduction of relations, in an indefinitely higher and higher order of abstractness, with correspondingly wider and wider capacity of utilization in the elaborated symbol; and (III) the eduction of correlates of the evolving symbol among

[* Charles Spearman, *The Nature of 'Intelligence' and the Principles of Cognition;* London: Macmillan, 1923.]

the existing available symbols, or, more remarkable still, beyond the physical confines of the organism (the "transcendental function").

We think not only in this manner of securing and elaborating symbols, but by the activity of those we have. Here, too, his analysis is helpful. By (1) reproduction, (2) disparition, and (3) clearness-variation, all the additional phenomena come about. The last mentioned process is of great importance in psychopathological theory. The following quotations from his text may elucidate it somewhat. "Every item in the cognitive field possesses some grade of 'clearness.' It stands between two poles, the one of utter obscurity and the other of perfect clarity. . . . The clearness would seem as if it were a mental configuration that is only attainable and sustainable by means of some special tension; on this tension being relaxed, the configuration automatically lapses." This clearness is composed of a factor of *intensity* ("degree of consciousness" of many psychologists) and one of *determinateness*. The latter is a factor pertaining to symbols only; "no real entity or occurrence can ever admit of any degree in respect of determinateness; it must be exactly of such and such a nature and exist at exactly such and such a particular moment, not in the least otherwise or otherwhile." By this factor of increasing determinateness, differentiation *may* be brought about among already existing symbols; in the reverse fashion, *inevitably*, a diminution of determinateness, and therefore also of difference, comes about such that symbols tend to be confused—Müller's "principle of convergence" (consider dream condensations). The intensity factor in itself determines the momentary locus of the symbols—whether in "focal consciousness," elsewhere in "manifest consciousness," or in the unintrospectable region, "foreconscious," "subconscious," "unconscious." *

[* Here Sullivan is dealing with the process of varying degrees of awareness, with an attempt to move this variation in awareness (postulated by Freud as foreconscious, subconscious, unconscious) into a new frame of reference, which he later termed "selective inattention." (See index references for this term, for instance, in *The Interpersonal Theory of Psychiatry*.) This passage shows clearly Sullivan's dependence on some of Spearman's thinking in his theoretic formulation of schizophrenic process and its relation to the ongoing interpersonal situation. The shift from "utter obscurity" to "perfect clarity" appears in the schizophrenic

These three processes pertaining to evolved symbols are derivatives of five inherent factors to which Spearman has made reference under the terms (a) general mental energy, (b) retentivity, (c) fatigue, (d) conative control, and (e) primordial potency. Briefly, each organism tends to maintain a level in respect of its "total simultaneous cognitive output," however varying be the intensity and the quality of the mental processes; the activity of a symbol produces both a tendency for and a tendency opposed to its further activity; "the intensity of cognition can be controlled by conation"; lastly, all these activities of elaborated symbols in their manifestations show the effects of primordial potencies highly variable among individuals, such as "high intelligence," "talents," and so forth. "Under this heading come pre-eminently the influences of heredity and of health."

Before this systematization of cognition can be carried over to the clarification of the thoughts of a schizophrenic, an additional consideration must be interpolated. It is not uncommon to find in the writings of those interested in such problems, a usage of the term "symbol" such that it applies particularly to words or other signs. Such is the case, for example, in the valuable text of Ogden and Richards (*The Meaning of Meaning*),* and in the so stimulating work of Korzybski (*Manhood of Humanity* and *Time-Binding*).** But the symbol of psychobiology is not by any means necessarily a word or label. It is true that a greal deal of thinking—and perhaps all the troubles which overtake one in his abstract thought—have, as their major "ingredient," symbols in the shape of words. To start with the general theory of Korzybski: From an infinite field of (potential) knowable characteristics of an event, we make a primary abstraction of a certain perhaps fairly large number of these characteristics, constituting this abstraction as our "object." Concerning this object, we make further correct or injudicious abstracts to constitute our symbol of the

---

productions at an accelerated speed; and Sullivan notes that the speed of the shift does not lessen the clarity of part of the production, once the psychiatrist has determined the interpersonal context around which the temporary clarity comes and goes. H.S.P.]

[* *Op. cit.*]

[** Alfred Korzybski, *Manhood of Humanity;* New York: Dutton, 1921. And *Time-Binding:* New York: Dutton, 1924.]

object, our "label" for it, what we call it. This word-symbol may be rather permanent, sharply definable, as the philosophical use of a term; or it may be distinctly changeable and vague, the "henid" of Weininger.*

The psychobiological symbol of lower order is in fact no more or less than one of these infinite possible characteristics of the event. Needless to say, many such primitive symbols escape elaboration into higher order symbols in awareness. Because their intensity is below the "threshold of consciousness," they remain subconscious. This does not imply that they are without effect. Evidence is available which indicates that they undergo elaboration, under these circumstances, but the process is not of comparable speed. Sometimes, this further elaboration develops symbols which erupt into and dominate awareness. The subconscious

[* The concept of henid is developed in Otto Weininger's *Sex and Character;* (New York: G. P. Putnam's Sons, 1906; authorised translation from the sixth German edition); see particularly p. 99 *ff.* In the Greek equivalent of the term, henid, it is "impossible to distinguish perception and sensation as two analytically separable factors, and . . . , therefore, there is no trace of duality in them," Weininger points out. "The very idea of a henid forbids its description; it is merely a something. . . . Later on I shall show that probably the mental data of early childhood (certainly of the first fourteen months) are all henids, although perhaps not in the absolute sense. Throughout childhood these data do not reach far from the henid stage; . . . In the case of mankind the development from the henid to the completely differentiated perception and idea is always possible, although such an ideal condition may seldom be attained. Whilst expression in words is impossible in the case of the absolute henid, as words imply articulated thoughts, there are also in the highest stages of the intellect possible to man some things still unclarified and, therefore, unspeakable."

Although Sullivan in later papers discards Weininger's term and its definition, Sullivan's *modes of experience* (prototaxic, parataxic, and syntaxic) as developed in his later thinking contain certain interesting parallels to Weininger's concept. For instance, Sullivan states that the mode "which is ordinarily incapable of any formulation, and therefore of any discussion, is experience in the prototaxic or primitive mode." In this mode of experience "it is as if everything that is sensitive and centrally represented were an indefinite, but very greatly abundant, luminous switchboard; and the pattern of light which would show on that switchboard in any discrete experience is the basic prototaxic experience itself, if you follow me." The syntaxic mode of experience is an ideal seldom attained in which increasingly differentiated perception is consensually validated with others through language, gesture, and so on. See *The Interpersonal Theory of Psychiatry,* pp. 28-29 *et passim.* H.S.P.]

elementary symbols, moreover, are quite as available for conative control as are any others; under the influence of a strong desire, they may contribute a large share in elaboration of symbols of higher order.

Such of the primitive characteristics as are constituent of the "object" are quite accessible to action within awareness. These, let us say, second-order symbols, however, are not what we are accustomed to refer to as "sense objects"; they are but rarely fully in awareness. It is at this point that we may review the genesis of "adult cognition." The infant is born with various more or less matured abilities, and with impulses to put these individual abilities into effect. The sensory group of these abilities provide innumerable data which undergo the transmutation into symbols and which tend to bear a relatively simple relation to the sense data. Needless to say, these particular symbols are neither general, nor even generic; they are quite concrete. Relations grow between them, however, and a world-representation of a characteristically concrete type evolves. Such a primitive world representation has both advantages and disadvantages.

To this situation, there are added events constituted by the parents' utterances. The symbols elaborated from these, too, are at first equally concrete. In part, however, from the greater importance of the head, and its early maturation on the sensory side,* and in part from the nature of the oral complex—the greatest of the infantile symbol cadres—these vocal productions, and the efforts to duplicate them, tend to assume an especially vivid or intense condition. Even while the infant's "words" are purely magic sounds, they are a predominant feature of his incipient self-consciousness, if for no reason other than their utility as tools. Without further discussion, it should be evident how readily the tendency occurs to substitute these vocal affairs for the second-order symbols—why, for example, one feels so much more illuminated when he knows the "name" of an object. It is well nigh impossible for one to avoid a central attention to these

[* Sullivan has cited two papers here: Frederick Tilney and Louis Casamajor, "Myelinology as Applied to the Study of Behavior," *Arch. Neurol. and Psychiat.* (1924) 12: 1–66. And Curt P. Richter, "Some Observations on the Self-Stimulation Habits of Young Wild Animals," *Arch. Neurol. and Psychiat.* (1925) 13:724–728.]

magic names, which seem to have such a simplifying effect in the infinite individuality of Nature. Thus it comes about that words are pre-eminently the tools in cognitive operations among us: Freud went so far as to locate a "metapsychological region" where thoughts joined their appropriate words. Helas! The fact is that a word is an articulate noise which we have picked up from someone or other—a noise of rather rigid structure, so that one is without caste if he takes liberties with its articulation. Convention attempts to attach to the word a definite meaning. Visual analogies of it are attached to it in the dictionary. But a word, when it is used by an individual, has anything but so beautifully simple a function as he may suppose. It has more or less (generally relatively little) true meaning, in the sense of being a correct abstract, a symbol, of some lower order symbols: it has less or more (generally a deal) of false "meaning," mythology acquired by faith, suggestion, belief, hope, and perhaps charity. The latter is a group of fictive symbolic affairs; they have at best an exceedingly complicated relation to events in the individual's time-mnemic series, or his momentary experience.

Word-symbols, then, are anything but simple psychobiological symbols. In so far as they are used in thinking, they function as very high order abstractions. As far as they are correct in relation to a particular person's experiential data, they are as individual as any symbols, and perfectly satisfactory in their place in *his* mental operations. When, however, it comes to communication, there is difficulty. At times, one can depend upon tacit convention as to the meaning of a word to the user and to the hearer; this does all right in commerce. If there is room for any uncertainty, it is necessary for the speaker to attempt to define the implication of his terms as explicitly as is needful or possible. If this is itself impossible, as in dealing with most psychotic patients, then not *your* meaning of a word, but its meaning to the patient must govern its use. The latter must often be constructed from the contexts in which the word occurs in the patient's productions. When there are no data to help in this procedure, we are but bucking ourselves up to talk about "scattered speech," incoherence, and so forth. In general, it is wise to be very wary of conclusions based upon the use by a patient of words well known to be highly ambiguous, or very diffuse in reference; these should be taken seriously only in "scientific" discussions, for which they provide an inexhaustible basis.

The last of our theoretical considerations is the relation to thinking—to symbol activities in general—of sleep and allied states. Mayo,* speaking before the B.A.A.S., Toronto, expressed as his opinion the notion that there was a continuous gradation from the most vivid awareness, through relaxed attention and revery, into hypnoid states, and finally sleep. Moore, in an article which should be read by anyone especially interested in the schizophrenia theory ["Hypnotic Analogies," *Psychological Monographs*, No. 121] traced the change from the "well-knit fabric of our normal waking thoughts" to the structure of dreams, as it is exemplified in the symbol activities occurring while one is dozing. The writer has convinced himself, by sporadic experiments over a period of years, that not only special conative sets— such as the mother "listening" for the cry of the child—but also some of the major conative dispositions remain active in fairly deep sleep. On the subject of dreams, there are statements enough for all, regardless of persuasion. But in spite of all this, there is need for great improvement in our knowledge of sleep, even in its bearing upon the schizophrenia problem.

Aside from the emotion-signs and the more or less inhibited motor phenomena which are seen as occasional accompaniments of mental processes not alone in man but in horses, monkeys, dogs, and some other mammals, as well as in birds, the data available for the study of symbol activity in sleep is principally the remembered dream. This is far from satisfactory: We know, for instance, that a wealth of detail is lost from most dreams in a few minutes following awakening. Again, we know that the "mechanism" known as secondary elaboration, by which logical incongruities are altered towards greater correctness, functions in the waking interval, so that the "remembered" dream undergoes falsification from hour to hour. The determinateness of dream contents, which may have been very great a moment before, may

[* Elton Mayo, speaking before the British Association for the Advancement of Science. Mayo of the Harvard Business School staff was well-known for his early studies of American industrial work groups. H.S.P.]

fade so swiftly that practically nothing can be reproduced at the very time of awakening: So great is the alteration of mental state in awakening that persons becoming fully awake in the midst of somnambulistic efforts with great emotional accompaniments, generally find themselves "blank" as to what it was about; if they start an experiential report, it trails off into nothingness before we have enough information.

The success of dream analysis in dealing with mental problems underlying "neurotic" adaptations does not prove that the waking associations to the dream elements, or the "latent content" of the dream, is *in fact* of the dream; it is undoubtedly, in fact, *of the patient* (when it is not an extraneous interpretation), and the method is of great value. If, now, we assume as a postulate that symbol activity always takes place under the influence of, and directed to the securing of, an end or terminal state which was more or less clearly foreseen; and assume, similarly, the existence of those dynamic situations termed condensation, displacement, dramatization, and secondary elaboration (the "dream mechanisms"); and also those adaptation-methods which we may call the clearly planned-satisfying, the depressive, the anxiety reaction, defense reactions, compensation, and perhaps sublimatory reactions—then, with this somewhat awe-inspiring foundation, we can bring dreams into line with the recognizable impulses of the organism and, moreover, understand them as intimately allied to the manifestations of events in waking life. A fairly critical attitude extended over some years has not eventuated in the discovery of facts which contradict any one of these postulates. (Space is too limited for definitions, here; fortunately, most of these terms are but beginning to grow ambiguous and diffuse.) We should like more general hypotheses, which would be correspondingly less numerous; but the list, for that matter, is several less than the number of our recognized "special senses," as far as that goes. The postulates enumerated, while derived from other data, seem thoroughly in line with observations from the genetic viewpoint.

These postulates, in contradistinction to Spearman's analysis above summarized, include within them major factors of conation, as well as of affectivity. These subjects being exterior to the scope of this paper, they must be accepted simply for what they are—inseparable aspects of life events alike, in that respect, to time and space. We find it good method to study *one* of the multi-dimensional aspects of symbol activity; we cannot envisage even this aspect of a concrete problem, such as the peculiarities of thought in schizophrenia, without dealing somewhat with the other aspects.

Discussion

Schizophrenic thinking shows in its symbols and processes nothing exterior to the gamut of ordinary thinking, including therein that of revery and of dreams. Even its extraordinary symbol situations have parallels in the extravagances of dreams. Neither is its occurrence explicable on the basis of any novel cognitive processes. It is, as a whole, a peculiarly inadequate adaptation of the cognitive processes to the necessities of adult life: This can be analyzed into a characteristic dissociated condition and a reversive (regressive) change within the dissociated systems.

Throughout the writer's experience, the complex etiology of the disorder has invariably been found to have culminated in a situation in which the *sexual* adequacy of the individual, according to the ideals which he had acquired, was acutely unsatisfactory. The term, sexual adequacy, is to be construed simply as referring to the sexual act and to its closely related behavior, the securing of a cooperating love object. In considering this statement, one must, at the same time, have regard to the peculiar facility with which more or less frankly sexual symbols are brought into relation with *conative dispositions* otherwise susceptible of but the vaguest cognitive treatment, yet in themselves but indirectly tributary to the sex impulses, derivative of the sex instinct.

Because of the great distortion (*vide infra*) of the mind of the child, on the one hand, and, on the other, the barely precedented upheaval [except for birth] which transpires more or less rapidly in the adolescent period, the major concomitants of the latter readily supply a "language" for awareness pertaining to a variety of desires, thereafter. This is quite analogous to the ramification of oral zone symbols throughout the thinking of earlier years.

When, thereafter, there is any outcropping of impulses which had been inhibited earlier in life, no matter how infantile be their character, there is always this sexual paradigm for cognitive operations pertaining to them; there is in fact much more difficulty in rationalizing them by the aid of symbols derived from another system, and they have, of course, no cognitive system of their own. There is no good reason for supposing that all or most of that which is not fairly accessible to awareness, is sexual; there is good reason for the sexual coloring, as for the easy sexual conditioning (in thought, particularly) of undeveloped impulses which finally escape inhibition, and of abortive cognitive operations regarding remote events, which had been repressed by the reduction of their intensity to a subliminal value through the action of powerful opposing conation.

Per contra, as Kempf has emphasized, from the beginning of adolescence, the importance of the symbol system subsumed in virility is unequalled in influence among the goals of the individual. The fact that it, too, like certain other important symbols shortly to be discussed, carries in its relations, all too frequently, the most impossible contradictions, incoherencies, and empty fictions, does not minimize the trouble it causes the adolescent in his rather pathetic effort to save his old world representations, and secure adequate new ones.

The child, having come to an exceedingly primitive but inherently coherent world representation, is not left for long in this happy state. By their behavior, especially speech, the parents convey to the child a wealth of cognitive items in the structure of which is much that is indemonstrable and false. From this, there grows up a body of relational symbols and fictitious correlates which, if the parents were always consistent, might be of use in the home life, but is certain to be a handicap in the later adaptation. As a result of this continued process, by the eighth or ninth year, the child has a truly awe-inspiring collection of magic words (words, "concepts," or what-not without adequate basis in reality). These began with his own vocal productions, developed through wonderful combinations of words—polite expressions, "smart" remarks, conventional excuses, catch phrases, invocations —up to mighty fictive symbols on a par with our Freedom, Justice, and the like. The words which make up the weak links in the juvenile world representation are, thanks to the spread of "education," quite well stereotyped—counters in the game of conformity, first to the home standards, then to those of the school, finally to a larger society. Unfortunately, however, the world representations are *not* uniform—they are terribly individual; not only is each different from that of another who "talks" the same language, but none comes within *reasonable* approximation to reality.

The childish representations pertaining to people are of the greater interest to us, for serious mental difficulties pertain chiefly to contact with others. In our type of society, that sort of an organization to which the psychoanalyst refers as the Œdipus complex is prone to develop. Instead of an attitude towards the father resembling adult awe and fear or respect or reverence, in keeping with his superior abilities, there grows up an attitude of more or less concealed jealously and hatred. That this is a cultural artefact, we attempt to show in "Erogenous Maturation." The unsound prolongation of the "mothering" period is another important source of distortion of these representations. The fragile creed prohibitory of the husband's extramarital sexual life, with its supporting fictions when the wife is cold and struggles to hold him to it, with its confusing family jars when the husband is unstable in his affections or feels compelled to rebel against the yoke—particularly with its terrible "raising the boy so he won't be like his father," when there is actual philandering—these are some of the damnable situations. Even more destructive is the situation in which the woman is the "boss"; in such homes, any possible good which might derive from a benignant matriarchy is utterly swamped in the child's reaction to the woman's effort to be a man, yet conform to society, and the man's efforts to protect his self-esteem. When the father is a fanatic, from paranoid feelings or what-not—but this discussion of modern situations could be prolonged indefinitely: The matter of wretched adjustment of one to another parent, and of one or both to the conventional pattern to which they strive to conform, grows more and more important as we try to understand the coming of subsequent disaster to the offspring.

All too generally, these factors effect a castration of the boy, sometimes by frank fear of a penal amputation, more usually by placing in him the fiction of fictions—that system of symbols to which we may refer as the notion of Sexual Sin. Well before the occurrence of puberty, when such generic notions *might* have a real referent, the youth has come to a clear "appreciation" of the black wickedness of all things sexual. He is then loaded with dogma completely divorced from his biological necessities, taught more or less clearly that his hand on his penis is his hand against God. Filled also with the most fanciful notions about feminine goodness, if he had the misfortune of being the boy amongst girls; warned against the "wild" girls, if he had no sisters—with such additional ballast he enters upon the phase of his existence when it is certain that he *will* masturbate (or develop a severe neurosis as a substitute)—a phase in the course of which he must so reorganize his juvenile ideals as to permit him at least outwardly to be a young man among men.

If now he is one of those who has ovarian tissue in his testicles, as Gibbs demonstrates in several patients; or if he has an equally effective fixation of mother symbols as his complex of the other sex, with complications to protect himself from "incest" situations; if, to escape the maternal influence and save himself from the fate of the father, he fears or devaluates all women: in all such cases he is confronted by a problem of no mean proportions. It is not strange that such boys attempt to carry on the late juvenile attitudes and to satisfy the new impulses by the stimuli obtainable from members of their own sex. But this usually requires, in our so advanced society, an infinity of rationalizations.

Moreover, the homosexual love object all too frequently fails to "stay put," and the youth is subjected to one disappointment after another. When the love objects recant the covenant of friendship to enter the sacrament of wedlock, so much the greater is the shock to this youth. If the relationship with the homosexual love object does go smoothly, there is great likelihood of frank homosexual activity. This stirs up a hell of disapprobation from "conscience," the child-ideals. If, perhaps because of preadolescent experiences, he is able to adjust to frank homosexuality, there is still Mrs. Grundy, and the possibilities of an unfaithful paramour. If he "sublimates his homosexuality," it generally passes muster among the uninitiate, but there are the sophisticated. A "final adjustment, complete or incomplete, but at any rate clearly planned so as to give a feeling of satisfaction and completion," in the words of Adolf Meyer, being quite beyond him, owing to his ignorance of the internal situation and to his fictive representations of others, there now appear one or more of those subordinate and imperfect symbol activities to which we refer by the terms depression, anxiety, the more benign of the defense reactions, and compensatory efforts.

If these suffice, he continues a psychopathic personality, or a psychoneurotic, or perhaps remains in a paranoid state. If he is of stuff that cannot be satisfied with such a crippled adaptation, or if his multiple misfortunes are of such a nature as to render these reactions insufficient to secure the requisite balance between desire and satisfaction, then he recoils from the world—either physically, by flight into the hinterland or suicide, or by the route of symbols, schizophrenia.

The unwitting recoil from the world, which constitutes schizophrenia, will not be fully explicable until we are better informed concerning the phenomena of sleep. Some sort of parallel between the two states becomes increasingly evident as we collect observational and experimental data. At the present, it is perhaps worthless speculation to suggest that in deepest states of sleep, the individual has accomplished a function regression to an approximately palæ-encephalic level. We have data showing a sort of crude maintenance of postural tonus in certain protective attitudes, even in rather deep sleep. We know that certain particular conative dispositions which might be supposed to have much neural apparatus caudad of the cerebrum, may actually function even in deep sleep, so as to initiate behavior which, in its abortive development, is by no means unlike that seen at times in catatonic states. Too, these reactions are of that blind, nondiscriminative sort which impresses one with their purely "integral" character—with their being essentially purposive and specific as to the disposition, but without any features of adaptive elaboration to the particular requirements of the external situation with which the organism would deal. This same "integral" character is a feature of some of the most perplexing of catatonic motor phenomena. Again, with reference to certain postural sets of that musculature to which we refer as the oral zone (roughly, the lower part of the face and the mouth-throat-larynx muscles) and to which the writer is inclined to relate an essential rôle in those mental factors called conation (this is both a striking analogy to, and yet a total difference from, the views of Ramsay Hunt), we have observed modifications transpiring during sleep which could be correlated closely to alterations in the determinable conative situation brought about during that sleep. Here again, similar, if exaggerated, postural sets are observed in schizophrenics, and are noted to undergo modifications over periods of time—brief or extended—with strong suggestion of parallel alterations in the persistent conative situation. Parenthetically, the reader is reminded that the writer is inclined to believe that conative factors will prove fundamental in explaining schizophrenia.

In a great many cases, the difficulties which the youth is having in his adaptation to others are abruptly altered for the worse by the occurrence of an irrational fear. Even if these affective experiences seem to be lacking, one can observe in retrospect, that there always came a time when the load placed upon the symbolic functions of the organism caused a failure of some fictive links in the structure. With this collapse, which the youth may or may not have experienced as the ending of some systems of belief about the world (animate and inanimate, "causal" relations, possibilities and impossibilities, and so forth), there comes a swift or gradual reorganization—"things looked different from then on," or perhaps "I was never the same from then on"—with dissociations not alone in the correlations maintained by fictive links, but in much that is correct symbolism, but uncoherently organized. Along with this, the inherent neotic tendencies produce symbols to cognize the internal and apparently external events. It is here that those peculiarities of thinking which so closely parallel the dream make their appearance. Beliefs grow up which expend the universe—delusions of the well-known varieties—which are in part attempts to fill the gaps, and in part fantastic attempts at solution of adolescent problems. Along with this, the interrelation being still to be discovered, there are more or less obvious "alterations in consciousness," such that the state of the patient's awareness of both external and internal events changes from that seen when one is fully awake and closely attentive, towards types suggested by the state of one just awakening from a nightmare—when the internal symbol situations dominate the perceptions of all reality, which are terribly distorted into a diminishing approximation to the figures of the dream. In some schizophrenics (notably in the sixth case, G. H.) who make efforts to express their experiences, one sees also an intimate parallel between somnolence, drowsiness, inactivity, etc., and the increased fantastic thinking—this with, be it noted, parallel increase in the difficulty in speaking, in the sense of longer and more numerous gaps, less ability to keep to the goal, less critique over peculiar expressions, errors, and so on, as well as greater superficiality of logical thought. This roughly indicated alteration of symbol functioning and "state of awareness" can be traced into the deep stupor of still another patient, Y. C., whose attitude towards the physician was peculiarly favorable to efforts at communication, and whose pre-psychotic personality was so well-knit that the dissociations progressed but slowly.

A transit from quasi-normality to deep stupor may occur with great speed. There is much to suggest that this is brought about by the activity of symbols pertaining to death. As we have indicated in earlier papers, the primordial symbols in this case are closely related to the *event* of birth. The intimate relation of death symbols and stupor, and of rebirth symbols and the termination of stupor, has been discussed by Hoch and others. In our parallel concerning somnolence, above, we again encounter utterances to such effect as "I feel half-dead," "I am about done for," and so forth. We must leave this topic without further comment.

When the schizophrenic has effected his recoil, either from everyone (literally, as in some stupors, or relatively as in occasional paranoid manifestations and in hebephrenic developments), or from any but a few who are highly illusory to him, the thinking is almost entirely a matter of dreams in which his problems are dealt with in activities the peculiarities of which result from the dream-dynamics mentioned in our theoretic section. The striking differences from ordinary dreams arise in part from the magnitude of the conative backgrounds, and in part from the fact that his sensory channels are not nearly as impervious as in sleep, so that the events which transpire in his proximity take their place in the dream-thinking, in lieu of day-remnants. Since, too, the greater systems of symbols are now more or less dissociated from each other, and can function quite independently, and since the more ordinary trivial preoccupations and the trifling but very numerous reminders of the limits of reality are no longer experienced, the limits of phantasy are wide-spread, and we encounter cosmic dramas quite frequently. In these, everything for which the patient did not have correct symbols is turned to representations of the dominant purposes.

We cannot take up a group of major catatonic preoccupations: the extermination of symbol activities pertaining to the adult sex rôle; the successful (nonpainful) adaptation in fantasy to more infantile levels of conation; and the attendant attempts at repression of the adult goals. Before closing, however, let me emphasize the point that the general structure of personality, if such an expression may be used—that is, the relation of inhibiting, governing, symbol-systems of the nature of ideals, to those at the disposal of "lower nature"—is not abolished in schizophrenia, but constitutes the basis of conflict, quite as in other cases. It is not impossible to see these "ego-ideals" functioning in a pathetically normal way, at times. The outcome of the psychosis would appear to be a matter of readjustment here, and then readaptation to the altered world representation.

Lastly, a word about "blocking": This has seemed intimately parallel to those occasional states in which we "dream that we dream"; it represents the effects of awareness of the incongruity of conatively directed symbol activities not in keeping with the intention of the patient. To that extent, it should be anything but discouraging. As one patient (Y.C.) said, shortly after an amazing negativistic performance, the blocked patient is aware that things are not going right in his thoughts, and he may be interested in how he "can get out of this foolishness."

3

Commentary

THREE PAPERS published in 1926 have been omitted at this point in
the historical progression. "Erogenous Maturation" [1] is closely allied
in content with a paper published in 1930, "Archaic Sexual Culture
and Schizophrenia," which appears later on in this book; the content
of the omitted paper will be noted at that point.

A second paper "Regression: A Consideration of Reversive Mental
Processes" [2] is an interesting and valuable paper, and I regret its
omission in many ways. The main rationale for its omission is the
fact that Sullivan came to give the concept a kind of garden-variety
position in the explanation of schizophrenic and human process; in
his final formulation, he notes that "the conception of regression is
often utilized as a pure verbalism; that is, psychiatrists often use the
term to brush aside mysteries which they do not grasp at all. I do not
want anyone to think, when I use the term regression, that it is some
great abstruse whatnot that can be used to sound intelligent about the
mysterious. And the notion that regression is something rare, something highly morbid, and so on, can be dismissed on the strength of
one very easy observation: that in the course of the life of any child,
you can observe, practically at twenty-four hour intervals, the collapse, when the child gets thoroughly tired, of patterns of behavior
which are not very well stamped in. . . ." The concept is discussed
in less than a page and appears nowhere else in that book.[3] As I myself have seen the concept used in case conferences on schizophrenic

[1] "Erogenous Maturation," *Psychoanalytic Rev.* (1926) 13:1–15.
[2] "Regression: A Consideration of Reversive Mental Processes," *State
Hosp. Quart.* (1926) 11:208–217; 387–394; and 651–668.
[3] See *The Interpersonal Theory of Psychiatry,* p. 197.

patients, it is still a handy device for avoiding any discussion of a possible beginning solution for the patient; he is "regressing," the picture is grimly outlined in classical psychoanalytic terminology, and professional staff shake their heads over the sad prospect for the patient. If the patient fools everybody and begins to move out to a more satisfactory living pattern, then somehow the regression has been stopped, in some mysterious way, by the good offices of the psychoanalytic procedure. I think that this kind of exposure to case-conference verbalizations led Sullivan finally to feel that the less said about regression the better. In the paper written in 1927, however, Sullivan presents a scholarly approach to the concept of regression, its history and its meaning.

In addition, the paper contains some new case material and the first (and perhaps only) mention of the fact that Sullivan employed hypnosis at times with schizophrenics. Three of the cases are cited in "Peculiarity of Thought in Schizophrenia" (Case B is E. K. in the earlier paper; Case C is probably G.H.; also he makes reference to E.W.); the case data, however, is in a new framework and would prove interesting reading in conjunction with the data in the earlier paper.

Section II of the paper makes special reference to the work of Kempf and to W. H. R. Rivers, "who brought to psychopathology the training of an anthropologist." The influence of Rivers' thinking on Sullivan's development was considerable; I am indebted to Patrick Mullahy for bringing this to my attention.[4] As early as 1898, Rivers was one of three trained experimental psychologists who went on the famous anthropological Expedition to Torres—work which is generally considered a historical background for the 'new' anthropology of such people as Boas and Sapir. There is beginning evidence in "Regression" that Sullivan regards his hospital experience among schizophrenics as an opportunity to do a kind of cultural anthropo-

[4] In particular, Mullahy recommended the reading of Rivers' book, *Instinct and the Unconscious: A Contribution to a Biological Theory of the Psycho-Neuroses* (Cambridge Univ. Press, 1920) as a background for some of Sullivan's theories, and I found this book eminently worthwhile. Several of Sullivan's favorite terms appear in Rivers' writings: "unwitting," "diffuse," and so on. In addition, Rivers sets up a "protopathic stage" for a mode of experience that has no exactness in discrimination or localization; this is closely akin to the meaning Sullivan had for "prototaxic," although Sullivan's term is also derived from Thomas V. Moore's "parataxes."

logical study. Both Rivers and Kempf were engaged in *observation;*
and Sullivan notes that in order to answer the question of the process
by which any person may regress, "one may turn to the schizophrenic
phenomenology—not, I must emphasize, to draw glittering generalizations, but to view *a patient.*"

In this paper, Sullivan is still heavily dependent on psychoanalytic
thinking, but he has begun to stand more sturdily on his own convictions—for instance, he notes that Jung "never has escaped from
the material, hydraulic terms which disfigure so much of psychoanalytic writings." He has begun to correct more systematically his
mother discipline, and many of his criticisms are accepted as valid
in social psychology today.

In his conclusion, Sullivan states that regression is "a process which,
while pertaining to the past of the organism, does not make refer-
ential use of the past as in the case of functional memory; but rather
is an *inadequate reference to the present* and future. In other words,
as progressive processes extend in their goal from the situation at
hand to an imagined situation about to arise, the regressive processes
suspend this imagined reference to the future goal situation, and put
in action references *as if* the present *were actually* the future. . . ."
This is a powerful foreshadowing of the later formulation of the
importance of *foresight* in the recovery of the schizophrenic—the
necessity for something, however meagre, that was *happy* in the life
of the schizophrenic, so that he can foresee, however dimly, the
possibility of future happiness. (See, for instance, the end case in
Clinical Studies in Psychiatry.)

The third paper, also published in 1926 and not included here, is
"The Importance of a Study of Symbols in Psychiatry." [5] This paper
is of particular interest to those trained in philosophy, but is somewhat tangential to the subject of this book. In one part of the paper,
however, he gives a pertinent example of the way in which schizophrenic perception is only one special possibility of perception among
many and, in a sense, takes its place in the human symbol activities
which cluster around any particular object, in this case a *tree.* He
notes that a schizophrenic may determine "to his satisfaction that he

[5] *Psyche* [London] (1926) 8 [1] 81–93. I am indebted to Sandra Rudnick
whose training in philosophy helped me in the evaluation of this paper.

is 'perceiving' instead of a tree, a gigantic woman with arms extended and hair wide-flung to the breeze," and notes that the "phys-
icist must conclude that the individual is insane; the neuro-physi-
ologist that he has disease or malfunction of the integrative apparatus;
and the psychologist of cognition, that the study of illusion is in need
of much development. If now, our schizophrenic friend rids himself
of the troublesome woman by hiring someone to chop down the tree,
saw it into appropriate lengths, split them, and sell them as stove-
wood—yet still insists that the tree was the aforementioned woman—
then, amongst other things, (I suppose) the neo-behaviorist would
feel justified in his contempt for experiential report. . . . And when
the small boy's 'response' to the presumably identical bundle of light
waves is climbing the tree, in spite of a threatened spanking; the
photographer's, a meditation on the optimum hour of illumination;
the biologist's, a disquisition on genotypes; the psychoanalyst's, a
statement concerning phallic symbols; the realtor's, a calculation as
to how he can turn the landscape into fabulous profits; in view of
such diverse reactions, one cannot but realize that the symbol activities of which the tree was at root are not only strikingly private to
the individual, but in fact pertain enormously more to the individual
than to the tree. It must be evident that the relation to external reality
is confined utterly to the 'zone of interaction' with the individual's
personality" (pp. 87–88).

The next paper, "The Onset of Schizophrenia," first published in
1927, contains the first use of "interpersonal" by Sullivan, as far as
I know. The case material in this paper illustrates the fact that the
onset of schizophrenic process often first appears in adolescence and
goes unrecognized by a variety of medical specialists.

The Onset of Schizophrenia[†]

STUDY of onset of disorder in male patients of this hospital seems to establish two factors preliminary to schizophrenic psychoses. Firstly, the appearance of the disorder is late in a long series of subjectively difficult adjustive efforts. Secondly, it seems never to occur in those who have achieved if only for a short time a definitely satisfying adjustment to a sex object. We have not been successful in our effort to identify exactly the factors which cause milder maladjustive efforts to pass over into schizophrenia. Neither do we believe we are justified by accumulated facts, to stress the sex factor as of exclusive importance. Much more data is needed in regard to the onset of the malady; at this stage, however, there seems little reason to doubt that cultural distortions provided by the home are of prime importance. We have not seen maladjustment which was without a foundation of erroneous attitudes which parents or their equivalent had thrust upon the child. We have found all sorts of maladjustments in the history of patients who suffered the grave psychosis, but regardless of vicious influences subsequently encountered, the sufferer had acquired the tendency to such an illness while in the home situation. Interpersonal factors seem to be the effective elements in the psychiatry of schizophrenia.

Objective manifestations of maladjustment are now divided among the three classes of psychoneurotic, psychopathic, and

† Reprinted from *Amer. J. Psychiatry* (1927–28) 84:105–134. Read in abstract before the joint meeting of the American Psychiatric Association and the American Psychopathological Association, New York, June 11, 1926.

psychotic. The static implications of current teaching is unfortunate. The medical man in general envisages schizophrenia as a strange entity which befalls the predisposed. Teaching should emphasize the dynamic view of these situations.

The great number of our patients have shown, for years before the break, clear signs of coming trouble. A number of them were brought to notice by the outcropping of behavior of a simple psychoneurotic sort. Unwitting attempts at hysterical incapacitations not only precede many psychoses, but actually make up much of the psychotic picture in some cases. Reactions by obsessive substitutions are seen in a small number to have preceded for years frank schizophrenic phenomena. Here, too, the maladjustive "psychoneurotic mechanism" is continued in the psychosis, and we may find with the autochthonous thoughts of schizophrenia, a mingling of doubts and scruples of a simple psychoneurotic nature. The gradations from neurasthenic picture into schizophrenia would be easy to observe, did we but attend more clearly to the mental state of quasi-normal adolescents. Anxiety conditions which deepen into schizophrenic panic occur in numbers.

The psychiatrist sees too many end states and deals professionally with too few of the pre-psychotic. To him, "ideas of reference" are apt to imply psychosis; to one who has comprehensive data on psychoneurotics, psychopathics, and eccentric "normals," such delusional content is recognized as wide spread and simply one of the signs of inefficient adjustment to the demands of life. The institutional physician, for that matter, cannot but realize that those who require supervision are but that portion of the psychotic who are so in the grip of their eccentricities as to be rendered conspicuous. He knows that many who leave as "social recoveries" have achieved nothing more remarkable than the ability to conform outwardly to certain standards—that they carry quite as extraordinary delusions as those of some others who cannot conform. With this in mind, it would seem as if we should lay great stress on the prompt investigation of failing adjustment, rather than, as is so often the case, waiting to see what happens.

Most schizophrenics have shown evidences enough to excite

even lay curiosity during more or less extended periods before mental disease was diagnosed. Not family physicians alone, but specialists in rhinology, laryngology, gastro-intestinal maladies, in urology and in gynecology, all these see the incipient schizophrenic and all too often "let things ride." I feel certain that many incipient cases might be arrested before the efficient contact with reality is completely suspended, and a long stay in institutions made necessary.

If there is anything at all in our present views of mind and its disorder, watchful expectancy is not the method of choice in the difficulties of youth, and the provision of useful experience is the only hope for insuring such patients against trouble.[1] If there is any good reason for a policy of delay, it must reside in our lack of certainty as to what is to be done. In attempting to indicate promising lines, I shall review some of our notions of psychodynamics.

Ignoring that section of the population in the case of which serious physical factors exist,[2] we can distinguish three sorts of maladjustive processes which do not lead immediately to arrest of the individual's struggle.[3] They include *sublimatory resymbolizations* and *compensatory motivations*, neither of which interests us particularly here excepting in so far as they may antecede those processes more intimately related to schizophrenia. The *defense reactions*—infinitely diverse in their combinations, individual goals, and explanatory rationalization—these are the mal-

[1] Experience as here used refers to anything lived, undergone, or the like: to that which occurs *in* the organism, rather than directly to events in which the organism is involved. Experience is mental; *i. e.*, it is reflected to a greater or lesser extent in behavior and thinking. At the same time, experience often occurs without conscious awareness.

[2] Roughly divisible among (1) the defective, whose equipment has low potential educability, so that he cannot undergo many varieties of experience, and so does not profit from many events; (2) the physically handicapped, *e. g.*, the hunchback; and (3) that group typified by the epileptics, in the case of which there appears to be a strong tendency to bizarre destructive reactions wholly injurious to the individual. Needless to say, "psychogenic" factors are important in every individual case in this group, as they are apt to be in the other two.

[3] In contradistinction to (a) depression, and (b) the anxiety processes, both of which are not only maladjustive but also methods which present no real attack upon the troublesome situation; as such, they may be regarded as a means of "standing still" before a problem.

adjustive processes which can be seen to form a gradient from mere poses and trifling evasions of the obvious to the essential schizophrenia. They all show the characteristics that they are unwitting evasions and distortions of simple experience—means by which the organism interposes something artificial and relatively abstract in the complex of the individual and his environment, physical and cultural. From an objective viewpoint, the interposition seems "intended" to protect the creature from discomforts either internally conditioned as in conflict of deeper desires and ideals, or externally conditioned as in disconformity of supposed potentialities and environmental demands. Whether the individual struggles unwittingly to be other than he is, by poses and exaggerated reactions even amounting to psychotic excitements on the one hand, or substitute activities, rituals, etc.; or seeks peace by transference of guilt and blame from himself to others or to social institutions; or, again, effects a modification of the stress by partial or total incapacitation as in the hysterical disabilities of the invalid reactions; [4] in all these cases we find the irrational, "unconscious" protection of the self a central theme. The *barrier* subvariety of defense reactions, more particularly, are of a piece with schizophrenia. Here we find a structure, so to speak, thrust between the creature's accepted self and everything else. Whether he has unwittingly adopted (1) an attitude of repulsion to those around him, or (2) a "physical" concealment by secretiveness or even seclusive behavior, or finally, (3) erected a complex relation which subtends all contact with personal and extrinsic reality (schizophrenia)— all these processes reflect an increase in the complexity of life and a necessarily destructive influence upon personal efficiency.

It may be taken for granted that a clear appraisal of the factors entering into any difficult situation should precede efforts at its resolution. In our potential patients there is to be found a significant grouping of irrational factors. We find that the youth has developed many misapprehensions as to his real potentialities of achievement. He has come to exaggerate, misunderstand, and

[4] Invalid reactions, in particular, may partake much of the nature of compensatory efforts. In these cases, all of which probably start as defense reactions, the acquisition of sympathy becomes a goal in itself, the kindly feelings of others making up for disappointments in more practical striving.

conceal various requirements for his satisfaction, to believe that he needs certain end-situations which are superfluous and that he can dispense with certain others which are a part of the common biological heritage. Finally, we find him unwittingly elaborating a fabric of personal ideals which have but a complex order of relationship to possibility, and of notions concerning the estimation which others make of him that are simply fantastic. All these factors interlock in astonishing combinations, and his energy is dissipated in pseudo-problems and defensive processes. Feeling that an admission of his unhappiness—even to himself—is an indication of inadequacy or peculiarity, such an individual appreciates but vaguely that he is thwarted by an agency over which he has no control. That any increase in his correct insight would be helpful to him goes without saying.

Obvious though it should be, one must stress the factor of persons in all adolescent difficulties. The family physician seems often to accept the "physical" causation to which most patients refer their illness. Overwork, for example, enjoys great popularity as an excuse for mental disorder. Long hours, unsatisfactory working facilities, strain, even undernourishment—these masquerade as important much more frequently than not. The uncolored data from analytic investigation of patients quickly disabuses one of this "common sense" notion. Mental stress arises from societal relations, not from impersonal physical factors.[5] The question always to be answered is why the individual has proceeded into the state of physical depletion; what underlying

[5] Fatigue as a phenomenon of the total organism has thus far escaped scientific measurement and study. That it includes an important psychic element cannot be gainsaid. Rest and recreation also belong largely in the category of mind, and physical quiescence—in so far as it can in fact be achieved under such circumstances—is unavailing in the presence of ineffective mental activity. *Vide*, in this connection, Elton Mayo, "Revery and Industrial Fatigue," *J. Personnel Rsc.*, (1924) 3:273-281.

Nothing herein is to be construed as denying to ill-health, toxæmia, loss of sleep, malnutrition, etc., an important place in the sequence culminating in many mental disorders. The point to be stressed is their entirely subordinate role. The data of our study do not minimize the importance of the *efficiency of the somatic apparatus* in the life situation. There may well be times when a cup of coffee would delay the outcropping of a mental disorder. We have observed incipient depression and neurasthenic states follow unwitting denial of the accustomed caffein dosage.

societal factor has driven him to overwork, to deprivation of sleep, etc. When thus regarded, we find generally that the alleged causal factor is but a preliminary compensatory, sublimatory, or defensive maneuver, to be regarded as the prodromal maladjustment which facilitated the more dramatic failure.

Of all the preliminary maneuvers by which youths seek unconsciously to safeguard themselves against the stress of conflict involving their societal relations, the use of alcoholic intoxication is probably the most impressive. This is to be regarded as a subvariety of the defense reactions; it is seldom that one finds a case in which other defense processes are not also in evidence. Among alcoholic youths, one finds a continuous gradation of simple "comfortable" dissociation bolstered by much drinking, to states of extreme discomfort with phobias, anxiety attacks, and hallucinatory phenomena.

It is never easy to say just when the schizophrenic patient has crossed the line into actual psychosis. In several cases we have found that there had occurred a brief phase of marked psychotic condition some considerable time before the final break. A patient, for example, when 17 underwent an operation firmly convinced that he would not survive the anaesthetic. He awoke minus his normal "grasp on reality." Things seemed for days to be quite entirely unreal—he "lived in a dream" in which all sorts of trifling and wholly unrelated occurrences seemed fraught with great personal import, to bear in some signal but incomprehensible way upon him: the operation had been the occasion for some strange mutilation: he was changed in some curious fashion. Then, one morning, all this was past; he "awoke his old self." He went on to the age of 25 years before the stress of heterosexual adaptation pushed him over into an exceptionally paranoid incipient schizophrenia. Another, receiving cocaine anaesthesia for a nasal operation, at 22, developed an extraordinary excitement like that seen in catatonia. This passed in some 30 hours, and nothing bizarre was shown for the next three months. As the date of his marriage approached, he passed swiftly into a severe catatonic schizophrenia. Yet another, having accidentally discharged a gun in the direction of a beloved uncle, developed blocking and phenomena of stupor which lasted a few days.

Eight months afterward, in circumstances when both his hetero-sexual efforts and his strivings for prestige among his fellows were baffled, he underwent a catatonic dissociation. In these few, from a number of such cases, we observe fairly well demarcated psychoses following a major event.

Each one of this group of patients had come to a psycho-pathic type of adjustment quite early in life.[6] By this is meant a group of peculiarities in behavior and thinking which seem to be manifestations of, firstly, an unconsciously determined inability to profit from certain particular events. Unlike the defective, the psychopathic has no fundamental defect of educability; he has experience of unrestricted variety, but certain of it fails of elaboration and synthesis into a practical whole. This we mean when we refer to his "inability to profit by experience"—the im-portant point being that the experience from which he shows no practical learning lies in one or more circumscribed fields. These "resistant" areas are found to be the results of well known dynamics identical with those which we have identified in the psychoses and psychoneuroses. Secondly, psychopathic mani-festations include characteristically a more or less distinct aware-ness of personal defect or abnormality, and this is accompanied by an exaggerated tendency to rationalize. Finally, there is a striking inability to advance considerations of the future into con-trol over more immediate satisfactions. We know that the last

[6] In "Regression: A Consideration of Reversive Mental Process," we refer to this subject of the psychopathic personality, emphasizing the value of its study for the general theory of mental disorder. "Psychopaths" are not regarded as results of hereditary factors. It is true that germinal in-fluences may prepare the soil for individual mental evolutions, for the maturation and growth by experience of the individual mind. There is nothing explanatory of the case before one, however, in this reference to hereditary defect or peculiarity. He is no product of pre-existing harmony or disharmony, but a product of growth, like anyone else. The analytic investigation of such individuals is most profitable research, even though its prosecution for therapeutic purposes may be discouraging.

It is regrettable that clinicians have not taken care to separate the group which they please to call "psychopaths" into (a) those who show psycho-pathic type of maladjustment evolving from a basis of mental deficiency, and (b) the true psychopathic personalities, relatively stable maladjust-ments without mental deficiency in its accepted meaning. The former are problems of preventive medicine. The latter are an important field for study, and one almost entirely neglected.

mentioned characteristic applies to the immature, and, perhaps for this reason, we sometimes regard the psychopathic as instances of a selective arrest in mental development. Such a notion is permissible if it is understood as a general explanatory conception throughout psychopathology, rather than a specific conception of psychopathic states. By this, I refer to the identity of developmental sequences in this and all other groups. "Selective arrest" then refers to distortion of customary development rather than to any stoppage in the accumulation and organization of experience. We have yet to determine what becomes of experiential material which is thus distorted; that problem is no less acute, however, than are many that we gloss over in our discussions of psychoneurosis.[7]

Psychopathic maladjustment is a product of the preadolescent phase of personality development. The adolescent upheaval in these individuals includes destructive phenomena of distinctive character. Schizophrenia is much more likely as an outcome than in those who have more coherently integrated the experience of infancy, childhood, and the juvenile period. It is interesting, however, that the longer psychotic collapse is escaped, the less the chance of a grave disorder, and the less typical any illness which ensues. In other words a psychosis occurring in a psychopathic youth under, say, the age of 22, is in all likelihood frankly schizophrenic; but an initial psychosis occurring at, say, 30 will probably be a brief excitement—even if decidedly schizophrenic in type. This suggests that the psychopathic sort of maladjustment grows more effective as experience is accumulated, notwithstanding the fact that its interference with social efficiency may continue unchanged, or even increase.[8]

[7] To their credit be it said that the psychoanalysts are attacking the problem in their study of "neurotic dispositions." The outcome of investigations in this field has been somewhat concealed by the uniformity of "causal" factors that they uncover in all mental disorder. Analytically isolated factors have preoccupied them. We need to consider maladjustive syntheses as they occur in society, now that we have a grasp on abstract "mechanisms."

[8] Brief excitements with schizophrenic "coloring"—which are sometimes indistinguishable from the gravest psychoses—are a profitable field for investigation. The fact of their occurring fairly late in the course of a relatively stable maladjustment, and their disappearance with as residuals an exaggeration of the pre-existing peculiarities, connects importantly with

Search for the phenomena actually constituting the onset of schizophrenia has brought several interesting facts to light. As already indicated in the case of delusions of reference, a great deal of the early phenomenology is an accentuation of what can be elicited from almost any mild case of mental disorder. A clear to vague content indicative of [the feeling that other people show] an unfriendly interest in him is general in psychopathological states. A great proportion of all maladjusted individuals believe that they suffer invidious discussion. The "neurotic tendency" to detract in a relatively unwitting effort to reduce others to a lower level than that adjudged to self, is evidenced not only in more direct behavior and thinking, but indirectly by projection as these persecutory trends. With any excuse, this progresses into notions that one is being slighted, annoyed, or definitely wronged. Were all those who entertained mild delusions of this sort to be assembled in institutions, the state would collapse immediately from depopulation. Fantastic meanings attached to the behavior of others, to one's own action, and even to events among inanimate objects—these too are nonspecific. A remarkable number of those who are not regarded as psychotic entertain beliefs closely akin to delusions of mind-reading and of more or less mysterious control by another. Hypochondriacal notions form the rationalizations for innumerable maladjustive processes. Somewhat grandiose self-appraisals, on the one hand, and depressive depreciations and self-criticism, on the other, are easily uncov-

---

certain types of post-psychotic personality. We see after some cases of frank schizophrenia "social recoveries" amounting in fact to severe psychopathic states; e. g., the paranoid personalities which arise from catatonic schizophrenics, in the case of many "spontaneous" recoveries. These post-psychotic states sometimes arise *de novo*—they are not foreshadowed materially in the pre-psychotic personality. In the one case, a decidedly peculiar person undergoes a brief schizophrenic dissociation and comes from the process with accentuated warp. In another, an imperfectly adjusted person (lacking marked psychopathic traits) undergoes a severe schizophrenia and achieves from it a relatively stable maladjustment. Something of the implication of this was outlined in "Schizophrenia: Its Conservative and Malignant Features." See, for an interesting consideration not unharmonious with our views, Anton Boisen "Personality Changes and Upheavals Arising out of the Sense of Personal Failure" [*Amer. J. Psychiatry* (1925–26) 82:531–552].

ered in a great many patients. "Peculiar thoughts" and even pseudospontaneity are not very uncommon: Obsessions and pre-occupations typify one large group of maladjusted.

In a study centering upon cognitive features,[9] I have demonstrated several points bearing particularly upon the evolution of schizophrenic panic, and somewhat upon the insidious forms. We have come to regard all initial manifestations of these illnesses as strikingly uniform. From the standpoint of content, there appear those processes and symbol elaborations customary in dreaming. Instead of turning "day-remnants" to the purpose, the schizophrenic cognitive operations deal with perceptions of reality, personal and impersonal. All these—like the figures of the dream —are distorted into use for representing the personal situation and for efforts at solving it. It is at this stage that the patient believes he is watched and followed—the observers personifying in some cases the ideals which cannot control his desires of lower cultural value by ordinary activity. In others, they are personifications of the "evil" desires which pursue him to assault or "rob" and degrade him. In the first situation, exteriorization takes the form of the "voice of God" and in the second, the hallucination of threats or foul epithets. This sort of content connects with a more or less terrible affective situation of a primitive sort—an "insane mood" which has pre-existed the clear-cut cognitive phenomena. The motivation at work is in a general way conflicting groups of elaborated (and more or less successfully repressed) personal tendencies opposed by tendencies of the nature of ideals (cultural controls). The disturbance in reality-appraisal which has been slow in the prodromal stages, is now very swift, progressing to a state in which everything is involved in the cognitive efforts. This stage in which nothing is without an incomprehensible meaning, and the ordinary exchange of intelligence is palsied, may continue in relatively simple elaboration. This is the catatonic type of schizophrenia. In it, the conflicts remain unresolved, the struggle expands into cosmic dramas, and the psychic processes revert through the ontogenic repertory, perhaps down to the most primitive. At any time, however,

[9] See "Peculiarity of Thought in Schizophrenia."

this situation may pass into one of a few typical attempts at re-adjustment. There may be a massive resynthesis amounting to recovery with profit. There may be a fragile reorganization prone to relapse under fresh difficulties. Of grave portent, however, is the readjustment by paranoid processes. If it succeeds, we have a persistent paranoid state with more or less of schizophrenic residue (paraphrenias of Kraepelin). If it fails, we have an unhappy jumble of schizophrenic projections, any hopeful aspect of which is lost through the destructive hateful attitude of the patient ("paranoid praecox," and many now classed as hebephrenic).

Finally, there is the practically irremediable hebephrenic type in which destruction of the conflict is achieved by disintegration of the acquired socially adopted tendencies, and along with this there is a dilapidation of the evolved structures influencing manifestations of simple native tendencies. The motivation of such patients then becomes juvenile, childish, or even infantile.

That which we have called the prodromal period of schizophrenia often includes characteristic features which should receive special attention. One sees many who were "depressed" for a long time before the outbreak of frank psychosis. The behavior and utterances of these individuals reflects much unhappiness, but is to be distinguished from the psychosis of depression. They do not slow up physically and mentally nor suffer preoccupation with a certain few grief-provoking notions to the exclusion of more practical thinking. Expressed loosely, they feel not that all is lost as a consequence of personal sins and errors, but that all is wrong for some more or less inscrutable reason, which may or may not pertain closely to some weakness or inadequacy or peculiarity of the individual—often alleged results of masturbation. The situation is always a maladjustment to assumed personal inadequacy, but this may elude the patient's awareness entirely. While the true depressive is preoccupied with thoughts of the enormity of the disaster, of punishment, hopelessness, and the like, the incipient schizophrenic is not the host of any simple content, but is burdened with pressing distresses and becomes more and more wrapped up in fantastic explanation and efforts at remedy. The distinction is one fundamentally dynamic: Pure depression is practically a standstill of adjustment; the schizophrenic depression is a most unhappy struggle. Instead of literally or figuratively sitting still, these people are striving to cut themselves off from painful stimuli, escape the situation by mystic and more or less extraordinary efforts, and justify themselves by heroic measures. While the pure depression may end in suicide of a practical sort, the schizophrenic depression leads to fantastic methods of self-destruction often preceded by fear of being killed.

Perplexity also is an important phenomena of the incipient state. In this condition, extraconscious material influences perceptions of reality to such end that the patient becomes more and more entangled in contradictions, alternative notions, and illusions. Autochthonous thoughts appear and interfere unpleasantly with rational efforts. Insignificant characteristics of events persistently hold the attention and give rise to disturbing analogies.

Fear-states covering the gamut from phobia through terror, and from anxious feelings through apprehension, to the full-developed primitive panic,[10] are factors important in many incipient conditions. Whether or not rage—fighting fear—will make up part of the late picture depends in part on the character of the individual's former experience, in part on the particular explanatory delusions which he is entertaining.

All three of these phenomenon-groups combine in the evolution of most schizophrenic psychoses.

CASE 8

Admitted December 24, 1922, æt. 24. The only surviving child of three; one, two years older, survived until the patient was about seven and one-half years old. The father living and well at 60, of a family showing considerable mental disorder; himself "excitable when engaged in business and things go wrong." Does not drink. The mother

[10] Affective experience related to fear can be divided into two major categories. Genetically it is evolved from the primordial experience including preliminaries to birth—the death-evil preconcept, as we have called it. See "Schizophrenia: Its Conservative and Malignant Features," and "The Oral Complex." The differentiation proceeds along two lines, the basis lies in the external and internal character of reference. The former is through terror to fear. The latter is through apprehension to anxious states.

six years the father's junior, living and well, "quite aristocratic and proud of her family."

Gestation, birth, and early development are reported to have been normal. No night terrors or nightmares can be recalled by the parents. There is some suggestion that the boy showed considerable determination to have his own way. Did well in school and graduated from a university. Puberty at 15; no mental changes noted at that time. Entered Naval Reserves and was given training in aviation, which was completed a few days before the Armistice. It is alleged that early in this training course he was caused to swim in ice cold water, following which he had some difficulty with his legs: some short time before the acute psychosis he said that he first became nervous "when they made me swim across the lake while I was in training—it was in February and was icy cold"; one gathers that he was under treatment thereafter for two or three months and it is interesting to note that during his psychosis he at times spoke of stiffness in his calf muscles.

On discharge from the service, the father "noticed that he had dreamy spells. He was much more irritable, the least little thing seemed to agitate him." He resumed his schooling "but became very much worried by it so that he was very glad indeed to be home for the summer vacation." He then took a year's post-graduate course and entered employment in the fall of 1921. Things went fairly well until early in 1922.

He had never shown a great interest in women excepting for one prolonged engagement with a girl of about his age, whom he called "buddy." She taught a group of children and he a class of 13-year-old boys in Sunday School. During the years they were in different colleges "they wrote each other every few days—then he would let a month pass, thereafter writing apologies stating that he had been sick, when he hadn't been at all." His fiancée's mother remarks: "He was morally the cleanest boy I know. Very attentive and thoughtful but sometimes showed astonishing forgetfulness. He was the most wonderful man to her; always took such wonderful care of her— about a year ago, in a bunch of sorority girls and boys there was a little drinking going on, and he brought her right home because of it."

In February, 1922, the patient began to show insomnia, sometimes getting no sleep at night. There were times when he would cry; he said his nerves were bad and that his legs would start twitching and bother him. Decided to have an operation to repair a deformity of his nose which had resulted from an injury at hockey. Was much disturbed after the use of local anaesthetic and on leaving the hospital called at his fiancée's home which he refused to leave, so that they put him up for the night. "At 5 a. m., he was singing and whistling in his room and having a great time. He came down and took a record my 14-year-old son had put on the victrola and took it out on the porch and threw it away." He returned to his home that day, and there "talked of the Ku Klux Klan and was down on Catholics. This all passed away in some 10 days."

In March, 1922, it was noticed that his work showed lack of initiative and inefficiency. His salary was reduced and this stimulated him to greater effort as a result of which he was to have received a raise at the time when psychosis became evident. In October, one of his fellow employees sustained loss of an eye, for which the patient gave first aid. He was much upset that night, but "seemed to get over that pretty well." In November another employee, while standing alongside the patient, was caught in gearing and destroyed. The patient assisted in disengaging him. He did not mention the incident on returning home, wept to himself most of the night, discussed it with the family next morning, and took out accident insurance forthwith. "After the last accident at the plant his sleep was very much broken—would not want to go to bed—would take spells when he did not want to go to bed, said he could not sleep." Around this time he spent a night at the fiancée's home, and her mother reports: "He was afraid of his hands—they were swollen and then they were shrivelled up—but they were always red; some poinsettias were in his room and he had to have them taken out because they seemed bloody. My daughter was using a curling iron on her hair and he jumped up from the bed where he was lying and said that they should take it away, that it was pointed toward him."

On Thanksgiving Day the patient refused to wear sufficient clothing on a hunting trip, going out with khaki shirt and breeches and catching cold.

"Two or three weeks before Christmas . . . [the fiancée and the patient] came out of a room and asked if they could get married at Christmas. His face got red and his eyes were bloodshot—didn't seem able to say anything but 'I love . . . —I love her awful much —wanted to ask you—now feel better that I have.' A couple of days later he acted as if had taken a shot of something." During the next two weeks he was observed to be abstracted and said that "I'm all wrong mentally." On the afternoon of December 20 he went with the fiancée for their marriage license. On reaching the Court House Square he straightened up and marched sharply at attention, executing the turns in a military fashion. To the question [required in that state] as to whether he was white or colored, he became very indignant. He remarked later to the girl that his city "needed an ensign." That evening he attended a banquet of his employing company and received a bonus check. He was emotional and wept much during the banquet. Called on the fiancée for an hour thereafter, giving her the check and other souvenirs and "sat there and smiled and looked at the floor."

Next day, December 21, he went with a fellow employee on business to a city at some distance. On his way he attracted his companion's attention by crying. When questioned, he made no response. He acted sufficiently peculiar so that he was sent back. At 4 o'clock the next morning he called his father by telephone, hanging up the receiver when the father answered. That morning he took the wrong train to work, walked a considerable distance across country, and said to his mother on reaching home: "Mother, you never told me anything about the relations of a man and woman after marriage." The father made some efforts in this direction, later that afternoon. The patient then went to his fiancée's home where he was observed to be badly confused. He said to her: "I think we ought to get married, sweetheart, don't you?" On being reminded that the wedding was set for two days thereafter, he said, "Oh! that's right." At 3 o'clock the next morning he was found standing on a bridge, a mile from home. He went to the fiancée's home, arriving very early in the morning. At breakfast "he would not eat anything until she had put a piece into her mouth—would chew when she told him, would ask 'fast or hard, sweetheart?' Talked constantly of mixing chemicals, smelling things and testing waters." He was quite violent to his mother who visited him. Was given hypnotics and slept until about 1 a. m., December 24, then rose, "washed for a long, long time, stood on one leg and spun around, leapt around the room, took a spoonful of medicine and played with it in his mouth, thereafter going and expectorating it in the bath room. Then put everything, towels, paper, etc., all in the commode. Took off all his clothes and got noisy, shouting for my son . . . all the time, slamming the bathroom door and hitting the light." The police were called and the patient brought to the hospital.

When received, the patient was in an acute catatonic excitement, very antagonistic. He insisted upon being nude, was destructive to clothing and took very little food. There was considerable rigidity, statuesque postures and auditory, gustatory, and olfactory hallucinations. Spoke of peculiar burning sensations in the skin of his face, the result of having poisonous gases blown upon him. At times he was in panic. In the next few days he remarked: "Oh! I know that I'm sick, but I don't know what's the matter." Misinterpreted everything which he heard, and hallucinated many obscene names applied to him and accusations of various sexual perversions. In response to these, he frequently cried bitterly and threatened to "get even" with those thus abusing him. He was assaultive, but always in a defensive fashion. Had tactile hallucinations "like electrocution," and said that he was constantly bothered by odors "like that of analine dyes."

Became fairly accessible and showed marked improvement after each interview for a time, this change following a dream in which he was the recipient of pederasty and fellatio. In his convalescence, he was at times perplexed and distressed as to his having venereal disease, although he said, "I have always been virtuous and know that I have never had any venereal disease." It was discovered that the distress which he referred to his legs might be due to enfeebled arches, and measures for their relief improved his confidence, somewhat. As his perplexity diminished, he made a rather paranoid readjustment, clinging to some somatic ideas, in which he was discharged.

CASE 24

Admitted May 23, 1921, æt. 30; under care, one year six months. Readmitted June 30, 1923; under care, two months. Readmitted September 22, 1923; under care four and one-half months; transferred to St. Elizabeths. The eldest of five children, two brothers and two sisters younger. One, a brother 22, married. The father living and well at 65. The mother, 10 years her husband's junior, living and well. The patient resembles her in physique and physiognomy strikingly.

Gestation and birth reported normal. Night terrors, temper tantrums, enuresis, etc., denied. He was "very precocious" in learning to be tidy. Prior to the age of one, he had become so active and was so given to standing while in a carriage, that he was spanked three times in close succession, after which he discontinued the practice. Up to the age of nine months, he was very nervous and restless and suffered a great deal with colic. "He was very active and talkative by the end of the second year." During his third year he was burned by over-turning a container of hot potatoes—subsequent to this it was noted that he became increasingly quiet, much less showy in his activities. He was very easily weaned, and this ease of discipline was also noticeable at the time that he was taught to sleep alone.

The patient did well in school and finished high school at 18; the first evidence of mental disorder occurred in the course of the last year. He then did two years of work in engineering and then quit the university and entered an office where he began to study law. This was part of a plan to become a thoroughly competent patent attorney.

Masturbation began at 12 and has continued. At the age of 25 he had his first heterosexual experience; has had but two since.

"The first signs of his illness took the form of some ideas of a self-deprecatory nature in regard to his English teacher, when he was about 17. Because he had been good in his work in this class, the teacher gradually omitted calling upon him and he developed the idea that this was because he was failing in his work." As the mother recalls it, this cleared up promptly after a talk in which the teacher explained that it was quite the contrary. In his 24th year when he was studying very hard late at night, he developed a disorder of the right arm and subsequently the right leg. The condition was painless: "At times when he attempted to grasp things he would do so with great force so as often to crush breakable things in his hands, at other times he could not grasp them at all, and always he was uncertain whether he could hold a thing or not." He showed depression and lack of initiative. He went to the West and there rehabilated himself in three or four months. Resumed work in a patent office, whereupon the condition returned. Around this time, he had a rather vague interest in a woman which led to nothing. This increased his depression and after an absence of about two and one-half years, he returned at the age of 26. He resumed work on specifications connected with patents and in four months "suffered another collapse." In 1917 he tried for the Officers' Training Camp, passed the physical examination, and was to have gone up a few days later for mental examination. The day preceding this appointment he began vomiting, with severe retching, from 11 p. m. to 2 p. m. the next day. He was much weakened by this and did not take the examination. He later registered for the draft. His father claimed exemption, but the patient declined it, his brother having already enlisted and gone. He was drafted and sent to Camp Meade on June 30, 1918. The second day there he was found to be acutely disturbed and was sent to the hospital. In interviews had in September, 1923, the patient relates that when he went to camp, the first two nights he did not sleep well, as he was occupied with planning how he could make most rapid progress in the Service. On the afternoon of the third day, he developed a condition of exaltation, went off by himself for a walk in the fields.

The following is *verbatim:*

"The first delusion I recall occurred shortly after my arrival at Camp Meade. It seemed to me that I took a very enjoyable walk about the entire camp and was so exhilarated that it seemed to me that I was just touching the high spots and in actuality really flying over the surface. This dream or rather walking dream occurred at sunset about the second or third evening of my arrival at the camp. I remember after walking or flying rapidly for a short time about the entire encampment, I came to the sun-warmed platform of a warehouse. This warm surface felt very enjoyable and nice to my touch, so I rested on its surface for a while and enjoyed the various activities which I could observe. After resting here a while I continued my walk dream flight until reaching a pump. Here I stopped a while and rested on a log alongside of the pump and was much interested in observing the various groups of soldiers who came to the pump to secure a supply of drinking water. Shortly after this episode at the pump, it became dark and I then endeavored to retrace my steps to the quarters where I was encamped. After several blunders in locating the proper shelter I reached the right encampment.

"The next day I was feeling too ill to drill on the field and secured permission of my captain to rest from maneuvers that day. After this I became quite sick and only remember in a vague indefinite fashion being carried or partially carried as I staggered along to the camp doctor.

"For three months [actually six weeks: considered as 'very exaggerated form of maniacal excitement; suffered from visual hallucinations and was dissociated in all spheres'] following the foregoing episodes I was quartered at the camp hospital and remember very little except that during this time my mind was occupied with dreams of vast hordes of soldiers being drilled in the hot sun, much against their protest, until they were about ready for rebellion. I seemed to take no part in these maneuvers except as an observer. Seems to me that they thought that I was in some way responsible for the severe drilling that they were being subjected to.

"I remember being driven in a motor omnibus to St. Elizabeths Hospital. This was a trip of 25 or 30 miles and I had two illusions or hallucinations during the progress of the ride.

"The first concerned the nature of the ground over which we progressed. It seemed to me as though we were driving through a rubber plantation. I could see evidences of tropical vegetation and also see what I thought to be black people working collecting gum from the rubber trees. This interested me during the first part of the 30-mile drive and then it seemed to me as though we were being pursued by an automobile driven by a person with whom I had had some business relations when in Los Angeles. The pursuing car never succeeded in overtaking us and for the remainder of the trip I was keenly interested in escaping from the pursuer or pursuers. The road over which we traveled seemed to be crossed at frequent intervals by other roads and at each intersecting point this car following us would seem to shoot by—sometimes ahead and sometimes behind us, but evidently it would be off the right track and thereby we succeeded in not being overtaken.

"On arrival at St. Elizabeths I was much impressed by the terraced lawns around the entrance to the hospital and by the masses of red flowers blooming profusely about the entrance. I had no idea where I was being taken to and thought, perhaps, it was a monastery or some retreat located in Switzerland." This idea was elaborated into a recurrent fantasy somewhat as follows: "A monastery or some Catholic church—in the basement or cellar was a thick layer of grease or tallow which, it seemed, might be renderings from dead bodies, in what corresponded to the Catholic purgatory. I used to see an old priest walking in through this mushy layer, and then my cousin who is a very light and spirited girl [a Catholic six years younger than the patient who lived with them from his tenth to fifteenth year] would join him in his walk." It appeared that he had gotten caught in this subterranean cavern and was tolling a bell at the time. He had lost hope of ever being remembered. It seemed that the priest may have lost faith in humanity, still he seemed a faithful follower of the church and a very lovable person.

"My year or more [actually only 11 months] at St. Elizabeths was filled with dreams, most of them very pleasant, but unfortunately they made no lasting impression upon my mind and I do not recall the great majority sufficiently clear to express them in words.

"I remember that in one ward I was under the delusion that I was Sitting Bull, an Indian chieftain, whom I thought at the time was living in the neighborhood of the Montana mountains. This chief, whom I seemed to feel that I saw, had been captured by the United States regulars and was in dreadful fear of torture. There was an attendant, who because of his cowboy dress conveyed to me the impression that he was Buffalo Bill's son and I liked this boy very much and at the same time stood in fear of his actions."

["Admitted in a confused manner, showing considerable psychomotor restlessness. Stream of talk free, irrelevant and incoherent. Emotional status and attitude of mind: patient lies in bed, at times quiet, then chatters senseless unconnected words and phrases. Patient evidently has both hallucinations and delusions. Disoriented in all spheres. Could give no sensible answers to questions."]

In addition to this material, he recalls another series which pertain more or less directly to Napoleon, the content of which occupied a portion of several excitements. He is sure that the first occurred at St. Elizabeths. Napoleon has always been a sort of ideal to him and in the course of the illness, one of the dramatizations took this form: Napoleon would appear in the midst of battle (European war), would ascend a hilltop and stand gazing about, expectorate into the palm of his hand and slap the hands together, whereupon lightning-like phenomena would proceed from between them; this lightning was not destructive, but was a channel by which he issued commands to his subordinate officers. Of the other fantasies, perhaps the following is the most remarkable: again and again Napoleon would go for the most intensely enjoyable rides on a remarkable black mare. In the course of these enjoyable rides the element of battle would intrude. The mare would change to an extraordinary black stallion and in the course of the fantasy, Napoleon would secure semen from the yard of the stallion, which in turn he slapped between his hands with the production of lightning-like flame which similarly proceeded to invigorate and direct his subordinate officers. There was a quite clear identification of the patient with the hero figure throughout these fantasies, as was the case in most of the following:

"For many hours I was entertained in my room by the actions of a fly on the surface of a small table which used to be used in serving my meals. This fly I termed a 'Benjamin Franklin' fly and it seemed to me that it was endowed with superhuman intelligence and it used to keep me entertained by its antics on the top of the table.

"At Laurel Sanitarium [removed there, by parents] I used to dream occasionally of being [perhaps a bull] locked in close sexual embrace with a cow and flying rapidly over the surface of the earth from one rich luxuriant valley to another. This cow seemed to embody or seemed to be the embodiment of Miss S. and she seemed to take a maternal interest in my companionship. This dream of being a cow [he cannot recall this one] and flying in close embrace with a cow was the first of a series of dreams in which the other party always seemed to be Miss S. [See insert below concerning Miss S.]

"I remember thinking that a picture hanging on the wall of the Laurel Sanitarium was Miss S. and that she was the Czarina of Russia. Myself and the other patients of the hospital, I thought in the dream state, were very much opposed to the treatment and the meals which we were receiving and I planned a petition to Miss S. when she made her annual Christmas visit to the hospital for release from the place. This petition which I had in mind was of course never presented and the lady never made a visit so far as I dreamed but I thought that her presence had been evidenced by a supply of candy which we received during the holidays and by a thorough cleaning of the hospital.

"I recall a young fellow named Curtis whom I thought to be the son of a Turkish nobleman and, perhaps, the crown prince of Turkey. He interested me very much—first, perhaps, because of his soldier-like bearing and refinement of features and later on because he gave me what is known as the 'queen's salute' [cannot recall]. I dreamed or had hallucinations to the effect that Curtis was visiting the United States and carried with him a retinue of servants and harem, and that it was my duty to entertain him during his stay in the United States. I arranged, in my dreams, for his entertainment at dinner parties, cafes, and theatre parties. Later when he returned as I thought to Turkey it seemed that I went along with him and became acquainted with Turkish and oriental customs." He has additional recollection to the effect that while in Turkey he was connected with the rescue of a great many women who had been falsely imprisoned, and that they were brought before him in very bedraggled condition, after which he caused their rehabilitation.

"Leaving Laurel Sanitarium I went to the Trenton State Hospital [admitted July 17, 1920] and while there I had a series of dreams or hallucinations. One again was concerned with Russia and it seemed to me that Miss S. and her sister appeared to me once when I was sitting alone in the ward and once when in the yard. On both occasions they were dressed in skating costumes and I enjoyed skating with them over the large limitless expanse of Russian ice.

"For a time my dream thoughts were concerned with the feasibility of some perpetual motion arrangement. I knew that perpetual motion is not practical nor thought feasible by the United States patent office and yet my thoughts seemed to center about the fact that this earth is supposed to be continually in motion and that would seem to point to the fact that one form of perpetual motion, at least, is known. Then along with this trend of thought I thought of the universe, and forgetting what little I knew of astronomy I used to ponder on what kept the stars in their orbits and wonder as to the whole meaning of life and creation. This thought was not conscious thought but was indulged in by myself in a condition of dream sleep.

"From Trenton Hospital I returned to Laurel Sanitarium and during each of my bad spells was entertained by dreams of a very fantastic content. In one of these dreams I seemed to see a picture of North and South America as though the under surface of these two continents was plated with gold. It seemed very delightful in the gold lined cavity existing under the two continents of North and South America and I delighted in drifting about thinking that I was reposing contentedly on a bark." As originally related, the caverns in this case were under the Central American portion of the Western Hemisphere and it seemed that the South American portion was female and the North, male. This fantasy is intimately related to another series which will be mentioned after that of the Egyptian slave.

"From the Laurel Sanitarium I went to Sawyer's Sanitarium at Marion, Ohio. The first continuous dream I remember at this latter place was concerning Monte Carlo. It seemed that Monte Carlo was a flourishing gambling establishment located in the center of Africa and that the two colored hydro attendants were serving as croupiers. I thought that Jack Johnson was the proprietor of the gambling establishment, and at the same time as it seemed to me he was the king of Africa. The establishment seemed to have many floors similar to a department store and these different floors were reached by an elevator which it seemed to me ran up and down through the center of the earth. On each floor was gambling paraphernalia and as the sum of a person's bets reached larger volume he was permitted to gamble on a higher floor. The top floor was the most exclusive one of the establishment and each evening the winner of that night's play was regaled by the appearance and dancing of Mrs. Jack Johnson, the colored queen of Africa.

"There was a young lady at the Sawyer Sanitarium who interested me very much and during my bad spells I often saw her in visionary form dancing before me in the room. It seemed to me as though she was supplied with a pair of wings, not suggestive of angels but merely to further her agility and ease in dancing. I used to dream while at Sawyer Sanitarium and when I was slightly excited that I was in Russia. There was one young man, a major in the British aviation service, whom I was thrown into close association with and whom I always dreamed of as being one of the Russian nobility. Several of the nurses at this sanitarium I always thought of when abnormal as being Russian princesses.

"At the Sheppard and Enoch Pratt Hospital I have had many interesting and peculiar dreams, most of them occurring when I was confined to Ward Three [for disturbed patients]. I remember a series of dreams in which I thought myself to be an Egyptian slave and I worked very hard and faithfully pacing up and down one of the rooms on the third ward and sticking my finger into a little opening in the wall. It seemed to me for a time as though my task was to scrape the sand forming the cement from out of this opening and I worked apparently for hours at the useless task." In another fantasy the greatest pyramid is being built with tremendous labor. Great numbers of elephants are employed under the domination and guidance of a milk-white elephant, vaguely identified with the patient. In the interior of the unfinished pyramid is a pool, and as the elephants become worn out they climb over the edge and fall into the pool —this was not so much fatal to them, rather their lives left them and were deposited in a small cupboard-like space elsewhere. Another fantasy clearly recalled was to the effect that the patient was one of a number occupied with the work of building a great pyramid. On the outside of this, life was very hard, rigorous and painful. From the exterior, where he worked, there was a tortuous and difficult channel with a peculiar kind of entrance by pushing back a stone, and this passage led to the interior which was superbly gilded, hung with diamonds and precious stones [which no one thought of taking but enjoyed] and contained a great pool in which one floated in small vessels in sublime contentment.

"Miss S. again featured prominently for a time in my dreams. It seemed to me for a while that she had strayed from the straight and narrow path and had become a very high class woman of the street. I had fallen into her toils and had to obtain for her a supply of opium which it seemed to me she was very determined to obtain and use. I do not recall how I thought I obtained this drug but I remember that it was my task to obtain it and that I always pleaded with the user to break away from the habit and endeavor to regain her former place in society." It developed that Miss S. is the mother ideal, having all the great virtues of the true mother, with all the real mother's defects replaced by their opposite virtues. In a fantasy pertaining to Miss S. while in this hospital, she desired the life-giving opium. She lay in his bed and he struggled and struggled to keep out of it, but the attendants would pick him up from the floor and put him in. He could reproduce no thoughts which followed his being put into his bed under these circumstances. "For a while I used to dream almost nightly that I was in Russia and that Miss S. was a lady of nobility and very fond of classical dancing. I would be granted the privilege of a private audience and she would appear before me on a stage draped with heavy velvet hangings of a golden brown color then I would become very much interested in the display of nude dancing which followed. For a time I was entertained during these bad spells by arranging for a meeting in the woods. It seemed to me that I had constructed a retreat of logs somewhere in the vicinity of this institution and that Miss S. was to drive over from Washington and spend a pleasant evening with me. I remember after making these arrangements and waiting in vain many evenings when finally the lady appeared and we spent a very pleasant time together.

"Another dream concerning primarily Miss S.'s sister at whose funeral I had acted as one of the pall bearers—I dreamed that this girl's spirit had become embodied in a pigeon ring, such a ring as I had often placed upon the leg of a bird. I dreamed that the pigeon carrying this particular ring had flown to Peru, there died and that the ring was placed on board a ship along with a quantity of guano. Then it seemed to me that Miss S.'s sister, Lilian, reached this country in much the same form that she had embodied when she died. Her relatives and friends with the exception of myself would not believe that the girl had returned to life but I remember dreaming that I had no doubts as to her identity. For a time after this it seemed to me that Miss S. appeared in the form of a turtle carrying a loaf of bread under her arm. The bread was to be used to nourish her deceased sister. It seemed that Miss S. was always headed for the cemetery and I think that this delusion was, perhaps, furthered by the fact that outside of the room which I had on ward three some excavating was being done. The ditch which had been dug looked somewhat like an open grave and suggested to me a cemetery.

"Some of my dreams at this institution and a number of those which I have had at other institutions were concerned with Chinese. I used to dream here, for instance, that the god of the Chinese people made his home on the top of the mountain and that in order to keep his subjects happy and employed he used to direct that they tunnel continuously round and round through the mountain, with the idea that by working hard and faithfully they would in the next world obtain a higher position in society. I used to see a Chinese princess who it seemed to me had a position upon the cap of this mountain and she was fed on opium and was there as an incentive to the workers below to do their best in anticipation of marriage with her.

"My last dream or hallucination was concerning spies. For several days when I was ill at home I questioned my mother as to the identity of my brother and asked her if she thought he was a true soldier of the United States Army and if my brother was in the secret service agency of some foreign government. This trend of spy thought persisted for a couple of days when I returned to this institution. I remember picking out in my dream sleep about 10 people around this institution whom, because of their foreign language, made me feel that, perhaps, they were not true to the United States. I directed Mr. R. [an attendant] to have them executed as spies at sunrise, later in the evening I called him in and told him that they had better be shot at once because I thought, perhaps, they might escape before morning. Mr. R. demurred at this request to shoot the suspected men so I told him that if he would bring them to me I would be pleased to do the shooting. For a while during the second evening of my stay here I thought that Mr. S. [night supervisor] and Mr. R. were connected with foreign governments, Mr. S. being a colonel in the Scottish Army and Mr. R. being an Italian diplomat in the service of his government. I thought it was incumbent upon me to invite them to my house and arrange for their entertainment. I remember that the party which I had planned never came off—that I was much disappointed because Colonel S. was unavoidably detained."

Following the wave of illness in which these productions were secured the patient left the hospital in one of his stupor equivalents which passed as normal periods. Sleeplessness gradually developed and he was brought here before disturbance made itself evident. By the first of October he was very restless, boisterous, sleepless, and silly. In an interview with the writer, he saw the Pope standing in the shadows behind the physician's chair [patient is Presbyterian; the mother's family is Catholic]. He improved rapidly and on October 8 produced the following:

"My last illness was the mildest of any similar experiences which I have passed through during the last five years. The attack was so mild that I do not think I lost consciousness during the entire period. I was slightly stimulated for several days and really enjoyed the time when I was slightly abnormal because then my thoughts were very pleasant and moved very rapidly.

"I recall believing that the second ward where I am at present located was the quarters of a Masonic fraternity and various gentlemen there were putting me through a mild ritualistic test. I thought, for some reason, that I was a Mason of rather high degree and that it was my duty to instruct some of the younger men on the ward and teach them the sacredness of the mutual vows which we had all taken in this fraternity. I stood before one of the older men on the ward, thinking that he was an exalted Mason, and held a stiff position as long as possible. While standing very still and tense, I wanted to faint and be revived by some one secret sign which it seemed to me the senior members of this wonderful fraternity were aware of and could put into play at their wish. After standing still as long as possible I fell over against the wall and gradually assumed various well-known poses until I became tired of the phantom play which I was indulging in. For awhile I seemed to pose as Mercury, then tiring of this, I assumed various other well-known poses and finally took the position of Rodin's Thinker and held this last pose

for a considerable length of time. Later when my excitement sub-
sided a little I realized that no one else was interested in what I was
doing and so after reading awhile retired for the evening.

"The next evening I got to thinking about the battle of the Alamo
and for a long time my mind was occupied in a dream sort of way,
with a rehearsal of the events which I believe took place at this well-
known battle.

"After thinking along this line for a while I became interested in
an art catalogue of the Corcoran Gallery in Washington and halted
for a considerable length of time at the picture of Stuart's painting
of Washington. This picture appealed to me very strongly for reasons which I will not trouble to write here and I even went so far
as to show it to Mr. McK. without any comment as to its significance.

"Since coming here this last time my interests in horticulture, medicine and occupational therapy have revived and at present I wish
to center my thought upon one of these three subjects but as yet
have not decided which is best to follow. Horticulture has been of
interest to me practically all my life and the beautiful flowers which
are to be found around this institution are very interesting to me
and I should like to know more about them in a scientific fashion.
I have been thinking for some months of taking up the study of
medicine but just at the present am undecided whether I want to
study osteopathy, chiropractic or general medicine. As occupational
therapy has helped me considerably I have come to the belief that
it is a very helpful and a large growing field of endeavor and I
should like to go into this subject in great detail at some time with
a view to following that as an avocation."

The patient has been under practically continuous treatment in
St. Elizabeths since August 26, 1924. The most recent note is as follows: "Has come out of one of his stupors almost completely. He
answers slowly, relevantly and coherently; denies psychotic content
and has some realization of the malady from which he suffers. He is
oriented. Is neat in appearance. Has had many stuporous periods
during the past three months and does not emerge as before. Is
seclusive on the ward. Works a little."

CASE 52

Æt. 38, admitted November 12, 1924; discharged unimproved
seven and one-half months later. The second in a family of four; the
other three girls, married. The father died 22 years ago of cardio-
vascular renal disease. The mother five years her husband's junior,
living and well. A maternal cousin had mental disorder. Little is
known of the early life of the patient. He graduated in pharmacy at
the age of 19, and went to work immediately. Fourteen years ago he
set up in business for himself and has been most successful. The

mother and one of the sisters lived over his store. He has had but 17 days vacation in 14 years. His work kept him at the store from 7 a. m. until 11 p. m., with the exception of two nights a week, which he would spend with his mother and sister. While popular as a boy, he was not much of a mixer and had very little social outlet, though much respected in the community.

His sex life began at 13 with masturbation, which continued to the 19th year, being then discontinued "because I began having wet dreams and they satisfied me, I didn't have any more desire, I guess." Father died when patient 17: "I was too young to appreciate it, you know." Says that he had been one of a gang of boys that practiced mutual masturbation, but that he has had no other homosexual experience. In his twenties he had his first heterosexual experience, "All right, but it was weak." Since then he has had three or four other contacts with women, always unsatisfactory, usually due to precocious emission, complicated by defective erection. The last was about four years ago and was a failure. He feels that this situation and the continuance of contentless sexual dreams throughout his life ("I'd just wake up, knowing I had had one, so slight they barely wet the sheet"), have had something to do with periods of tremor and "nervousness" in public places. It seems that he had gradually become more uncomfortable in the past two years whenever away from the store and out of doors.

Some six months before admission he had notions that he had developed a hernia. He decided that he should sell his business. He slept so badly that he took chloral by mouth. Within the next two months he showed agitation and depression concerning the hernia. A brother-in-law came to stay with him to convalesce from a tonsillectomy which had been performed for the relief of rheumatism. The patient decided that his own tonsils were troublesome, had them examined and found that they were in bad condition. This worried him although the family attempted to pursuade him to undergo operation. He sold his business at a fair profit early in September, and on the 22d of that month consented to tonsillectomy. He was afraid that he would die of the operation. His mental state deteriorated progressively. By October 1 he was quite sleepless. He was taken to see a cinema, "The Ten Commandments." This worried him considerably. In the morning of November 3 he drank iodine and cut his throat with a razor blade. On admission he said that he could not understand the attempt on his life as he felt afraid to die. The second night in the hospital he dreamed that "there was blood coming from my mouth, and I was dead." It woke him up, but he realized it had been a dream at once. In the early days of his stay he showed a persistent stupor-like reaction in which he appeared superficially in very fair condition but actually wore a mask-like expression and paid no attention to flies, etc. lighting on his face. He was constantly apprehensive and at times had acute attacks of general tremor. The seventh day in the hospital he made an impulsive attempt on his life, beating his head against a brick wall. Seen 25 minutes later he said that he had answered "all their questions"; this seemed to relate to an idea that the attendants had obtained from his mind the answers to a number of very personal questions without his having said any- thing; that they had discovered the crimes which he had committed and for which he was to be punished; to wit, having very frequently lain in bed with his mother and having engaged in masturbatory pro- cedures upon himself under these circumstances; and having handled the person of Ruth, the daughter of a friend of his. He had seen and heard Ruth and her father on the ward, the latter having spoken of shooting him. He was "drilled" a great deal on the subject of his relation to his mother, the auditory hallucinosis being so acute that he repeatedly asked, "Don't you hear them too." He asked the physician to "stop playing that machine on me," the machine being a device to influence his mind. He became inaccessible and progressed into an unhappy paranoid dilapidation in which he was removed by the family.

CASE 75

Admitted July 22, 1925, æt. 26; second of two boys; the elder 30, unmarried. The father died following accidental infection when the boy was about 20; he was "deeply interested in the upbringing of the children. Did more for them than he should have done—swimming, shooting and the like. They were very close to him." The mother living and well, seven years her husband's junior. Mental disorder on both sides of the family. Gestation, birth and early development re- ported as normal. The mother recalls that as a child the patient was "fascinated by clothes and loved to dress as a girl. Has always loved costumes and finery." He was rather precocious in development and for years entertained himself with sexual fantasies. "He matured earlier than the average boy and was rather more sophisticated." "He did not take the same interest in clothes that most boys take." "He read Petronius, etc., and was full of curiosity about sexual matters but he never sowed any wild oats. He was exceedingly cautious and loose women disgusted him. He regarded sexual intercourse in itself as an animal act." To young girls "he always made himself most charming but. . . . had more in common with older women. . . . he was taught to have great respect for women."

The mother taught her sons to realize that she never felt safe until they were in at night. They always reported in her bed room and discussed what they had been doing. The father stressed to him that he should never cause a girl to love him until he was prepared to offer himself to her in marriage. "This necessitates several conditions. First and foremost, a clean past life."

Some of his early associates remark, "He was a most interesting talker with great independence and poise. He was not widely popular, not a man's man and some people thought him conceited, pompous and a treacherous cat. He was a bit uncertain as a friend. He did not stand by friends when they got into trouble. He was extremely selfish." In college, he felt at one time that he was "near a breakdown"; details are lacking.

He went to Europe to complete his studies and there found his morals a source of much levity and crude by-play on the part of fellow students. On one occasion he went with a friend to a house in which a peep show was maintained. What he observed "revolted" him. He remarked that the atmosphere of the city in which he was located was all sex and that he was unnaturally repressed. He became concerned about his health, feeling that his tonsils ailed him; did much gagging and belching. He began to think of getting married; "most peculiar emotions have developed in my adolescent nature." The girl he selected had already found a satisfactory swain and he was considerably upset when she declined him. The sexual horseplay at his school increased. He began to find certain of the teachers repulsive.

Developed an interest in automatic writing and felt that he was receiving communications from deceased relatives. An acute disorder of sleep appeared. Became so uncomfortable that he concluded he was suffering an attack of brain fever. Went to visit a relative, previously making a memorandum which he carried with him, as follows: "I feel under a hypnotic power of someone. And if I should marry, it will be against my will power." Immediately before this trip he had consulted a physician on the assumption that he had venereal disease. On arriving at the neighboring city he complained that he had a dual personality, that he was hypnotized, and that he was hermaphroditic; "I know the trouble of the whole matter; it's sex." He talked much to the physician who was called, of censorship from his father, being married, having attempted Coué's method, and that he was a woman—having been castrated. Great excitement ensued; he became disturbed and combative and much hallucinated. After some weeks of care he was returned to the United States.

On admission to this hospital he was much disturbed and made many attempts to harm himself. There was a great deal of antagonism and pugnacity, this frequently most impulsive. Went nude at times and often refused his meals; had feelings that he was being impersonated by some one outside the hospital.

His marked improvement was foreshadowed in a dream somewhat as follows: he stood naked in a close triangle formed on the right by a board fence, on the left by a large horse and behind him a tub full of water. He became accessible, shortly afterwards. The following is an extract of his productions concerning the psychosis:

"My brother and I were brought up on fear, and it was this fear of venereal disease that kept us from asserting our manhood. Mother brought us up and it was from her that we got most of our instructions. She took the dominant part until anything went radically wrong. The chauffeur was the first source of information regarding these matters. Later mother explained certain things and talked of them as not clean. Sex had a great deal to do with my illness. I had masturbated. I had never done anything worse than that. I felt that I should have been with a woman.

"I was run down and lonely. The girl of whom I have spoken was coming to the city. I expected to propose and was therefore particularly anxious to see her. I felt that she was coming to settle the matter and that she expected a proposal. She told me about her other sweetheart and later told me that she was going to cable him instructions to announce her engagement. I had the impression that she was in love with me, but that I was not sufficiently in love with her to make the proposal. I felt I had led her on. This matter worried me a great deal. The chief attraction between us was a mental one, not a physical one.

"About a month before I left [the city in which he was in school] there was a young chap visiting the house. I was playing extremely hard and drinking a good deal. My main reason for drinking was to be sociable—never made me ugly—always drank from sociability. One evening I was with this young friend of mine and we picked up a couple girls. You know the sort that make their livelihood by dancing and that sort of thing. We fooled around with them and I would have liked to have a wild time, but they did not appeal to me. Whenever it comes to that type of girl that I could take liberties with, the romance always seems to be lacking. Sometimes their voices were not pleasing, or possibly it was the odor. This evening, I had dinner with this friend and I had a number of drinks. We then went to a dive. There were a lot of young ladies in negligee and I picked out what seemed to be the prettiest one. I petted her, but had no desires to go to bed with her. I think this rather provoked the girl that I didn't. My friend was off upstairs with his girl. Then following this, we went to a peep-show, which was low and vulgar. The next day, I felt very cheap, because of the vulgarity of the thing, and the money I had spent. At the time I had enjoyed it, because I had just enough liquor in me. The actions of my friend revolted me. I thought it was so crude and bestial [he had observed the act] I hated to see my friend go to bed with that girl. [Asked as to which girl seemed to be the more interesting after this performance.] My girl still was most interesting: I felt sorry for her, feeling that it was too bad that anybody should have to earn their livelihood in this way. Therefore, I gave her 30 francs. At the peep-show, they performed all the sexual aberrations. I had a bad taste in my stomach for a week. That night

I felt it was a very valuable experience, but it all seemed a sham. The picture that other fellows had painted of a good time did not seem to come through, it all seemed very sordid. My sex interests were probably stronger when I was younger: I was near a breakdown in . . . . [college].

"I was working hard, drinking, and felt at times as if I were on the verge of a breakdown. I was acutely self-conscious, I lacked energy, I was mentally slow, I thought that people did not like me. My hearing seemed poor, and I would often fail to answer questions, I suppose because I was preoccupied. The day following the episode I saw my friend and we went to a dance. He showed one of the girls very much attention, and since the girl did not like it, I felt worried and responsible. Hearing French [much spoken in this city] all the time rather worried me. One of the girls asked me why I was preoccupied. It was no one particular thing. I was not happy and I was trying to find out what particular thing I liked.

"Mother had always been interested in spiritualism, and I always rather pooh-poohed the idea. For some reason or other, I began to have an idea that I would try some automatic handwriting. I put a pencil in my hand and it maneuvered around. After two or three twitches, the pencil started writing, but I had some difficulty at first, because the hand would go off the page. Then things seemed to be under control and I wrote two or three pages. My hand just dancing over the paper. It was all very spooky and then I read it. It was incoherent, and difficult to understand, but one line in particular stood out. It was a line from my grandmother, which was as follows: 'Life after death, very enjoyable' signed Grandmother, father, and other members of the family who are dead. When I attempted to do this automatic writing, father's photograph was on the desk beside me. I felt as if somebody were behind me. I also got the idea that my father was unhappy in his last illness, that there had been something wrong in the last illness. I had the idea that he was not keen to live, and was glad to die from the operation. He was like a brother to me. At that time I was anxious to leave but I was bored and lonely. I would have gotten out of town and gone home on the next boat if it had not been that I was staying for the examinations.

"I was unhappy, I was specially worried, and the doctor told me to go away, but I lacked self-confidence. I was afraid to go away and be sick where I knew nobody. So I went to . . . . and there at the theatre one night, it was practically impossible for me to follow the play. There seemed to be a congestion in my brain, my hands were sweaty, and I was extremely self-conscious. It seemed as if people were looking at me and I felt as if I had talked out loud. I felt in a panic, but there was really no adequate reason for this. I was not conscious of what took place. I remember being in two nursing homes, but I don't remember being transferred from one to another.

I remember fighting with the nurses. I had a feeling of affection toward the nurse, and I had some idea of proposing, but I got out of that situation without any embarrassment. There was another nurse, a rather simple little thing, but nothing special came of that. I had an idea that they were trying to play tricks on me, and they were not playing square. There were some ideas of being persecuted. Sex had a great deal to do with the sickness. In the first nursing home they gave me some modelling clay, and I attempted to make figures. It seems my mentality could not have been more than that of about 10 years and I worked in a sort of daze. All the models seemed to take the form of male genitals, and this was both fascinating and repulsive to me. It seemed as if I was the medium for another artist. I rather liked the doctor. He was a big fellow, and I felt he sort of had a hypnotic influence over me. When I entered the nursing home, I told him everything, and then later I felt that he was not looking out for my interests. I felt that there was a negro in the woodpile. One night I had a terrible time and I felt as if my brain were disintegrating. I began to hear voices, also, at about that time. The first time I heard voices was probably one night when there was a special nurse on duty, and there was a sort of screen between my bed and her desk. There were some white bed clothes on the floor, and this made me rather suspicious. The nurse was weeping, coughing, and then later said that they would perform an operation. I thought I had been chloroformed when I woke up the next morning, and I thought that an operation had been done on my brain in order that my brain might be turned around, in order to give me a great deal of will power. Voices said the operation had failed. Another voice said that the doctor whom I wanted was not available, and then said he had been bribed to perform the operation by Mr. P. [father of the alleged sweetheart]. At one time in the nursing home, I had the idea that someone was trying to shoot the doctor from the window of an adjoining building, and I tried to protect him by running in front of him.

"In the second nursing home, the voices were worse. I would hear them just as if I had telegraph receivers on my ears. They would say 'hello, old friend, you are away on a trip to the country. Don't you believe in brotherly love? It is the greatest thing in the world.' Then later, in the second nursing home, when I would sit in certain chairs the apparatus would commence, and it would only say 's.o.b.' 's.o.b.,' and repeat until I was scared to sit on the chair. The bath tub was the same way. It was just as if there was an electric attachment to the bath tub, that started when I got in. I got weak and clammy. It was spooky.

"We motored to the boat. There were a couple of young chaps along, and I didn't know that mother was on the boat until we had gotten out to sea. She had come up to talk to me on the deck, and the

doctor offered me a cigarette. He also offered mother one. She said
'don't you think you had better give up cigarettes?' and it seemed
to me as if there was something wrong. I felt that for every cigarette
I smoked, mother had to sleep with a sailor. This gave me such a
shock that I said I would be the king's cock sucker. There was fear,
and I felt that I should make some sacrifice to protect my mother.
The doctor said at one time 'you are not on to ship ways,' and I felt,
for some reason, that the doctor might have the power to nationalize
women, and when I didn't see mother for several days, I felt that
something had happened to her, or that she was cutting me. I used
to be afraid of the deck chairs, and when I would sit down I would
hear words like whore—more—war, etc. When the wind was in a
certain direction, the port holes would give me objectionable ideas.
When I made the remark about the king's cock sucker, Miss . . . .
got up and said she would go to the other side of the boat, in order
to see another boat that was passing. I took this to mean that virtuous
Miss . . . . was to be assaulted.

"On the steamship the nurse slept in the bunk place, so that he
would awaken in case I tried to go out of the room. The morning
following we were on deck and I asked to put on his spectacles and
he remarked that I had eyes like mother's. I thought this meant that
I had slept with mother, and had gotten her eyes. I had an idea he was
a crook. Later, I saw writing on the wall just as plain as I could see
anything, and they were the names . . . . and . . . . Then I saw two
crosses in the eyes of the nurse, and I put my fingers on my fore-
head and wrote *Judas*. From that time I began to be afraid of him,
more from my own actions than from anything he did. I was afraid
I would be kidnapped by him. I had the idea that they had locked
me up for some reason that I didn't understand. The male nurses
scared me. They came into the room about eight o'clock and gave me
paraldehyde. It had a revolting taste and odor. I thought it did funny
things to me. On one night, I threw up my supper, and then went
to sleep. When I woke up, my nostrils were dirty, and I thought they
had made me rub my nose in the vomitus. At times, my stomach
would seem to swell up specially when I had indigestion. And also,
when I was shaved, my spine seemed loose, and when I put my head
very far back, it seemed as though my spine buckled up. I also
thought I was a hermaphrodite. I thought that I was going to become
a woman. When my stomach swelled up from indigestion, I thought
that I was pregnant. The doctor explained the term hermaphrodite
to me in the second nursing home, when I thought I was pregnant.
I had the idea afterwards that my penis would drop off. They gave
me paraldehyde at night and salts in the morning, and I didn't know
what happened at night. The voices never explained what happened
at night. There was no desire on my part to become a woman. I
did not have a fear of perversion, because I had never slept with a

woman. I was over-suppressed. I had the fear that I would be more attracted by the male. I always thought the male figure more beautiful than the female. At the start of my sickness, the only perverted desire I had was a wish to throw my arms around persons whom I developed a fondness for.

"The walks on deck were almost too much for me. They would give me four pills, and this would make my face flush, and I would look healthy, and then they would parade me on the deck. In the cabin, I would feel faint, and I thought my legs would shrivel. It seemed on deck as if I were losing all my weight."

4

Commentary

Research on Affective Experience in Early Schizophrenia.—In 1927, and again in 1928, Sullivan published reports on this ongoing research at Sheppard.[1] The experimental design for this study had been originally proposed to the Association for Research in Nervous and Mental Diseases, on December 28, 1925. As late as 1930, this research was still going on at Sheppard, but no further reports on it are extant after 1928. The two published reports have not been included in this book, since (1) the instruments used in the experiment have been long superseded in modern psychology, and (2) Sullivan, after 1930, abandoned the necessity for 'proving' that there is affect in schizophrenia. The rationale for the experiment has, however, some historical meaning for this book, and it will be reported on briefly. Today it is rather hard to imagine that in the 1920's the general opinion in psychiatry held that the dementia praecox patient had a disturbance of affect that meant he did not experience 'normal' emotions. Sullivan aimed to demolish this notion completely. He specifically attacked the concept of "apathy," often used at that time in an unscientific manner to describe the patient—and still used all too frequently. In effect, he hypothesized that even if the schizophrenic patient appears apathetic at times, he has affective experience related to the content of his thoughts and delusions and to the people in his immediate environment; in other words, the patient's affective ex-

[1] "Affective Experience in Early Schizophrenia," *Amer. J. Psychiatry* (1926-27) 83:467-483. And "Affective Experience in Early Schizophrenia," in *Schizophrenia [Dementia Praecox]*; Vol. V of series sponsored by the Assn. for Research in Nervous and Mental Disease; New York, Paul B. Hoeber, Inc., 1928; pp. 141-158.

perience is more like 'normal' affective experience than different from it. In order to 'prove' this, a galvanometer, a light source (extensively described in the 1928 paper), and a recording camera and control were used; the equipment was housed in an ordinary-looking desk. Since some of the equipment was visible and might upset even a 'normal' person, an extraordinary attempt was made to have visible equipment 'make sense to' the schizophrenic patient; for instance, the patient was led to believe that he would benefit from exposure to therapy from the light used to supply proper illumination for the camera. The Conclusions from the 1928 paper are as follows:

Both from crude observation and from detailed study of the facial expression, the alleged indifference, apathy, and emotional disharmony of the schizophrenic patient are more a matter of impression than a correct evaluation of the inner experience of the patient. It has followed that the study of inner affective experience is urgently indicated if the nature of the schizophrenic processes is to be elucidated. Attempts along this line do not seem to have produced valid results, owing largely to the susceptibility of schizophrenic patients to disturbing delusional reactions. In order to prevent interference by such reactions, considerable variation from ordinary psychological technique is required.

The elaboration of apparatus and technique has been undertaken to the end that study of the fine movements and tonic postures of the facial muscles (particularly of the perioral group) may be *correlated absolutely in time* with alterations in the electrical conductance of the body—the psychogalvanic response—a phenomenon known to be related very simply and uniformly to affective experience. In addition, it is planned to supplement these records with phonograms in some cases, with pulse tracings in some, and perhaps with respiratory records.

Finally, an effort is made to reduce distracting factors, and to insure definite timing of stimulus reception, as well as the integrity and simplicity of sentience "conveyed" to the subject, by the use in selected cases of purely visual stimulus situations in place of the verbal and the autochthonous [pp. 153–154].

The next paper in the book is also related to research—"The Common Field of Research and Clinical Psychiatry." Research is seen as an adjunct to good therapy—a viewpoint which is somewhat at variance with the current competition between research and clinical operations in some mental hospitals. This paper represents one of the early operational statements of participant observation—the way in which the observer participates so that he has explicit knowledge of what contribution he has made to the patient's productions and to the beliefs of staff.

The Common Field of Research
and Clinical Psychiatry†

PSYCHIATRY is one of the group of useful arts. As such, its origin antedates that of science by several centuries. One need not discuss the history of medical evolution from magic and more primitive religious thought and behavior. It can be accepted, it seems, that the empirical psychiatry of today includes ever more finely rationalized magical notions, excepting only that part based either on scientific discoveries or on the intuitive knowledge of the practitioner. As to this last mentioned *intuitive knowledge*, one might justifiably inquire as to how it is different from magical notions. This inquiry would entail discussion of the entire field of subconscious and nonconscious mental processes, and so would include the whole of mental affairs with which psychiatry is particularly concerned. Suffice it, therefore, at this juncture, if we attend only to the scientific groundwork of our art.

Even in demarcating here that which is scientific, one encounters discouraging situations. As Bernard Hart has expressed it: "Psychology has clearly established its right to deal with the phenomena of human behavior, and to formulate psychological concepts which will serve to explain those phenomena, provided that they are constructed according to the rule of scientific method. It has to be recognized that psychology is at a disad-

† Reprinted from *Psychiatric Quart.* (1927) 1:276–291. This paper was the basis for an address before the Neurone Club at its meeting in Rochester, N.Y., January 22, 1927.

vantage in that its method is of a character which presents inherent difficulties to the complete satisfaction of those rules, and this disadvantage is equally apparent in the section of psychology constituted by psychopathology." He continues, "Nevertheless, many of the simpler conceptions of psychopathology, such as dissociation, fail to satisfy the canons of science by so small a margin that it can safely be neglected." [1]

Dissociation, suggestion, conflict, adjustment and maladjustment are the conceptions to which Hart would refer as fully scientific. The conceptions of the defense reactions, compensation, sublimation, and regression may well be added to that list. Beyond these we can scarcely claim full scientific justification.

Many of the other conceptions which Freud and other psychoanalysts have produced cannot be regarded as true scientific hypotheses, regardless of their utility in the treatment work of their originators and analysts at large. Utility of a conception may be said to hinge on its providing a ground for successful prediction of events, and for the construction of crucial experiments. Its plausibility of application to facts of observation already at hand is not a scientific sanction if the hypothesis cannot be *tested*. The therapeutic "test" is no test at all; witness, chiropractic and Eddyism.

Without extended digression on the cause of this peculiar dearth of scientific formulations, I wish to emphasize certain factors, widely recognized but not very much studied. First of all, one must look to the notion of demoniac possession, until fairly recently an accepted explanation of mental disorders, and still a potent magical notion among the body of citizens. Not that there are many Americans today who will admit or recognize that they believe in evil spirits—certainly not as interlopers into the human body, with mental disorder as a result. Study the reaction of most laymen to the mental patient, before dismissing the devil-notion, however. The ancient horror of leprosy is not so exaggerated an analogy to this aversion of the "normal" for the "insane." Their remarks often suggest a notion that the miasm

---

[1] "The Development of Psychopathology as a Branch of Science," published in *Problems of Personality;* New York: Harcourt, Brace, 1925; pp. 231–241.

or evil spirit might readily extend to the psychiatrist; their remarks as to the "depressing effect" which such patients have on them require more than naive acceptance if they are to be understood.

The obverse of the devil-doctrine—which you recognize as the antitheses God-Satan, angels-devils, good-evil—is the old doctrine of mind and body. The demented have lost their "mind," if not by dispossession by an evil spirit, at least by some strange machination which is formulated in the likeness of other magic. This is a glaring instance of magical thinking; the more enlightened do not tolerate it. No, indeed. They show the same superstition, however, in their anxiety to *eliminate* "mind." They are the laymen who relate Johnnie's psychosis to a bump on the head, and the psychiatrists who write of psychology as a division of "brain physiology." This is materialistic twaddle, and the succeeding mechanistic explanations are energized by the same old magical idea of antithetic mind and body, plus cultural accretions in the shape of "disbelief" in dualism, the whole ensuing as monism.

It shows again as the feeling of natural scientists either that psychology and psychopathology are entirely metaphysics, or that they are realms of investigation in which the usual methods of science are unavailing, and mystical, esoteric methods required. In the one case we see the behaviorism of Watson and his less regenerated followers; in the other, the raconteur and spook-research varieties of alleged psychology. These factors operate unfortunately to provide the community background for psychiatrists.

Even more unfortunate, however, is the situation of many psychiatrists themselves. Either they are "physicians of the soul," lamentably detached from biological viewpoints, or they are "hell on focal infections" or "cortical degenerations" or "endocrine failures," etc. It is perhaps observation of these extreme attitudes added to their conventional superstition which leads some medical men to say that "the psychiatrist is an internist who failed," instead of realizing that the good internist is also a successful psychiatrist.

When these false attitudes of the silent majority, the more

enlightened, and the medical profession at large enter into the dissemination of educative propaganda, the giving of research funds, and the creation of medical curricula—then the unenviable state of psychiatry is accentuated. With open support of popular prejudice, superstition, and shame of mental illness; with millions pouring into cancer research, tuberculosis control, investigation of yellow fever, etc., even into research on racial, social, and industrial psychologies, with perhaps a cent for general and abnormal psychology; and with the psychiatric teaching staffs spending their semioccasional hours in futile effort to overcome the blindness of the students—native and acquired from the rest of the faculty—with all this, needless to say, progress of the art of psychiatry is uncertain, and healthy expansion of its scientific foundations a comparatively rare phenemenon.

That New York, Massachusetts, and a few other states have been led to accepting the far-sighted policy of furthering psychiatric research is the most promising effort toward the remedy of these situations. That a few institutes have been endowed for psychopathological research is exceedingly gratifying, the more in view of the widespread aversion of the wealthy to the association of their names with anything pertaining to mental disorder.

With this overlong peroration, I return to my topic, which may be reduced to the proposition of making the best of what we have. In other words, let us consider what the specialist in psychiatry—in his moments of leisure from administrative and quasi-satisfying professional duties—may accomplish as a research worker.

Perhaps another series of quotations will facilitate the presentation of the gloomy side of this matter. Knight Dunlap, the eminent experimental psychologist, has written: "In planning an investigation the most frequent mistake into which experimenters fall is in making the scope of the problem too wide, to include too many problems. . . . [Not] all the scattering of labor that comes under this category can be attributed to youth either of the investigator or of the topic. In some cases, the scattering is due to lack of grasp on the real problems involved. Without a sufficient grasp the fundamental small problems which ought to be attacked cannot be determined with clearness. . . . [Also] the lengthy and copious working out of a simple small point is extremely tedious, and nobody likes tedious work. The covering of a large topic superficially is much more thrilling." [2]

In this quotation, is expressed the most regrettable truth concerning much would-be research in psychiatry. Large topics are covered most superficially and thrilling "discoveries" [*] and reports produced. All to no end, so far as permanent improvement of the art of psychiatry is concerned. So huge a field as that of the schizophrenic is charged across by our enthusiasts, and "retreat into narcism," "regression to archaic unconscious," "dilapidation of the gonads," "disorder of the basal ganglia," or whatnot of bushwa is "discovered" as etiology. After the discovery, the enthusiast sees *nothing but* evidence of his correctness from thenceforth. His disciples rediscover and rediscover his genius; they amass "evidence" in support of his theory. But if you sift the whole business you find that there is nothing. You must begin all over from the beginning. The most elementary canon of science has been ignored; his data are wholly subjective or so tainted with his preconceptions as to be useless. Behind this situation, all the fundamental questions which bear on his data have been ignored or begged. In fact, in general, you have little or no real investigation—merely an occasional uncontrolled observation here and there as cornerstones for huge arches of speculation. In the "archaic unconsciousness" business, many of the cornerstones are so-called facts deduced not by psychiatrists but by dilettantes who culled them in the library from the garbled accounts of untrained and prejudiced missionaries who had about the same contact with primitive culture that the writer has with equine conceptualization, who had less scientific training than the average elevator boy. Poets and literati have been another fruitful source of psychiatric cornerstones.

Another great nuisance, nay, prime evil, of psychiatric research

[2] "The Experimental Method of Psychology" in *The Psychologies of 1925;* Worcester, Mass.: Clark University, 1926.

[* Throughout this paper, Sullivan makes extensive use of quotes to indicate that he is using words to express fringe meanings. In later papers, he used single quotes for such usage. The most reliable meaning for such use is found in Korzybski's *so-called.* H.S.P.]

is unwarranted generalization, in the more restricted sense of passing from a few particular instances to universals. This has been a peculiar difficulty of psychology and is the most vulnerable weakness of psychoanalytic doctrines. Once a proposition has been universalized, the observation of negative instances dies a natural death. The most tenuous generalization seems a perfectly sound buttress for any theorizing. Because of our native reasoning ability, relations spring up, correlates are taken for granted, new and ever extending propositions grow like fungal hyphae, and we have a plausible "system," ever ready, like the astronomy of Ptolemy, to receive a new crank to "explain" a stubborn fact which intrudes itself.

Observation is the touchstone of psychiatric research. Pure research would preferably be observation under rigid and carefully arranged conditions susceptible of ready duplication by another. Such situations are for several reasons impossible in the field of psychiatry. No human subject is ever quite the same on a series of occasions. No schizophrenic is apt to respond in even approximately similar a way to a series of observers. The setting of observational situations is a task requiring rather uncommon gifts on the part of the observer, not to mention rather unusual facilities for his work.

Surpassing these great difficulties is another inhering in the nature of the subject matter, human behavior and thought. Experiential report, the subject's statement of "what went on inside," of what he thought, felt, wished, intended, etc., this is a vital part of observation in psychology and psychopathology. This is not only subject to direct complications and interferences, but introduces a great variable in the shape of the linguistic factor.

Speech, while less important as a means of concealing thought than our efforts at anamneses might suggest to us, is a ticklish channel for scientific data. Words cannot be conceived as having inherent, "objective" meaning. There is no word in common use which can always be depended on to "mean" what it means to you when you use it. The degree of intrasocietal variation of certain relatively common nouns and a lesser number of verbs, adjectives, etc., may be sufficiently small to permit of ready exchange of intelligence about "external" situations. In reporting subjective situations, be they relatively unimportant and comparatively unemotional, common words may be accepted as data in psychological experiment. *But for reporting subjective situations important to the self-esteem, self-respect, etc., of the subject, or situations for other reason definitely tinged with emotion, verbal reports are but mediately available as scientific data.* There must be rather elaborate contexts which include not only the verbal report, but, if possible, also extensive data about the situation and state of the subject, his relations (real and fancied) to the observer, and so on. This is the problem of all problems peculiar to psychopathology; the observations necessarily must carry with them a broad context if they are to be relied on for scientific purposes.

Finally, there is a factor of general biological research which enters most importantly into psychopathological studies. A fundamental characteristic of the living is found in the effect of previous experience, the mnemic function. Mental disorder and the individual phenomena of mental disorder have as an essential, contributions from certain past experience. It is necessary for understanding a phenomenon that we have not only our objective observations and the subject's reported experience at the time, but also as complete as possible a *genetic background,* the cogent material of the subject's life-experience *as experienced*—i. e., what he actually lived or underwent, not what he is alleged to have experienced. Free-associational investigation is intended to correct and expand data ordinarily secured in history taking. If it is to accomplish this purpose, it must be entirely autogenous, not a reproduction of suggestions, gratuitous interpretations, etc., from another. In the end, the genetic data must be arranged accurately in time, so that it represents the true life-series, not a fictitious or confused string of incidents.

Perhaps these brief references suffice to preface a statement that the common field of research and clinical psychiatry is found in the observation of patients. Lacking an enlightened social backing which would permit the arranging of several crucial experiments, research psychopathology must depend for its greatest aid on ever more nearly perfect observation of human behavior and thought. This is imperative upon it; it can choose nothing else. As to clinical psychiatry, however, there is no such imperative. Clinical psychiatry can be, and in some cases is, most slipshod. The psychiatrist may entertain himself with ribald fancies, he may preoccupy himself with most unscientific theories, he may—and, curse the luck, he too frequently does—tread clumsily upon the delicate balance between accessibility and inaccessibility, between relatively observable and relatively opaque states in patients who show most important phenomena.

In fine, the clinical psychiatrist has a choice of almost any conceivable position between an extreme of exquisite scientific rigor of observation, and one of blissful meandering through the day's alleged work, with results of no therapeutic importance to the patient or scientific importance to anyone. With the schizophrenic, he may seem anything from the personification of an all-wise impersonal Deity who in some way causes light to shine in the darkness, to an indifferent or even a malignant judge who seals the verdict of society—failure, hopeless, despised, damned.

What can pyschopathology suggest as a program for clinical psychiatry? Firstly, one may venture a statement that scientific research can be and often is a thoroughly effective therapeutic tool. Leaving out of consideration the crucial tests which are of but indirect concern to the clinician, we reemphasize that observation is the touchstone of psychopathology. But on the other hand, observation in the sense above discussed puts us in a preeminently satisfactory position as to *understanding the patient, his manifestations, and his purposes.* I can conceive no more necessary factor in successful psychotherapy. I admit freely that there are situations in numbers in which a measure of understanding on the part of the physician cannot be communicated in any direct fashion to the patient. If we come to understand more in these cases, perhaps the limitation of communicability will disappear. Whatever may be the case, the patient is apt to be benefited by the incommunicable understanding of the physician. Sympathy phenomena are of great importance in these cases. In fact, the more one understands, the more he will find accessible, as a rule. And we all know of social recoveries which we have assisted without any real exchange of information and yet with affection of the discharged patient as a sign that we are not succumbing to wish-fulfilling fantasy.

May I take the liberty of discussing a pitfall in this under-standing of the patient. That it is one of my own difficulties will perhaps negative an appearance of preaching. The personality of the observer must either be exterior to the scientific observations which he secures or be represented explicitly in their context when it enters into them. Now, there are numerous instances among my acquaintances in which observational situations in re-gard of schizophrenics have been reported and interpreted in fashions widely at variance with fact. Our lay assistants, nurses and attendants, and our lay quasi informants—relatives and friends of the patient—these groups show the reaction under discussion most clearly. Emotional situations, sentiments elabo-rated in regard of the patient, exercise a powerful influence on what is perceived, and on interpretations, retrograde amnesias, and pseudo-recollections concerning what actually transpired before the observer. Even more unquestionably, however, does the sentiment of self of the observer play tricks on his reliability. There is no one among you who does not appreciate the dubious character of reports arising from situations in which the observer knows that he has been guilty of fault or shortcoming. A fact the existence of which stirs a feeling of shame is a fact prone to much garbling in the report. Surely this needs no special stressing in this presentation. But how curiously opaque we are to our own observational scotomata. How easy it is to overlook things which do not fit into our tentative explanation. How more than difficult it is to see evidence of an unpleasant theory. It is sad indeed that medical men are so human as to find theories pleasant and unpleasant. There is no scientist but should blush at an accusation that he liked or disliked an hypothesis, on the basis of ethics or aesthetics, or—and this is the important ground—on the basis of his own early training. Convicted of such an accusa-tion, he is adjudged no scientist; he is but a bigoted layman thrusting his likes and dislikes into the serious business of ob-servation, the method of knowledge.

The effect of personal warp, however, is much more insidious than mere overlooking of negative instances and resistance to disturbing theories. It seems to be the principal factor in the production of a number of our current theories. For examples, one might point to the quaint notion of MacCurdy, G. V. Hamilton, and others, the gist of which is to the effect that emotional reactions are abnormal, or to McDougall's theory of schizophrenia which makes it a development of stubbornness, or the old notion of the psychoanalysts which makes it a narcissistic neurosis —thereby justifying failure of easy-going therapeutic approaches. Even better illustrations may be culled from the psychoanalytic literature, probably because the psychoanalytic theory formulations include a good deal that is repugnant to the puritanical. That certain of the most important investigators in psychoanalysis reach divergent results from contact with supposedly identical or homologous facts is one manifestation. That certain individuals amongst them move the accent of importance to this or to that "mechanism"—as for example Ernest Jones with anal erotism, Isador Coriat with urethral erotism, Rank with the birth trauma, Adler with the masculine protest—seems to reflect more than a little of personal warp. There seems at times to be a considerably overdetermined attitude toward these individuated factors; the writer's work on the ramifications of the oral zone in personality genesis is readily accepted by these investigators as a similar "all-embracing idea." Surely it is not the method of science to see everywhere manifestations of one particular theoretic prepossession especially when much that is thus seen as proof is identical with that which another proponent identifies as proof of his notion.

The greater difficulties which one encounters in the conversion of clinical work to psychopathological ends have now been mentioned. Perhaps an illustration may be offered from a recent interview with a patient to show how these combine to vitiate valuable work in the writer's service. We have elaborated a working hypothesis of schizophrenia which relates it closely to the phenomena and situations which go to make up sleep. As mentioned in "Peculiarity of Thought in Schizophrenia" and elsewhere, there seems to be very little in schizophrenic phenomena observed in the incipient and catatonic varieties at least which are not paralleled by sleep and dreams. Having worked out this tentative hypothesis, our research service is naturally on the *qui vive* for data which sustains the hypothesis and, I hope, for data which will indicate its limitation and the need for revision. In an interview with an incipient schizophrenic who is showing an ominous tendency to develop hebephrenic maladjustment, the following took place: * * * * [Doctor: *You tell me a lot of things; then you say it isn't so.*] "I say, that is what I think I am going to be doing. I haven't been here but 10 days. Great Day!—When I talk to these other people they have been here months and months. I can't expect to do that right now— and I am not doing it." [*What are the things you don't understand about it?*] "Nothing. Understand about what?" [*The situation in which you are.*] "I think I have clarified it." [*All right, what was there to clarify?*] "You said I was in a dream— you said it was sort of mysterious." [*When did I say anything was mysterious?*] "I probably said it—I don't know—I said I was in a dream and I have been talking to try to explain to you what I meant by that." [*I don't understand that and I wish you would explain.*] "Good God—I have been talking about that ever since I have been here." * * * [*Try to tell me what you mean by being in a dream.*] "That sort of a—I think my ideas to me— how to spend the time and everything like that. I explained to you about feeling sort of—when I jigged a little—light and springy—I think that's what—but come right down right now— I think I feel fine. I think I am perfectly clear about it. That was another man's idea. May be his interpretation and you and Dr. X. —maybe all could explain that sort of thing—it sounded darn good to me—anything that's particularly impressive, that comes back to a person—that did come back to me and was exemplary of my opinion of how I felt since I have been here." [*I am trying to find out what you base it on.*] "I base it on being—feeling in such shape—of more good—base my whole ambitions and hopes just on getting better. * * * "

This extract from 35 pages of verbatim, representing three interviews, is a classical instance of defeat which one sustains through lack of scientific critique on the part of the best-intentioned assistants. The recollection of the examining physicians in this case does not impress one as complete enough to be certain that one of them was not carried by his enthusiasm into supplying this interpretation to the patient. While certain of our colleagues have a convenient theory that interpretations which are accepted by a patient are, to the extent accepted, true of the patient, this notion is more delightful than scientific. The reproduction of an interpretation by a patient showing positive suggestibility may be one hundred per cent in the case of any interpretation which has not come into direct conflict with a powerful motivation of the patient. Perhaps a reference to the ease with which the hypnotic subject is convinced that he can mimic a squirrel or a turtle illustrates this better than would extended quotations of interviews with schizophrenics.

The clinical psychiatrist who asks leading questions produces a record which is very difficult indeed to transfer to the purposes of psychopathological research. It is much better, if one cannot take the time or make the effort to get information without offering an answer, that his questions shall be misleading. As a matter of fact in the hasty examination in a hospital conference, the nearest approach to scientific investigation has frequently to be to a considerable extent misleading questions. The ideal interview is one in which the physician offers only the orienting questions to cover the most recent activities of the patient, mention of the particular topics on which he desires the patient to talk, and such provocative interjections as "And—," "And then," "Continue," "Which seems to mean what," and the like. With comparatively inaccessible schizophrenics it is often possible to obtain two or three thousand words in an hour without supplying the patient with anything of "explanation" or "interpretation." In favorable cases it has been possible to secure about as complete a record as that secured by the psychoanalysis of a psychoneurotic from quite paranoid schizophrenics without offering them any interpretation or explanation whatsoever. Needless to say, the impression had been given in these cases that frank discussion would do no harm and would probably accomplish much good. It seems scarcely necessary to invite your attention to the fact that frank discussion does do good by bringing the genetic background and the subconscious motivation of the patient's peculiar thoughts and behavior into the region of his logical consideration and volition.

The problems of research which seem to have important clinical implications are remarkably numerous. A good many of these can receive material aid toward solution from efforts primarily directed to the assistance of patients. The addition of scientific critique—a close attention to what can be seen and heard from the patient and about the patient with careful avoidance of premature interpretations and explanations—increases the difficulty of psychotherapy, but also increases the probability of success. No patient is harmed by an effort on the part of the physician to know what he is really driving at and to understand comprehensively what the patient believes or suspects. It is true that the ontogenetic psychology needs studies of the intrauterine state from the neurological, the stimulus and response, the visceral neurological, and the dynamic-symbolic aspects. We are badly handicapped by our ignorance of the neonatal and infantile periods of personality genesis. Our child psychology and our juvenile psychology are far from coherent because of the lack of knowledge of infantile psychology. Several very large topics and a wealth of small points need to be worked out. For instance, we know very little as to the actual *attitude* of individual parents for individual children. We know very little as to the mental state and attitude of individual teachers to individual pupils. We have only a beginning of data on nursery, kindergarten, and school group life. We know woefully little as to the actual facts concerning high school society per se and its relation to the adolescent resymbolization. In spite of the long time during which we have been rather intensely interested in adolescence as an epoch of personality genesis, and the great number of individuals who have addressed themselves to this topic, our information is meagre and much of the work will have to be repeated on the basis of more thoroughgoing study of the preadolescent periods. The psychology of college entrants is but now engaging us. The psychology of the grammar school juvenile on entering the world of employment has not concerned any scientist of note. The adolescent developments in this latter group is still an uncharted realm for psychology and psychopathology.

We believe that the schizophrenic disorders are restricted in their occurrence to individuals who have never if but for a brief period effected a thoroughly satisfying adjustment to a sex object. This hypothesis is of enormous scope; it is not only a purely tentative proposition but it is one the demonstration of which requires a vast amount of tributary work in all the fields which I have so far enumerated. Besides them it must receive contributions from all other divisions of psychopathological research: from the scientific study of such topics as symbol dynamics *in utero*—a subject which can be approached only indirectly through delicate psychophysical research; a number of exact psychophysical studies of the new-born and the growing infant (so limited a thing as exact photographic studies of the postural changes from birth will give an important assistance to both psychopathology and neurology); a wealth of real data rather than suppositions about the pleasure sources of the infant, child, and juvenile; a wealth of data about the subjects which have in particular been the preoccupation of the psychoanalysts; an understanding of speech and graphic procedures from the genetic side; an understanding of the evolution of logical thinking; knowledge of the growth and vicissitudes of self-consciousness and the evolution of personal fictions; and many many others.

For the understanding of schizophrenia, in addition to all the great fields of investigation which have been indicated above, it seems as if we must make some real research into the nature and dynamics of sleep. The present status of this field of study is that of entirely unexplored territory. Nothing of any real moment has been contributed throughout the years that an occasional worker has turned to this vast subject. Of all the aching voids we find in psychology, there is not one which remotely approximates the omissions on the subject of sleep. One can go so far as to say that the first work which approximated scientific character in this connection is the work of Pavlov and his followers in connection with sleep as an outcome of general inhibition. Without taking time to discuss the breadth of utility of this conception, let me point out to you the rather paradoxical fact that from the genetic standpoint sleep is the normal state of living organisms and that wakefulness begins as an occasional disturbance of sleep originated by the activity of chemical needs, cravings, etc., which have arisen within the sleeping organism. Theories of dreams can scarcely be valid when we lack any real insight into the distinctive character of the state in which dreams occur. So-called theories of symbolism can scarcely concern us as other than rather far-fetched speculations until we know more about the dynamics of sleep and dreams. So typically wakeful a thing as motivation has important ramifications in sleep, in which the writer has been able to discover abortive behavior reminiscent of the more profound motivations of waking life and also reminiscent of the so-called inexplicable motor performances of catatonics.

Again from the ontogenetic standpoint we have to know something of the effect upon personality genesis of experience characterized by overstimulation, if not exclusive stimulation, of each of the primary "emotional tendencies." At present we have data which are but barely suggestive as to the ultimate importance of the overactivity of fear responses and rage responses from the neonatal period onward. The data which we have as to the ultimate evolution of personalities in which overemphasis has attached to the "satisfaction responses" are largely fantastic. If now you will consider the complicated picture of the individual who from infancy onward for some time has shown comparative freedom from markedly emotional responses in the waking life, but has suffered from panic dreams, fear dreams, or anxiety attacks during the night, you may envisage the breadth of research in this connection.

The ontogenesis of stable maladjustments of the type roughly classified as psychopathic personalities, their fate, and the dynamics of experience which lead to the various developments in these patients—schizophrenic or otherwise—is another great topic.

The nature and manifestation of the warped personalities which leave us as social recoveries following psychoses is a tributary to this field. The understanding of chronic and periodic alcoholism, drug addiction, and the huge field of sexual peculiarities ties in with all these problems.

Another research problem, which has the widest ramification in psychopathology, is that which pertains to the growth and vicissitudes of self-esteem in its widest and narrowest connotations. It has seemed that the pre-schizophrenic is all but characterized by unusual difficulty in the evolution of this sentiment, so that he comes to think of himself as peculiarly inadequate or definitely abnormal. A good deal has been contributed which tends to demonstrate that this situation is due to homosexuality which in turn is related to earlier influences to which the individual has been exposed. The psychoanalytic conception of the Oedipus complex has been produced with a view to explaining this situation and the "normal" progression to heterosexual satisfactions. The conception of the castration complex has been added to this to fill certain gaps. The writer has speculated from insufficient data, a theory of sexual evolution. In "Erogenous Maturation," the complexity of this problem has been outlined and a number of tentative paths for research attack suggested. We have to be cautious in accepting data already accumulated in regard to homoerotic impulses. That sexual inversion is an ultra-important fact in psychopathology cannot be gainsaid. That a reference to homosexuality explains the manifestations of any mental disorder is incorrect. Anyone moderately familiar with homosexual society must have observed the stable character of a proportion of its members quite as large as the proportion of stable people in admittedly heterosexual society. The overt homosexual who develops a mental disorder, mild or severe, is a most profitable subject for study, more profitable by far at this stage of our knowledge or ignorance of the evolution of sexual impulses than is the man who encounters difficulty in living with a woman.

The utilization of the conception of repressed or unconscious homosexuality is probably more justified than is use of the notion of universally repressed polymorphous perversity. At the same time the carelessness of psychiatric workers by which they find only what they are looking for and record only conclusions with an occasional excerpt of data torn from their context, leaves the whole conception of latent, repressed, and unconscious homosexuality in the condition of an interesting speculation rather than a scientifically demonstrated hypothesis. To revert again for the moment to our work at Sheppard Hospital, I may mention that—in spite of my firm conviction that this conception will prove a very valuable one—in the really considerable quantity of rather exact observations which we have accumulated, I am unable to find what I would regard as scientific demonstration of the conception. We have not yet hit upon crucial matter which would determine the acceptance of this hypothesis rather than other perhaps less plausible explanations, but explanations the application of which have not been disproved.

The great wealth of material which could more or less properly be offered in a paper on our broad theme overwhelms one. May I conclude with the plea that little be taken for granted of the traditions, speculations, and theories which have sprung up in the field of abnormal psychology and psychiatry, and that we seek whenever opportunity is afforded for data which are exact and comprehensive—data which carry their history and their context so that they are facts to the best of our limitations. While the few who by great good fortune have at least limited facilities for intensive research in psychopathological topics are attempting to fill many theoretic gaps and provide a sound basis for the development of precise hygienic and curative measures, we cannot do justice to our public responsibilities by waiting through the years until research shall have been properly supported or through the decades until the few shall have solved the many problems. The principal increments in our understanding of mental disorder must for some considerable time come from the scientific acumen of clinical psychiatrists.

5

Commentary

THE TITLE for the next paper, "Tentative Criteria of Malignancy in Schizophrenia," is somewhat misleading, since Sullivan is generally concerned here with criteria for favorable outcome, or at least some degree of social recovery. Some of the terminology used in this paper —oral-erotic, anal-erotic, and so on—is not characteristic of Sullivan's later writing. These terms are used, however, within an interpersonal frame of reference: ". . . we find ample confirmation," Sullivan notes, "for the conclusion of Kempf as to the prognostic importance of the 'attitude of the ego to the perverse cravings.' To the extent that representations in awareness of the motivations—which have escaped repression—continue to be regarded by the individual as criminal and subversive, to that extent the mental disorder which ensues is to be suspected of an unfortunate outcome." Thus the attitude toward the event is seen as more of a determinant of the outcome than the particular zone of interaction involved.

Tentative Criteria of Malignancy in Schizophrenia[†]

PSYCHIATRIC prognosis may best be considered as a specialized technique in social psychology. Its problem is the prediction of the future adaptability of an individual within some more or less clearly envisaged milieu composed principally of people. To reach a judgment of prognosis, facts are accumulated in regard of (a) the personality of the patient, (b) the morbid process which he is suffering, and its effects on his personality, and (c) the significant factors in that cultural environment to which the patient may presently be returned. In no case an easy achievement, prognosis of those individuals who suffer schizophrenic disorders is peculiarly difficult for several reasons. The personality of the patient is hard to appraise: his cooperation in such procedures as free association and dream study are difficult to secure; facts contributed by previous associates are meagre, owing to his "shut-in" responses to pre-psychotic social situations; and the parents are almost always psychopathic in their reaction to investigation—perceiving more or less dimly their part in the illness of their progeny and smoothing over and falsifying liberally. Again, the fundamental characteristics of the schizophrenic process itself are still in doubt. We are but beginning to free our-

---

† Reprinted from *Amer. J. Psychiatry* (1927–28) 84:759–782. Read in abstract at the eighty-third meeting of the American Psychiatric Association at a joint meeting with the American Psychopathological Association, Cincinnati, Ohio, June 3, 1927.

selves of many misconceptions concerning "dementia praecox," and the majority still revise diagnosis when the patient recovers. The Kraepelinian diagnosis by outcome has been a great handicap, leading to much retrospective distortion of data, instead of too careful observation and induction. Finally, it is no small task to distinguish in the environment to which the patient may expect to return, those cultural factors which are potentially effective in his adjustment. Without accurate data as to his own valuations, we are prone to serious errors in deciding which factors are the significant ones and our efforts to weigh their influence are relatively futile.

With the view to rendering explicit the processes coordinated in formulating prognostic expressions, a summary has been made of 140 consecutive admissions to this hospital of male patients in whom schizophrenic processes were shown. No diagnostic criteria have yet come to light the application of which would make possible a rigid classification of these people as victims of schizophrenia and of other disorders. A considerable number of the individuals concerned in the summary would ordinarily be regarded as "mixed" states, or psychoses associated with psychopathic personality, or eccentric alcoholic psychoses, and the like. From another viewpoint, a number of them would be considered as cases of malignant hysteria, extreme psychaesthenic reactions, or "grave parapathias, unclassified." Continued experience with mentally disordered persons weakens the writer's hope of finding clear nosological entities. The more one learns of what is going on in his patient, the less faith he can retain in the alleged types of anomalous and perverted adjustive reactions. The field of mental disorders seems to be a continual gradation, in which little of discrete types is to be found.

At the same time, it is irrational to attempt a discussion of schizophrenic illnesses if the meaning of the term schizophrenia is not at all explicit. No scientific investigation can proceed even so far as empirical accumulation of relevant data unless some working hypothesis exists in the mind of the investigator. The writer assumed some time since that there was some distinctive peculiarity in the "associational" processes reflected in the verbal and other productions of dementia praecox patients, such, for example, that these productions would invariably impress one as difficult of understanding. This seemed to be a distinctive feature of Bleuler's descriptions, among others. The inherent vagueness of such a view was recognized, but the hope was entertained that it referred to something definite. That hope reached no fruition. The mysterious characteristics of the productions invariably faded when some familiarity with the life experience of the patient was secured. Study of the work of other psychiatrists who seemed to be favorably inclined towards this conception revealed that not "absence of rapport" but some particular peculiarities in the verbal and written interchange between patient and physician were effective in bringing about a diagnosis opinion. The notion of emotional disharmony or peculiarities in the affective features of mental life in schizophrenics (Kraepelin's disorder of will and emotion) was next accepted as a tentative basis for clinical investigation. So long as the writer was content to use his subjective appraisal of the emotional life, based on crude observation of the patient in exceptional situations—e. g., when required to stick out the tongue in order that it might be injured—there seemed to be some uniformity. As soon, however, as more minute observation was applied to this aspect, the alleged criterion tended to become vague and nonspecific.

Finding no distinctive cognitive or affective features of mental life which could serve as criteria of the presence of the schizophrenic process, he concentrated investigation on those aspects called by the traditional psychology, conation. It is still too early to express final judgment in regard of distinctive peculiarities of motivation in individuals suffering presumably schizophrenic illnesses. The inclination at this time is to distinguish the functional prominence of certain motivations as typical of these processes and to look upon the untimely appearance of these motivations as notably diagnostic.

Schizophrenia is considered tentatively as an evolution of the life process in which some certain few motivations assume extraordinary importance to the grave detriment of adjustive effort on the part of the individual concerned. This disturbance of adjustive effort is shown as an interference in the realm of social experience. Social experience refers to anything lived, undergone or the like in adjustive or maladjustive contact with at least one other person or with surrogates of persons. It excludes experience pertaining wholly to the individual's bodily sensations, emotions and the like; and also experience of the inanimate physical universe, as well as of all creatures excepting those invested with valuations and meanings approximately anthropomorphic. It includes cognitive, affective, and conative phenomena pertaining to persons and groups and to animate or inanimate objects which for various reasons have magical or religious relationship to the individual. It is approximately correct to say that experience is distinguished as social rather than extra-social when the "external" objects which have important relation to it are invested by the experiencer with potentialities which are more or less human or anthropomorphic in character. Besides the quasi-passive aspect, there are, of course, the aspects including the subject's action in the social situation and the response of others to that action; and finally, there are factors which we can conveniently identify as social motivations, tendencies, or impulses which give immediate origin to the actions, and indirectly govern the content of more passive experience.

As we consider the infantile and childhood periods of personality genesis to be prior to the real socialization of the individual, it is cogent to enquire if schizophrenic processes can occur before the juvenile era. It is easy to assume that the mental life in infancy and childhood is of too recondite a nature for us to identify preschizophrenic phenomena within it. It is equally easy to assume that the rich fantasy life in infancy and childhood is of a piece with the schizophrenic psychosis. The writer is disinclined to either of these views. There are phenomena occasionally to be observed in infancy which have a certain relationship to schizophrenia. The night terror and terror dreams of childhood are so closely related to schizophrenic panic states that it does violence to scientific method to arbitrarily separate the two groups. As was pointed out by Clouston,* these eruptions of fear during sleep are important omens of future mental disorder. Even more in point are those manifestations of childhood thought to

[* This is obviously Sir Thomas Smith Clouston, British psychiatrist and neurologist, although the exact work is not known. H.S.P.]

which we refer as temper tantrums. While incidents of occasional nocturnal panic are often lost from the anamnesic information conveyed by parents and can only be recovered when the patient becomes accessible to analysis, the temper tantrum makes sufficient impression upon the complex-driven parents so that once their conceit has been abated, such history is obtained in a considerable percentage of cases. As has been mentioned elsewhere,[1] our observations would give much prominence to these several evidences of imperfect adjustment in the home milieu. In so far as the nocturnal disturbances represent the suspension of sleep by emotional states accompanying tentative solutions of childhood problems, they may be taken as a sign that there is great discrepancy between the adjustive demands to which the child finds himself subject on the one hand, and the growing system of adjustive tendencies which make up his personality.[2] Such a child is apt to pass into the juvenile period of personality growth with a handicap that eventuates in mental disorder, mild or severe. On the other hand, it is quite possible that he may secure additional experience from his compeers, etc., that will resolve his conflicts or reduce their malignancy to such extent that he escapes material maladjustment. When the history of a schizophrenic patient includes the incidence of pavor nocturnis, nightmares, and the like,

[1] See "Schizophrenia: Its Conservative and Malignant Features," and "Regression: A Consideration of Reversive Mental Processes."

[2] No allegation is intended to the effect that all those disturbances of sleep in infancy and childhood that are attended by fear, are to be interpreted on a "purely psychogenetic basis." The writer knows himself to be without sufficiently extensive material to dogmatize in this premise. The pediatrician's explanation of night terror on the basis of adenoids, etc., is certainly open to serious question. I have pointed out ("The Evaluation of Fear" and "Some Notes on the Investigation of Sleep") that a considerable number of people continue late into adult life to show fear and terror reactions on falling to sleep, in the cases of whom the content is of a highly inaccessible character. A number of these cases which have been under observation show conspicuous freedom from somatic maladies. *Per contra,* several cases of children with adenoids and tonsilary enlargement of considerable degree have been found to be entirely free from these nocturnal disturbances, as have also cases of childhood cardiac disease, etc. In short, this matter of sleep disturbance, like that of schizophrenia itself, can be explained on an organic basis only by the aid of carelessness, overlooking of negative instances, and lively pathological imagination.
[I have been unable to locate the two papers referred to in the preceding footnote. H.S.P.]

these are to be considered in prognostication as events showing those periods in personality genesis during which exclusion from conscious awareness was used unsuccessfully in dealing with life experience. If they occurred very early—*e.g.*, in late infancy—then the *character* of the experiential material concerned must have been primitive and preverbal, and its elucidation will be correspondingly difficult. If they occurred in late childhood or only after the juvenile epoch was reached, then the experiential material involved may well have been fairly easy of formulation in speech, and so fairly readily obtainable and convertible into adult experience, with complete relief of the conflict.

Temper tantrums—outbreaks of rage behavior—however, represent not repressed material which makes its presence painfully felt in the dream-work, but material freely elaborated in the growing sentiment of self which renders the submission of the child to necessary or unnecessary adjustive demands, an intolerable insult to self-esteem. As such, they represent a rigidity of the self-regarding sentiment which bodes ill for any adjustment in a situation in which the youngster is not practically omnipotent. Only the possession of elasticity in the tributary structures, or of remarkable talents—*e.g.*, high general intelligence—can save such a person from very great stresses in juvenile and adolescent epochs. These extremely unfortunate children, who have never modified their aggression and demands for instant and unconditional satisfaction, enter into the juvenile period (initiated by socialization of language habits and progressing through socialization of play, etc., up to the "gang" or homosexual stage of adolescence) with adjustive handicaps which are hard to overcome in time to prevent grave warp of social relations, and psychopathic, psychoneurotic, or psychotic developments. Prognostic implications of these factors may be expressed as a rule to the effect that the earlier were the appearances of rigidity in the self-regarding sentiment, the greater the difficulty of its therapeutic reorganization, and hence of securing a stable recovery. In other words, if the child showed very early a marked tendency to temper tantrums, and never "outgrew" this tendency, a subsequent postpsychotic adjustment of the personality to reasonable demands of social life is not easy to bring about, and can scarcely be expected unless the individual's abilities available to us are of an unusual order of merit.

There is a certain difficulty in distinguishing the specific differences between childhood fantasies and the content of dilapidated schizophrenics—particularly comfortable hebephrenics. It is quite possible that there is little distinction to be found in the character of childhood fantasies and those which go to make up the life process in the rare cases of "simple dementia praecox." In all other cases the fantasies seem on close scrutiny to be entirely different. Even at regressive levels of revery such that the recollections, backgrounds, value scales, etc., are those of early childhood, the motivation easily inferable from the contextual content (the revery itself) is of an adult nature.[3] Schizophrenic fantasies deal with societal relations; relations of the individual to one, two, or many other people. Even the Oedipus fantasies of the child are not of a piece with those which occur in any of our patients. Sexual fantasies—incestuous, autoerotic, and homosexual —are naturally of a late juvenile or adolescent nature. Despite the fact that the schizophrenic often achieves a regression below the level of socialization and into the era of childhood (or even infancy) in which the interpersonal relations are of the order of child-parent only, and that in this retrogressive process the sexual motivation regresses also and in its true sense is lost, still the fantasies which we recover from these patients show the radiation of sexual impulses which have been resymbolized in primitive figures. And these sexual impulses still effect a complete change of the reveries from childhood analogies. It even seems as if the process of regressive castration implies the elaboration of extensive symbol cadres, the like of which is inconceivable as an ingredient of childhood personality.

[3] Regression of "the level of symbolic integration" (*vide* "Erogenous Maturation") is found to be remarkably evident in the dreams of an individual accumulated on unexpected awakening from sleep at various "depths." While the writer is unable to set up criteria as to depth of sleep and therefore can make no indubitable correlation in this particular, he has been able to discover in the case of four subjects that recollections, etc., used in the dream-work during that period of sleep in which there is the most marked reduction in blood pressure, peripheral temperature, psychogalvanic response, and increase in nonspecific sensory threshold, are material originating in childhood experience.

Prognosis by the "depth of regression" is therefore not rational. The hebephrenic, whose behavior seems to rest at the "depth" of early childhood or late infancy, is of much more grave outlook than is the catatonic who has approximated an "intrauterine regression." In this connection, outcome of psychosis is a function not of the general level of behavior, but rather of the disparity of regression of the various phases of personality (see "Schizophrenia: Its Conservative and Malignant Features"). And the importance for outcome of this factor of disparity of depth in the regressions is significant only in so far as it implies disorganization of the personality, of the individual's interaction with and within the social environment, and of therapeutic access to the life experience of the sufferer. It may well be that this factor bears some important measure of relationship, also, to the unwillingness or inability of the sufferer to accept the personal source of much of his psychotic phenomenology.

It is in the juvenile and adolescent epoch of personality genesis that all schizophrenic processes have their locus.[4] Among our patients are several in whom the onset of *recognized* psychosis was quite early; one under thirteen and another under fourteen years of age. We have encountered no case of recognized schizophrenic psychosis below the early or homosexual phase of adolescence: the so-called dementia praecoxisima * seems rather scarce. One would conclude that psychotic manifestations sufficiently obvious to excite attention usually appear rather late in adolescence, and but rarely as early as the juvenile epoch. On the other hand, we have some material which shows the frank appearance of the motivations which we are inclined to call schizophrenic, well down the scale below adolescence. None of the cases shows any-

---

[4] In "The Onset of Schizophrenia," evidence is shown to support the belief that adolescence as a phase of personality genesis should be regarded as reaching its terminus in the incident of a really satisfying adjustment to a sex object—hetero- or homo-sexual. Until such sexual adjustment has been experienced, if only briefly, there are characteristics of the life process which identify it (regardless of chronological age) as adolescence. Once such experience has occurred, the chance of schizophrenic illness seems to become nil.

[* This is a term coined by De Sanctis to describe a condition similar to catatonia which is reported as appearing in very young children (as early as 4 years of age). H.S.P.]

thing more characteristic than pavor nocturnis, terror dreams,[5] and temper tantrums occurring before the socialization of language habits and association in play, etc., with compeers. All of those from whom data have been available have shown disorders of social tendencies in the course of the juvenile and adolescent periods. Our knowledge of these disorders is not furthered by grouping them as manifestations of introversion (hormonic or otherwise). They do not seem to be ordained by constitutional or innate factors. They impress me as the relatively clear outcome of experience. They show as modifications of common social activities brought about in efforts to secure desired ends (or to avoid undesired results) and are the effect of peculiarities in the conditions which have surrounded the individual. They are by no means "conditioned reflexes" in the accepted sense. There is no simple stimulus-response situation. That which is given to the individual is not what is given to his more "normal" compeers, and in order to continue to live with them he has modified his social acts, elaborated eccentric social tendencies, and finally altered the nature of the given—that which he selects for experiencing from the situation in which he exists. In the process he has become eccentric, psychoneurotic, or psychotic.

Unfortunately, our study of social phenomena from this scientific viewpoint is quite new. We begin, for example, to see why "silliness" is of bad prognostic omen. The act of laughing in that peculiar way in an attempt to satisfy a social tendency manifests given objects or conditions widely removed from those which we select for attention and activity in our successful interplay with others. It reflects a self (as an important one of the objects given to the patient, as subject) quite far from the intelligent rational self which we accept as ours. Perhaps these sketchy remarks will serve to indicate the promise of further investigation along this line.

[5] It may be well to emphasize the magnitude which these disturbances of sleep may assume. One of my cases, who developed a psychopathic personality with unusually difficult evolution of his sex life, culminating finally in a homicide, had at intervals in childhood attacks in which he would "awaken" into a twilight state of some considerable duration during which he would perceive the hangings, pictures, etc., of the room in flames. He showed nothing of epileptic tendencies.

Prognostication by age at onset of the recognized psychosis is of but indirect value. In so far as one can find in the history evidence of maladjustment extending back for years before the serious collapse of personality, one is justified in drawing some conclusion as to the abilities of the individual, and as to the stability of his personality integration. The former bears upon the chance of recovery; the latter is of but most indirect bearing on outcome. It is not infrequently the case, however, that the very freedom from such *observed* signs of adjustive strain is entirely fraudulent, and deceives us in our estimation of the factors that resulted in the psychosis. One hears of the bad outlook where the break was dramatic and the situation in which it occurred, practically without unusual features that might "explain" the illness. This opinion may include nothing of the facts. If the schizophrenic psychosis actually occurred "out of the blue"—without material individual-environment factors of causation—then surely the prognosis might be anything, for understanding of the illness would elude us entirely (unless we revert to the doctrine of predestination). Other things being equal, the age-at-onset factor may be appraised as follows: The younger the patient in the age group from 35 to 17, the better the outlook; in earlier years, the younger the patient, the poorer the outlook because of the improbability that he has ideals and valuations of other persons such that we can establish good rapport in our attempts at therapy. If we can secure good data on the significant people from whom he has derived his ideals and valuations, and these include no extreme cases of psychopathy, we may be able to adjust our approach in such a way as to "reach" the patient. In such a fortunate case, the general rule applies—the younger the patient, other things being equal, the better the outlook for recovery.

Study of the evolution of personality has led us to a number of tentative conclusions which, at first glance, may seem rather bizarre. Had not schizophrenic individuals provided considerable data of confirmation, they must needs have remained far-flung speculations. We have come to look upon the human organism as at first a purely hedonistic process. Its first acts tend to satisfy needs which are unpleasant, and the satisfaction is pleasant and eventuates in a return to the quiescence called sleep. The skeletal musculature is more or less tensed and functional enervation is maintained so long as needs remain unsatisfied. On their disappearance, there is musculature relaxation and almost complete abolition of contact through sensory channels and consciousness with the "outer" environment. As chemical (or other) necessities accumulate, the tonic factor of enervation grows more and more conspicuous, until the tension suffices to suspend sleep—with attendant restoration of permeability of the sensory channels and more or less coordinated musculature activity of the appropriate parts. Some effort has been made in "The Oral Complex" and elsewhere to suggest the great importance of the oral zone of interaction with the environment. In "Affective Experience in Early Schizophrenia," stress has been laid on the importance of postural tensions of the peri-oral region in the expression of impulses, particularly the more persistent tendencies. It seems now that these persistent tendencies which are expressed by alterations of tone in the peri-oral musculature are generally tendencies of a social rather than hedonistic, etc., nature. It is being borne in upon me that a great deal can be inferred concerning the attitude of the patient in relation with the physician and other significant persons, from noted changes in these postural tensions. It has been possible in several cases where considerably affective relations had been developed to provide experience the effects of which have appeared in correctly anticipated alterations of these postural tensions.

The mouth and nose may be considered as apparatus by which the subject secures and incorporates in himself objects from the "outer" world. One *acquires* for his body by the mouth. One feeds his life through the nose and mouth. Knowledge may come by the eyes and ears or by the sense of touch, but "substance" is taken by us through the nose and mouth. This comes not as interpretation, but as the precipitate of crude fact from the days before speculative thinking—infancy and early childhood. This positive taking in by the nose and mouth antedates all cultural experience. It is well established as a function before there is any differentiation of the creature from his "outer" environment, represented by the nipple and later the mother, crib, etc. In contradistinction to the case of controlling the sphincters, training (cultural inhibitions) in this zone has as its end restriction of objective-choice only, rather than the production of wholly new habits of control to interfere with automatic reflex processes. The oral function of material acquisition is therefore one which grows on the basis of the most primitive innate abilities, without suffering any marked distortion or redirection from its crude biological "end." Again, from before birth, the oral-nasal-pharyngeal apparatus is capable of good representation in whatever consciousness there exists. In this respect also it is distinguished from the sphincter zones in that awareness is but secondarily directed to them, in the shape of attention to cultural requirements thrust on the child.[6]

As Ferenczi has remarked in his *Versuch einer Genital Theorie* (Int. Psychoanal. Verlag., Leipzig, Zurich, Wien) * the urethral function is one of giving out, and the rectal-anal is one of retention or hoarding. This is in the language of the child, but the thoughts of the child are the caissons on which is erected the super-structure of juvenile and adolescent thought. Furthermore, the fantasies of the child, as the psychoanalysts have demonstrated, are fantasies which we lose only by consciously elaborating them to an adult level. Substances are taken in through the (nose and) mouth and thrown off by the lungs, skin, kidneys, and bowels. Not alone in childhood fantasies but in folk-lore and quasi-philosophical ruminations we see the translation of these physical matters-of-fact into the realm of "mental" things.

Personality may perhaps be considered with a view to the prepotency of one of these zones of interaction with material substances (in turn, considered *as personal surrogates*). We see (1) the oral-erotic, so called, who, among other traits, is eternally tak-

---

[6] No implication is intended to the effect that the acquisition of anal and urethral sphincters control is *necessarily* accompanied by awareness of unpleasant demands of a cultural character. Well-directed training can make this habit-formation a matter of impersonal fact, rather like our acceptance of the weather, gravitation, etc. In such "normal" cases, the character traits called anal-erotic and urethral-erotic, respectively, are not developed, and the preponderating symbolic importance of the mouth zone is all the more clear.

[* For a related statement, in translation, see Sandor Ferenczi, *Thalassa: A Theory of Genitality;* New York: Psychoanalytic Quarterly, 1938. H.S.P.]

ing in, without regard of retention (the emissive function may be more or less displaced in this sort of schizophrenic, so that expectoration becomes an important act—the saliva often assuming equivalence of sperm); (2) the anal-erotic, who *retains*, hoards, and gives out but unwillingly; and (3) the urethral-genital, the characteristics of whom depend importantly on the developmental emotional bias and on the degree of evolution of adjustment of the sex impulse.

Personality may be thought of as elaborated with principal reference to one of the primitive emotional situations. Thus the overemphasis of anger responses may be conceived as leading to violent and aggressive personalities, and to epileptics. The exaggerated anticipation of all the child's wants may eventuate in an attitude of passive omnipotence, and a secondary obsessional type of personality. Where the infantile and early childhood experience has been accompanied principally by fear, we anticipate individuals who manifest "defense reactions" as their characteristic. Among these latter, we expect to find most of our schizophrenics.

A combination of these rough classifications has seemed to give us some insight into differences to be identified in our clinical material. To us the oral-erotic obsessional patient is a very different sort of person from the anal-erotic. The problem presented by his treatment is quite different. The oral-erotic epileptic, rare though he may be, is a clinical problem of some promise; the anal-erotic, by no means to be sought.[7] These generalizations seem peculiarly cogent in the case of schizophrenics. On the other hand, it is not too easy to formulate "rules" by which to place patients under these rubrics. The oral-erotic seems to be a fairly clear cut picture. Anal-erotic tendencies show early in the disorder period, by unpleasant fantasies of money, gas attacks, color

---

[7] The most destructive epileptic with whom the writer has established some measure of contact was of the oral type. He was accessible and showed good promise of profit by psychotherapy. Circumstances rendered this impossible. The few other cases of these maladies which have been under care have been prevailingly anal in type. They have been difficult, tedious, and their material has in each case reached back into the comparative inaccessibility of early childhood. *Passim*, no data has yet been accumulated (from a very small epileptic material) in regard of postural tensions of the face, to compare with the findings in individuals suffering schizophrenic processes.

displays, etc. To the urethral-genital class, I refer those adolescents in whom the early training (complex of sexual sin) incest
barrier, and homosexual elaborations have not operated to prevent some evolution of prepotent value in the genital sensations.[8]

Cases Regarded as Prevailingly Oral-Erotic

CASE 13

Patient admitted February 6, 1923, æt. 20; illness observed six
months previously; the elder surviving of two boys. The father has
been semi-invalid for a long time; the mother, nine years the father's
junior, is rather nervous; nothing is known of more remote relatives.
Information concerning birth and early development lacking; finished
high school æt. 17, entering business in which he received two pro-
motions. Mother was very strict as to the kind of company he kept
and on one occasion when he produced a condom she staged a
grand scene. Masturbation began at 12 and continued to date of admission, averaging two or three times per week. He regarded this as
disgraceful. He day-dreamed considerably of becoming financially independent and a social success. He quit masturbation about a year
and a half ago for about three months; gradually a feeling of sexual
inferiority developed and he brought himself to taking a loose
woman for an automobile ride. She stimulated him, but instead of
engaging in intercourse masturbated him; this distressed him considerably. He had shown little interest in women previous to this and
he now began to drink with fellow employees. Shortly afterwards,
after taking a few drinks and going to a cinema with a boy friend,
he developed some interference with his vision and was helped out
and taken home. During the night he felt that mice were running over
him. He stayed in bed the entire day, obsessed with erotic feelings
which he struggled to control. When an elderly chambermaid
entered his room, he made a feeble attempt to attack her. He had in
mind performing cunnilingus. She escaped. In the evening he felt
that he must go out and mail a letter, and when on the street he became dazed and walked about, pursued by "imaginary" lights, etc.
He could not orient himself and felt that something terrible was
about to happen. He was obsessed by sexual desires. He walked for
hours and finally got home, stayed awake all night, and worried lest

---

[8] Genital sensations normally become superior, during adolescence, to
pleasure returns from any other sensory area of the body.

That there is an "urethral character" seems to be dubious. Prolonged
enuresis seems often to be associated with anal-erotic traits. The title
"urethral-genital" is explained in the origin of genital pleasure. *Vide*
"Erogenous Maturation."

his name "be dragged in the mud." When a doctor was called he refused the medicine, feeling that it contained poison. In the next day
or so, he again attacked the elderly chambermaid and attempted to
perform cunnilingus on her because he "needed some transference
of blood from the womb to get well." She was rescued and he was
taken to a sanitarium where he remained three days, being then
taken home.

He continued extremely erotic and one afternoon attacked his
mother, throwing her on the floor, thinking that he "had to extract
blood from the mother's womb in order to purify myself." His
courage failed him and he gave up the attempt; he became restless,
walking aimlessly in the street; he tried to read newspapers and books
but saw the "wrong side of everything." He saw some news item
pertaining to crime and immediately became fearful that he was involved in it, believed that actions of others had reference to him,
hallucinated voices and noises at night, and was quite fearful—feeling,
however, when morning came that his experiences had been largely
imaginary.

He was received in a condition bordering on panic. Under treatment for three and one-half months he was then discharged as a
social recovery. Toward the end of his stay, he attempted an extensive heterosexual adjustment.

After a time on the outside, he resumed his former type of employment and continued approximately well for over three years,
thereafter developing mild paranoid psychosis with feelings that he
must not eat where he could be observed. This illness followed his
securing a position which was really beyond his ability.

CASE 17

Admitted March 10, 1923, æt. 26, from the Henry Phipps Psychiatric Clinic to which he had been admitted January 29, 1923. The
youngest of four children, the eldest a boy distinctly effeminate in his
manner, the second an army officer, the third a girl one year the
patient's senior; the father living, well, a successful merchant; the
mother eleven years his junior is fairly well. Birth and early development reported normal. Did very creditable work in high school and
was winner in an interscholastic oratory contest. While in the university, he began to complain of difficulty in concentrating, returned
home and went to work. Enlisted in the navy during war, making
frantic efforts to secure his discharge immediately after the armistice.
Then observed to be nervous and dissatisfied. Had several positions,
each of which he lost due to business depression. In the summer of
1922, it was noted that he was depressed and worried—his response to
questions being "I can't tell you." Made vague reference to relations
with a woman at the university, after which a number of incidents

occurred which had aroused his suspicion to the effect that she and another were "going to tell on him." Entered pre-medical school; did very poorly, and was hospitalized.

In retrospect the family realize that for three or four years he has been irritable and fault-finding; that for two years past he has been noticeably seclusive. For a long time he has prided himself on his knowledge of women, boasting that his "specialty" was married women. For two or three years, he devoted much time to writing letters to girls and carried with him at all times a book full of their addresses. Much complaint of tonsil trouble and several guillotine operations in the past four years. He said to his eldest brother that since he had his tonsils removed he had been better able to think about the events of his early life; on several occasions he frequently remarked that he "was gradually becoming straightened in my mind." It was finally discovered that he had a most elaborate system of delusions to the effect that his mother was carrying on a liaison with a barber in town. This was based on many extremely trivial incidents having no such meaning. He began to carry a revolver. He refused a drink by his brother on the belief that it was poisoned, rapidly extended his delusions of the mother's immorality, and was hospitalized.

On reception here he was found to be very paranoid and markedly hallucinated, chiefly at night. In spite of the markedly paranoid reaction, he profited by psychotherapy, developing insight to the extent of recognizing intense fellatio cravings. In spite of a very thorough examination by competent specialists, with entirely negative findings, he insisted that something must be cut out of his throat, saying finally that he didn't care what, just so something was cut out.*
He recalled that as a child he had been given to thumb-sucking, and that some time when he was about five, when he accompanied his mother to a dry goods store, one of the clerks called him behind the counter, exhibited his penis and said to the patient, "If you want to suck anything, suck this." After withdrawing most of his retrograde falsifications and delusions about the mother, he was frightfully harassed by acute fellatio desires and vowed that he would commit suicide. He secluded himself from other patients, claiming that they protruded their tongues at him as an invitation to perform fellatio: he believed the drinking water was doped (with quinine!). Some suicidal attempts were interspersed amongst many threats. He gradually developed an ability to conceal his difficulties. Under cover, he continued to see invitations when patients or attendants licked their lips, protruded their tongues, etc.

Under pressure from the family he was discharged.

Less than two weeks after reaching home he remarked that he wished he was dead; a few days later he renewed most of his old

[* This is the same patient briefly mentioned in *The Interpersonal Theory of Psychiatry*, p. 363. H.S.P.]

ideas about the mother. The impression is that, notwithstanding the unpromising nature of paranoid maladjustments, this patient might have been brought to insight into the underlying incest situation with recovery.

CASE 34

Reported as patient E. K., in "Peculiarity of Thought in Schizophrenia."

CASE 37

Admitted December 8, 1923, æt. 32; married and divorced; an elder sister, stable and successful; the mother died when he was 22, after ten years of invalidism. The father and some of the paternal relatives are heavy drinkers. Birth and early development alleged to have been normal. Finished grammar school and took up a trade. His habits were exemplary until his mother's death. Thereupon he began to drink heavily at intervals. On outbreak of war, attempted to enlist. Was rejected and later drafted. Shortly before the war he married a very loose woman with whom he lived but six days, leaving her because of her extreme looseness. In the service he developed a great intimacy for a Belgian cook who was his drinking partner. His service amounted to about eighteen months; some time after his return, his wife, with whom he had had no contact, died. As a measure of his feeling for her, it is noted that he disbelieved the notice of her death and had to be persuaded to go with his landlady's son to the hospital to identify her.

He secured a rather good job after the war; continued to live in the home of a widow with ten children, with whom he has spent in all over fifteen years. Not long before his admission, a married woman began to pursue him and secured from him considerable furniture purchased on the installment plan. He finally grew weary of this drain upon his finances and broke off this relation. In the meanwhile he had begun to drink a great deal.

One night he was profoundly shocked to dream of performing fellatio upon one of his landlady's sons. The next day he had difficulty at his place of employment and began to feel that bootleggers were going to kill him. This was quite irrational, there being no explanatory rationalizations. Became sleepless, actively hallucinated, afraid to go out of the house, and was received into the hospital. For a considerable time he was panicky and the subject of many abusive and threatening hallucinations. A visit from his much dilapidated father produced considerable disturbance in him. Treatment was undertaken, but it was not possible to break down his conviction that many of his psychotic experiences were genuine. His superficial adjustment, however, became so good that he was paroled after four months, and after a time returned successfully to his former occupation.

CASE 39

Reported as patient Q. R., in "Affective Experience in Early Schizophrenia."

CASE 46

Admitted May 3, 1924, æt. 23; the sixth of a family of nine; four sisters and one brother older; two sisters and one brother younger. Of the last mentioned he is very fond. The father is a successful professional man who has suffered for many years from the fear that he will be regarded as a chronic masturbator. The mother, two years his junior, is living and well. There is considerable mental and nervous disorder on both sides of the family. Birth and early development are reported to have been normal; he was "sweet and pleasant and loved by everybody," good-natured, agreeable, quiet and unobtrusive. "Girls are attracted to him but he does not reciprocate." Left high school in the third year to enlist in the navy, April, 1917.

He was one of those chosen for special training; in the entrance examinations for this he failed. Upon his return to his ship, he found that he was no longer "one of the boys" and shortly thereafter secured his transfer to another vessel, where he was promoted to the rank of petty officer. He was discharged æt. 18. Refused to go back to school and entered the merchant marine service in which he reached the rank of mate in the first year. Was inveigled into a stock promoting business in which he lost all his money. Thereafter, somewhat disheartened, worked for his father, in the course of which his mental disorder became evident; patient felt that he and his father were the victims of persecution by the Klan. The father thought that his son's illness might be the result of masturbation and sent him to a sanitarium. The father has marked religious tendencies, and often he prayed with the patient for his recovery. The family physician recommended outdoor work, and not long afterwards the patient shipped as mate on a vessel which made a trip around the world. His behavior was rather erratic; he began to write home to the effect that he had been married for more than five years to the daughter of a high government official, by whom he had a child five years old. He began to fear that he was suspected of performing fellatio. He struggled with the psychosis until the vessel finally docked at an American port, and then attacked all the ship's officers; was taken to a hospital where he was violently excited; moved rapidly through two or three hospitals, and was received here deep in catatonic condition. He had been considerably bruised before arrival and erysipelas developed in the facial wounds. We were successful in avoiding any considerable excitement during the period of pyrexia, the only incidents being an occasion on which he struck an attendant who coughed in his presence, and another during his convalescence from the septic process when he came unexpectedly from his room one night and struck an attendant. Coughing was regarded as constituting an invitation to him to perform fellatio, and the attack on the attendant followed a nocturnal emission which the patient felt had been brought about by the influence of the attendant.

It developed in the course of his prolonged and somewhat difficult treatment that he had had but one approximately serious love affair, and it was terminated. He had lost all interest in this girl some years before her marriage to a fop for whom he had no special regard. Around the time that he first expressed delusions of persecution, he encountered her one day on the city street and she made mention to him of plans to secure a divorce. This he felt was a joke, but soon afterwards learned that they had actually separated. He felt that this was on his account and felt it his duty to go out to see her to convince her that she need not expect him to play attendance upon her as he had once done. Around this time he was entertaining a grandiose fantasy which made it probable that he would be heir to a very wealthy property. When he called at the girl's home he learned that the couple had patched up their differences and confined himself to expressing to her mother a number of fine Christian notions about marital harmony, etc. This impressed her mother, and led to his being complimented by one of the Sunday school classes he taught, a couple of days later. Knowing his own motives, he was struck by the unconscious irony of this commendation. In the next Sunday's sermon the preacher expressed "a lot of soft soap" which seemed directed at him and his "noble attitude." He rationalized all this as the work of the good or religious section of the Klan and presumed that the sinner section of the Klan, which "knew me for what I really was," became jealous and prepared to retaliate.

Shortly after visiting the couple, he went for the first time in years to a house of prostitution. One day while riding with a friend of his, the friend started to turn a corner, swung back into the street and remarked that the druggist at the next corner was addicted to fellatio. Some days later one of the "good" Klansmen mentioned to the patient that a sailor just in from a European port had been picked up by the police for performing fellatio. The particular port mentioned was one to which the patient had planned to go to study shipping. From this period onward he was preoccupied with a wealth of schizophrenic fantasies in spite of which he maintained superficial adjustment until the incident at the port already mentioned.

Throughout his stay he was very sensitive to "challenges," signs, symbolic activities, etc., of those about him: all these were related to invitations that he perform fellatio. He was able to deal with some of the incest material and was progressing satisfactorily when he was removed from the hospital. In a neighboring hospital to which he was admitted as a veteran he had a somewhat rough time at the start, but renewed and continued his transference until his discharge to his home.

There, in the past two years, he has maintained a remarkably good social recovery, including sublimatory activities of the nature of singing, etc. He would be described as a paranoid state following upon prolonged catatonic schizophrenia.

CASE 47

Admitted May 30, 1924, æt. 22; the third of three boys. There were three boys by an earlier marriage of the father, who is foreign-born, supposedly in good health. The mother, foreign-born, twenty-three years her husband's junior, is "sickly and nervous." He had a sister somewhat younger than he, who died æt. 12. Birth and early development alleged to be normal. Attended two years high school and night school. Worked as a clerk for some time, then enlisted in the merchant marines four and a half years ago. In his year of sea service he was very happy. On returning to civil employment he showed decreased efficiency and changed jobs frequently. On returning home he talked a great deal about how pleasant his home was and frequently said, "Thank God I am home." About three years ago he began to complain about his stomach; said that he felt rough and shabby, that he was unable to eat various types of food because they did not agree with him. He developed a great fondness for ice cream, consuming as many as ten or fifteen sundaes at one sitting. He grew very much dissatisfied with the home. About a year and a half ago had an appendectomy, but was disappointed as his stomach symptoms continued. His gastric complaints increased and he had a tonsillectomy. For four or five weeks before admission he spoke of having "that all-gone feeling." Said he had no sensations when he ate or drank. Said that after taking water it put him to sleep. Once or twice he said he had no stomach, that "it is gone."

In the hospital, he showed disordered sleep, preoccupation with somatic ideas, and seclusiveness. He seemed to secure satisfaction from discussing his symptoms. Said he felt very changeable; that "at the time my meals come I feel sleepy, then after I've finished I am dizzy, choked up." He stated that he had had anxiety attacks for years past and quoted as a recurrent dream the following: "I dreamed that I am lying in bed, trying to go to sleep. A man comes into my room and annoys me. Just as he leaves I have a feeling of electricity running through my body. On awakening I feel tired and afraid." He grew restless, expressed more bizarre ideas—e.g., does not feel the blood circulating through the arteries and veins as he did before he became ill—became more and more difficult in regard to taking of food, and [had] bearing-down sensations in his abdomen, etc. It became necessary to resort to feeding by the tube for a considerable time. Much of his time he was occupied with an obsessive progression of the names and characteristics of the people who made up his environment here. He became a moderately cooperative patient, but because of the wretched cooperation of the family he was discharged, after about six months' care, as much improved. It is understood that he continues to be most eccentric, but is able to make an economic adjustment.

CASE 75

Reported in "The Onset of Schizophrenia."

It should be evident from the above cases that the pleasure returns from genital manipulations, intercourse, etc., in each of these cases was not sufficiently great to take precedent over the interest and "libidinal" returns which derived from the oral zone. Such situations would be regarded as arrests in the genital localization of the "libidinal" components of motivation. Some of these oral-erotic individuals have had sensitizing experience. Fully as frequently we encounter oral-erotics who have not had anything particularly notable in the way of sensitization. The promise which these patients hold forth seems to reside in the fact that they are *set* to take in from the environment, and that this set works in cultural terms so that they are amenable to constructive experience. It is believed that the favorable prognostic outlook in such cases arises very largely from the working of this factor.

For cases regarded as prevailingly anal-erotic see Cases 8, 24, and 52, reported in "The Onset of Schizophrenia." It will be noted that Case 8 made a rather stable paranoid social recovery after less than three months' treatment; that Case 24 had many remissions with gradual dilapidation; and that Case 52 degenerated into an uncomfortable hebephrenic dilapidation.

As to the urethral-genital type, several cases will be found in the earlier studies. It will be noted that they showed various degrees of genital adjustment—none, however, approximating complete sexual satisfaction with a partner. Those who seemed to include factors of exaggerated anal-erotism tended in general to unfortunate outcome: a number of those whose behavior and content indicated a retention of libidinal elements in the oral zone include a much higher percentage of favorable outcomes. Much more striking than the recovery rate, however, was the element of rate of dilapidation. Those showing anal "mechanisms" in psychosis seemed very much more prone to disintegration of the personality, in the sense of collapse of social tendencies. For what little interest may attach to it, the following rough classification of our material is appended: oral-erotic personalities 38.8 per cent; genital type 35.2 per cent; anal type 18.7 per cent; no data for classification 6.3 per cent. Since the period of hospital residence of most of our 140 cases preceded the elaboration of these tentative prognostic criteria, these figures are to be regarded as of no general reference—not even as just to our material.

In further consideration of personalities and symptomatology on the basis of prepotent zones of interaction, we find ample confirmation for the conclusion of Kempf as to the prognostic importance of the "attitude of the ego to the perverse cravings." To the extent that representations in awareness of the motivations —which have escaped repression—continue to be regarded by the individual as criminal and subversive, to that extent the mental disorder which ensues is to be suspected of an unfortunate outcome. On the other hand, because of the receptive attitude of the oral-erotic who has not progressed to a paranoid maladjustment, the appearance of violent negative response to the erupting motivations in such patients does not carry gravely pessimistic implications, if only because this sort of person is very often able to acquire experience which will lead to more just valuation of matters-of-fact pertaining to himself.

A subdivision of particular importance among psychiatric material is made up of those who have—in alcoholic intoxication or other circumstance—engaged in the gratification of their unapproved motivations. Emphasis need not be laid upon the fact that in the but slightly imperfect or complete adjustments of incestuous or homosexual types, mental disorder does not develop excepting in response to accident. These people have constructed, in their sentiment of self, a friendly attitude toward behavior, interests, and sexual motivations which they know to be contrary to the prevailing social ideals. They therefore have little or no internal conflict. Such perverse sexual adjustments are usually established in early adolescence, if not as behavior, at least as ideal. Sometimes, however, experience transpires which enforces upon such an individual the judgment of society, or impresses him with his helplessness to contest for the mate against the biological odds which function to carry everyone through the incest and the homosexual stages to heterosexual adjustments. In such cases, mental disorders of any kind may ensue. We have several cases of schizophrenic disorder which arose under these circumstances.

There is a large number of people who—some during the juvenile period, most of them during the adolescent epoch—have been seduced to participating in perverse practices. Many of these have found to their chagrin that they are not devoid of motivation making for perverse acts. To others, appreciation of that situation has come as a result of the reduction of ideal censorship through influence of intoxicants. It has been interesting to observe the relationship which exists both in nature of psychotic maladjustment and in progress and outcome of personality disorders in this group, as compared with the group which had encountered "perverse" motivations in fantasy only. In this group the distinction of emotional bias is probably determining. It is the opinion of Elton Mayo, who has worked with much obsessional material, that these perverse experiences increase the therapeutic problem presented by such patients; the writer has seen only a few cases of schizophrenic disorder which has developed in obsessional personalities—usually appearing in the course of an obsessional neurosis. In general, in the oral-erotic schizophrenic material, history of perverse practices has appeared to reduce the therapeutic problem rather than to increase it. In the small number of prevailingly anal-erotic illnesses in which sufficient cooperation was secured to uncover perverse experimentation, a number of social recoveries was secured.

In the field of the urethral-genital type, we encountered a distinctly different problem in this connection. Such of them as are importantly oral in organization have generally attempted heterosexual adjustment without complete success and often have included extensive oral perverse relations with the mate. It is almost a rule in therapy of male oral-erotic personalities that fantasies of cunnilingus will precede frank fellatio fantasies. We take this to be an effort to preserve a measure of self-respect by attempting to establish capacity to satisfy and be satisfied by a woman. What may be called the primitive oral motif is the taking in of substance. Most oral perverts take in, take away from, and absorb the sperm of their partner as the symbolic equation of his strength, manhood, virility, or other admired quality. This feature, which seems to have escaped so-called sexologists, is the outstanding characteristic of such acts.[9] Having ample data to support this conclusion, the writer doubts the satisfaction values derived from cunnilingus, per se, and suspects in all cases it is a compromise and that we are here dealing with people whose sentiment of self finds homosexual satisfaction intolerable, or whose judgment has chosen this less dangerous means of satisfaction.

In addition to the prognostic factors directly referable to prepotency of the oral in contradistinction to the sphincter zones, we might venture a subdivision in the oral type of personalities. One occasionally encounters, among definitely oral-erotic patients, certain ones whose attitude towards the environment constituted by others is markedly malicious. This is not to be taken as an evidence of "anal erotism." There are some schizophrenics in the case of whom prepotency clearly attaches to the oral zone, yet whose attitude is prevailingly sadistic: they tend to *hurt* with the mouth. This may expand as fantasies of biting, tearing with the teeth, and the like. It may find expression in uniformly abusive utterances. It may take the form of sarcastic and otherwise annoying speech. It sometimes—usually episodically, only—man-

[9] Without digression into the general psychopathology of sexual activities, I would mention that the male oral pervert rarely wishes to cooperate in an active role. His relation to his partner is either one of feminine love or, much more commonly, one of lustful aggression devoid of any sentimental elaboration. Homosexual love as a distinctive sentiment-formation seldom occurs excepting in case of the comparatively rare active homosexual and that of the bisexual persons. These, when oral-erotic, establish sentiments making for behavior in the shape of *soisante-neuf* and in these and similar arrangements there is libidinal interchange equivalent to complete satisfaction of demands of the socialized personality.

ifests in actual aggression, during which the patient bites someone, in preference to inflicting some other form of injury. These
patients are more difficult to handle, therapeutically, than are
others of the oral type. Their necessity for injuring or annoying
anyone who becomes significant to them is a serious handicap. On
the other hand, they none the less have the good prognostic implication of the oral type in general; they deteriorate but slowly,
if at all, even though their recovery is delayed. The following is
a fragment, classically illustrative, from an interview with one
such patient:

[Doctor: *What is the trouble?*] "Well, I don't know. Nervousness,
I suppose." [*How does it show itself?*] "What?" (this in a most annoying fashion). [*Is there anything that distresses you?*] "Oh, I
don't know. Yes, perhaps, somewhat." [*What is it?*] "What?"
(Question repeated.) "I really don't know." [*When did it begin?*]
"I really don't recall, now." [*How are you troubled, now?*] "What,
oh, I don't know. I feel pretty good, now. That is, practically speaking" (this with much sarcasm). [*Are you getting better?*] "Well,
probably—yes." [*How have you changed?*] "Well, I don't know."
[*Tell me what impresses you as signs of improvement?*] "Well, just
general feelings, I guess. I don't know, really."

Supplementary to the considerations heretofore discussed, some
attention may be given to the dynamic situation revealed in the
abnormal sensory experiences of the patient. In general, pleasant
hallucinations are to be regarded as wish-fulfilling fantasies which
are so valuable that they have been awarded precedence over
reality. This is an ominous situation. Reassuring and encouraging
voices—particularly God—when they become the prevailing feature of the hallucinosis, represent the awarding of excessive reality value to the inhibitory ideal structures in order to control or
suppress the undesirable matters-of-fact constituted by the un-
acceptable motivation. They represent an extreme effort through
the sentiment of self to disown the basis of conflict and frequently can be pushed aside by a vigorous attack by the therapist.
Accusatory and abusive voices in the oral-erotic sort of illness,
even if accompanied by hate, are a fairly good sign. The hate
behavior of this sort must be distinguished from that of the prevailingly anal-erotic individual. The latter is of grave omen.

Rather remotely connected with these considerations is the empirical observation that psychoses including as prodromals illusions or delusions concerning unpleasant bodily odors are of unfavorable outlook. Auto-erotic conflicts which carry with them many eye symptoms and mannerisms of the orbital region * are frequently resistant to therapeutic approach but do not entirely preclude social recovery. Lastly, a word concerning the role of alcohol and its relationship to prognosis. It has seemed that the use of alcoholic beverages as intoxicants may be credited with supporting the partial integration of a great many people and saving them from graver maladjustments. When alcoholic overindulgence is closely related to the outcropping of schizophrenic processes, these processes, other things being equal, have a somewhat more favorable outlook than those in which such history is lacking. This is believed to arise from the fact that the underlying conflict has been so near awareness for some time before dissociation of the personality that it is relatively easy to bring to conscious formulation.

In conclusion, let me stress the view that outcome under treatment in schizophrenia depends largely upon two major factors: the nature and organization of previous experience, on the one hand, and the facilitation or the reverse towards new experience, on the other. Regardless of other seeming criteria, the prognosis of younger oral-type patients is not bad, and thoroughgoing efforts should be directed towards salvaging such individuals. As our understanding of the schizophrenic processes is increased, we may confidently look forward to a considerable percentage of recoveries among this type of patient.

[* See Phyllis Greenacre, "The Eye Motif in Delusion and Fantasy," *Amer. J. Psychiatry* (1925–26) 82:553–579.]

6

Commentary

SULLIVAN attended a series of conferences from 1927 to 1929, which appear crucial in terms of his association with scientists from other disciplines. At least the papers which appear in the rest of this book seem to show a sharp expansion of perspective, and all of these papers seem to have been written after at least one or more of these conferences. The first such meeting that I have any record of is a Social Science Research Council Meeting, held at Dartmouth College in Hanover, N.H., in August, 1927. Sullivan was a discussant of a paper by William Alanson White on "Psychiatry and Its Relation to the Social Sciences." [1] In the discussion, Sullivan reports that in his opinion there was no need to consider (for certain research into the dynamics of groups) "aggregations larger in number than four because one found in aggregations of people living intimately together or working on one project reactions which seem in no way more distinguished or more complex than the reactions that had appeared in the experimental society of two or three or four. I should say the studies of groups of two or three came pretty near to giving us for our purposes an understanding of the social forces as they appear in the relation of individuals and as they affect those individuals in relation to each other." Obviously Sullivan is reporting on his experience at Sheppard and is noting that the social forces on a small ward of schizophrenic patients are basically undistinguished from other groupings in the society.

[1] From the Proceedings, mimeographed, of that Conference; see, in particular, the evening session for August 26, 1927. White's paper was later published under the title of "Psychiatry and the Social Sciences" [*Amer. J. Psychiatry* (1927–28) 84:729–747], but Sullivan's discussion appears only in the mimeographed Proceedings.

At the 83rd meeting of the American Psychiatric Association, held in June, 1927, (at which Sullivan presented the paper which precedes this commentary), Sullivan and William Alanson White were instrumental in helping to create a committee of five, directed to "survey the field of interrelations of psychiatry and the social sciences, with view to greater cooperation among those concerned in studying the nature and influence of cultural environments." This committee succeeded in December, 1928, in bringing together for a 2-day meeting a distinguished group of social scientists and psychiatrists in a First Colloquium on Personality Investigation (already mentioned in the Introduction to this book). Sullivan's contribution to this Colloquium was considerable, and it is obvious that he was very much stimulated by the contributions of others; Sullivan spoke on the necessity for adequate communication between social scientists and psychiatrists—some common meeting ground. In a sense it represents an early formulation of the purpose of the journal, *Psychiatry*, which he helped found in 1938.

A second meeting of many of the same people was held a year later, in November, 1929, this time under the joint sponsorship of the American Psychiatric Association and the Social Science Research Council (the Second Colloquium on Personality Investigation). Sullivan's formal presentation at this second meeting, with excerpts from the discussion, is included in this book under the title, "Schizophrenic Individuals as a Source of Data for Comparative Investigation of Personality."

The next paper, "Research in Schizophrenia," which was presented and published in 1929, clearly shows some of this expanded interest in the social sciences. Noteworthy in this paper is the fact that Sullivan mentions the necessity for comparable data on nonschizophrenic persons and the importance of a study of schizophrenic process in adolescents for explaining many adult personalities: ". . . I am convinced that in the schizophrenic processes and in the preliminaries of schizophrenic illness—so common among adolescents who are having trouble in their social adjustments—can be seen, in almost laboratory simplicity, glimpses which will combine as a mosaic that explains many more than half of the adult personalities that one encounters."

Research in Schizophrenia [†]

ON THE basis of some thirteen years [*] of preoccupation with problems concerning schizophrenia, the writer concludes that existing formulations concerning this subject are misleading. Proceeding from certain widely accepted fundamental postulates, physical and biological, he has come to believe that progress in the direction of practical understanding of the schizophrenic disorders in particular and towards the formulation of preventive and hygienic measures in general cannot appear until an extensive revision of prevailing conceptions is made in the direction of an increased attention to super-personal or social factors operative in human life. Research in schizophrenia has proceeded in many of the possible directions: physical, physico-chemical, bio-chemical, chemical; anatomical, histo-pathological, neuro-pathological, endocrinopathological, cardiovasculopathological; by studies of abnormalities in metabolic physiology, blood physiology, kata-physiology, etc. Alleged light has been thrown on the problems by general psychoanalytic investigations, studies in "narcissism," contemplations of the Oedipus complex, doctrines of "autoerotic regressions"; by formulations as to reduced consciousness, as to

† Reprinted from *Amer. J. Psychiatry* (1929–30) 86:553–567. Presented in abstract at the eighty-fifth annual meeting of the American Psychiatric Association, Atlanta, Georgia, May 14–17, 1929.
[* This is apparently a reference to Sullivan's first analytic experience in Chicago during the winter of 1916–1917, in which he undoubtedly began to insightfully explore some of his own difficulties as well as those of the patients he was seeing as a medical student on hospital wards. Sullivan received his M.D. in 1917 from the Chicago College of Medicine and Surgery. H.S.P.]

synæsthesia, as to perversion of cœnæsthetic sensations; by speculation on the effects of various toxic agencies such as mescalin, bulbo-capnin, etc. Doubtless there are impending data from the field of nutrition, vitamin searching, etc.

When one strives for a measure of detachment from part-aspects of the organism and undertakes to contemplate the schizophrenic individual as a *person*, the cogency of many of these attacks is enfeebled. One perceives in some cases a human being strikingly close to the most acceptable form of physical development, vitality, and opportunity. Some students then proceed with commendable diligence to seek out "psychopathic determiners" resident in the stock of the patient and arrive thereby at immensely satisfactory if woefully diffuse hypotheses. Here again we witness the spectacle of a broader perspective withering into a monocular and rather bemoted view of the person as a sub-biological entity, the victim of hereditary factors. And all this occurs notwithstanding the known achievement by people of widely diverse hereditary endowments of comparable measures of success in living. This notwithstanding also the negative instances which only an overwhelming devotion to the mystic-hereditary henid could obscure from one's view.

We know that there is behavior *in utero;* at least we know that activities of a highly integrated character occur before birth and that it is epistemologically safer to assume their total-reaction character than it is to contemplate them as extraordinary instances of local action. Only those blinded by ancient prejudice will now deny to the infant an ever expanding field of behavior. We know that, whatever we call it, there is a potent influence brought to bear upon the evolving organism from the earliest days through activity of the relevant adult environment. We know that everything favors the view that environmental influences have a tremendous role in determining the growth of human personality.

The peculiar characteristics of the parents of schizophrenic youths are represented by such precipitates of psychiatric experience as is the statement, "You can never secure a history from the mother of a schizophrenic." The only question that can be raised by fair-minded critics is one as to the universality of the

influences which some of us allege to be determining in the occurrence of schizophrenia. It has been the misfortune of so-called
dynamic psychology or psychopathology that it has proceeded
over an enormous field of factual material with a large measure of
disregard for inferential control by statistical and similar methods.
This question of control is one fundamental to great progress in
psychopathological research: the extreme difficulties inhering in
this aspect of the general problem must not prevent the amassing
of data on nonschizophrenic individuals if we are to come to a
definitive formulation in this field.

Schizophrenia is regarded by the writer as a term to be applied
to a large and variegated group of life-processes, showing as characteristics, (a) regressive preponderance in implicit total activity
of fantasy as compared with the previously acquired—and temporarily inactive—"externally controlled" "thought processes";
(b) a regressive preponderance of overt total activity of the type
of irrational ritualistic and magical behavior; and (c) an underlying extraordinary preponderance of certain motivations normally
accorded by occasional expression in life. This statement implies
a certain genetic-evolutionary view as to the limiting possibilities
of total activity. It eliminates from the definition of schizophrenia
all considerations of duration of the schizophrenic processes and
of their outcome. Their duration and their outcome are two perhaps intimately related subsidiary problems, the solution of which
is perhaps to be expected from our investigations. The statement
directs investigation toward mental content, conscious and unwitting; toward a thoroughgoing investigation of activity of the
total kind—with careful distinction of the neuromusculogland-
ular activity which is local action; and toward exhaustive inquiry
into methods of study of human motivation. If current theories
are well founded, the motivation problem is the fundamental one.
To that the principal work of research must be directed.

The most obvious manifestations of motives are emotional situations. If we assume that primitive emotional situations are entirely subsumed in primitive fear, primitive rage, and primitive
satisfaction, and if we continue the application of our genetic-
evolutionary doctrine, we then come to the question: Is it the
case that only those personalities in whom the principal emo-

tional direction is along the channel of fear are liable to the development of schizophrenic processes? Grave doubt is cast upon this otherwise attractive hypothesis by the frequent discovery in the history of our patients of temper tantrums and other instances of rage behavior. Are we then to think that it is in personalities principally developed along the channel of rage impulses that schizophrenia appears? Or are we to combine the two and accept, for example, McDougall's easy definition of schizophrenia as morbid "sulks"? Perhaps the very inclusion of rage behavior with this "dangerous condition" of sulking is sufficient to eliminate this group; we still find a problem in "explaining" the "termination" of sulking in "amok." Shall we then consider only those who show the supernal omnipotence tendencies as outstanding evidences of the underlying primitive emotional development as likely to eventuate in schizophrenia? A few obsessional neurotics become schizophrenic; a good many of those who have substituted rumination for more effective adjustive action pass through this to schizophrenia. All in all, however, we cannot find in the emotional developments of infancy any useful key to the evolutionary explanation of the schizophrenic processes. It is fairly well demonstrated that certain very grave deviations of personality—e.g., primitive genital phobia—have their source in the interpersonal relations which exist in the first year and a half of extrauterine life. It is equally evident that certain somatic factors such for example as obstructions of the respiratory tract, gastrointestinal structural or functional anomalies, circulatory disorders, endocrine peculiarities, anomalies of the mother's milk, nipple, etc., etc., are potent in determining serious personality deviation variously evidenced as pavor nocturnis, perversions of the sucking behavior, and the like.

But the causal series of later schizophrenic processes, so far as it passes through infancy, seems wholly nonspecific: Infantile maladjustments ensue in fundamental warp of the personality and load its development heavily in favor of later disaster. More than this we cannot say.

Taking childhood as the epoch ushered in by the appearance of articulate speech, one may seek in it for primary determiners of schizophrenic processes. One discovers without much difficulty a group of abnormalities arising from incoherence in the senti-ment-formation pertaining to the two parents and can trace from this certain grave personality developments such as the obses-sional neurosis. One finds infantile deviations now developed in the field of feeding disorders and speech disorders. One sees the effects of vicious "external" influences applied to the teaching of sphincter control in the shape of "anal erotic" deviations of per-sonality. One discovers clear-cut beginnings of psychopathic per-sonality arising from irrational training as to sufficient causes for reaction on the part of the personal and impersonal "outer world." One sees the inculcation of maladjustive dependence on various defense reactions such as incapacitation by "sickness," etc. In general, childhood shows much of the psychopathology of the adjustment to imposed authority but little that is directly illuminating in the study of the evolution of schizophrenic proc-esses. There are mentally disordered children in abundance and some of them progress, in a manner easy to rationalize, into grave schizophrenia. Our study of motivation leads us to a denial of the possibility of any true schizophrenia in childhood. (It is true, in this connection, that if one ignores the factors of motivation, schizophrenia may be said to be something that is outgrown by everyone except schizophrenics; this may be a useful conception, in some ways, but it is by no means an accurate one.)

It is first in the juvenile era—that phase of personality growth ushered in by the appearance of true socializing tendencies, mani-fested as strong motives making for adjustment in and within an environment of other juveniles—that we come upon factors in abundance pointing toward the evolution of schizophrenic ill-nesses. In this era, powerful curative processes occur against over-individuation or rather malindividuation which may have resulted in childhood. On the other hand, if any influence prohibits the satisfaction of the juvenile socializing tendencies, there ensues grave warp of personality of the sort which seems to be rather clearly related to the appearance of schizophrenia. Thus in the cases where family tradition dictates the exclusion of juvenile playmates and the use of tutors and so forth, we see a satisfac-tion of the socializing urge by the use of imaginary playmates and by other forms of highly organized fantasy which naturally fails to provide a satisfactory basis for the adjustments to other people which will be demanded subsequently. The imaginary playmates may approximate within workable degree the necessities of the personality in some cases where parental influence is not well integrated and in those cases where some adult influence directs the juvenile to books and other educational sources in which the cultural precipitate of this era is successfully reflected in myth, fable, and the like. Such a vicarious socialization, however, while decidedly better than nothing, is woefully inadequate. It makes for a great prolongation of the early and mid-adolescent periods. Special schools are seldom peculiarly well designed for the great purpose of this era, and large public schools are perhaps the most useful haphazard measure at this time. The attitudes toward authority and toward adults are sufficiently consolidated during childhood so that only close individual study suffices to provide opportunities for good juvenile socialization in individuals already badly warped. The partition at this age of the time used in adjustment in and within an environment of compeers and that devoted to adjustment in and within an environment of adults, is such that the latter is still able to vitiate, by its emotional linkage and imposition of valuations, many of the fortunate developments toward a social norm in the case of handicapped children. The warp from childhood later identified as psychopathic personality is not markedly influenced during this time because it includes a fundamental difficulty of self-appraisal and therefore an inability to evaluate other personalities in a sufficiently realistic fashion to encourage the growth of abilities to adjust in and within the personal environment. Hysterical warp is readily continued through this period as a result of continued interest by the disabled parent or parents who encourage the juvenile's escape from his difficulties by recourse to "illness." The obsessional warp is continued because of its fundamental characteristic of substituting implicit processes characterized by doubt and uncertainty for overt behavior: it thus favors superficial unsatisfactory contact with other juveniles and their developing an attitude of dissatisfaction with the subject. The deviations that reach even further back in the evolutionary history of the personality have ultra-important influences in preventing the development of the normal juvenile reference-frames and thus in continuing over-individualized self-appraisals and morbidly phantastic appraisals of others. In addition to all these factors, we have in the juvenile era the growth of a certain stabilization of interpersonal adjustive processes which appears as the basis of "personality type."

An understanding of this aspect of the subject is greatly assisted by abstracting from the totality of innumerable personality factors the more or less unitary group subsumed as the *self*. Proceeding by differentiation on the basis of experience (to some extent influenced by maturation of abilities) from a background of universal subjective participation characteristic of late intrauterine and early infantile life, to some measure of clear-cut differentiation of (a) things characterized by objective reality of the physical kind, (b) things characterized as purely personal subjective reality, and (c) things characterizable as socially valid —what we may call the sentiment of self is evolved in one of several fairly distinguishable types.

We probably have enough data at this time to organize a fairly systematic beginning of human typology. Attempts such as those of Jung and of Hinkle, of Roback, and the important (if somewhat obscure) efforts of Edouard Spranger may be cited in this connection. As the last mentioned well says, "I have never heard of a case in which Fate, *i.e.*, external influences, radically changed a mature man from one type to another, except for the above mentioned transition to the religious type . . . [in old age]." While Spranger has the impression that puberty "is always the time of life in which mental personality first awakens . . . and the self for the first time confronts the world as something for its own sake . . . ," our considerations move this point backwards into the juvenile era. This is not to be understood as meaning that the first stage of adolescence finds each male established in a comparatively unyielding pattern as to the self-world complex, but only to say that the freedom of choice of such pattern begins to shrink in the juvenile era and that the pattern is established during the next phase of personality growth; *viz.*, the preadolescent or homosexual phase.

When there appears in the growing social tendencies of the boy impulses making for intimate adjustment with one (or two)

other boys, we see the beginning of preadolescence, early adolescence, or the homosexual phase of adolescence—whichever
one wishes to call it. Already in the juvenile era it has in many
cases come to pass that such interpersonal adjustments are made
impossible by warp of the life processes. It is to be surmised that
in such cases hebephrenic deteriorating processes will follow the
occurrence of schizophrenia. Per contra, if any measure of true
interpersonal adjustment is achieved in early adolescence, then
we surmise hebephrenic deteriorating processes occur, if at all,
only after prolonged illness.

Puberty may be taken to be susceptible of objective establishment by reference to somatic modifications. The appearance of
the early (or pre-) adolescence on the other hand is not by any
means so clear-cut a point in time and may precede physical
puberty by many months. It is the stage commonly called the
gang age and as such studied by Furfey, Thrasher, and others.*
In it there first appears motivation making for the development
of true sentiments for others. The primitive mother sentiment—
the *anlage* of religious beliefs—and the differentiating sentiments
for the real mother and the real father, for certain adult figures,
for abstract idealistic formations, etc., which have gone on to this
point, are not of the type which we designate by the term "true."
We wish by this to emphasize their highly fantastic individual-
ized and unrealistic character. In the intimate adjustive effort
during the early adolescence period, however, in so far as a personality continues to possess the ability for elaborations of experience about another person, "true" sentiments are formed;
these are characterized by a new degree of realistic approximation, consensual character, and objectively effective influence
over behavior and thinking. Along with these very important
aspects of the personality growth there goes a growing prepotency of the sexual impulses with consequent adjustive effort.
At this point it may be well to emphasize the positive value of
overt behavior and to stress the destructive influences of inhibitory factors already inculcated in the personality. Whether

[* See, for instance, Paul H. Furfey, *The Gang Age;* New York: Macmillan, 1928. And Fred M. Thrasher, *The Gang: A Study of 1,313 Gangs
in Chicago;* Univ. of Chicago Press, 1927, H.S.P.]

from primitive genital phobia or from later accessions of inhibition, a number of early adolescents find it impossible to make
realistic adjustment to the impulse of sex. The matter of deviations in this connection is very important for study if only for
the reason that it is in this particular field that not only is repression now clearly manifest but also the effect of social forces conspicuously demonstrated. Here we find for example that the boy
who cannot go along with his compeers in the gang in regard of
behavior concerning the genitals, either is detached from the
group or is required in maintaining his standing to compensate
vigorously by manifesting unusual abilities of some other kind.
We thus find in this very circumstance two important sources of
delinquency and crime. Gangs in which sexual inhibition is general often maintain some measure of mutual complacency by
group behavior characterized by a persistent juvenile drive
against authority. On the other hand, individuals insidiously os-
tracized from gangs, individuals who by reason of serious previous personality warp with or without the misfortune of being
unable to find others enough capable of socialization to amalgam-
ate with them in forming a low order gang, tend to pseudo-
cooperative or "lone wolf" drives against the world and eventuate in what may be called the true criminal modus vivendi. It
is to be observed—and a great deal of careful investigation should
find its locus here—that to the extent to which an individual is
now able to adjust himself with another individual, to that very
extent he becomes certain of a comparatively prompt recovery
from schizophrenic processes if they occur, and proof against
deterioration of the profound or hebephrenic type. In this era
of personality growth also we can study with great profit certain
maladjustive modi vivendi at the social level such as the roots of
hysterical superficiality, of inadequate homosexuality, of paranoid superficiality and the like. It is again in this era that we are
to find clear understanding of certain other inadequate people
who burden the social fabric—e.g., the "spender."

Mid-adolescence ends and late adolescence is considered to begin with the establishment of habitual sexual behavior, laying
aside consideration of the other very important phenomena in
progress throughout this time of personality completion. It is

untimely to develop in this paper the wealth of implications of adolescence and we must content ourselves at this point with one statement: the establishment of habitual sexual behavior (and concomitant implicit processes) depends in part on opportunity; opportunity is in part "externally" determined and is very importantly determined by previous experience; and finally, the character of habitual sexual behavior includes as it were in brief an abstract of the total personality growth to date. One can delineate preliminary research classifications in this field which have appropriate divisions for each of the types of maladjustive situations (see Scheme of Classification). Certain of these stand in a direct serial relation to the outcropping of schizophrenic processes following certain types of rebuff.

HUMAN DYNAMICS

SCHEME OF CLASSIFICATION OF ADJUSTIVE PROCESSES ON THE BASIS OF THE DEGREE OF RESOLUTION BROUGHT ABOUT IN THE ORGANISM-ENVIRONMENT-CONFIGURATION—DEGREE OF KINESIS.

I. Adjustment: complete kinesis: total resolution of the configuration so that there is no remaining *stress*.

II. Partial Adjustments: by which stress in the organism-environment-situation is more or less reduced but the configuration is not resolved completely.

A. *Compensation:* by which simpler activities and implicit processes are substituted in lieu of difficult or impossible adjustment.

1. Day-dreaming in lieu of constructive thought or action.
2. Sport, theater, reading and the like instead of effort.
3. Seeking and preying on sympathy.
4. Unsocial lying, pathological lying of idealizing type, etc.

B. *Sublimation:* by which more complex activities and implicit processes which are in conformity to systems of ideals, social or derived, are unconsciously substituted for more direct adjustive processes which if carried out would create new organism-environment situations because of the disapproval of others.

1. Altruistic activities.
2. Religious practices.
3. Other ritualistic behavior of social value.

C. *Defense Reactions:* by which more complex activities and implicit processes not in close conformity with the systems of social and derived ideals, are unconsciously substituted for more direct adjustive processes which are blocked by *conflict* within the personality, the stress of the conflict being avoided or reduced thereby.

a. In which the "inner" aspect of the situation is the more impressive:
   1. Forgetting.
      i. Suppression.
      ii. Repression.
   2. Rationalization.
      i. Elaborative.
      ii. Retrograde falsification.
      iii. Detractive.
   3. Excitement.
      Including many "abnormal sublimations," reformers, etc.
   4. Transfer of blame.
      i. Impersonal—luck, fate, etc.
      ii. Personal—"my sickness," "my views," etc.
      iii. Paranoid—suspicion—blame—persecution.
b. In which the "outer" aspect is the more impressive:
   1. Negativism.
      i. Passive.
      ii. Active.
   2. Incapacitation.
      i. Special.
      ii. General.

D. *Dissociation:* by which some of the systems of experience and some of the somatic apparatus are disintegrated from the rest of the personality and engaged in activities and implicit quasi-adjustive processes not in harmony with those of the rest of the personality.
   1. "Psychogenic" tics, mannerisms, and stereotyped movements.
   2. Automatisms, including automatic writing, crystal gazing, etc.
   3. Mediumship, etc.
   4. Hallucinosis.
   5. Multiple personality and the like.

E. *Regression:* by which more recent experience, and the resulting elaboration of complexes, sentiments and tendencies, are disintegrated in such fashion as to remove them as discoverable factors in the organism-environment situation; thus resulting in the reappearance of adjustive efforts of a chronologically earlier state of personality.

III. Nonadjustive Processes: by which stress in the organism-environment-situation is not reduced, and no resolution of the
configuration is brought about.

    [A. *Panic:* in which the acts are reflex and of a primitive im-
pulsive order, and the implicit processes, primitive. An
uneven regression most striking in the awakening of
primordial fear.]

    B. *Anxiety*, varying from more or less frank attacks of fear to
pessimistic worrying.

    C. *Obsessive Preoccupations*, including morbid doubts and scru-
ples.

    [D. *Grief:* in which the prevailing process may or may not be
quite nonadjustive.]

    E. *Depression.*

*The above is an abstract scheme, not an exposition of genera and
species of adjustive processes, which are processes in, of, and including the organism in communal existence in, of, and with the environment. A scheme of this sort is useful only as a frame of reference to
aid one in orienting himself in the problem of understanding an individual personality and its problems; static terms are used to refer
to sorts of process (change).*

Research in the schizophrenia problem must proceed in two
directions. In one, the interest is in the evolutionary path which
we have just outlined. The data of child study institutes, controlled data from child guidance clinics and data from such
sociologic investigations as that now in progress under the direction of Thrasher in New York City; all such material is grist
for the research worker in his efforts to organize and classify
important factors. In the other direction minute study of life
processes actually occurring in adolescents on the one hand and
in patients suffering schizophrenia on the other provides the
clues, the negative instances and the emphasis on lacunae in data
on human nature otherwise secured. Without taking up the
former we must emphasize the magnitude of the research field
constituted by the latter. Not only is it necessary that at least
two methodologies be applied at every point over the whole
fields of adolescence and schizophrenia—*viz.*, the personality
study (life reconstruction) method and the method of more
objective investigation—but also the enormous significance of
some factors usually overlooked by the investigator must be

kept in mind. A great body of error has been incorporated in psychiatric tradition. The investigators have not maintained awareness of the general factor of interpersonal interaction. Moving in some strange hypothetical detachment they have recorded and thought as if their contact with the patient was without significance to him. Here we touch upon one of the most fatuous errors of the humanistic or "un-natural" sciences: to wit, that by some technique—poker-face or other—the "observer" gazes down from a pinnacle of scientific detachment upon subjects from whom he is concealed as if by the *tarnkopf*. This error is even more to be criticized than is the conventional logical error of assuming that in spite of preconceptions one is very likely to discover unexpected data. When these two influences so gravely prejudicial to sound understanding of human nature are considered, research problems of rare intricacy make their appearance even in regard of the most simple point.

In the course of our study it has seemed that in every case of schizophrenic illness there is to be found in the history of the individual a point at which there had occurred what might well be called a disaster to self-esteem. This event is attended subjectively by the state which we identify by the term, *panic*. Panic customarily results from the utterly unexpected collapse of something very important in the life process of the individual: the sudden failure of a side-walk or of a stair-step is perhaps the instance most frequently encountered. Injuries to self-esteem are by no means uncommon experiences. Most of the youngsters whose doting parents and relatives have permitted them to grow in belief in the prodigious nature of their attainments come to a time when some less patient victim reacts to their exhibition in an anything but gratifying manner. These unfavorable reactions are not uncommonly so organized as to lead to a sudden unexpected and very unpleasant diminution in self-esteem. The subjective concomitants of such an event may or may not amount to panic. Usually the individual by appealing to a "principle" rationalizes the situation to his comparative content. In the case of the spoiled child some worshipful adult usually applies satisfactory balm in the shape of depreciatory rationalization of the offending mortal. Wit, humor, anger and vituperation, and vari-ious other social gestures usually resolve such situations occurring later in life without much permanent effect. In some such situations, however, panic passes over into a chronic feeling of insecurity or inadequacy. In these cases there has occurred a grave break in the solidarity or dependability of the frames of reference which the individual possessed concerning the synthesis or complex of his self and the world (especially other people). Such a break or failure takes the form of a vaguely formulated but clearly felt uncertainty in the cosmos. The individual is no longer able to proceed in the elaboration of his life with the same unthinking directness which was previously the case. A number of typical chronic maladjustments in interpersonal relations may be referred to such an event. Such events stand apparently in a necessary relation in the series which culminates in schizophrenia. In other words, there is always such a collapse of that cosmic security which is perhaps our heritage from an exceedingly early developmental period, to be found in the history of a schizophrenic.

It is imperative for the solution of the schizophrenia problem and likewise for illumination of many social difficulties that we should understand (a) the evolution and character of self-esteem and (b) correlated types of events which can culminate in these disintegrations of security. There is a whole "psychology" of panic which is yet to be elucidated. There is a wealth of correlative material pertaining to socially inadequate persons, eccentrics, and the like, which is directly relevant and as yet unstudied.

In regard to the schizophrenic processes themselves, whether they follow immediately as the resolution of the above-mentioned panic or appear abruptly or insidiously in the course of the modified life after the panic experience, we are confronted by a problem uniquely difficult in that the state of consciousness of the individual is not the one customarily encountered in investigations of human nature. As Thomas V. Moore, for example, has indicated in a related paper, there is not the clear-cut reference to socially valid reference-frames in the thinking, but a decided preponderance of fantasy-thinking of the kind best illustrated for the average person by reference to his remembered dreams. Coupled with this is a curious consciousness (which may be vestigial) of the false or dramatic character of much that is thought and done, and along with these continued peculiarities of consciousness there is the occupation of the individual with motives difficult for the inexperienced to apprehend. Far more than in the case of less disordered life processes, the productions, verbal and otherwise, of the schizophrenic require minute observation. It is only as one develops some familiarity with the probable content that one develops sufficient "set" to apprehend many of the remarkable (and frequently barely audible) statements that the patient makes. It is only by similar experience that one can learn to note the truncated, purposefully distorted, emotional signs that he shows. It is only by thorough acquaintance with the implications of this fragmentary content and emotional expression that one obtains clues to the interpretation of much of the bizarre gesticulations, posturings, etc.

Preliminary investigations have impressed us with the probability that schizophrenic phenomenology requires for its complete exposition nothing different in essential quality from the elements of commonplace human life. It is preposterous, however, to imagine that the individual in the depths of schizophrenic processes is to be understood by a reference to an "average" individual of corresponding chronologic age or the like. There is no room for doubt as to the regressive simplification that occurs in the interests of these patients, and one major problem of research occurs here. We must study with reliable criteria the problem of the type of situation which has lost *meaning* for the schizophrenic. In so doing we will obtain information not only of explanatory utility but also very valuable in organizing the sorts of situation in which these patients will show maximum benefit in recovering from their illness. As has been mentioned elsewhere, one way of attacking this problem is the study of visceral responses (*e. g.*, radiographic study of intestinal tone) to situations presented in the shape of visual stimuli—especially prepared animated cartoons and the like.

Many questions await investigation pertaining to the character of content hallucinated in schizophrenic illness, its origin, the factors permitting such dissociation of sensory projection fields, and the processes by which such dissociations are remedied. We have here material bearing importantly upon the question of *belief*. At this point also there arises the problem of the escape from control of reality-valuation pertaining to the fantastic life-drama which the individual conceives himself to be playing. We learn from our patients that this particular problem will take us far into the phenomenology of sleep, for one of the classical symptoms of incipient schizophrenia is a difficulty in awakening from sleep. I refer here to the fact that in addition to "dreaming he dreams" many an individual reports very uncomfortable periods occurring between "real" sleep and full awakening. Other patients show in the deeper illness "lucid periods" during which they are quite fully aware of the factitious character of much of seemingly important matters, only to relapse promptly into apparently complete domination by delusion.

The problem of disturbances in partition of interest between inner and outer events such that hypochondriacal preoccupations and delusions make up a good deal of some schizophrenics' content also awaits study. Somewhat of the same nature is the problem pertaining to the extraordinary distribution of meaning over irrelevant aspects of circumambient reality. In the catatonic conditions almost anything that can be noted is equally apt to fit in as apparently relevant to certain trains of thought, and the energy of the patient seems to be dissipated in perplexity about what ought to be done concerning innumerable trivialities.

Time forbids any real survey of these problems. It must suffice that I add a statement pleading the urgent necessity for much broader investigation as to adolescence and as to schizophrenia than has been anywhere so far recorded. Our perspectives must include far-reaching and intensive study of the whole subject of interpersonal relations. We must proceed carefully with great regard for many potent factors in human life that have not yet received even a measure of our psychiatric attention. What we will come upon in such a really scientific attack upon this major mental disorder will in all likelihood exceed any returns that we can obtain from any other field of study. I say this because I am convinced that in the schizophrenic processes and in the preliminaries of schizophrenic illness—so common among adolescents who are having trouble in their social adjustments—can be seen, in almost laboratory simplicity, glimpses which will combine as a mosaic that explains many more than half of the adult personalities that one encounters.

7

Commentary

IN SEPTEMBER, 1929, Sullivan presented a paper at the Third Congress of the World League for Sexual Reform, meeting in London. This paper, "Archaic Sexual Culture and Schizophrenia," which is included next in this book, is somewhat comparable to two earlier papers, "Erogenous Maturation" (1926) [1] and "Mental Hygiene and the Modern World" (1927),[2] which have been omitted. All three of these papers are early formulations of the need for remedial action in the cultural attitudes toward sex.

The Proceedings of the London Congress were published in book form; papers were presented by such well known figures as Bertrand Russell, Bernard Shaw, Marie Stopes, and Vera Brittain. This book, which contains much new and exciting material in the field of sex reform, seems to have been largely lost in the literature. I consulted one of the few copies available in United States libraries; it was in a vault at the Harvard Law School Library, and I had the impression that I was one of its first and only readers. It should be remembered that the Congress was held a year after the initial furor over D. H. Lawrence's *Lady Chatterley's Lover*, which was first published in Italy in 1928, but did not receive a favorable legal opinion on

---

[1] This paper, here omitted, contains some brief data on two infants that Sullivan obviously observed. [*Psychoanalytic Rev.* (1926) 8:1–15; see p. 6 *ff.*] Since Sullivan was himself an only child and never married, his knowledge of children was extremely limited, as he, himself, often noted; but the data he presents in "Erogenous Maturation" is cogent and arresting.

[2] *The Modern World* (1927) 1:153–157. This monthly magazine, with editing and publishing offices in Baltimore, Maryland, appeared for a few issues in 1927 and is now almost unobtainable.

its publication in the United States until 1959. Undoubtedly, the London Proceedings were selectively inattended by the same general forces in the society of the twenties.

One of the central themes of the paper is the important role that homosexuality may play in the 'normal' development of the male toward satisfactory heterosexual adjustment. Although the Kinsey report on male sexuality placed this possibility within the grasp of contemporary social psychologists, Sullivan's thinking in this paper was radical for the twenties.

It should be borne in mind that Sullivan did not consider himself an expert on female sexuality and schizophrenia. His focus of attention is on male sexuality. The only relatively extensive statement on female sexuality is found in a chapter of his unpublished book, *Personal Psychopathology*, which he wrote in the late twenties and revised during the early thirties; but this chapter was written with the active collaboration of Clara Thompson, M.D. At variance with much of Freud's thinking on female sexuality, Sullivan noted in "Erogenous Maturation" that he does not accept the "allegedly identical Electra complex in girls. I will say only that I believe we have thrust upon women altogether too many conclusions derived from the genetic study of the male; in fact, the adolescent developments in the female, as now described, clearly include such artefacts, so that we are expected to believe that the vaginal erogeny is due to a regression! Perhaps, if investigation will follow a path among the facts appertaining to the female child, in some such manner as I have tried to indicate in the other case [male child], we shall come to an entirely satisfactory and self-contained hypothesis which will regard the woman's psychology as no more a caricature of the male's than is the mare's a regressive distortion of the stallion's."

The end of this same paper, "Erogenous Maturation," carries a summary statement on the archaic sexual culture, as it pertains specifically to the male, which might profitably be read as prologue for the article which follows:

When the gonad function has matured to the state of semen production, and activation of the neural apparatus pertaining to its ejaculation, there comes the adolescent resymbolization. Here the youth has a field of experience of the very greatest pleasure-value coming with unprecedented suddenness, its dramatic appearance being made on the stage of a to him practically complete world-representation, leaving (after its first appearance) that representation a mass of crumbling systems which he must rebuild—secretly and helped only by the equally unfortunate—always under the eyes of that devil, "Sexual Sin," formerly a mysterious, vague, wideflung influence, now a rapidly crystallizing symbol system including fictions of the past, present, and future, of hell fire, insanity, and everything else anti-biological. The conflict between this gigantic mental fraud and the indomitable sex impulse, spreading to well nigh every symbol, provides the "language" of all ill-defined cravings, of every pleasure source ever inhibited, and forms thereby the justification of Freud's use of the term "sexual," in so far as in it he voices the Jewish and Christian repressions erected in the path of human biology to insure a man-designed, and perhaps none the less wonderfully useful, arti-ficial culture. I leave you with this question: Cannot careful study of the facts of individual personality genesis, carried on by a strictly scientific method, give us a real (not fantastic) program for parent and child guidance which, while preserving our cultural achievements, will avoid this damnable adolescent situation, the fruits of which, now, are mediocrity or some degree of mental disorder in the case of most of our promising children?

Archaic Sexual Culture
and Schizophrenia†

BEFORE EXPRESSING the weighted opinion that archaic institution-alized attitudes and beliefs pertaining to manifestations of the sexual impulses are important tributaries to the occurrence of the gravest forms of mental disorder in adolescence, one may well take cognizance of the unwitting mental operations which so frequently eventuate in troublesome or even destructive "up-lift" and similar sublimations. One may propose to himself the question: Is the singularity with which conflicts and stresses pertaining to the development of the sexual phases of personality appearing in all accessible sufferers, the result of his preconcep-tions or his technique of investigation rather than a sequence existing irrespective of his views? There is no difficulty in psy-chological inquiries in arriving at erroneous but gratifying con-clusions. The very history of the theory of schizophrenia, or dementia praecox, epitomizes the situation. The whole tendency of modern psychiatric method is colored by an appreciation of the peculiar futility of ordinary methods of investigation when applied to the field of mental disorder. Observation is inadequate and interrogation woefully ineffective in elucidating the mental process actually making up the content of the graver mental dis-

† From *Sexual Reform Congress* [Proceedings of the Third Congress of the World League for Sexual Reform, London 8.–14.: IX: 1929], edited by Norman Haire; London: Kegan Paul, Trench, Trubner & Co., Ltd., 1930; pp. 495–501.

orders. Five different investigators can easily arrive at five strikingly different conceptions of the current situation of any one patient. It behooves one to scrutinize closely each intellectual step by which he progresses toward his conclusions about any patient in this field—or for that matter about any personality that may be the subject of his investigation.

It is traditional that sexual manifestations, and for that matter the less conventional or more abnormal sexual manifestations, are an outstanding factor in the picture of schizophrenia. It is common belief among the group of psychopathologists most probably really acquainted with schizophrenic phenomena that homosexual manifestations are almost all but invariably conspicuous in some stages of this illness. As observations of the former category have eventuated in one school in the notion of a primary degeneration of the sex glands, so a view is now among us to the effect that schizophrenia is to be regarded as a manifestation of dysfunction of the endocrine processes of the gonads. It is the writer's opinion that these views are wholly beside the point. In the category of homosexual manifestations there have appeared views relating schizophrenia to things as concrete as developmental anomalies amounting to ovarian substitution for testicular substance and vice versa. In this latter connection attention may well be called to the wide dissemination of the view that homosexuality itself, posited as a fixed condition, is an inborn developmental matter having a curious (and, needless to say, mythological) organic basis.

The experience of years in research into the nature of schizophrenia has impressed upon the writer certain considerations which seem cogent for the attention of the Congress. Schizophrenia seems to have hereditary origin only in the sense that any material organic deviation acts as a handicap in the development of normal personality and therefore can lead to deviations which increase the probability of collapse of the personality in the period of adolescent resymbolization of the ego and the world. That there is any uniform specific factor or factors conveyed in the germ plasm which function to produce a schizophrenia, the writer finds nothing to substantiate. The youths who make up the material of research include a large number who, when seen, present a variety of anomalies * and physical deviations. The facts are all these anomalies and functional deviations can be found in the nonpsychotic community and that many showing them in high degrees go through life without material disturbance of their mental functions. It is equally the fact that of those who come to the psychiatrist there are none in whom cautious study fails to reveal a great mass of experiential factors which have in a clearly understandable fashion collaborated with physical functional limitations to distort the individual's self-esteem to that low point at which the grave disorders manifest themselves.

Since the homosexual manifestations seem so conspicuous among incipient and acute schizophrenics, considerable study has been devoted to the life processes to be found in homosexual individuals generally. The writer is unable to make any definitive contribution in this connection, as his study has tended for a long time past to be circumscribed in a fashion which must be explicated at this point. It has seemed that human personality may be roughly classified into some such groups as the oral erotic, the anal erotic, and the urethral genital. Criteria for the absolute placement of any personality are impossible at this stage of our knowledge. Individuals are found who might well be called polymorphous as to these tentative types, and some individuals seem actually to have shifted in their recent developmental history from one to another type. In spite of this, there does not seem to be very much difficulty in placing a great majority of human personalities that have been subjected to close study in one of the three. As is the case with most schemes for classifying humanity, there enters in a considerable degree of interpretation by the student, and this is the more impressive when he is compelled to formulate an individual, for example, as "a passive pederast using

[* The use of the term "anomalies" throughout this section of the paper is of some interest in terms of an anonymous book published in 1927, which Sullivan cites several times in his published and unpublished papers. The author's name is listed in the Library of Congress Union Catalogue as "Anomaly": *The Invert and His Social Adjustment;* Baltimore, Williams & Wilkins, 1927. Sullivan refers to it as "a remarkable document by a homosexual man of refinement . . ." (see Appendix C, section on Sex, in *Proceedings: Second Colloquium on Personality Investigation;* Baltimore: The Johns Hopkins Univ. Press, 1930). H.S.P.]

this procedure as a defence reaction to powerful cravings for the passive role in oral sexual behaviour—being in fact prevailingly of the oral type of personality." While it is beside the purpose of this paper, brief examples from psychopathology may be given to somewhat illuminate this confusing situation: a homosexual given rather contentedly to fellatio, and being incarcerated for "offences" of this kind, and being there compelled to submit to pederastic assaults, develops that form of schizophrenia called Acute Homosexual Panic. Again, a passive and active pederast, finding that many of his companions are progressing into hetero-sexual adjustments, develops a minor mental disorder, resorts to more blatant pursuits of sex objects, and after some discouraging experiences, becomes preoccupied with cravings for fellatio, whereupon he immediately progresses into Acute Homosexual Panic. Among schizophrenic patients it has been found that there is a conspicuous preponderance of the oral type of personality among those who recover (or, if you will, experience prolonged remissions). This observation has restricted the study of homo-sexual personalities largely to those prevailingly oral in type. It seems demonstrable that there is an early phase of personality de-velopment in which the prepotent zone of interaction between the individual and his environment is oral, and it seems equally certain that there are no small number of individuals in the case of whom the oral zone continues to chronologic adulthood as the zone prepotently gratifying in contact with the environment. It seems that the principal processes connected with the adjustment of such an individual in and within environmental situations is by direct oral process or processes easily analogous thereto. It ap-pears that the actual appearance of a homosexual type of behavior in these individuals is the direct outcome of personality deviations that in turn have their nucleus in abnormal attitudes and beliefs cultivated in the parent-child relationship combining with later extra-familial experiences. No amount of homosexual experience impinging upon any type of personality will fix a homosexual modus vivendi in the absence of deviations of the kind mentioned.

In other words, in a hundred youths customarily homosexual in their adolescent gratification, only some small percent en-counter particular difficulty in evolving into the heterosexual phase of personality. In this small percent, on the other hand, only thoroughgoing and extensive reorganisation of the personality will permit of the achievement of comfortable heterosexual adjustment; and only the most emphatic environmental pressure will interfere with the continuance of a homosexual habit of life.

It is unsafe to think loosely of homosexuality. Homosexuality as a term must be appreciated to be generic only. There is no stuff or group of characteristics which by its presence or absence distinguishes an individual as homosexual or heterosexual. Homosexuality refers to a group of processes the nucleus of which may be identified somewhat as follows: mental processes, behavior and thinking, that are motivated by impulses more or less specifically sexual in nature and tend to be carried out in situations or configurations including another person of the same sex. Under such a formulation, so much of an individual's life is homosexual as consists of fantasy, thoughts, and witting and unwitting behavior directed toward the securing of more or less obviously sexual satisfaction from an individual of the same sex. It is most important to have this broad dynamic view in mind rather than to regard homosexuality as a static entity characterized by a degree of frank sexual activity with members of one's own sex. With it as the postulate in one's investigation, one readily finds a distribution among individuals which amounts to a continuous gradation between what might be described as the ideal pole of purely homosexual personality and the equally ideal pole of purely heterosexual personality. While there are no statistics worthy of the name, one cannot but surmise from fairly extensive clinical material that the modal point of distribution of the average American male aged thirty-five in the cultural area of the Northern Atlantic seacoast is some reasonable distance removed from the ideal heterosexual pole, decidedly more than is suggested by the traditional five percent. As one considers younger material, say the mode for males aged twenty-five, one finds it approaching the mean. And when one come to, let us say, age nineteen, one is impressed by the approximation to the middle point which might be described as the bisexual mode. These considerations, coupled with extensive data from retrograde study of personality growth by the methods of free association and dream analysis—in other words, by psychoanalysis—lend pragmatically sufficient justification for the doctrine of a "normal" homosexual phase in the evolution at least of male personality. The phenomena of gang life are markedly elucidated by the use of these conceptions, and the fact to which reference is made in the last preceding paragraph concerning the preponderance of heterosexual development among youths who lived for a period in comparatively comfortable homosexual adjustment is seen to be only what one should expect. The writer wishes to stress these views because of their great importance in formulating a realistic program of sex reform.

Attention must be called likewise to a fact pertaining to the great mental disorder under discussion in its relation to actual sexual experiences of the less conventional or "abnormal" kind, prior to the onset of mental disorder. While the writer is advised by certain colleagues that a history of "traumatic experiences," such as actual homosexual seduction, is not of good prognostic significance in the average case of psychoneurotic individuals, he has been impressed with the contrary significance among schizophrenics. It is to him certain that in this form of mental maladjustment any actual material arising from voluntary or unwilling concrete sexual activities has a beneficial effect in bringing conceptualization and fantasy of a sexual nature within the frame of real criteria. The patient who is harassed by cravings to perform fellatio in the history of whom there is nothing clearly related to the actual experience is a patient capable of regressive distortions in fantasy such that he can escape from any therapeutic effort at present available to us. If the personal origin of such harassing cravings has been *real*ized by so insignificant an event as the eruption into consciousness of a craving to duplicate the passive role on an occasion when he was undergoing fellatio, that experience incorporated into his personality is, as it were, a mooring from which he is not apt to tear away even during the most gravely fantastic phenomena of his illness. In brief, if the general population were to pass through schizophrenic illnesses on their road to adulthood, then it would be the writer's duty, on the basis of his investigation, to urge that sexual experience be provided for all youths in the homosexual phase of personality genesis in order that they might not become hopelessly lost in the welter of dream-thinking and cosmic fantasy making up the mental illness.

Let us proceed to the question: If in a hundred youths only some small percent encounter difficulty in evolving into the heterosexual phase of personality and of this small percent some go on as homosexual personalities engaging in more or less frank pursuit of gratification, while others progress into seriously maladjustive mental states including a large proportion of schizophrenic illnesses; what of the explanatory factors, consideration of which may give us a rational basis for sex reform? Without digressing into the extensive field of the psychopathology of uncommon sexual adjustments, and without subscribing to the oversimple formula that "perversion is the opposite of neurosis," which we can ascribe to Professor Freud, the writer would point out that any sexual adjustment which has brought a large measure of satisfaction (and implicitly a small measure of dissatisfaction, conflict, regret, or guilt) seems to guarantee an individual from subsequent grave mental disorder (this statement refers to individuals in peacetime cultural situations approximated in Western Europe and America). If, however, the personality of an individual includes (*a*) ideals which render any sexual activity unholy or "sinful," and his character is so organized that he does not dissociate his ideals rather completely from his unconsciously determined behavior and thought, then any sexual processes— activity or persistent fantasy—bring in their wake depreciation of self-esteem and resulting psychopathological phenomena which are liable to grave issue. Again (*b*) we find personalities including ideals as to some particular form of sexual gratification being the only accessible one and these ideals are constructed without any real regard for methods of attaining the approved goal or for adjusting to compromises in this connection: among such are what we call the resistant homosexuals, a particularly unvaluable group of the community, including many criminals. We may again hypothesize two poles, one at which the ideals (superego processes) are childish (interfamilial type rather than socialized type) and very powerful; and the other at which ideals are very highly evolved, fully socialized, and while equally powerful are, however, of a fully rationalistic, realistic type. Again our material shows nothing at either pole; the average among schizophrenics approaches the first mentioned; the average among frank homosexuals tends slightly toward the second pole; the average among psychoneurotics tends noticeably toward the first mentioned; and the average among the comparatively limited material that can be called normal adults tends noticeably towards the second pole. We find persons belonging nearer the first pole who maintain useful and comparatively comfortable lives by sublimatory activity, this being wholly unwitting. We find people approximating the second pole who are bisexual in their fantasy and behavior. We find two groups of individuals to whom this study of ideal-ethical classification applies in a more complex fashion; the one are the mentally deficient; the other are the psychopathic personalities. In the latter, which include a considerable proportion of the actually homosexual, and a larger proportion of distortedly sexual persons, we are dealing with personalities in which the integration commonly called character is so imperfect that domination by unconscious motivation does not eventuate in sustained conflict with contrary ideal formations.

From the consideration of this ideal-ethical classification, one comes to a conception of revision to which fundamental notions of sex ethics must be subjected if the purposes of mental hygiene are to be furthered. It is obvious that the origin of difficulties is not to be found in institutions to which individuals past the seventeenth year are directly subjected, but that instead their origin lies in institutionalized attitudes and beliefs which are applied to and inculcated in individuals in the early stages of personality genesis. The writer has discovered, for example, in certain cases a group of manifestations clearly pointing to the inculcation of what he chooses to call *primitive genital phobia*. This primitive genital phobia may be considered as an ideal formation derived in the months of infancy and abstractly formulable as a powerful feeling of terror about manipulation of the genitals. It is not conveyed by verbal injunction nor by punishment of the infant, but is instead a product of the empathic linkage which existed between the significant parent and the offspring. In other words, deeply unconscious motivations are built up in the infantile mind by direct emotional contagion.

Briefly, a person cannot develop normal personality in the formative years unless he shall have as the significant persons to whom he adjusts himself wittingly and unwittingly in infancy and childhood, [people] who are free from certain destructive attitudes and beliefs. He himself will infallibly grow up a personality warped in the direction either of direct or of compensatory maladjustment to sexual considerations. His children will continue the vicious circle. A certain number of such a series will eventuate as relatively unhappy "normal"; a certain proportion frankly homosexual; a certain proportion psychoneurotic; a certain proportion psychotic. To break the chain, to accomplish something in the prevention of avoidable misery and futile living, one must attack the situation at the adult level of parents and the institutionalized attitudes, beliefs, and so on to which they [the parents] are effectively subjected. It does not do to legislate for his [the child's] guidance. Unless they are prepared by extensive educational movements, the parents are not capable of profiting from the distribution of accurate information. The child guidance movement, in so far as it attempts to adjust not only the child but also the parent—having for the latter purpose the leverage of the child's welfare—can do something. It is a method costly not only for organization but very costly indeed for personnel, since it must depend on good psychiatric insight for its efficiency. It requires social workers not only excellently trained but also of satisfactory personalities.

By the development of a wise, farsighted program of parent teaching, supported by the powerful agencies for dissemination of accurate information, press periodicals and popularizing booklets, we can destroy certain archaic cultural factors which make for mental disease and abnormal living. To accomplish this, we must be most scientific in determining what is to be done—taking counsel not from our own emotions, warps, and unhappinesses which life has thrust upon us, but from intimate studies of normal and of disordered personalities. When we turn to this source of information we find our facts are of a comparatively simple and convincing nature. They are couched in terms which are the common terms of human life and as such very impressive when properly presented. In their presentation, however, we have to contend with defence reactions on the part of the hearers and we have to guard ourselves against fanaticisms on the part of assistants suffering from morbid sublimations, and we have eternally to remember that the processes of evolution are very slow so that we must be prepared for a long campaign from which rewards will be slow indeed in coming and during the course of which campaign the workers may well be subjected to assault by sick minds.

Schizophrenics become sick because their self-esteem has sunk to a very low ebb. The self-esteem on which most adolescents depend for mental security must survive the eruption of the sexual impulses with resulting resymbolization of ideals and purposes. There are very few adolescents today who know that there is a homosexual phase in the evolution of each human personality. There are very, very few indeed of the adolescents of today who can learn that homosexual activities of a frank sort, engaged in in the period of personality growth when such things are most likely to come to them, are experiences which contribute to the growth of personality and not sins, crimes, and the like. Just as a great step toward mental health will be achieved by suppressing misinformation and fantastically stupid views about masturbation —this even among the medical fraternity—so also may we look toward a conspicuous diminution in the extremely destructive psychosis of youth by the widespread promulgation of sane ideas as to the universality of sexual manifestations, the evolutionary course followed by the sexual impulses, and the real origins of deviations of sex life. So long as this group of human impulses are called upon to carry the principal burden of religio-ethical formulations suited to other ages and purposes, so long may we expect many of the most talented of our youth to spend their otherwise productive years weaving unhappy cosmic dramas within the mental hospitals. It is by an attack upon delusions and institutionalized absurdities in the home instruction of children as to ideals which are later to assume tremendous importance with the coming of puberty, that the burden of mental disorder and general unhappiness, including domestic infelicity, and so on, is to a large extent to be controlled. Sex reform has its great objective in correcting this situation, and to the correction of this situation the best efforts of public-minded individuals may very well address themselves.

8

Commentary

ON NOVEMBER 29, 1929, Sullivan went to New York City, to attend the Second Colloquium on Personality Investigation, which was jointly chaired by himself and Harold D. Lasswell. Sullivan's formal presentation at the Colloquium is presented as the next paper; an excerpt from the subsequent discussion has also been included in order to give some idea of the liveliness of the interchange. The calibre of the interdisciplinary communication is extraordinarily high.

Some of the suggestions made at this Colloquium eventually came to fruition. For instance, W. I. Thomas made a suggestion which seems to have captured Sullivan's imagination. The question under general discussion concerned adequate training for personnel in the whole field of personality investigation; Thomas' comment is as follows: "Speaking for the sociologists, it would certainly be a great experience if we were able to enter your hospitals and have contact with your patients as your interns have it. Would it be possible for a young sociologist, following a training under Dr. Burgess [Ernest W. Burgess, Professor of Sociology, The University of Chicago] and Dr. Sapir, to have an internship or something like that in a psychopathic hospital in association with Dr. Sullivan and others who have an appreciation of the whole meaning we are trying to get at here? . . ."

Almost twenty years later, such a project was sponsored by the Washington School of Psychiatry then under the leadership of Sullivan. A sociologist from the University of Chicago, Morris S. Schwartz, came to Chestnut Lodge Hospital in Rockville, Maryland (where Sullivan had regularly lectured and consulted) to collaborate with the psychiatrist, Alfred H. Stanton, M.D., (a student of Sullivan's), on a study of "institutional participation in psychiatric illness and treatment." The results of this study are found in *The Mental Hospital*,[1] which is one of the great interdisciplinary studies of the institution as affecting the day-by-day life of the patients (most of whom were diagnosed as schizophrenic).

[1] Alfred H. Stanton and Morris S. Schwartz, *The Mental Hospital;* New York: Basic Books, 1954.

Schizophrenic Individuals as a Source of Data for Comparative Investigation of Personality[†]

ASIDE FROM perhaps the most significant of my activities—the attending of conferences with social scientists—my attempts at collecting data on personality take the form of living with schizophrenic individuals. In the address from the chair, it was stated that general familiarity with the work of each other would be assumed. As, however, there seems to be no particular consensus even among my psychiatric colleagues as to the connotation of the term schizophrenia, it is perhaps rather in the interest of this conference that I say something by way of explanation.

Schizophrenics are individuals who have undergone a severe mental disorder which is characterized variously but is significant, for our purposes, because of a dissociation of the mental aspects of the life processes in such fashion that the victim no longer amalgamates readily in ordinary social activities but instead finds himself surrounded by extraordinary caricatures of other people, engaging in bizarre activities more or less definitely injurious to him, the whole of his interpersonal relations resembling the phan-

† Reprinted from *Proceedings, Second Colloquium on Personality Investigation* (held under the Joint Auspices of the American Psychiatric Association, Committee on Relations of Psychiatry and the Social Sciences, and of the Social Science Research Council, New York City, November 29–30, 1929); Baltimore, The Johns Hopkins Press, 1930; pp. 43–55 *passim*.

tasmagoria of the nightmare. His motivation is correspondingly (perhaps fundamentally) altered in a fashion leading him to what is popularly called "insane activities," and he becomes a "menace to himself and/or to others."

The people who are later to become schizophrenic are usually relatively inconspicuous in the social fabric up to and into adolescence; but in the course of the latter they more or less abruptly become conspicuous indeed, and are thereupon conveyed hastily to the mental hospital—if perchance, they have not effected a sudden termination of their life.

In the mental hospital, they tend to follow one of a few fairly definite courses of behavior—being, respectively, extraordinarily shy and uncommunicative, bitterly hostile because of the fancied enmity of everyone, or shy, silly, and childishly employed; they are all alleged to suffer "emotional disharmony," "apathy," and certain other phenomena, some of which are unknown to students of human nature—known only, in fact, to a particular variety of psychiatrist.

They tend markedly, under existing regimen, to remain thenceforth and forever in the mental hospital, until, at the end of a rather long life—and a terrible one—death removes them. They are expected, more or less by definition, to deteriorate in all or various of the human abilities, to some curious vegetative state termed "deterioration"; and they are ordinarily dismissed by comment to the effect that they are "completely wrapped up in autistic fantasy."

Their number is legion; the cost of their care is vast; and the economic and other social loss occasioned by the incidence of this mental disorder is appalling.

The disorders which these unfortunates suffer were alleged by an eminent but now defunct psychiatrist * to be of a nature of an hereditary degeneration—I believe he concluded that the determiners were recessive. As I am but one of many who no longer entertain his views, I shall be content with stating that his formulation—the dementia praecox concept—has been a great handicap to psychiatric progress, a death sentence to many schizophrenic individuals, and an important factor in justification of

[* This refers to Kraepelin, who died in 1926. H.S.P]

the continued anachrony of the Institutional Care—one of the outstanding peaks of our so humanitarian culture and probably of a piece with our "more and poorer children to the poor" policies, our "greater venereal disease" campaigns, and our general procedures for destroying the future of offenders against our fossilized criminal codes.*

Some schizophrenics impressed me, years ago, as singularly interesting, in part, because of their striking manifestation of some of my own most highly esteemed traits. I refer, of course, to my personal appraisal of my traits. I therefore cultivated them and this gave such complimentary returns to my self-respect and feeling of well-being that I have continued it since, alternating chiefly with attendance upon scientific deliberations and the like.

I find many such individuals very human indeed, particularly when they have not been exposed for a long period to "good" psychiatric care. It has seemed to me that in these schizophrenics one finds in almost laboratory simplicity the manifestations of complex processes which are combined in the more fortunate of us in such great complexity that they can scarcely be grasped and subjected to anything approximating scientific critique.

The schizophrenic's life is, on the surface, an excessively simple one. On the surface he is completely divorced from social influences. He no longer reacts in any ordinary graspable fashion to the social forces which are impressed upon him. He no longer is interested in many of the cultural values which inflame most of us. He is no longer interested in "fine ethical traditions." He is no longer interested in objects of art. He is not even interested in such crude things as the taking of food, the avoidance of "contamination with excrement," and so forth.

One discovers on acquaintance with these individuals something different indeed from the traditional psychiatric picture that I have been reproducing—a picture which may be found elaborated in concise expressions and fine verbiage in almost all textbooks of psychiatry.

[* Here Sullivan is attacking, respectively, the then current fight against dissemination of birth control information, the campaign to eliminate prostitution as a method of controlling venereal disease, and the use of capital punishment. H.S.P.]

One finds that the individual who has had a schizophrenic illness has not, in the first place, developed the abrupt manifestations of hereditarily-determined deterioration in the life processes. Instead, he has stood in a significantly and distinctively difficult position in the social situation in which he has lived; he has developed a striking, more or less specifically distinct technique in dealing with people with whom he has lived; in the course of this peculiarly distinguished life he has come upon certain situations which were most serious in their negative effect upon his self-esteem; and after encountering these situations (which include as significant factors only other people), after, perhaps, a rebuff to his self-assertion, he has shown a significant and characterizable failure to react by any of the methods of reacting to rebuff which are more or less well known to all of us from our personal experience (which, in turn, might well be made the subject of study if anyone can be encouraged to leave the realm of more pure science and take up so personal a matter).

We find that the stricken individual, following the peculiar and characterizable failure to react to rebuff, has lost a great part of that confidence in the integrity of the universe, the goodness of God, and so on, which is our common human heritage from infancy; and that from thence onward he goes on feeling decidedly uncertain about life. Apparently, if one is sufficiently uncertain about life, one loses the cognitive assets which serve us in distinguishing products of autistic or purely subjective reverie from products which include important factors residing in so-called external reality; and when one has lost this ability to distinguish between such reveries and such objects having more external points of reference, one begins to sink into mental processes significantly like those that we experience when we are asleep.

With the appearance of a partition in which considerable waking time is spent in a condition in which one is without the ability to tell what has true, genuine, and consensually acceptable, external references, and what instead is purely personal fantasy, there appears a peculiar disorder of social activity (and I might say even of nonsocial activity), and it is these peculiarities that seem to constitute the essence of schizophrenic behavior.

Now it appears that one does not thus lose one's ability to distinguish externally conditioned realities excepting after certain very significant losses of self-respect, and it appears also true that such significant losses of self-respect arise from but a small group of weaknesses or alleged weaknesses in the individual. Only from this two-factor situation does there derive a state in which dominating autistic reveries or fantasies take the place of the more realistic thinking; these reveries arise from and work out the comparatively few important tendencies in the individual to one or more of which the rebuffs had application—rebuffs which led to the failure of self-esteem and belief in the dependability of the universe. The reveries, therefore, take a markedly asocial or actually antisocial type, and the patient becomes a difficult person to have in the house, the school, or elsewhere.

When they are received into the mental hospital, they have been by that act removed to a degree from manifestations of the accustomed structure of society and from anything clearly in line with their previous experience, and are instead entered into a distinctive and characterizable new social situation. In it they make various adjustive efforts. Some of them go on to the point which we call full recovery. Many of them go on to what we call institutional recovery, which means that they are able to sort out reverie and externally conditioned reality to the point that they can live to the satisfaction of the relatively simple institutional environment (consisting however solely, significantly, of people). Quite a number of them do not progress to an institutional recovery. The number who succeed in making this reapproximation to consensual reality vary rather widely with the institutional situations to which they have been exposed.

It occurred to me some time since that if in receiving these patients we regarded them as persons, we attempted to discover what continued to be of interest to them, and we attempted to adjust the environment to which they are exposed in a fashion in harmony with these particular findings, we might then discover a rather remarkable recovery rate, if you will. In other words, we might find a way for restoring a lot of these people. I am now rather convinced that that notion is true, and the contribution, if any, that I can lay before you—in the hope solely that it will bring out a great deal of response from you—is the following:

We find that the schizophrenic is an extremely shy individual, extremely sensitive, possessed of a singular ability to get his feelings hurt, who has rather naturally erected an enormous defensive machinery between himself and intimate contact with other people.

Now, given such a person, one might expect that a detachment from reality, from externally conditioned reality, and a getting lost in autistic reverie would be moderately easy to achieve. At the same time, the fact remains that these patients continue to be very sensitive. You must take my word for that, because it is not recorded in the well-known textbooks.

I found some people running around loose who seemed to have a good deal of this same sensitiveness but who still seemed like myself to maintain a measure of contact with external conditioned reality; and when we put these people in positions to care for some particularly young schizophrenics, the results achieved approximate miracles, so far as the well-known traditions about schizophrenics are concerned.

We found that situations of affection, striving for esteem among others, cultivation of favorable reactions on the part of these particularly selected attendants, and so on, went on very much as they are supposed to go on in ordinary human society.

That was promising. But many of these chosen employees didn't seem to function satisfactorily; and so we looked further, and we discovered that if we changed the attitudes of these sensitive, shy, and ordinarily considered handicapped employees so that they had some notion of the schizophrenic as a person— in other words, if they ceased to regard him in more or less traditional ideology as "insane," but instead had stressed to them the many points of significant resemblance between the patient and the employee—we created a much more useful social situation; we found that intimacy between patient and employee blossomed unexpectedly, that things which I cannot distinguish from genuine human friendships sprang up between patient and employee, that any signs of the alleged apathy of the schizophrenic faded, to put it mildly, and that the institutional recovery rate became high. In other words, in an environment intelligently adjusted to the schizophrenic, the schizophrenic seemed to prosper and to be able to do almost everything but get quite ready to go back into the world. . . .

I would like to mention at this point the frequency with which the recovery process takes the form of an urge to leave the hospital, with almost an inevitability of relapse preceding by from a few hours to a week or so the actual date of discharge. In other words, here again we seemed to have a simple social situation: The strivings of the patient, his conformity to the social ideal of leaving the mental hospital and becoming an independent individual, carries him to the point of making extensive adjustment to the demands represented by the hospital staff conference, and so on (necessary to secure permission to leave); but when he has succeeded, when he has worked these interpersonal relations to the point that we, the staff, are willing to discharge him, then contemplation of what is ahead of him seems to sink the ship and he is back again, quite sick, but rather willing to get on his feet again as soon as we have removed the danger of success in the attempt which he can scarcely be said to wish to succeed in.

Let me recapitulate what I am attempting to say: We have found in the most disorganized group of people—I believe the psychiatrist would agree that the schizophrenic is the most disorganized of the functional mental illnesses (by this term "functional" I am excluding those who have suffered actual serious damage to their integrating systems)—a continuation of very much that is simply human.* They seem to react to social techniques and after they have reacted to social techniques—after they have reacted to them to the extent of again becoming members of a human group—we then find them susceptible to the same therapeutic maneuvers that we apply to the neurotic who needs some understanding of himself, some reorganization of his personality.

But in our dealing with schizophrenics we discover what I would describe as a decided simplification of the ordinary life situation; and in this simplified situation we see manifestations of

[* This is probably the first formal use of the term, "simply human," which became such a crucial term in the one-genus postulate (see Frontispiece of this book). H.S.P.]

the subject matter of each of the social sciences. The result of all of this is that we have developed an hypothesis of personality—which I am not presenting for the well-known reason [probably lack of time]—and a schematization of personality growth, suggesting that a good deal of excellent material (material which, as Dr. Thomas has said, is presumably excellent at birth) is converted into grave failures in adolescence; that the path by which this conversion is brought about is moderately reproducible already; that it shows important warping in infancy, in some cases; that in others this does not appear until childhood when it is largely a matter of disorders in relation to authority, submission to dominance, perhaps; that thereafter there comes a period during which the individual develops true social motivations and in the era thus ushered in, most important tributaries to the adolescent disaster make their appearance; that, following this, there comes a period of close interpersonal adaptation or adjustment, developments corresponding roughly to what we call love, and that it is under this last circumstance that the final disintegration of development ensues in what we call schizophrenia.

This ontogenetic notion seems to be quite lucid, quite within the grasp of such minds as mine, and the final state, schizophrenia, seems to provide us with a field in which there are simplifications, disorganizations of large complexes, which should provide a remarkable opportunity for studying each of the preoccupations of each of the social sciences—for in it are data which could easily be adapted to the usages of each of the social sciences, if each of the social sciences could in some fashion present to us a notion of what they could expect from this type of disorganization, and what they can contribute, of course, in the way of techniques for our securing this data for them.

Discussion

CHAIRMAN HAROLD D. LASSWELL.— . . . Dr. Sullivan has used the instance of the community formed by psychiatrist, attendant, and schizophrenic patient for the purpose of suggesting that a somewhat extraordinary social situation might reveal factors about every social situation, which we have failed to see. I wonder whether it would be possible for those present to detach themselves in some measure from their preoccupations with the details of their own research enterprises, as was suggested in the President's opening discussion, and think somewhat at large about the kinds of marginal situations which we would like to be able to study or to have studied in the modern world. One sees in this group Dr. Sapir, representing those who study primitive cultures, and it might be advisable (as a follow-up to Dr. Sullivan's suggestion) to ask Dr. Sapir to improvise at some length about the situations which one finds in certain types of primitive societies, and which would seem to offer special possibilities for the exposure of some neglected aspects of social relationships.

I wonder if Dr. Sapir is in a position to indicate some of these possibilities, placing them side by side with the suggestions which Dr. Sullivan made for the study of another group which lives in a world of unusual presuppositions.

DR. EDWARD SAPIR.—You mean, I presume, with reference to our basic interest. The first thing that occurs to me in connection with a study of primitive society—the major interest being personality—is simply this: that every society presents the individual with well-developed patterns of behavior, entirely conditioned in character, that either favor or do not favor certain of his innate tendencies. To rephrase this somewhat awkward statement, I do not think that it is quite as correct as it is often assumed to be that an individual, taken at random, has quite the same chance of success or failure in all societies. I think that there are certain preferential differences owing to the fact that characteristic behavior patterns get socialized in different ways in different societies.

To give an example of the sort of thing I have in mind: In our modern American community there is little tendency to indulge in visions. To prophesy out of a spirit of conviction not based on hard facts is to be considered pretty much of a loss on the whole. One would have to indulge in one's prophetic fancies in some very indirect way, via all kinds of academic techniques, via the use of an accredited jargon and all that sort of thing. This social cramping, necessary in our society, would deprive the expression of the "visionary tendency" of much of its value to the individual possessed of it. But there are a good many primitive societies that are somewhat favorably disposed to individuals of that kind. Such individuals could more easily be made to fit into a social groove, because their society encourages, rather than discourages a man possessed of "the spirit," one who can look into the future and lead others on to important types of activity. To that extent the chances of his breaking with his society and developing what our society would call a psychosis are somewhat less than they would be among ourselves. We might say that the potential psychosis is capitalized by his society and given an evaluated name, which makes such an individual less abnormal in his social environment than he would be with us.

A good actual example of this sort of thing would be the incidence of hysteria among the Eskimo and some of the peoples of Siberia. The calling of the medicine-man is, as a matter of fact, one that requires the ability to put one's self into a hysterical trance. Those who are by nature pre-disposed to that kind of conduct have a better chance of being significant as medicine-men than others. In other words, it would seem that it is not altogether a question of an individual's adjustment to society as such; it is not altogether a matter of society's standing for a generalized act of human values which either make or break the individual. That is looking at the question of adjustment too broadly. It is a question of one's preferential pattern of expression or behavior fitting in or not fitting in so well into the socially transmitted patterns of behavior. . . .

DR. W. I. THOMAS.—Take the Crazy Dog society; what can you say about the severity of exaction of conformity among these ethnological groups in comparison with modern life? Is the strain greater among the groups that you worked with?

DR. SAPIR.—That is a rather large order. I don't quite see how we are going to measure the strain that society imposes upon us. We may feel ourselves living a rather soft and contented and passive life and yet the actual strains will be much greater than we realize. On the other hand, I am not at all sure that even these excessive demands, as we would call them, are felt as severe by the Crazy Dogs of the Plains Indians. Much depends, of course, on the social background. You can project your own estimate of strain of course.

DR. THOMAS.—If it is not felt as strain, it is not strain.

DR. SAPIR.—On the other hand, I don't think it is quite as simple as that either, because undoubtedly there is a very definite tendency to preserve one's life at all costs. There must be a strain caused by the threat of death under set social conditions; otherwise we wouldn't have the neurotic and psychotic breakdown that we do have in our own wars, for instance. I think, by the way, that it would be a very interesting thing to study just such crisis situations among primitive peoples from the psychiatric viewpoint.

DR. LAWSON G. LOWREY.—Do I understand correctly that in those social groups in which there is this seeking of death, there is a strong belief that in that way the individual chiefs have them without further difficulty, so to speak? Is there another complex system that is easily submerged completely in a desire to drive for self-preservation?

DR. SAPIR.—It may be in particular cases.

In the case of the Crazy Dogs of the Plains, I am sure there is no belief in happiness in heaven beyond the happiness accorded to any individual, but simply the feeling of loyalty to one's comrade. Perhaps I ought to explain that in the Crazy Dogs fraternity two or three individuals go out on the warpath, risk the utmost and vow to come back as a group or to stay behind dead as a group; if one dies, the other one or two have to die as well. It seems to me that before you can estimate custom of that kind psychologically, you have to know how strong is the underlying sentiment.

DR. LOWREY.—In both instances, however, you have to do with very strong emotional conditions, which easily have greater value than the single value of life itself.

DR. SAPIR.—Certainly. There would have to be some great value to overcome the mere value of self-preservation.

CHAIRMAN SULLIVAN.—Dr. Sapir, you speak of this formation among these particular Indians, of groups of two and three who are sufficiently closely knit that a survivor would prefer death. That seems to me significant indeed for the understanding of many phenomena with which I deal. As it has appeared to me, so also it seems from some of Dr. [Clifford R.] Shaw's studies that the magnitude of intimate social groups is distinctly limited. I wonder if it would not be valuable to have your views as to just what constitutes these groups —by that I mean the forces. How can we talk about that which constitutes these groups in which survival of the remaining one is not worth the trouble? What binds them together? How do they happen? What has been done to investigate that?

DR. SAPIR.—In the case of the Plains Indians, I think the social background is comparatively easy to understand. The man becomes a man of real importance insofar as he distinguishes himself in war. The greatest value that the Blackfoot or the Sioux Indians recognized was the value of being a distinguished warrior, particularly from the point of view of having been caught in danger, whether actually escaping from it or not. It is rather important that the taking of a scalp isn't really the important thing that it is supposed to be, among these Indians at least. It is rather having been in contact with a live enemy, risking a very great danger. The so-called touching of the enemy with a coupstick is really a sign of greater honor than the getting of the scalp. The getting of the scalp might mean that you simply scalped a slain enemy. There is no particular credit in that as compared with the other. That is, these Indians have constructed for themselves a real value in the courting of danger, regardless of whether they individually survive or not in the pursuit of war.

With that as a sort of obsessive background, and with constant horse raids and other military expeditions undertaken, often, by just a handful of people for the sake of going through this dangerous process, it isn't so difficult to go further and develop the extreme form of military prowess which the Crazy Dogs illustrate. Of course there is much more than that to it.

I am afraid we don't know enough about the social psychology of these patterns of behavior. The meaning of friendship among males, for instance, is a thing that suggests itself as highly important in this society, just as it undoubtedly was in the society of the Spartans and among some of the feudal classes of Japanese. It seems to me this would be well worth looking into.

As to the question to what extent the primary psychology has gone out of the fixed behavior and to what extent it is being revalidated all the time in the lives of particular individuals, I suspect you would find very great differences as you went from individual to individual. Some would follow the pattern very blindly, in a sense unemotionally and unintending; others would realize themselves much more fully in these patterns. It is the same story that we find illustrated among ourselves in religion, for instance. We are all given the opportunity, as it were, for certain typical kinds of religious expression, but few avail themselves significantly of these opportunities.

CHAIRMAN SULLIVAN.—Now you touch upon a problem which seems to be identical, except in matter of approach, with one of the conspicuous situations in the psychiatry of schizophrenia. The sort of rebuff which most of my patients seem to have suffered is in that very field of affection among males. They have not been able to establish the little group that they felt, for a reason that someone might tell us, they should establish. What is the anthropologist's approach to the understanding of that situation in American culture, let us say? How can we arrange any experiment for elucidating that matter?

DR. SAPIR.—Possibly the psychiatrist could contribute much to the enrichment of the anthropologist's study. It looks almost as though there were certain types of human association which crave certain tokens of personal intimacy, and as though there were some societies that granted these tokens more freely than others. One of the very distinctive things about modern American culture is the relative difficulty of establishing highly emotional friendships between males, and between females for that matter. The emphasis is rather on the disruption of too great intimacies of these types. But where society, with a complete distinction of the roles of male and female, rather favors that type of expression, certain individuals at least are provided with an outlet that perhaps saves them from the schizophrenic debauch. It is perfectly possible.

CHAIRMAN SULLIVAN.—In turn the parallelism increases because that is precisely what we do in the mental hospital. We lead to complete distinction of the roles of the male and female and try to set up groupings between intelligent and sensitive employees and psychotic and sensitive patients of the same sex, and it seems to be remarkably successful in reducing the stress and strain of living, and thus in reducing the necessity for psychotic behavior.

DR. SAPIR.—I may mention another detail in regard to the military expeditions of the Plains Indians. It was necessary for those who entered on an expedition to confess all sexual irregularities. If one of the followers had committed adultery with the wife of the leader, he would have to admit that publicly, and no redress could be taken.

CHAIRMAN SULLIVAN.—In the mental hospitals we again parallel these more or less primitive people in that while there is not any public confession, one of the most helpful things about treatment is the acceptance—as having occurred—of the sort of thing that your Indians might be confessing. In other words, in my particular group it becomes common property by tradition that presumably these irregularities happen, and what of it? That situation certainly facilitates the thing that the Indian is required to do—to wit, more or less direct confession; and in psychiatric material it seems to relieve a vast amount of tension, with marked improvement of the patient's adaptability.

DR. THOMAS.—May I ask whether this confession is made in order to assure group solidarity, or as a device for efficiency in the spiritual sense—that is, in a sense, perhaps that if one carried a load of guilt one might not have spiritual cooperation or personal confidence in oneself?

DR. SAPIR.—I am afraid that isn't very easy to answer. The ethnologist is glad to get enough facts together to establish some sort of a case. You can't always get behind the facts and find out the ultimate motivations. Very often questions which are intended to elicit such information are not answered cooperatively, or are not fully understood. Then again you have to deal with the question of tribal rationalization. I think you have a number of problems there that need to be looked into.

DR. THOMAS.—How widespread is confession?

DR. SAPIR.—I couldn't say offhand; it is pretty common among a great many primitive peoples. The Eskimo have it in another form. I think the point is worth looking into. It may have escaped us in many cases. The opportunities for public confession of transgressions, whether sexual or otherwise, is a real ethnological problem. It might very well be worked on in connection with these problems of psychiatry that we are interested in here. We don't know the full extent of the confession pattern, but I think it is widespread in one form or other.

CHAIRMAN SULLIVAN.—Dr. Thomas, if I may go back to your question, what do you see as the distinction between confession as a device to bring about social solidarity and as a device for discharging the feeling of guilt of the individual?

DR. THOMAS.—That is what I was asking Dr. Sapir.

CHAIRMAN SULLIVAN.—It struck me that you asked him "whether or not." Now I am asking you what is the distinction between these two things.

DR. THOMAS.—I had in mind the case of the Eskimo, in which the content is not necessarily sexual but might be the violation of a taboo. You had perhaps eaten seal at the wrong time, and you would be punished if you were not pure from the taboo standpoint.
   May I ask you a question? Does the schizophrenic continuously elaborate the same body of memories or experiences, or does he practice discursive, random fantasy?

CHAIRMAN SULLIVAN.—There is a double process at work. The same sort of problem seems to preoccupy many, but an enormous amount of irrelevant trivialities can be involved in the process of, first, occupying one's self and thereby evading an insoluble problem, and secondly, in reaching out, sort of groping for solutions of the insoluble problem. Do I make myself clear?

DR. THOMAS.—But the core is the same?

CHAIRMAN SULLIVAN.—Oh, yes. For example, on six different days one patient of mine who was very sick, on three occasions progressed immediately from an approach to a certain fairly concrete problem of his to a discussion of the unsatisfactory character of the shoes that he was wearing, and on the three other occasions, progressed to something which was accidentally more convenient, in one case the fact that the telephone rang. The point is that it is at a certain particular moment when a certain content is before him that he seizes upon these trivialities.

Before we go on with that, to go back to this question of confession as a means of securing group solidarity and confession as a means of discharging a feeling of guilt, it is my perhaps overindividualized belief that these are identical. I would particularly like to hear from the people who are working with children, with people who are not nearly as elaborate as the adults we are discussing, to see if they find anything which distinguishes the feeling of guilt from what it seems to me to be, namely, a socially originated entity, a thing thrust upon the individual by the traditions and standards of the people with whom he is adjusting. . . .

9

Commentary

BETWEEN October 12, and November 9, 1929, Sullivan gave a series of five lectures at the Sheppard and Enoch Pratt Hospital, which are referred to as the Farewell Lectures.[1] These lectures, mimeographed and privately circulated, contain the first full-fledged statement of Sullivan's theoretical position and, in essence, form the first two chapters of the unpublished book manuscript, *Personal Psychopathology*.[2]

The next paper represents a summary statement of Sullivan's work at Sheppard in respect to the relation between onset and prognosis in schizophrenia. The Discussion of this paper is included, since it gives Sullivan an opportunity to stress the fact that acute stormy onset of schizophrenia, whether or not it is recognized by the patient's family, is a favorable prognostic sign at the time that the patient finally comes to the attention of a physician, even if this takes place several years later.

Since this paper is the first one written after Sullivan's move to New York City, it seems appropriate to pause briefly and consider the nature of the move from Baltimore to New York City. In reviewing Sullivan's work, it is clear that the Baltimore years had a flavor of their own. He was 38 years old when he went to New York City; his reputation as a clinician had gone before him, and he was never again free from the pressures of his clinical fame; he still found time for research, teaching, and a variety of "remedial attempts" in the society at large, but he engaged in such work while maintaining an increasingly heavy clinical load.

[1] Sullivan officially left Sheppard in June, 1930.
[2] An excerpt from this manuscript is the final paper in this book.

The years in Baltimore and at Sheppard had been busy ones, but they permitted Sullivan a certain freedom to develop a variety of interests—for instance, in printing and publishing. In 1928, Sullivan had acted as editor of the *American Journal of Psychiatry* for three issues, substituting for the Editor, Edward N. Brush, M.D. In this way, he came in contact with Mr. Donald Reeve at the Lord Baltimore Press, who was actively involved in bringing out the *Journal*. Sullivan became infatuated with the idea of bringing out his own journal; and he spent many happy hours exploring with Don Reeve the readability and aesthetic appeal of various fonts, the advantages of a two-column page for a technical journal, paper specifications, and so on. Reeve has described Sullivan as energetic and determined in pursuing what seemed, at the time, a pipe dream. Eventually Sullivan came up with several elaborate job proposals; in this way, as Reeve described it, Sullivan became known to various rival printers in the area, as he flew around the city in a "classy, yellow Franklin with an air-cooled engine," getting competitive bids on what seemed nebulous projects. Incidentally, one of these pipe dreams became a reality in 1938 with the first issue of the journal *Psychiatry*, printed by the Lord Baltimore Press on yellow paper with double columns— in many ways as classy and as much of an innovation as the Franklin.

In the Baltimore years, Sullivan also began his career as an editorial writer and book reviewer; from 1926 on, Sullivan's fine Irish-American hand is found on many pages of the *American Journal of Psychiatry*. Three book reviews will be mentioned briefly as examples of this work. In a review of Znaniecki's *Laws of Social Psychology*,[3] there is clear evidence that many of Sullivan's postulates as formulated in his final theory of psychiatry were closely related to Znaniecki's approach; social action is seen as *interaction* "in and within the individual-environment complex," for instance. In a second review, Sullivan looks at Norman Fenton's book on *Shell Shock and Its Aftermath*,[4] based on a study of 3,000 patients from World War I. Fenton's finding that the "liability to neurotic symptoms is practically universal" is quoted by Sullivan and is an interesting datum for Sul-

[3] *Amer. J. Psychiatry* (1927–28) 84:674–685. Review: Florian Znaniecki, *The Laws of Social Psychology*; Univ. of Chicago Press, 1925.
[4] *Amer. J. Psychiatry* (1927–28) 84:367–368. Review: Norman Fenton, *Shell Shock and Its Aftermath*; St. Louis: Mosby Co., 1926.

livan's growing conviction that we are all more alike than different. Fenton's book was also probably tributary, in some part, to Sullivan's decision to undertake work on the relationship between schizophrenia and the obsessional disorders—a study which formally began with his move to New York City and his first extensive encounter with neurotic patients, in private practice. A third review is of the Blantons' work with new-born and young infants at Johns Hopkins.[5] Sullivan approves of the fact that the Blantons disperse "the myth of will power" and postulate the learning of the infant through muscle tensions. He also takes occasion to note that "the fetish of inheritance [is] the lazy man's retreat." Many of these book reviews are long and detailed; through them, one has the opportunity to read over Sullivan's shoulder as he carefully sorts out knowledge which will prove useful to him in the productive years ahead.

[5] *Amer. J. Psychiatry* (1927–28) 84:166–168. Review: Smiley Blanton and Margaret Gray Blanton, *Child Guidance;* New York: The Century Company, 1927.

The Relation of Onset to Outcome in Schizophrenia†

Introduction

THE writer will assume that the concept of schizophrenia has been stripped of an implication of inevitable chronicity and deterioration. He will not accept recovery as "remission" or "arrest," but instead will hold that an individual who has undergone a schizophrenic illness, ceased to show schizophrenic processes, and resumed social living with a gradual expansion of life-interests, has in fact to the limit of the meaning of such terms actually *recovered* from the schizophrenic illness. Having noted that such recoveries are by no means infrequent, he will then offer some tentative notions bearing upon crude observational factors seemingly sequents of the favorable outcome, and useful to the psychiatrist who cannot engage in any detailed study of his patients.

Review of Cases

In the seven years during which the research staff of the Sheppard and Enoch Pratt Hospital has been occupied with the problem of schizophrenia in males, about two hundred and fifty patients have been subjected to more or less elaborate investigation. To simplify this orientation, the discussion will be limited

† Reprinted from *Schizophrenia [Dementia Praecox]: An Investigation of the Most Recent Advances* 10:111–118; Baltimore: Williams & Wilkins, 1931.

to the first hundred, of whom fairly dependable correlations of the crude (nonstatistical) sort can be made. This hundred occur in the first one hundred and fifty-five serial admissions. Fifty-five patients were eliminated from this study for the following reasons: (*a*) defective information coupled with failure of the physician to establish satisfactory contact with the patient, 30 patients; (*b*) mentally defective patients coupled with defective information, 11 patients; (*c*) schizophrenic nature of the illness questioned (often in earlier admission elsewhere), 14 patients. In other words, there is useful data in 64.5 per cent of the consecutive male schizophrenic admissions. This higher percentage results in part from such factors as the hospital's policy and prestige, so that the patient-material cannot be held to be a representative cross-section of the general schizophrenic population. Many of the notions derived from this study, therefore, may or may not be of general application. The positive conclusions, however, which are the subject of this paper, must be accepted as only very modestly related to defects of the clinical sample, and as generally valid.

Of the one hundred cases on which comment is made herein, the onset of mental illness was insidious in twenty-two. In other words, in each of these twenty-two individuals, there was a life-course in which the patient underwent no dramatic separation from ordinary living, but instead became gradually more and more peculiar until finally, by reason of some more or less spectacular occurrence, his mental illness was recognized. In no one of these was the prolonged phase of insidious divorcement from approximate mental health a matter that was overlooked because of the indifference or stupidity of the persons making up the environment. The insidious characteristic of the change may be accepted as genuine.

Of these patients, a liberal figure for those improved is seven. That is, less than 32 per cent of these patients showed marked modification of the processes towards that state of approximate mental health. Of the seven, two patients are in perhaps as good mental health as is the general population, three are definitely paranoid states, one is a defective without psychosis, and one is decidedly reduced in the interest and activity range.

Of the basic one hundred patients, the onset of schizophrenic mental illness was acute in seventy-eight cases. In other words, in each of these seventy-eight individuals, there was a life-course in which the patient underwent a rather abrupt change in behavior and expressed thought such that the personal environment was emphatically impressed by his transition from a state of approximate mental health to one of mental disorder. Of these, forty-eight, or somewhat over 61 per cent, have shown marked improvement; in a considerable number, the change has amounted to a recovery from the mental disorder.

Of the thirty patients in whom the onset of grave illness was acute, but improvement did not follow, the following data may be of interest: four are dead, two having killed themselves; four are defectives, two of whom improved greatly under care, but relapsed to grave disorder under social pressure after discharge. In two instances, the illness appeared late in life; these are now both in chronic paranoid states. Nine younger patients have progressed into chronic paranoid states from which recovery is not to be expected, since the disorder is preferable to the real situations to which the patient might hope to return. In five hebephrenic cases, deteriorating processes are evident—one at least as a result of errors in the psychiatric handling of the patient. Another one progressed swiftly into a dilapidated paranoid state, but continued subacutely ill for some years, killed a bystander while on parole, and was in turn killed by a policeman. This was the fifth death in the group. Of the remaining five, one has had recurrent waves of psychosis over a period of about eleven years, and is rather badly disintegrated; one has been in a subacute catatonic state with great hostility to the personal environment—a form of paranoid state, according to a descriptive psychiatrist—for about four years; one slipped into the acute psychosis owing to the extraordinary fragility of his personality, which had been held to some semblance of integration only by a quite bizarre disregard for ordinary standards, coupled with a wife willing to co-operate in his extraordinarily perverse *modus vivendi;* another is a subacute catatonic of several years duration, tending strongly to paranoid maladjustment, also the result of poor therapy on the part of the writer; the fifth is a man singularly handicapped by physical factors, who stumbled along until about thirty-six years of age before failure, and has little indeed to recover to—he is progressing into a paranoid state.

Impervious barriers generally keep one from establishing rudimentary interpersonal relations with the unfavorable patient of insidious onset. This is probably a direct result to be expected from consideration of the environmental personal situation in which the personalities had their development. In the seven cases of improvement after the insidious onset, to which reference is made above, a rather good superficial contact was established with six of them. One proved to be of extraordinary intellectual equipment, who had had only a small number of truly schizophrenic processes in the course of an insidious deviation from conventional life, towards a life of extreme radicalism. He underwent partial psychoanalysis and is now studying medicine. Another was of decidedly superior intellectual equipment, had very few schizophrenic processes, but early retired from active social life and efforts towards achievement. He has been gainfully employed for two years or so. Another is a seriously defective boy *in whom the onset had been acute*, but in the course of such chronic maladjusted living that the change did not impress the personal environment. He made a "transference cure" of low grade and has been working for about a year. He thus comes to belong among those cases of acute onset, but is reported here because of the *apparently* insidious onset.

The Significance of the Type of Onset

In brief, an insidious onset of schizophrenic processes is of much more grave omen as to outcome than is an abrupt onset. Two theoretical considerations may be advanced in this connection. Either the insidious disorder is *different from* the acute, or the personality distortion underlying the insidious onset is more severe, although of similar nature to the distortion underlying the acute onset. Moore [1] has presented some evidence derived from statistical operations with tetrad differences, pointing to the

[1] T. V. Moore, "The Empirical Determination of Certain Syndromes Underlying Praecox and Manic-depressive Psychoses," *Amer. J. Psychiatry* (1929-30) 86:719-738.

existence of a syndrome of "cognitive defect" positively related
to so-called praecox conditions. This author finds that "cognitive
defect" has positive correlation with "what are probably two
phases of dementia praecox: the uninhibited and the catatonic."
This is taken to move the "praecox" disorders off into the realm
of neurologically founded maladies. It is easy to divide the material under consideration into "praecox" illnesses based on organic pathology and "schizophrenic" illnesses based on functional
pathology. The division, however, is irrational and unprofitable,
for some of the former cases recorded a good measure of mental
health just as did most of the latter. In other words, in frankly
defective patients, undergoing severe and relatively typical schizophrenic processes,[2] nothing fully distinctive from extraordinarily
talented individuals suffering schizophrenia has appeared in this
investigation.

Moore's syndrome includes the "shut-in" personality factor.
This inclusion results from mathematical operations, and not directly from descriptive psychiatric procedures. How does the
material under discussion bear on the "shut-in" factor? Taking
the forty-eight patients in whom the onset was acute and recovery considerable, there are, roughly, thirty-six clearly negative and twelve more or less positive. Taking the thirty of acute
onset without material recovery, there are, again roughly, ten
showing what might be described as a "shut-in personality." Of
the seventy-eight acute onsets, then, fifty-six did not impress the
writer as occurring in personalities to be placed under the rubric
of "shut-in." The question arises as to those showing insidious
onset. Of the twenty-two, there were fourteen distinctly "shut-
in"; these did not include any of those that actually improved
markedly.[3]

---

[2] In other words, not typical "psychoses with mental deficiency." [See
Statistical Manual for Use of Institutions for the Insane, prepared by the
American Psychiatric Association; N.Y.: National Committee for Mental
Hygiene, 1918.]
[3] If all defectives are to be accepted as, by definition, "shut-in," then
these figures are subject to revision, for several of the mentally defective
patients did not impress the writer as having shown a "shut-in" personality.

Comment

Very briefly, quite in keeping with the work of Edward J. Kempf and with the other findings of the Sheppard study, a crude correlative study such as that any hurried psychiatrist might make, indicates that an acute dramatic divorcement from more or less commonplace living is of good prognostic omen in schizophrenic illnesses. This sort of psychotic onset implies a personality that has *grown farther* towards adulthood than is the case with insidious illnesses. In this is the factor of promise. The acute onset means that one is dealing with a personality integration that has gone on a long distance in spite of the dissociated homosexual cravings or the masturbation conflict from which the illness has finally taken origin. It, therefore, includes a good deal that can be re-integrated into a "going concern." The insidious onset means that the growth of the personality has failed long before the hospital admission, and that there is relatively much less that is useful for a re-integration of anything like an average life-situation. Disregarding all the factual material which can be elicited in psychopathological study of individual patients, one is justified in prognosticating on the acuteness of the divorcement from reality in the schizophrenic illness, and may give a heavy favorable weighing to the dramatic outcropping of the psychosis. The chances for "recovery or remission from dementia praecox" are alleged to be in the neighborhood of one in four or five of the younger patient. This may be amplified by saying that the chances for recovery are twice as good in the patient of acute onset as in the one insidiously separated from reality.

Discussion

The following questions submitted to Dr. Sullivan before the Commission, together with the answers to them, are here reported verbatim.

DR. STRECKER—In Dr. Sullivan's excellent presentation, I was particularly interested in the fact—and I take it this is the point of the paper—that what has been designated as an acute stormy onset is a relatively favorable prognostic sign. It is an old observation and one which I think is well borne out in clinical practice.

The other point is that I do not think we should be too much disturbed about what might be called the criteria of restitution. I wonder if some of our disturbed frame of mind about the matter is not due to the fact that we tend to lean over backwards in regard to the possibility of favorable outcomes. In discussing my presentation at the meeting of the Association when this subject was previously presented,[1] Dr. Jelliffe put it very well when he said that every one of us, not only these restituted patients but every one of us found it necessary to carry a mental potato with which to get on in life. By that he meant (referring to the old Irish superstition of carrying a potato to ward off rheumatism) that we all needed perhaps a crutch or two. Now, when we ourselves need that sort of help, which we extract from our environment as best we can to meet our individual needs, it seems hardly fair that we should expect the ex-schizophrenic patient to get on without anything at all. Therefore, I should like to point out that we should not be too rigid in our definition of what constitutes restitution.

DR. SULLIVAN—Dr. Strecker's comment, stating the point, if any, of my talk, requires reply. I shall also amplify my presentation, although I had intended nothing more than a crude prognostic indication for general use. As to the prevailing notion regarding the type of onset and outcome, not only does an acute stormy outlook indicate a relatively good prognosis, but an acute stormy onset is frequently overlooked or unrecognized by members of the patient's family. It is the character of the onset as it actually occurred in the patient that bears on the outcome. Sometimes the outcropping of schizophrenic phenomena is very clearly reproduced by the patient and shows an abrupt appearance of the abnormal content. This may have occurred when his behavior was not observed to be seriously disordered. The prognosis in such cases is good. The consideration of the sufficiency of the exciting situation seems to me to be practically of very little value to the institutional psychiatrist. I have attempted in other studies to show that the sufficiency of the exciting situation is an almost irrelevant consideration—certainly one on which I would accept the patient's opinion rather than that of the investigating psychiatrist. Since the insidious onset does not arise out of an "exciting situation," this consideration is wholly irrelevant, in every sense, to the group of patients in whom, in my opinion, the prognosis is most gloomy.

As long as I am led to touch upon the dynamics of the schizophrenic break, I feel that I should mention certain considerations which have appeared to me to be valid and which I presented at a recent meeting of the New York Neurological Society. Study of the life history of a considerable number of people, including those patients men-

[1] E. A. Strecker and G. F. Wiley, "Prognosis in Schizophrenia," in *Schizophrenia* [*Dementia Praecox*] (1925) 5:403-431.

tioned in the present paper, has convinced me that the onset of schizophrenia can frequently be divided into two stages. A considerable number of people experience the first step towards schizophrenic phenomena a considerable time before the psychosis makes its appearance. The interval between the initial *stadium* and the appearance of psychotic experience may be a matter of moments or the matter of a lifetime. I call the first stage the collapse of the individual world synthesis.

Individuals come to a certain age with a body of what I suppose one might describe as implicit assumptions about themselves and the universe. We all depend upon a large number of things that we are really not justified in depending upon, but we have never had any reason to suspect them. The sun rises pretty regularly and our alarm clocks work if we give them a chance, and so on and so forth. A great body of assumptions is the foundation upon which our life processes rest. In a remarkable number of adolescents, however, there comes a time when their faith in this background of implicit assumptions about their own abilities or about the consistency of the universe, and so on, is abruptly shattered. Then, instead of building the rationalizations as we do when someone points out that we have been an ass, these individuals go on feeling terribly upset about things. From that time on, instead of building the sort of rationalizations with which we heal the wounds to our self-respect and all that sort of thing, these people are different from what they were before. Perhaps I might mention three or four groups. In one case the individual becomes a superficial individual from then on; he deals with social contacts in what we call a sort of hysterical fashion; he has all sorts of enthusiasms and distresses and what-not, but acquaintance with him shows that this is just a sort of surface play. In another instance the individual becomes retiring, secretive, he seeks a much more restricted environment and avoids all social contacts. As a third case I might perhaps mention the resort to a wild compensatory program, this often leading to schizophrenia.

I believe we can isolate by further study a type of situation which I will call the first stage of schizophrenia (because it is so very frequently associated with the second or definite schizophrenia), in which there is a rapid loss of faith in the self and the universe, without the remedial maladjustments or actual remedial processes which go on with most of us when we receive a severe bump in life. Such situations are not, however, in any necessary close association with the gradual separation of the individual from reality, of which I have spoken.

Briefly, the second stage of schizophrenia, as it has become formulated in my mind, is somewhat as follows. The individual, with serious impairment of the dependability of his self and the universe progresses into a situation in which the dissociated parts of his personality are the effective integrating agencies. The factors which he experiences are then of two varieties. He lives the sort of life to which he is accustomed; this under the domination of the accepted egoistic structure. And he has from momentary to extended intervals during which the experience which he is having is dominated by the dissociated systems. The result is a condition which I cannot distinguish by any important characteristic from that undergone by an individual in attempting to orient himself on awakening in the midst of a vivid nightmare. To all of this condition I apply the term incipient schizophrenia. If it goes on, the clinical picture becomes that of catatonic illness. So far as I can see, an individual may remain in this state of difficulty almost indefinitely. On the other hand, he may, as a result of appropriate experience, undergo one of three changes—this at any time in the course of a catatonic illness of any duration. An integration may begin between the dissociated and the dissociating systems of his personality—in which case all proceeds toward recovery. A massive transference of blame may occur, as a result of which he progresses into a chronic paranoid state, the particular type of which is related in a simple fashion to the conflicting systems. Or there may be a dilapidation of the dissociating system and a regression of interest and impulses to an early childhood or infantile level—in which case we see what is called hebephrenic dilapidation.

You will notice that my considerations imply that a gradual detachment from reality, occurring rather early in the evolution of personality, follows an ominous course quite distinct from that of the more dramatic type to which I have invited your attention. Further, that in the latter connection, it has appeared to me from study of the problem, that so-called hebephrenic and paranoid præcox illnesses are separate processes from the essential schizophrenia, incipient or catatonic.

10

Commentary

THE NEXT two papers are companion pieces, both written during the same period. The first paper, "Environmental Factors in Etiology and Course Under Treatment of Schizophrenia," was delivered to a general medical audience and is less well known than the second, "Socio-Psychiatric Research." The latter, delivered to an audience of "psychiatrists and mental hygienists," is an oft-cited minor classic in psychiatry and sociology. In it, Sullivan states emphatically—and sometimes with sardonic humor—the essential social psychological or interpersonal nature of schizophrenic illness and treatment. In both papers, he proposes the use of convalescent camps for transition from hospital to community and eventually as a substitute for the mental hospital, particularly for the care of young patients.

Environmental Factors in Etiology and Course Under Treatment of Schizophrenia†

As a result of some years' study of male patients suffering from schizophrenic mental disorders, I am inclined to the opinion that the occurrence of these illnesses is to be explained on the basis of experiential factors rather than by reference to an hereditary, or to a primarily organic, disorder. In other words, certain people, when caught up in the course of certain events, undergo a change in total activity, behavior and thought, to that which we call the schizophrenic psychosis. Two considerations immediately arise: Are these people average people, or are they instead people *predisposed* by innate constitutional factors to such an illness? Again: Are there certain "necessary" organic predisposing factors, vicious physiological functioning, disease, morbidity of the endocrine functions, or the like, that constitute a "morbid disposition," in turn the "fundamental disturbance" in schizophrenia? I shall offer a provisional answer to these questions in the shape of the following formula: It may be that only certain of the various combinations of constitution determiners may permit the final occurrence of schizophrenia, but the particular constitutional situations that are permissive of schizophrenia are probably widespread among the general population, and only a

† Reprinted from *Medical Journal and Record* (1931) 133:19–22.

small part of those *capable* of undergoing schizophrenic processes come to such an illness. Secondly: Intercurrent illnesses, certain intoxications, and perhaps certain endocrine dyscrasias (e.g., hypothyroidism), may be factors determining the failure of the individual to handle the events that precipitate the illness. Any factor, innate or intercurrent, which effects a serious limitation in one's facilities for biological adjustive action, may and does predispose to mental disorder, mild or severe. That we can go further than this along the lines of either a specific constitutional or a somatological determination of schizophrenic illness, I do not believe. There are probably only *some* young people that are reasonably apt to undergo a schizophrenic psychosis; of this number, however, only a small portion ever do so undergo the grave mental disorder. Hereditary and somatological factors are probably contributory, but may prove, when finally we learn to measure them, to be so general in their occurrence among the population as to be of but slight importance.

Following on the great systematization of Kraepelin by which the schizophrenic (or dementia praecox) disorders were distinguished from the manic-depressive psychosis, Jung and Bleuler, under the inspiration of Freud, worked out the psychogenetic nature of many of the schizophrenic symptoms, while, in America, Adolf Meyer propounded the dynamic conception of schizophrenia. After a quarter of a century, however, Bleuler still teaches of a "certain predisposition of the brain [which] . . . in schizophrenia seems to be a progressive disease," [1] as the *cause* of the disorders. While I do not comprehend his argument in this connection, and am indeed much more impressed by the late Charles B. Dunlap's negative autopsy findings than by any of the numerous crop of "specific dementia praecox lesions" reported from time to time, it is not relevant to my present theme to marshal evidence against the 'disease' doctrine. The enlightened *Journal of the American Medical Association*, somewhat amusingly, referred in a recent editorial to the psychogenetic and dynamic approach to understanding "mental disease" as

---

[1] See the abstract by Dr. E. Bleuler of his December 1929 address before the Massachusetts Psychiatric Society; *Amer. J. Psychiatry* (1929–30) 86:203–211.

"conveniently designated as psychogenetic philosophies," "savoring of the nonmedical, if not unmedical," against which it is necessary to "keep the banners of medicine over the mentally ill." The fact is that until medical training is made to include some information about human living, there will continue to be plenty of armchair philosophizing about "brain diseases" and "lesions" (with the "neurologizing tautology" criticized by Meyer) on the part of our numerous nonpsychiatric psychiatrists and helpfully inclined medical men, generally. Bleuler, and, for that matter, anyone seriously concerned with the study of actual schizophrenic patients, knows that improvements "up to what is practically a recovery" do occur, that the "psychic" treatment accorded the patient has an important relation to the outcome in *some* cases, and that "all attempts to separate deteriorating forms from nondeteriorating ones have failed." For the resolute believer in underlying organic disease, then, this paper may be taken to refer to the numerous *favorable* cases, which he cannot isolate among those whom he sees.

The etiology of a schizophrenic illness is to be sought in events that involve the individual. The significant events seem to me to lie wholly within one category—viz., events relating the individual with other individuals more or less highly significant to him. Interrelation with significant people constitutes the most difficult sort of action required of us. People are decidedly the hardest things we have to deal with. Not only does this task require a great amount of skill learning, but also the full value of achievement at this task does not begin clearly to appear to the individual until he is in the second decade of life. While one may have learned very well the management of his parents and other more or less authoritarian figures in childhood and the juvenile era, it is only after the appearance of a real need for interpersonal intimacy (which ushers in preadolescence) that one finds himself called upon to develop delicate adjustments of his own to and with another personality.

This personality, the entity that has to enter into interpersonal relations, if one (or more) of the most powerful of our biologic drives is to be satisfied, is to a great extent a product of culture. By this I mean that it is chiefly composed of experience with people and with the traditions, customs, and fashions produced by people. The human neonate is marvelously equipped with the rapidly growing rudiments of apparatus for dealing with situations and integrating itself with very complex environments. In other words, once matured, the human integrative apparatus can function with a great number of highly diversified factors. A very large part of these many factors that every person comes finally to integrate into situations is of the nature of culture, indirectly factors of other people. In the first months of extrauterine life, unless he be an idiot, the infant will learn a great deal of the most pervading culture of the parents, particularly the mother. In the first three or four years, he will have acquired so much of this that he is apt to be from thence on a "typical American," or an "Italian," or an "East Side boy," or whatever. In other words, before he enters even the nursery school or the kindergarten, he is very largely a cultural product. Moreover, the part of the cultural heritage that has been built into him is of a primitive and infantile character; it is not likely ever to be the subject of any more adult type of thought—e.g., of rational deliberation. And some of this very primitive material is also of high emotional value; it has been transmitted with much expressed (and empathized [2]) feeling on the part of the parents or their equivalents. In these particulars, it is different from most of the later cultural acquisitions. The school and playground experience is susceptible of more or less conscious consideration, and of a measure of valuational reappraisal. In other words, later group experience is of not nearly so final a form or of such extreme import within the personality; it is much more easily reorganized on the basis of subsequent experience.

There is within the personality a system of experience to which we apply the terms, the ego, or the self. This is built up of all the factors of experience that we have in which significant other people "respond" to us. In other words, our self is made up of the reflections of our personality that we have encountered

[2] By *empathy*, I refer to the emotional linkage existing between the mother and infant. For a discussion of the general evolutionary course of personality, and of the importance of empathically conditioned "primitive genital phobia," see my forthcoming *Personal Psychopathology: The Pathology of Interpersonal Relations*.

mirrored in those with whom we deal. Its most primitive, and perhaps its most important, part is contributed by the mother and/or her equivalents, nurses and the like. Very important complementary or supplementary parts are contributed by the father and/or his equivalents. These parts, in so far as they are infantile in character, are extremely inaccessible and resistant to change by later experience. If they are too far removed from resemblance to later accretion to the self, the growth of the personality will be seriously distorted, and the individual may come to have that extraordinary organization to which we refer as psychopathic personality. If the deviations are less grave they may take, in boys, the form of a continuing rather childish or juvenile appraisal of the self as it is reflected by the mother. To these people, a weaning from an attitude of unique dependency on the mother is very difficult. An incorporation of her value attitudes is the rule. A progression of values to a proper placement of girls as objects of interest does not occur. Either the mother only, of all women, or only older women, are eligible to him for interpersonal intimacies. He cannot progress smoothly to the biologically ordained heterosexual goal. When such a person comes to the time of outcropping of the need for close interpersonal relations, he may be found very badly crippled: he may not be equal to integrating the interpersonal relations with boys necessary for a normal "gang" life. So grave a handicap is, fortunately, relatively infrequent. The handicap in the evolution of personality, and in particular in the sorts of experience sought by the self—the things one wants to undergo—generally shows most restrictively in the next stage of personality growth—viz., the progression to heterosexual activity. The morbid youths to whom schizophrenic illnesses are likely to occur, often succeed measurably in the preadolescent socialization, become members of a gang, and may even proceed to great intimacy with some other youth. They may achieve a good measure of success in this interpersonal field, being perhaps very popular with other boys—even, sometimes, leaders. Quite often, however, their success in the preadolescent socialization is but mediocre.

After the coming of frank genital sexuality that initiates mid- or true adolescence, these people begin to have serious troubles.

If they have established good status among their compeers, it is now necessary that they proceed to become interested in girls. Their personality organization precludes the growth of such interests, and their status is thereby endangered. They must do something to preserve their self-respect. They must resort to extensive subterfuge of the nature of a fictitious sexual life; they must segregate themselves out of the general gang and continue a nonheterosexual sociality with similarly handicapped individuals —in which case, owing to the increasing pressure of the sexual drives, they are apt rapidly to proceed toward an homosexual modus vivendi; or they must get out of it all and regress toward an earlier type of interpersonal living, a new dependence on the parental and related adult environment.

It is in this group of persons that we seem to find all schizophrenics. I have come to believe that in peacetime no one becomes schizophrenic who has achieved a really satisfactory sexual integration with another person of comparable status. If the individual achieves, even once, an interpersonal intimacy primarily sexual in motivation, in which there is neither a gross discrepancy in social status of the persons concerned, nor a body of complex "extra" processes of the shape of hysterical dissociations, projection of blame, feelings of guilt, or the like, then in the ensuing satisfaction of the sexual impulses, the individual, it seems to me, achieves both a long step towards adulthood, and a great measure of safety from the sort of processes that go to make up the schizophrenic illnesses. He has convincingly demonstrated to himself his competence at the technics of interpersonal intimacy necessary for comparative mental health, and will, in all likelihood, be able to handle most of the problems that life brings him with a sufficient measure of self-respect.

If the progress of adolescence includes a severe rebuff in interpersonal relations, and there is warp of the personality of the type indicated above, the outcropping of schizophrenic processes is apt to occur. If the personality is rather well developed in fields other than those making for sexual intimacies of the fully adjustive (equal status) kind, then, while the break may be preceded by a long period of increased stress, it will be rather abrupt and acute in type. If there has been grave warping, such, for example, that the boy has retired from the realities of interpersonal relations to the juvenile world of authoritarian adults, then the schizophrenic processes are apt to make their appearance insidiously, and an acute outcropping of psychosis is not seen.[3]

Even after the schizophrenic processes are clearly in evidence, there is continued striving for self-respect, for status reflecting to the self from other significant people. Under the bizarre panoply of phenomena that make up the incipient and the (continuing) catatonic psychosis (which is closely related to the phenomenology of sleep), there goes on a struggle for status. The course of the illness is largely a product of the personal relations into which the patient enters voluntarily or in which he is forced to participate. He recovers if the schizophrenic processes lead to a repair of the personality warp, an escape from the old deviations toward a more normal evolution. If he is of a certain history, or if the persons dealing with him particularly facilitate such a development, the true schizophrenic illness progresses into a paranoid state, in which only so much of schizophrenic processes continues to be in evidence as deal with those drives of the patient that he cannot project by transference of blame. If there is nothing to which his bizarre interpersonal processes seem to attach, or if he is brutally discouraged by those who have come to be significant to him and yet cannot discharge the situation by exteriorizing blame on them, then a profound regression of interest takes place, and he becomes preoccupied with early childhood or late infantile activity-patterns, and we call him hebephrenic.

Obviously, if this formulation is even approximately correct, the persons with whom the schizophrenic patient is brought into contact are of very great importance in determining the course and outcome of his illness. And, *passim*, the persons peculiarly significant in the situation in which the onset of illness occurred are not likely to be helpful in the acute stages of the psychosis. A considerable body of actual experience in the institutional care of acutely schizophrenic males within the age group fourteen to

[3] That there is a peculiarly bad omen to be associated with insidious onset of schizophrenic illnesses is suggested in my brief note "The Relations of Onset to Outcome in Schizophrenia."

twenty-five has seemed to confirm both of these deductions. I have come to feel that the personality qualifications of all those with whom the acute schizophrenic patient comes in contact should be the primary consideration in any attempt to achieve good results from treatment. It has been demonstrated again and again that a great deal of good work is easily ruined by even brief contact of the patient with unsuitable personnel. This consideration often dictates the elimination of visits by relatives and the like and a restriction of visits to relatively neutral and intelligent friends only, during the acute stages of the illness. This sort of segregation, with restriction of the personal contacts of the patient to highly qualified personnel in a receiving service to which he is sent immediately on admission to the mental hospital, seems to be a very promising step toward the conservation of these patients.

Teamwork by all those concerned in the treatment of the acutely schizophrenic patient is essential. It is unfortunately all too true that personality is not a product of one's good intentions adopted rather well on in life. The capacity of subprofessional personnel to do more than intend well by the patient is a product of their personality established in turn in the years before they have become interested in caring for the mentally sick. The *sine qua non* of the successful receiving service in the mental hospital thus comes to be not alone teamwork inspired by appreciation of the significance of personal factors in the course of these illnesses, but also the careful selection of qualified personnel, with the exclusion of undesirable persons, however well-meaning.

Given a coordinated group of physician and subprofessional personnel—nursing, physiotherapeutic, recreational, and occupational—and all these of a personality organization suited for dealing with schizophrenics, one can certainly achieve results that are at complete variance (at least in cases of acute onset) with the traditional poor prognosis of the schizophrenic. True, it is unfortunate that the work of such a unit cannot be extended into the postinstitutional life of the convalescent patient, for all too many of them are taken back to a morbid situation, and this often happens before the patient has consolidated enough insight to enable him to avoid immediate damage—and frequently, recurrence. I suppose it will be a very long time before the public is educated to a rational view of mental disorder, with corollary willingness to be guided by good psychiatric advice. The distance of this much to be desired enlightenment is the greater in that, until the general practitioner has been rid of the older views concerning the schizophrenic psychoses, a reform in the direction even of good institutional care is all but impractical, and the demonstration of curability of these disorders will continue to be the exception rather than the rule in the larger hospitals.

When the general medical view shall have been reorganized along the lines I have indicated, the situation should change rapidly for the better. With this change, we may hope for the creation of convalescent camps and communities, in which the youth involved in the grave disorders of schizophrenia can pause long enough after leaving the institution to secure himself in meeting future interpersonal problems. Moreover, with this change in medical viewpoint, I surmise we shall have accomplished a great step toward the prevention of schizophrenia and toward the prompt restoration of incipient cases without the necessity of resorting to the ominous treatment by institutionalization.

If the medical curriculum comes finally to include as a fundamental an intensive training in the "psychogenetic philosophies" bearing on interpersonal relations, and psychobiological entities such as self-respect, submission and dominance, sexual tendencies and repressions, social status, group solidarities, traditions, customs and fashions, economic factors, and surfaces of human distribution as to factors of sociality, introversion, intelligence, and the like, then, and only then, the physician will be trained for his role in the management of preschizophrenic and incipiently schizophrenic individuals. In that fair day, the practitioner will deal with somatic ideology as such, instead of giving "medical" or "surgical" treatment for hypochondriacally (or otherwise psychogenetically) determined complaints about eyes, ears, nose, throat, heart, stomach, bowels, or genitals. He will have at least as much respect for concrete human personality as has his present-day representative for immune bodies, vitamins, and autocoids. He will know that if John Brown believes he is suffering some "loss of manhood" in his sleep, a "suggestion" as to the absurdity of the belief is *not* the remedy; but instead, that he must aid in searching out the factors ensuing in the belief. He will know that he serves no useful purpose in perpetuating among his patients the superstitions of his own forefathers, and so may be of some use to sufferers of autoerotic and other sexual difficulties. In fine, he will approximate the ideal of the psychopathologist, and function to remove personal handicaps, physical *or* mental, to the end that personal efficiency rather than mere somatic efficiency becomes the reward of consulting him, and the adolescent patient finds in him a guide to mental health.

We must give a large measure of new attention to the psychobiology and psychopathology of interpersonal relations, with admitted respect for questions of constitution and questions of physical health, but without the prevailing oversight of the fact that the patient is a *person* striving to live among persons, and susceptible, perhaps oversusceptible, of influence by interpersonal factors.

Socio-Psychiatric Research

ITS IMPLICATIONS FOR THE SCHIZOPHRENIA
PROBLEM AND FOR MENTAL HYGIENE †

WE MEET here in the capital of a country perhaps in the vanguard of a world-movement for the dissemination of information, to discuss problems the exact nature of which may or may not be comprehensive even to those who wish to communicate information to their audience. I am under an extraordinary handicap in the more-than-ordinarily handicapped business of psychiatric and mentally hygienic intercommunication, in that I can scarcely present to you in a brief paper various explanatory matter needed for a basic grasp of my hyphenated subject; *viz., socio-psychiatric* research. I am finding it difficult to compress the comments on the meaning of this viewpoint into a moderate-sized book.* I can scarcely expect of you, therefore, more than an optimistic surmise that I have at least the customary vague notion of that of which I am talking this morning—that I, in other words, am about to talk about something, of which I believe that I know something, and of which I feel that it is important for the assembled psychiatrists and mental-hygienists to have some information.

To begin: the *personality* that is the immediate concern of our specialties, I conceive to be less unique and space-bound than

† Reprinted from *Amer. J. Psychiatry* (1930–31) 87:977–991. Presented in abstract at the eighty-sixth annual meeting of the American Psychiatric Association, Washington, D.C., May 8, 1930.
[* The unpublished book, *Personal Psychopathology.* H.S.P.]

may be your prejudice. The personality indicated by my name, now functioning more or less to some point from the rostrum, in the admitted purpose of furthering *your* acquaintance with a viewpoint called "socio-psychiatric"—and in part functioning towards its ennoblement by your good-natured acquiescence in its allegedly exhibitionistic impulses, by your automatic submission to its fortunate position granted by your Program Committee, wondering betimes how much of its verbal content is lost on you by reason of its peculiarities of enunciation, of diction, of intonation (even by reason of its perhaps bizarre physical embodiment)—I say, this personality "telling you" about the socio-psychiatric viewpoint is *not* conceived by me to be limited to the individual standing and talking here, *but rather* is primarily limited by the length, breadth, mental and physical thickness, number, interest, motivation, friendly and unfriendly feeling-tones, and so on and so forth of each one and every one of you *in significant relation with me* as auditor to my audiation.* Secondarily, it is limited by factors significant *in* me, in this personality system, from a more or less illusory, hypothetical, reading and thinking public to whom the printed "record" of these verbal expressions will come as more or less meaningful provocations, and in whom there will grow up a complex of information and misinformation as to my alleged viewpoint, role in the psychiatry of schizophrenia, in the promotion, criticism, and curtailment of mentally hygienic performances, in the progress of human welfare, of Harry Stack Sullivan, of his friends, foes, and so very far forth. In astonishing brief: the alleged biological consideration of the "higher functions" of the human individual *as simply such,* claimed to be *psycho*biology, is an absurdity. Psychobiology, if it is anything but a body of intellectualized absurdities and self-contradictory rationalizations, misnamed neurology or endocrinology, or various philosophizing with empty words, is a study of human *persons* in dynamic interrelation with other *persons* and with *personal* entities (culture, tradi-

[* "Audiation" is undoubtedly Sullivan's own word, deliberately manufactured for the particular meaning here of the speaker hearing his own audition as well as participantly observing the hearing of it by others. H.S.P.]

tion, man-made institutions, laws, beliefs, fashions, etc.). To isolate its individual subject-matter, a *person*ality, from a complex of interpersonal relations involving most meaningfully other persons physically exterior to the subject-person, is preposterously beside the point and indicative of more perverted ingenuity than the speaker finds himself possessing. In yet more violent brief: psychiatry, if it deals with anything, must deal with disordered living of subject-persons in and within their *personal complexes*. It is not an impossible study of an *individual* suffering mental disorder; it is a study of disordered interpersonal relations nucleating more or less clearly in a particular person.

Psychiatry, for the purpose of this presentation, holds neither that the whole course of each human life is determined as to even its rough outlines of individuality by an arrangement of genes in the germinal chromosomes, nor that there is unlimited opportunity for each new individual for individuation. No more does it hold that the mental or psychobiological functioning of the person as *actually occurring* represents purely the effects of environmental influences that have borne on an infinitely potential infant, than it holds that the most minute study of anything structural in the individual will ensure in a comprehensive understanding of actions taken by the subject-person. It does not, in other words, believe itself to be either "natural" or "philosophical" in the pseudo-sense of E. Kahn, or "objective" or "subjective" in the pseudo-sense of G. V. Hamilton. Psychiatry, for the present purpose, is a *largely intuitive art* that some of its practitioners are striving to convert from this artistic, highly personal character to a body of interpersonally valid verbal formulations. In other words, some psychiatrists are striving more or less optimistically, more or less intelligently, to find *consensually valid* factors that will prove to be of real moment in *understanding our intuition* of psychopathological situations—and living, generally—and in understanding our ubiquitous errors in both of these. The slant on this effort to which I wish to invite your attention is perhaps, even probably, novel. To me, it is no "fact" that the "clinic has always been and always will be the foundation for psychiatry." The intuiting (fantasying) and subsequently thinking (formulating) mind is and will always be the "foundation" of everything consensually valid, everything scientific. This fundamental entity, this mind, can never effect its own apotheosis, be its verbal fog ever so dense, be its "logic" ever so shiftily propagandistic. No mind can exteriorize itself for complaisant meditation about less transcendent minds, because the mental or psychobiological—even considered as a purely fictional scientific abstraction—has a meaningful existence only in interpersonal complexes, real or *fancied*. The clinical psychiatrist, and the mental hygienist, just so far as he is "clinically" detached from appreciating the interaction, the chiefly immeasureable, imponderable interplay going on in and within the complex of physician-patient-and-others-relevant, so far is he "out of touch with reality," and a source of delusional utterances and shabby rationalizations, of fallacies of induction, and of *ignoratio elenchi*. His detachment cannot be more than a *fancied* detachment, his "observations" and "conclusions" about data received in this "detachment" can be no more than fancies about his fancies. As we acquire from the first day in the cradle onward a body of popular fancies (our fancies about which are at least moderately popular) the "detached" observer has a reasonably large field for his entertainment—but is scarcely to be expected to cross its boundaries and to create a novel fancy. To this extent, the "detached" observer of humanity is comfortable "in his mind," and, I surmise, pleasantly "objective" in his verbal formulations—he doesn't "have" any "funny ideas"; more accurately, he doesn't become acquainted with any of his "funny ideas"; they work themselves out in his sleep, in the "nonsense" of his dreams! Query: why not a study of psychiatrists' dreams?

For the purpose of this discussion, the infant is born with a great many potentialities, most of which he will never have opportunity to develop. Until he shall have become an adult, he is subject to many changes in the direction of the evolution of his personality—the dynamic realization of inborn tendencies as determined by experience—by processes occurring in his personal complex. There is probably a diminishing range of possibility for these changes from infancy onward. In other words, the longer one lives (towards adulthood), the less are the chances of a major redirection of his personality. The very events of mental disorder, however, indicate that there continues to be a considerable range of possibility for personality change, well into the epoch of adolescence.[1]

Just as our limited rather than unlimited equipment of special sensory receptors probably restricts our contact with the kinds of events actually progressing in subhuman reality, to such effect that we are acquainted with but some of the processes of the Universe, so also a limitation doubtless arises from the hereditary factors as to the extent and direction of each individual's *possibility* of individuation by experience. In other words, there are probably a great many different sorts of personality *not only* because there have been a great variety of organism-environment complexes in which these personalities were formed, *but also* because there have been a variety of predetermined (hereditary, congenital, somatological) limitations as to evolutionary potentialities. That is, some are born with the possibilities for surpassing any previous human personality evolution, and others, many others, are not. Maybe, some are born with the possibility of evolving a schizophrenic disorder, and some are not. I believe that the former, if such there be, greatly outnumber the actually schizophrenic.[2] Many indeed seem capable of schizophrenia— whatever, in the fullness of time, it may prove to be.

This paradoxical discussion of widespread hereditary permissive organization towards an event on the real nature of which I can claim no illumination, perhaps requires a digression. Epistemological disquisitions seem rather beside the point in a paper including practicing psychiatrists and, especially, mental hygienists

[1] It may seem that *adulthood* is defined by me as that stage of personality growth which *prohibits* the occurrence of severe mental disorder. This is not the case. The theory of personality evolution includes no stage at which mental disorder is impossible. It holds, however, that even as late an event as the involutional psychosis occurs generally (if not, in fact, exclusively) in personalities protractedly adolescent in character. This is not *merely* a matter of definition; there are many consensually valid data quite independent of my peculiar prejudice. The adolescent character of the prepsychotic personality in schizophrenics does not seem difficult to demonstrate.

[2] See also "Environmental Factors in Etiology and Course under Treatment of Schizophrenia." That paper, and this study, are in a sense complementary, having been prepared synchronously—for a general medical and a specifically psychiatric audience, respectively.

SOCIO-PSYCHIATRIC RESEARCH

as its objects. It may be taken for granted that no one can tell us about the ultimate nature of anything, or of reality as a whole. However, it may be asked by what perverted miscarriage of mind a psychopathologist, allegedly (and admittedly) somewhat versed in schizophrenia, comes to discuss something which he dismisses as only in the fullness of time to be grasped as a definable entity. . . . I shall seize this opportunity to propound what I trust will be a meaningful dictum: If the locus of psychobiological events is in a nexus of persons and their relations, then—in the new-found insight into this fact—we may very well be hesitant in using the old "objective" language and attempts at describing schizophrenia as a characteristic peculiarity of some particular fraudulently isolated patients. The road to knowledge of schizophrenia is now seen to lie in the formulation of the fundamental, differentiating characteristics of interpersonal complexes, the personal loci of which some dependable few of us intuit to be schizophrenic. That something will come of this newly oriented attack is guaranteed by one fact, if not by many, viz., that there are some persons about whom several of us will agree in "diagnosing" the phenomena as schizophrenic. Its promise is much more clearly indicated, however, by a body of facts of my personal experience, the immediate basis of this paper. I refer to experience in dealing with young male patients by deliberate and rather thoroughgoing modification of the personal social and cultural environment in and within which they continued their being during the earlier stages of hospitalization.

Some ten years' rather close contact with sufferers of schizophrenic disorders culminated in the firm conviction that not sick individuals but complex, peculiarly characterized situations were the subject-matter of research and therapy. About five years ago, the problem seemed to be a matter of peculiar fitness of certain people for dealing with schizophrenic patients. The major conclusion may be said to have been foreshadowed by my effort to discover the characteristics of this peculiarly useful personnel. These efforts gradually concentrated in a study of increasingly experimental interpersonal relations along various tentative lines (or categories) with this personnel directly and indirectly—

through the mediation of the patient. Some few illuminating and many obscuring phenomena were observed. Finally, as I have said, some ten years from the start of my more exclusive preoccupation with schizophrenia, it dawned on me that in personal interaction—even though it occurs chiefly extraconsciously—there is a valid, even if a recondite, field for observation, classification, and induction. The tentative surmise that, in good personnel for dealing with schizophrenics, we were observing that *similia similibus curantur*, so that the successful personnel would, had they instead been schizophrenic, have fallen in the group of patients with good prognosis, passed finally from the realm of amusing fantasy into that of meaningful reality. As soon as the emphasis in observation was moved from concrete characteristics of the person as an individual to the intuited characteristics of his interaction in some approximately typical situations with me, I found that—with one painful exception—a remarkably valid classification became possible; *viz.*, personnel segregated into the probably successful, the doubtful, and the certainly unsuccessful. The painful exception appeared in the inclusion in the first of these divisions of certain cases of psychopathic personality, the carriers of which, however successful they might have been in some ideal situation, possessed no competence for adaptation in a complex group—that is, in a ward organization. When the statistical experience with this technique of sorting people had impressed me with the great excess over probability of the successes, I know that I had something worth formulating. As I look back on the past eighteen months, during which the attempt at formulating has been my chief occupation, I cannot but envy the pleasant state of the paranoid who "sees it all." Ghostly forms of unclear preembryonic ideas have risen on occasion into my strained awareness. Repeatedly, I have tried the sure—but very slow—method of interpersonal relations to strike from my symbolic-verbal equipment a fortunate clue. I have not yet any typological categories, or any communicable intelligence on this matter of classifying persons by the phenomena of interaction, other than the age-old classification of the liked, the unliked, and the disliked. Those who stand near me in my work often respond coordinately with me in liking and disliking; there is a disconcertingly broad fringe of both groups into the indifferent or unliked group. Experience demonstrates that psychiatrists not judged to be suited for interview work with schizophrenic patients, classify identical personnel in a decidedly different fashion in these three hoary divisions. Experience also demonstrates that "really normal extraverts, good 100 per cent people" do not place a majority of the successful personnel (for schizophrenics) under the "liked" rubric; they sometimes invent a fourth division—the "peculiar"— for my chosen ones. Believe me most sincere in remarking, however, that not all the "peculiar" people of my personal experience have aptitude for the socio-psychiatric rehabilitation of schizophrenics, not even all the physicians whom unfriendly extraverts might thus classify.

Howsoever come these "signs and wonders" of successfully guessing hospital personnel for the study and treatment of schizophrenia—to which I shall presently recur in urgent pleading— the procession of events led to the establishment at Sheppard of a Special Receiving Service, in which it was proposed that a study be made of the therapeutic possibilities of carefully organized personal environments.[3] It was thus possible to facilitate the ap-

---

[3] A six (two 3-bed, intercommunicating) bed ward was used, physically approximating a detachment from all but the occupational and recreational services, and in part from these. In particular, the nursing care was independent. The hydrotherapy and physiotherapy were effectively independent. The administration, supervision, and patient-doctor contacts were segregated and entirely supervised. Specifically, by eliminating supervision of the Nursing Service (of those never-enough-to-be-admired miracles whose life is so glaringly illuminated by the professional ideal, often shining the more brilliantly—and casting the more perfect and Stygian shadows—because it is without any competing ideal) I was able to grow in the sub-professional personnel a lush crop of self-respect from good accomplished with the patient. The modern nurse is usually so well trained in (a) The Ethics of Nursing—including a tacit "my Profession, right or wrong, but always my Profession"—and (b . . . n) all sorts of valuable words, phrases, conceptions of diseases and treatments (especially for distributing blame), techniques and crafts, that her aptitude for integration into the complex uncertainties of the mental hospital milieu is vestigial, and only by a personal personality upheaval is she apt to come again to that intuitive grasp of personal totalities that was once her property in common with all pre-adolescents.

The graduate of our medical schools, for somewhat different reasons, is so detached from a "natural" grasp on personality that it usually takes him from 12 to 18 months residence on the staff of an active mental hospital to

parent tendency of personalities to enter into group relationships, and to form syntheses of attendants and patients which
were most valuable in promoting recovery of the patients. Once
freed from the inconsequentiality of ordinary ward service, suitable personnel could gain rapidly in appreciating the significance
of interpersonal interplay and come to be effective in reorganizing the sick personalities. Once energized by this growing insight, the personnel were motivated to personal approximation
to a sanifying culture, rather than merely to "catching on" to
the shibboleths, so widely articulated—when Doctor is about—
by the "more successful" of the ordinary hospital personnel.
Therapeutic notions were thus made effective, *living*, entities instead of formulae obviously ineffective in the governance of their
alleged disciples. Instead of spending most of my time in de-
naturing minor atrocities and stupidities of the patients' life in the
hospital, I could now devote myself to a coordinate cooperative
effort that *tended to endure*, instead of to end on the threshold
of my office.[4] The Institutional Care began to show brilliant prom-
ises, instead of continuing to promote my discouragement. . . .
Where previously one might tend to tears at the probable outcome of schizophrenic patients admitted in the age group 15–25,
one could now begin to hope for their early institutionalization.
The theoretical expectancy of recovery rate in inverse proportion to age of onset tended to realization. The mental hospital
became a school for personality growth, rather than a custodian
of personality failures.

    Before taking up the gloomy aspects of this venture, I wish to
refer to one of the patients studied. We have had several schizophrenics in the age group fourteen to seventeen, and among them
was one in particular [aged 14], whom I would unhesitatingly

---

crack his crust to such effect that he begins to learn "what it is all about."
The graduate nurse, however, harassed as she is by upstart internes, inefficient physicians, utterly unmoral male personnel, etc., etc., seems usually
too preoccupied ever to make this beginning.
    [4] That a majority of this psychotherapeutically effective personnel evinced
sustained interest in the betterment of their own personalities (even, in
two cases, progressing to personal analyses) is perhaps the most impressive
demonstration of success. To come to know one's inadequacies and unconsciously motivated mistakes in dealing with others is perhaps the *least*
likely effect of mental hospital work, generally.

pronounce hebephrenic. His course in the hospital—on a ward in which he was one of five patients, with five of the most satisfactory employees that I have ever been able to make contact with—was very unfortunate, attended by all the ominous symptoms that one associates with the hebephrenic picture. After this had gone on for about seven weeks with uniform downward course, fairly obvious impending dissolution of the personality and regression to early childhood interests, I for the second time saw the patient. I guessed at what might be among his problems and asked him if it had ever occurred to him that there were other people who had such problems, that in fact there were several in his immediate environment. He showed some feeble interest, and I elicited from him the information that one of the employees [attendants] interested him at least feebly. I then told the employee that in spite of the extremely unsatisfactory behavior of this patient and his singular lack of any promising and encouraging signs, I wished he would undertake to establish some sort of intimate relation with the patient, would show him some attention and attempt to get over to him . . . that he was really fond of him and wanted to help him. I told the patient, on the other hand, that it did seem as if it would do him no harm to be interrupted in his very regressive behavior now and then to the extent of being fairly human to this employee. It came about within a few days that this employee and another employee, who had been apprised of the situation, said certain things in the patient's hearing that referred to their own life experience and that also paralleled some very unpleasant experience that the patient had had;* they remarked in passing that it was too bad that so many people who had that sort of experience didn't seem able to think about anything else, and so never discovered that there was a much better way of handling things. I trust you will not consider me so naïve as to suppose that this byplay *in itself* turned any tricks. I use this to illustrate how crude and simple things, set in the right context, and done by understanding people to

[* For clarity, I have reworded this sentence somewhat. The original read: ". . . said in the patient's hearing things which referred parallels in their lives to some very unpleasant experience that the patient had had . . ." H.S.P.]

known ends, may accomplish great results. For the patient ceased his downward course, forthwith, and went on to a "social" recovery. The progress of the social disintegration was arrested; the growth of socialization was given impetus that carried him to the point of leaving the hospital with new enthusiasm for living. The initially poor prognosis was reversed. From probably the most unpromising of the patients I have undertaken in the past year and a half, he came to be as well as are many of those who have never entered a mental hospital. This result arose not by an analysis of his difficulties in a cooperative physician-patient relationship, but by utilizing socio-psychiatric factors. That his personal insight was not greatly increased is obvious; that his *social* insight, as distinguished from insight into the roots of certain of his motives, was increased to an extent *sufficient to abolish the schizophrenic situation* is evident.

The theoretic implications of this very distinction of *social* versus *personal* recovery might long since have turned the attention of research personnel on the processes concerned.[5] A study of "social recoveries" in one of our large mental hospitals some years ago taught me that patients were often released from care because they had learned not to manifest symptoms to the environing persons; in other words, had integrated enough of the personal environment to realize the prejudice opposed to their delusions. It seemed almost as if they grew wise enough to be tolerant of the imbecility surrounding them, having finally discovered that it was stupidity and not malice. They could then secure satisfaction from contact with others, while discharging a part of their cravings by psychotic means. The path to social recovery—so often a necessary preliminary to thoroughgoing treatment—thus seemed to be along the line of really sympathetic environment; perhaps this is the simplest way of indicating the thesis of this presentation.

Thus, regardless of all the factors that go to make up the picture of schizophrenia—regardless of the fact that thyroid deficiency is no asset to a person who has to live, and regardless of

---

[5] Presumably, the archaic conception of mental diseases and Kraepelinian preordination has had a good deal to do with arresting the clinical imagination and curiosity.

the benefits that will accrue to him if in some fashion we can overcome such deficiency, regardless of the fact that people who are hunch-backed have a very great handicap in establishing the kind of success, and particularly personal success, that they desire, regardless of everything except our common interchange with our fellows—there are in the course of schizophrenic illnesses (I can speak personally for the acute and I have no reason to doubt that it is true of the chronic) a great body of favorable and unfavorable results which arise from and are definite sequents to the most commonplace of all things, our ordinary contact with our fellows. Given an intelligent appreciation of the fact that the patient is very much in touch, as you all well know who have studied schizophrenics, given an appreciation that they are extremely sensitive and terribly unreasonable in their expectation from interpersonal relations, it would seem obvious that we must seek people who by their own past experience and personality organization are equally sensitive, put an equal value on the little details of life, if we are to elaborate anything even crudely approximating a situation of sympathy. Two people who know how severely one can be hurt by the other are apt to show consideration. An insensitive person living with a very sensitive one is not apt to learn consideration, be he ever so willing; and certainly, the thin-skinned one is not apt to become inured to suffering, for the escape from injury by others is a matter not of habituation but of reorganization of personality. And personality reorganizations of the type making for approximation to mental health are not outcomes of hate, humiliation, and the like, but of affection and intimacy. Given the correct situation, the "social" recovery goes far towards a "real" recovery and certainly includes much of a true reorganization of the disordered personality.

Two formulations in the above may need definition, because words of common speech are used in a particular sense and because the total-situation viewpoint gives them implications that may have escaped attention. I refer to *sympathetic* personal environment, and to *personality reorganization*. The social recovery in the ordinary hospital situation is, as already expressed, a matter of the patient's realizing the harmless stupidity of those who do not share his psychotic notions—this is its conscious formulation. Beneath this, there is a reorganization of the patient's integrative tendencies, such that it is no longer impossible to live with people thus divergent from the psychotic mode. A sympathetic environment, in the ordinary sense, [for the patient] is one in which there is no brutality but instead a more or less condescending intellectual tolerance or a pleasant indifference based on *unconscious* sympathy of the personalities concerned. The sympathetic environment to which I refer is a group of persons, some "psychotic" [patients], some relatively "sane" [personnel], in the latter of whom there is *conscious* formulation of *community* with the more disordered ones, and a deliberate, rather than a good-naturedly unconscious, purpose to enter into the life of the patient to a beneficial goal—this by reason of the *recognition of common motives, differentiated as to their manifestations by sole virtue* of different experience. Put somewhat loosely, the truly sympathetic person lives with the schizophrenic on a primary basis of assisting in the growth by experience of a body of *relatively undeveloped* tendencies to interpersonal relations; the situation is one of education, broadly conceived, not by verbal teaching but by communal experience—good tutoring.

Personality reorganization in our special sense is expressed in the preceding paragraph. It is not an active interference from outside, such, for example, as that of a mechanic who takes out worn parts of a machine and replaces them with new and perhaps more effective parts. It is a psychobiological procedure more in keeping with the behavior of a husbandman who removes from the organization of a growing plant, mechanical, physicochemical, and biological obstacles, and by providing optimum circumstances, encourages a superior growth and fruition. In our sense, the superior growth and fruition of this plant is the analogue of personality reorganization. It is *not* pampering and petting into living—this does not produce good results with plants or animals. The index of the difference lies in the word, *optimum.* Useful personality reorganization is manifested as a broadening, a deepening, or both, of interest in interpersonal relations—not by dependence on a "strong" personality, the adoption of fantastic rituals, or the development of paranoid situations.

To rise to the heights of prophecy, a recklessness that is scarcely to be pardoned, I surmise that the use of psychiatrically intelligent control of the personal environments of acutely schizophrenic individuals will lead to *a great increase in the institutional recovery rate*. I know that this will be attended by a corresponding increase in the *relapse* rate, for our improving patients will be hurried out into bad situations before they have consolidated enough insight, enough personality reorganization, to survive the morbific personal environments to which they must return. When, however, the efficiency of socio-psychiatric treatment has been demonstrated, I surmise that we will be encouraged to develop convalescent camps and communities for those on their way to mental health. In a not too distant time, these socio-psychiatric communities may come to be the great mental hygiene, with a great reduction in the incidence of major mental disorders, at least of the schizophrenic type.

The path to this Golden Age of psychiatry will not be by way of but financially supported propaganda, or faith, or hope, or even charity. It will be by the sound practice of science—that unremitting scrutiny of preconceptions and hypotheses that leads to ever-improving instruments and data. The apparatus of the study of man is man. Refining of instrumentality is refining of the research personnel itself. Until the processes of growth shall have sloughed off of each student of personality the ubiquitous superstition of *the unique individual completeness of human beings*, on which is based so many fundamental fictions of our church, our state, and our most intimate personal living, that student is almost blind to the very matter of socio-psychiatric research—interpersonal relations.

A great step forward towards the inscrutable goals of human life comes with a new insight into the interrelation of the substratum that is ultimate reality. Great psychiatric advances must be expected from an effective investigation into interpersonal relations. Just, however, as the contractor can build to the architect's specifications without knowing anything of modern physical theory, so can the psychiatrist of today turn his eyes, his intuitional insight, into the as yet unformulated realities underlying interpersonal relations, to the *processes* going on in the allegedly therapeutic situations that he is called on to guide. If my thesis pertains at all to the truth towards which one may surmise that man takes his way, then certainly the superintending physicians of mental hospitals may well give attention to the *control of the commonplaces of their patients' lives* and may well begin to use the knowledge at their disposal in the management of *personalities,* towards the goal of common knowledge,* the primary factor in determining everyone's measure of success and failure. Either you believe that mental disorders are acts of God, predestined, inexorably fixed, arising from a constitutional or some other irremediable substratum, the victims of which are to be helped through an innocuous life to a more or less euthanastic exit—perhaps contributing along the way as laboratory animals for the inquiries of medicine, pathology, constitution-study, or whatever —*or* you believe that mental disorder is largely preventable and somewhat remediable by control of psycho-sociological factors. In the first case, I have no message for you, being but deluded in believing that I have shown the possibility of profoundly modifying the processes called schizophrenic by the use of personality factors. In the other case, it must be evident that your subscription to a psycho-sociogenetic view *entails inevitably* a new scrutiny of your custodianship of the mentally ill, and the evolution of a program of study and technique-development in the utilization of the *persons* working under you. In this case, the delegation of nursing, physiotherapy, and every-day psychotherapy to the management of subalterns activated by archaic superstitions, destructive unconscious motives, and petty *laissez faire,* must rapidly become a thing of the past.

[* The original text read: "may well begin to use the knowledge at their disposal in the management of *personalities,* to common knowledge . . ." I assume that he means that the knowledge should be shared with all the staff. This is the beginning formulation of the concept of consensual validation as a therapeutic and research tool. H.S.P.]

11

Commentary †

THE FOLLOWING is an important paper because it so definitely asks for a *modification* of the psychoanalytic treatment in dealing with schizophrenia; it should be noted that it by no means discards the psychoanalytic perspective. Here, also, for the first time, Sullivan spells out explicitly the therapeutic theory and technique that he, himself, used in working with schizophrenic patients. One phrase in the article is especially worthy of note: "the difference is wholly one of degree, and not one of kind." In this instance, Sullivan is referring to the difference between the schizoid and the schizophrenic, but this also includes any differences between the well and the disordered. This is, again, an early formulation of the one-genus postulate which underlies so much of this book. The expression, itself, was later made memorable by Sullivan's colleague, Frieda Fromm-Reichmann, M.D., in her work with schizophrenics at Chestnut Lodge; see, for instance, *Principles of Intensive Psychotherapy* (The University of Chicago Press, 1950), *passim*.

The Discussion of this paper includes a report by William V. Silverberg, M.D., who took over Sullivan's ward at Sheppard. Silverberg ran the ward on Sullivan's design for a year (June, 1930, to June, 1931), and his results reinforce Sullivan's work as being other than a personal triumph.

† A paper not central to the theme of this book has been omitted at this point—"Training of the General Medical Student in Psychiatry" [*Amer. J. Orthopsychiatry* (1931) 1:371-379].

The Modified Psychoanalytic Treatment of Schizophrenia[†]

IN THIS presentation, an attempt will be made to contribute some factual material bearing on the nature of the schizophrenic mental disorders, and on their treatment by a procedure rather intimately related to the psychoanalytic method of Sigmund Freud. No argument will be offered as to the propriety of the use of "psychoanalytic" in referring to a definite variation from Dr. Freud's technique, nor will a review of the orthodox Freudian contributions to the schizophrenia problem be undertaken. The former cannot but remain a matter of personal opinion. For the latter we may await a presently forthcoming study by Dr. William V. Silverberg. Since a session of our current meeting has been devoted to the subject of schizophrenia, and since some of the views expressed therein are doubtless not consonant with those of the present writer, some attention must also be devoted to the meaning of schizophrenia as hereinafter used. No importance is attached, however, to the magnificent expression of my personal prejudices in these matters.[1]

[†] Reprinted from *Amer. J. Psychiatry* (1931–32) 88:519–540. Read in abstract at the eighty-seventh meeting of the American Psychiatric Association, Toronto, June 5, 1931.

[In the process of examining early in the paper the whole concept of "prediction" in medicine and psychiatry, Sullivan gives, somewhat facetiously, the historical and professional setting for the paper and its predictability. H.S.P.]

[1] The reader is respectfully referred to the perhaps redundant but no less relevant "Thobbing" of Henshaw Ward (New York: Bobbs-Merrill,

272

Firstly, it is held that if there is any difference between the "schizoid" and the "schizophrenic" mental disturbances, the difference is wholly one of degree, and not one of kind. The writer is no more entertained by "thobbing" about an essential organic disorder in schizophrenia, than is he by tedious speculation as to the relations of organic anomaly or defect to particular psychoses with mental deficiency. In contradistinction, for example, to Schilder's contribution at the earlier session,* this paper is intended to deal with consensually valid information about actual patients and actual procedures of therapy, rather than with ingenuity of thinking about hypotheses concerning possibilities of an unknown order of probability. It must follow the tedious scientific rather than the spectacular philosophic road, and its verbiage must be so carefully organized and so adequately elucidated as to provide the psychiatric reader with a formulation useful to himself and his patients. It does not set up any new frame of reference by use of which one can achieve a high percentage of "hits" at the game of prognostic prophecy: to the writer, the future of any particular person is a highly contingent matter, unless the subject-person be psychobiologically an adult —and in the latter case, unless also he be approaching the *senium*, the degree of contingency of his future is *distinct* if not still *high*. Had we persisted for many generations in an agrarian culture, and had this, improbably, been accompanied by extensive, well-integrated psychobiological research, so that we came to know a great deal about the living of our people, then, perchance, we would have come to a fair acquaintance with the actualities of *human probability*. Translated, however, in a few generations from such a culture to the unprecedented industrial situation, we are now in a state of almost complete ignorance of these facts of living, and therefore without any basis for prophecy as to the outcome of this or that poorly envisaged complex of more or less important but partly unrecognized factors. The future of each physico-chemical organism may subsist in some reality under-

1926). To *thob* is to *th*ink out something, which opinion is glorified as an extravasation of one's personality, and most vigorously *b*elieved and "defended," thereafter.

[* Paul Schilder, "Scope of Psychotherapy in Schizophrenia," *Amer. J. Psychiatry* (1931–32) 88:1181–1187.]

lying our hypothetical time-dimension, but the future of each *person* must be recognized as a function of the eternally changing configuration of the cultural-social present. Conceivably, the identical germ plasm evolving in monozygotic twins may be representative in the present of a path in the future such that the twins shall arrive synchronously at a physico-chemical fiasco in the shape of appendicial inflammation. Conceivably, it was in some ultimately comprehensible fashion ordained at the moment of the writer's conception that he shall cease to live owing to rupture of the middle meningeal artery at the age of 57 years, three months and five days, plus or minus less than 100 hours.* But that the present fact of his contemning what Dr. Gregory Stragnell has so aptly dubbed the scholasticism of certain psychoanalytically inclined psychiatrists—in this particular case Paul Schilder about real and pseudo-schizophrenia—that this activity was determined more remotely than the occasion of the last meeting of the Association for Research in Nervous and Mental Diseases, is not true.[2]

No one could conceivably demonstrate any preordination of the effect on the protagonist's future of this situation, prior to the date first named. That which at least two people cannot dem-

[* Sullivan was born on February 21, 1892. He died of a cerebral hemorrhage on January 14, 1949, aged 56 years, 10 months, 24 days. H.S.P.]

[2] The most significant determining factors in this particular situation, *so far as the writer is chiefly concerned*, may be "dated" as follows: March 12, 1931, psychiatric meeting at which the protagonist "presented" a case illustrating the alleged relations of the organic and the functional; March 18, 1931, dinner discussion; April 10, 1931, psychiatric meeting, as previous; April 24, 1931, psychiatric meeting, as previous; April 28, 1931, protagonist's discussion of "The Pathogenesis of Schizophrenia" by Dr. Gregory Zilboorg, New York Psychoanalytic Society; May 13, 1931, reading of summary of protagonist's paper in the program of the current meeting; May 17, 1931, realization that someone must be made a "goat" for illustrating pseudopsychiatric contributions; May 21, 1931, conclusion that the ends justified the risk of this sort of illustration before so kindly and democratic an audience as the present one.

The *situation* under discussion is *interpersonal*; involving, as major nexus, (a) the writer variously expanded, (b) his "impersonal" hearers and readers, (c) the person, Paul Schilder as protagonist, auditor, reader, and reactor, and secondarily those who "side" with him in the alleged "controversy" which many conceive all psychiatric criticism to be, (d) the body of valid and other information that is the psychiatry of schizophrenia; and so forth.

onstrate cannot be utilized in scientific procedure. It seems therefore fairly proven that the effects of the current interpersonal situation on the future of Dr. Paul Schilder, arise *de novo* from the configuration of the present; this in turn, in so far as it is focused in the writer, arising from configurations *actually existing* at particular moments on certain dates in the recent past; these, in further turn, arising from streams of events so complex in themselves, and so complex in their interrelations, that any prophecy of the current situation, on a date more distant than six months ago, would have been fantastic in the extreme.[3]

To return now to the crux of this point: *either no one* of the acutely schizophrenic young men received by the research service of the Sheppard and Enoch Pratt Hospital in the past two years was in fact schizophrenic but instead all were "schizoid"—in which case we might perhaps assume that schizophrenia *the* disease is not shown by native-born males before the age of 25—*or* there is no great importance to be attached to the organic substratum of personality in young acute schizophrenics, but rather great stress to be laid on the socio-psychiatric treatment to which they are exposed, in our studying of the factors relevant to outcome. It is my opinion that a consensus of qualified observers

[3] The best that could have been ventured is something as follows: The present writer, being deeply interested in schizophrenia, and having amassed consensually valid information which he interprets as evidence convincing to any intelligent observer to the effect that *no such illness of acute onset is apt to manifest a dependable sign of bad outcome regardless of treatment*, being moreover activated by a drive to insure the active attention of all concerned to the importance of early care in determining the outcome of schizophrenic disorders, being also interested in the growth of psychiatric knowledge and its refinement from fantasy, *will to a considerable probability*, sooner or later, subject the views of the protagonist to more or less effective criticism. If suitable occasion arise, this will doubtless occur in the course of a psychiatric meeting. Since the writer will be activated to reach the largest audience, it will probably occur at a meeting of The American Psychiatric Association. After reading the program of the current meeting —a prophecy the more probable in that it is but a few weeks "ahead of" the events—an astute prognostician might have said, "It is *quite probable* that this situation will arise on June 3 or 5, 1931." Even if, on May 27, he had read this paper, he would have had clearly in mind the fact that the occurrence of the present situation *continued to be contingent* on many actually unpredictable factors.

can be secured in support of the latter conclusion. The question of an "organic disorder" is therefore irrelevant to this consideration of schizophrenia.[4]

Secondly, in further delimitation of the term, schizophrenia, it is held that these disorders have not been defined psychoanalytically. It is necessary, before adumbrating the original communication herein attempted, to discountenance any conclusion that the writer's study of schizophrenia has "proven" or "disproven" psychoanalytic theory, or any part or parcel thereof, other than the doctrine of narcissistic neurosis. The psychoanalytic terms hereinafter utilized are terms as to the meaning of which, in the writer's opinion, a consensus of competent observers could be obtained. That these consensually defined meanings would be identical with or quite different from the most orthodox Freudian definitions, is unknown. Psychoanalytic formulations are extremely individualistic, in the sense that they are largely Prof. Freud's opinions about his experience with his patients, in the formation of which opinions—as in the great part of all psychiatric opinions—the social and cultural aspects of the thinker's opinion-formation have mostly been ignored. There could not be a meaningful use of the term schizophrenia in regard of a man who had grown from birth into adolescence in utter detachment from any person or personally organized culture. Again, it is possible so to organize a society that the living of its persons, normal to each other, would be regarded as schizophrenic by psychiatrists who studied any one of its members in sufficiently alien surroundings. In brief, schizophrenia is meaningful only in an *interpersonal context;* its characteristics can only be established by a study of the interrelation of the schizophrenic with schizophrenic, less schizophrenic, and nonschizophrenic others. A "so-

---

[4] The acuteness or insidiousness of *onset of the observed psychosis,* however, may finally give the question of underlying organic state new relevance. It is quite *possible,* in the writer's opinion, that an ultimately measurable something of great prognostic significance may be found to underlie these insidious disintegrations of personality attended by more or less of schizophrenic phenomena, that are now lumped with disorders of acute *observed onset.* Statistics of the Sheppard experience indicate so great a difference in course of the two groups, that one cannot but wish that effort might be directed to the comparative study of individuals of acute *versus* insidious observed onset.

cially recovered" schizophrenic is often still psychotic, but is certainly *less* schizophrenic than is a patient requiring active institutional supervision. To isolate the *non*-schizophrenic individual, however, is no small problem. It implies criteria of presence or absence of these processes, of which criteria there seems to be a marked dearth. One might use the following as a fundamental basis for classification: the non-schizophrenic individual, in his interaction with other persons, behaves and thinks in complete consonance with their mutual cultural make-up. Then, to the extent that one's behavior and thought in dealing with another diverges from the mutual culture—traditions, conventions, fashions—to that extent he would be schizophrenic. This seems to be a good working hypothesis, but it has not yet ensued in much consensually valid information. There is, as yet, no measuring of mutual culture; we know that being exposed to culture does not necessarily imply its incorporation in a personality; we know that there are certain personality differentials that greatly affect the incorporation of cultural entities; but we have not paid much attention to evolving techniques for distinguishing the cultural aspects of individual personalities.[5]

There is, however, an indirect approach to this problem—one, moreover, that has seemed to be of practical application. We know that the dream-life of the individual is to a very great degree, purely personal. This consideration applies to a lesser extent to the waking fantasy-life. While there is probably very little indeed of the waking fantasy that is uninfluenced by environing persons or personal entities not wholly of the self, we can assume that certain "primitive" dreams are almost entirely without external reference. We therefore conclude that the more like the dream of deep sleep a given content is, the more purely of the self it is. We can then surmise that a rough approximation to our basis for division into the schizophrenic and the nonschizophrenic can be hypothecated on the consideration of the more purely personal *versus* the consensually valid apperception of a

[5] The development of this topic—*viz.*, the cultural entities built into and going to make up the individual personality—is to be found in the writer's forthcoming text, "The Sickness of The Modern Mind: The Psychopathology of Interpersonal Relations" [probably *Personal Psychopathology*].

given interpersonal situation. If the "contact" with external reality is wholly unintelligible *per se* to the presumably fairly sane observer, then the subject-individual manifests a content indistinguishable from a dream, and is either in a state of serious disorder of the integrating systems, or is schizophrenic. An individual manifesting behavior when not fully awake would thus be clearly schizophrenic. An individual suffering the disorder of interest manifested in severe fatigue would likewise come under this rubric.

A psychiatrist's initial reaction to this formulation can scarcely be one of instant acceptance. He knows of people who "awaken" in nightmares and have trouble in throwing off the content of the dream. He knows that most of these folk are comparatively normal, in their daily life. He is not ready to identify their transitory disturbance of consciousness on occasional nights with the mental disorder shown 18 hours or so per day, day in and day out by the "dementia præcox" patients in the wards of the mental hospital. It is the writer's opinion that neither phenomenologically nor dynamically can a distinction be shown between the two situations. Schizophrenics, in the first hours or days of the frank illness, show just as abrupt transitions among distinguishable states as does our troubled dreamer. The dream-state in their case tends to become habitual, or at least frequently recurrent, and whenever this occurs, the individual is definitely schizophrenic.[6]

The questions that would seem to require answer before acceptance of this formulation of schizophrenia are somewhat as follows: How does it happen that most of us are able to sort out our dreams and our waking experience with a very high degree of success, while the schizophrenic fails in this? Why do only some of those who have night-terror or nightmares progress into chronic schizophrenic states? And, from the organicist, why, if this definition is approximately correct, should not a treatment by alternation of rest and the use of a powerful cerebral stimulant like caffeine bring about at least a suspension of the schizophrenic

[6] That this conception of schizophrenia is broad enough to include the clinical entity, *hysteria*, has not escaped the writer. This is not the occasion on which to develop the implications of a classification of levels of consciousness, nor of the dynamics underlying major and minor dissociations.

state? As to the first of these questions, the actual sorting out of *some little* of our dream-life from waking experience is a difficult or impossible task. The little that is "hard to locate" as to whether dream or "reality" is often quite transparently related to important but none too well recognized tendency systems within the personality concerned. We come thus to the answer of questions one and two: To the extent that important tendency systems of the personality *have* to discharge themselves in sleep, to that extent the dream-processes tend to exaggerated personal importance, and to augmented "reality value." That which permits tendency systems no direct manifestation except during sleep and other states of altered consciousness is their condition of *dissociation* by other tendency systems of the personality—systems apparently invariably represented in the self. At this point, a digression must be made anent a fairly popular psychoanalytic "thob" about the "strength" *versus* "weakness" of the ego. We learn that the superego is "weak" in the schizophrenic; also, that it is "strong" in the schizophrenic; that the ego and the ideal of ego are weak or strong; that the feeble ego is ground between the powerful id of instinctual cravings and the superego; and so forth. Leaving aside the fact that there is plenty of clinical material to be observed by anyone seriously interested in *finding out* what this is all about—there being at least 250,000 patients diagnosed as schizophrenic in the hospitals of the United States—the writer would point out that no night-terror, nightmare, or schizophrenic disorder *can occur* unless there is a waking dissociation of some one powerful tendency system by another powerful tendency system. And, by direct implication of the formula, a continued dream-state, schizophrenia, cannot occur unless there is continued an approximation to a dynamic balance between the tendency system manifesting in the conscious self and the one dissociated from such manifestation.[7] As to the chemotherapeutic employment of agents to provide rest alternating with cerebral stimulants of the caffeine group, it may be noted that this very program, applied during the first hours of schizophrenic collapse,

---

[7] Since it is not the present purpose to discuss the strength or weakness of the ego and so forth, no comment will be made on, for example, the highly relevant data provided by psychopathic personalities.

does delay the disaster. The cerebrum and the other areas responding to caffeine stimulation, however, are not solely the province of the conscious self, and the raised threshold of function is not solely at the service of the *dissociating* system. This topic, together with that of delirifacient drugs and of ethyl alcohol, has been discussed by the writer, elsewhere.

It appears, then, that no well-integrated personality—in whom there is no dissociation of an important tendency system—can show schizophrenic processes of more than momentary duration; and that any personality in whom there is a chronic dissociation of a powerful tendency system may show persisting schizophrenia after any event that destroys the balance by strengthening the dissociated tendency system, or by enfeebling the dissociating system. Physiological maturation and toxic-exhaustive states are frequent factors in this connection.

The partition of time to the schizophrenic processes—whether they occupy but moments during the time ordinarily devoted to sleep, or instead persist days on end in active psychosis—is determined by the balance between the dissociated and the dissociating systems. The "healing" process that ordinarily occurs in night-terror and nightmare is the source of an important insight into this matter. One "recovers" from the failing dissociation manifesting more or less lucidly in the nightmare, by reintegrating one's consciousness of circumambient reality, including one's "place," status, etc. If the pressure of the dissociated system is great, one "knows better" than to return to sleep until one has strengthened the dissociating system by a readjustment of interest and attention to one's waking world. In night-terror, the healing process is less conscious, but usually more directly *interpersonal*. In any case, in the writer's opinion, the restoration of balance in favor of the dissociating system is achieved by some *adjustment of interpersonal relations*. On the other hand, a persisting dream-state represents a failure of interpersonal adjustment, such that the tendency system previously dissociated is now as powerful in integrating interpersonal situations as is the previously successful dissociating system. The augmentation of the one may alternate somewhat with that of the other; the *degree* of consciousness may vary, but conflict and a consciously perceived threat of eruption of the dissociated system is sustained. It is evident that these dynamics may lead to the phenomena delineated in the paper of Dr. Mary O'Malley earlier in the program. It is equally clear that the "retreat" from the personal realities of others, the "seclusiveness" and the inaccessibility to easy personal contacts that are so classically schizophrenic are but the avoidance of accentuated conflict between the tendency systems, which integrate or "strive" to integrate the sufferer into mutually incongruous interpersonal relations, with the appearance of most distressing interests and attention.

We may proceed from this theoretic formulation of the facts of schizophrenia to consideration of the treatment of these disorders. It is to be noted that the basic formula of all psychotherapy is that of interpersonal relations, and their effects on the further growth of tendency systems within the patient-personality. Observation of the processes shown in improvements and aggravations of personality disorder is clearly in line with this formulation. One sees that there is no *essential* difference between psychotherapeutic achievement and achievements in other forms of education. There is, in each, an alteration in the cultural-social part of the affected personality, to a state of better adaptation to the physico-chemical, social, and cultural environment. No essential difference exists between the better integration of a personality to be achieved by way of psychoanalytic personality study, and the better integration to be achieved by an enlightened teacher of physics in demonstrating to his student the properties of matter. There are several differences in the technique required, but these are superficial rather than fundamental, and are to be regarded as determined by actual early training of the patient, in the end reducible to the common denominator of *experience incorporated into the self.* The principal factors responsible for the apparent gap between the ordinary good educative techniques and the orthodox psychoanalytic procedures are to be found in the peculiar characteristics of very early experience—*viz.,* that of the first 18 to 30 months of extrauterine life.[8] Since the char-

---

[8] Consideration of these factors is not directly relevant to the contribution herein attempted, and has been outlined elsewhere [*Personal Psychopathology*].

acteristics of this material are discussed in various psychoanalytic contributions—including that of Dr. Gregory Zilboorg in this session—and since the purpose of this paper is to present the necessary steps preliminary to dealing with the infantile and early childhood experience, we shall proceed immediately to a consideration of the *interpersonal requirements* for the successful therapy of the schizophrenic.

Psychotherapy, like all experience, functions by promoting personality growth, *with or without* improvement of personality integration. Pure suggestion therapy, if such there be, merely adds experience to one or more of the important tendency systems of the personality, thereby perhaps altering the dynamic summation manifested in behavior and thought. Even such a therapy could perhaps be useful in preschizophrenic personalities and, conceivably, even in acute psychosis. A purely rational therapy would be directed to the better integration of the personality systems, as well as to the provision of additional experience. Since it could apply only at the level of verbal communication, it should scarcely be expected to produce great affect in the field of extra-conscious processes. Hortatory therapy would generally be directed to the augmentation of the superego aspects of personality. This includes persuasion and the all too prevalent "bucking up" treatment. None of these procedures is in line with the information which we have secured as to the growth and function of personality.

Treatment in states of reduced consciousness, notably under hypnosis, could be more nearly adjusted to the total personality. Unfortunately, however, the integration of the treatment situation implied by the occurrence of the hypnotic or even the hypnoid states imposes a great responsibility on the physician. Unless he is expert indeed in dealing with the earlier experience incorporated in each personality, the net result of the treatment is sadly disappointing. Either there is little more achieved than could have been secured by a fairly rational exhortation, or there is disturbance of the superego functions and an increased severity of conflict. The integration of the hypnosis situation in the incipient or acute schizophrenic is difficult in extreme. This manipulation of the personality is therefore for us chiefly of theoretic importance. The attempt at hypnotizing distressed preschizophrenics should perhaps be emphatically discouraged, as the mandatory—even if self-determined—submission to the other personality is almost certain to cause a severe emotional upheaval, with the hypnotist thereafter in an unenviable role as chief personification of the goal of the dissociated system.

The only tools that have shown results that justify any enthusiasm in regard of the treatment of schizophrenia are the *psychoanalytic* procedures and the *socio-psychiatric* program which the writer has evolved from them. Before taking up these procedures, however, it may be well to note that the process of benefit by psychoanalysis seems none too clearly envisaged by many of its practitioners. One might be led to assume from the literature that a "cure" is achieved by a releasing of the libido from its "point of the fixation" existing somewhere in the past of the individual. A steadily increasing complexity of the map of possible fixation points is leading some of the outstanding thinkers in this field to doubt the importance of the doctrine of fixation. The writer has long since indicated his inability to discover anything corresponding to a point of fixation in schizophrenia, and has come to believe that "releasing the libido from its fixations" is but a figure of speech for something that occurs in recovery under analysis. Observation shows that psychoanalytic therapy consists of two major processes, the combination of which leads to growth and improved integration of personality. These are, firstly, a retrospective survey of the experiential basis of tendencies that conflict with the simple adaptation of the person to others with resulting growth to a more adult character; and secondly, the provision of experience that facilitates the reorganization of the undeveloped or warped tendencies such that adaptation becomes more successful. The achievement of this double process requires the establishment between the physician and patient of the situation called by Freud the "transference."

There has been a good deal written about "transference," and many peculiarities of technique have been originated with view to its cultivation and management. There seems to the writer to be nothing other than *the purpose* of the interpersonal situation which distinguishes the psychoanalytic transference relation from other situations of interpersonal intimacy. In other words, it seems to be a special case of interpersonal adaptation, distinguished chiefly by the rôle of subordination to an enlightened physician skilled in penetrating the self-deceptions to which man is uniquely susceptible, with a mutually accepted purpose of securing the patient an increased skill in living. Like almost all other situations tending towards intimacy the early stages of the psychoanalytic situation include a great body of fantasy processes that are not directly helpful to the achievement of the goal of the physician. Like all other interpersonal relations, this one includes a good deal of intercommunication by channels other than that of spoken propositions. As it is ordinarily applied, the psychoanalytic situation involves a patient the organization of whose self is not satisfactory, and whose self-regard is inadequate. This is very much the case in preschizophrenic and incipiently and acutely (catatonic) schizophrenic patients. By reason of the extreme distress caused by any threatened (or fantasied) reduction of the already distressingly small self-regard of these patients, and also by reason of specific painful experience with all previously significant persons, these patients are extremely uneasy about any situation in which the favorable cooperation of another is required for its resolution. The appearance of strong positive tendency towards the physician is thus attended by an extraordinary augmentation of attention for unfavorable signs, and very slight provocation may lead to a reversal of the tendency—from positive to negative, love to hate.

Before proceeding to develop the implications of these facts for the actual management of these patients, reemphasis must be made of the writer's distinction of schizophrenia from hebephrenic deterioration and from paranoid maladjustments. In brief, the patients to whom therapy may be applied with high probability of success are, firstly, patients in whom there has been a rather rapid change from a state of partial adjustment, to one of apparent psychosis, a matter of weeks, not months or years—this transition being the incipient schizophrenic state; secondly, patients who have not progressed into that regression of interests to early childhood or late infancy levels, to which we refer as the hebephrenic; and thirdly, patients who have not made a partial recovery by massive projection and transfer of blame, the "paranoid schizophrenic," or paranoid state with more or less of residual schizophrenic phenomena. The case of the chronic catatonic state is of potentially good outcome, this seeming to be but a chronic continuation of the purely schizophrenic state, but the actual duration in illness is a factor that is not to be ignored.

The procedure of treatment begins with removing the patient from the situation in which he is developing difficulty, to a situation in which he is encouraged to renew efforts at adjustment with others. This might well be elsewhere than to an institution dealing with a cross-section of the psychotic population; certainly, it should not be to a large ward of mental patients of all sorts and ages. The sub-professional personnel with whom the patient is in contact must be aware of the principal difficulty— *viz.*, the extreme sensitivity underlying whatever camouflage the patient may use. They must be activated by a well-integrated purpose of helping in the re-development or development *de novo* of self-esteem as an individual *attractive* to others. They must possess sufficient insight into their own personality organization to be able to avoid masked or unconscious sadism, jealousies, and morbid expectations of results. They must be free from the more commonplace ethical delusions and superstitions. Admittedly, this is no small order, and the creation of this sort of situation is scarcely to be expected either from chance or from the efforts of a commonplace administrative agent.

Given the therapeutic environment, the first stage of therapy by the physician takes the form of providing an orienting experience. After the initial, fairly searching, interview, the patient is introduced to the new situation in a matter-of-fact fashion, with emphasis on the personal elements. In other words, he is made to feel that he is now one of a group, composed partly of sick persons—the other patients—and partly of well folk—the physician and all the others concerned. Emphasis is laid on the fact that something is the matter with the patient, and—once this is at least clearly understood to be the physician's view—that regardless of the patient's occasional or habitual surmise to the contrary, everyone who is well enough to be a help will from thenceforth be occupied in giving him a chance to get well. From the start, he is treated as a *person among persons*.

There is never to be either an acceptance of his disordered thought and behavior as *outré* or "crazy," or a "never-mind" technique that ignores the obvious. Everyone is to regard the outpouring of thought or the doing of acts as at least *valid* for the patient, and to be considered seriously as something that at least he should understand. The individualism of the patient's performances is neither to be discouraged nor encouraged, but instead, when they seem clearly morbid, to be noted and perhaps questioned. The questioning must not arise from ethical grounds, nor from considerations of mere convenience, but from a desire to center the patient's attention on the discovery of the factors concerned. If there is violence, it is to be discouraged, *unemotionally*, and in the clearly expressed interest of the general or special good. If, as is often the case, violence arises from panic, the situation must be dealt with by the physician. If, however, the patient seems obviously to increase in comfort without professional attention after the introduction to care, the physician can profitably await developments. A considerable proportion of these patients proceed in this really human environment to the degree of social recovery that permits analysis, without much contact with the supervising physician. Moreover, in the process, they become aware of their need for insight into their previous difficulties, and somewhat cognizant of the nature of the procedures to be used to that end. They become not only ready but prepared for treatment.

If the patient does not respond in so gratifying a fashion to the special environment, the physician must discover the difficulty. In some cases, the previously dissociated tendency system is integrating personal situations that precipitate panic or panicky states. This requires reassurance by a technique of realistic acceptance of the underlying tendencies, a bringing out into the open of the cause for the fear experienced by the self, with the resulting beneficent effects of a new feeling of group solidarity in that the harsh appraisal of the tendency incorporated in the patient's personality is temporarily suspended or enfeebled, by acquaintance with people to whom the situation is a commonplace of life. In all too many cases, the ideal-organization is such that the appearance of this solidarity-reaction is judged by the self to be ominous, and the attempt to diminish the violence of reaction to the previously dissociated tendency system fails. It is necessary, however, that the conflict be abated, otherwise the development of interpersonal security that is absolutely necessary for a social recovery cannot be achieved. In such cases, recourse is had to chemotherapeutic agencies, notably ethyl alcohol, which impair the highly discriminative action of the more lately acquired tendency systems, and permit the at least rudimentary functioning of the more primitive, without much stress. After from three to ten days of continuous mild intoxication, almost all such patients, in the writer's experience, have effected a considerable readjustment. The *modus operandi* may be indicated roughly by remarking that these patients discover by actual experience that the personal environment is not noxious, and, having discovered this, have great difficulty in subsequently elaborating convictions of menace, plots, fell purposes, etc. It is the rule to have several interviews with the patient during the period of intoxication, and in them to carry out the reassuring technique above indicated.

Occasionally, an acute schizophrenic, showing a marked tendency to paranoid maladjustment, proceeds all the more rapidly in this direction under the type of care thus far outlined. Several devices have been used in combating the process, but the results are not yet satisfactory. It has become clear that this eventuality requires an extraordinary intervention, if the patient is to be saved; and some pioneering work has been done in this connection. The principle involved, however, is one sufficiently startling to justify hesitancy in reporting but two patients. For the present, it must suffice that patients who show progressively deepening paranoid developments or those who are received in florid paranoid states should not remain with the group under active treatment.

As the patient improves, and as his acceptance of the need for help grows, the efforts of the physician become more direct in their application. Energy is expended chiefly in *reconstructing the actual chronology of the psychosis*. All tendencies to "smooth over" the events are discouraged, and free-associational technique is introduced at intervals to fill in "failures of memory." The role of significant persons and their doings is emphasized, the patient being constantly under the influence of the formulation above set forth—*viz.*, that however mysteriously the phenomena originated, everything that has befallen him is related to his actual living among a relatively small number of significant people, in a relatively simple course of events. Psychotic phenomena recalled from the more disturbed periods are subjected to study as to their relation to these people. Dreams are studied under this guide. During this phase of the work, the patient may or may not grasp the dynamics of his difficulty as they become apparent to the physician. Interpretations are never to be forced on him, and preferably none are offered excepting as statistical findings. In other words, if the patient's actual insight seems to be progressing at a considerable pace, it can *occasionally* be offered that thus-and-so has, in some patients, been found to be the result of this-and-that, with a request for his associations to this comment.

One of perhaps three situations now develops. Firstly, if the patient is doing very well, the family insist on taking him home, and generally ignore advice as to further treatment. Secondly, the chronology of the course of recent events running into the psychosis is rather well recovered, and the patient is found to have great difficulty in coming to insight. He is then discharged into regular treatment at the hands of a suitable psychoanalyst, experienced in the psychiatry of schizophrenia—and not too rigid in devotion to technique. Thirdly, the stage of chronology-perfecting is accompanied by so much growth of insight that it is shifted gradually to a close approximation to regular analytic sessions that follow a liberal variant of the orthodox technique.

In the writer's experience, covering some 11 years, there have been regrettable events to be charged off to precipitate and to rigid techniques of psychotherapy. From these mistakes and from the singular opportunities provided by patients themselves, the socio-psychiatric technique above indicated has finally evolved. When physical facilities were made available, it was tried out rather thoroughly. The condition of no patient was aggravated by its use, and the social and real recovery rates obtained were extremely gratifying. It would seem that, for the group as defined above, schizophrenia is an illness of excellent prognosis. The treatment required, however, is obviously far from widely available, and the schizophrenia problem therefore continues to be very urgently one of prevention.

Certain considerations bearing on the professional personnel for working with schizophrenics may not be amiss. In the first place, it seems quite clearly demonstrated in the Sheppard experience that the therapeutic situations must be integrated between individuals of the same sex. Two male patients treated by woman physicians did remarkably badly, while "cooperating" much better than the average. A number of women, treated by the writer, also "cooperated" nicely, as they progressed into deterioration or paranoid maladjustments. Male patients treated by the writer are not as comfortable in the treatment situation as were these women. But they are correspondingly more successful in achieving actual rather than fantastic results.

In the second place, the unanalyzed psychiatrist and the psychiatrist filled with the holy light of his recent analysis are in general not to be considered for this work. The former have generally a rigid system of taboos and compromises which are rather obvious to the schizophrenic intuition, so that the patient comes early to be treating the physician, and to be fearing him. The analytic zealot knows so many things that are not so that the patient never makes a beginning.

Thirdly, the philosophical type of person is a poor candidate for success as a therapist of schizophrenics; they too love philosophizing—it is so much safer to "think" than to go through the mill of observation and understanding. Also, most of these people get systematized so early that they are blind to experience less than a personal psychosis.

Fourthly, those elsewhere identified as the "resistant homosexual types" are poor material for schizophrenia therapists; they are too busy finding "homosexual components" in everyone to note the facts flowing past them.

Fifthly, the reformer element, who "know" how life should be lived, and what is good and bad, if they must do psychiatric work, should keep far from the schizophrenic. Perhaps the manic-depressive psychosis is their ideal field.

Sixthly, perhaps of all the people least fitted for this work are those that are psychiatrists because it gives them powers and principalities over their fellows; to them should go the obsessional neurotics.

Lastly, sadly enough, those to whom life has brought but a pleasant flood of trifling problems without any spectacular disturbances, who have grown up in quiet backwashes far from the industrial revolution, within the tinted half-lights of the passing times—these are afield in undertaking the schizophrenia problem. It is one up to the last minute in its ramifications, and can but bring them a useless gloom and pessimism about youth and the times. There are some ecclesiasts who find joy in tinkering with the mild mental disorders, in Church Healing Missions and the like. These folk might learn much from, for example, the Rev. Anton Boisen, Chaplain of the Worcester State Hospital, who has come by the tedious and often deeply disturbing road of observation and experimentation to a sane grasp of the relations of religious thoughts and techniques to the schizophrenia problem.*

In conclusion, it may be restated that, at least in the case of the male, fairly young schizophrenic patients whose divorcement from fairly conventional behavior and thought has been rather abrupt, when received under care before they have progressed either into hebephrenic dilapidation or durable paranoid maladjustments, are to be regarded as of good outlook for recovery and improvement of personality, if they can be treated firstly to the end of socialization, and thereafter by more fundamental reorganization of personality.

Discussion

DR. SILVERBERG (*Washington, D.C.*).—I have no doubt that one of the objections that will be raised to Dr. Sullivan's paper is that the method and the organization which he has described may work very well in the hands of Dr. Sullivan, who has peculiar means of dealing with schizophrenics, but in the hands of another individual, even with a reasonably good medical and psychiatric training, the method would not work. I most emphatically refute this objection. I was Dr. Sullivan's successor at Sheppard and inherited, so to speak, the organization which he had perfected there. During the year that I was at Sheppard, I made no essential changes in the organization that Dr. Sullivan had created there. During that time I dealt with 16 schiz-

[* A description of this experience is found in Anton T. Boisen, *The Exploration of the Inner World: A Study of Mental Disorder and Religious Experience;* New York: Harpers, 1936. H.S.P.]

ophrenics in the special six-bed ward that he used, and had rather good results. Of these 16 patients, 12 either recovered or improved. Of the 12 cases that had been cured or improved, nine were discharged and three remained under care at the end of the period. Of the four unimproved cases, three were discharged, and one remained under care. Of the three unimproved, discharged cases, two turned out to be patients who had been ill for some time, without its being known by their families. They had been paranoid for at least two years before coming to the hospital.

On the basis of these statistics, one sees that 75 percent of the cases going through this organization have been either recovered or improved. If one omits the two chronic cases for whom, as Dr. Sullivan has already said, such a method of treatment or any method of treatment seems to be of no great value, it will be seen that about 85 percent of these 14 cases have been either recovered or improved.

Another objection that might be made to this plan is: What is going to happen to those patients when they leave a situation of this sort, which is perhaps from a superficial point of view rather artificial? Will they not, in coming up against the world of reality again, have a return of their symptoms? I should say that this objection is rather more theoretical than real. The same question occurred to my mind when I first took over the ward. The patients, however, passed from this ward to the parole ward and from the parole ward out into the world without any significant difficulties.

I might also say that this particular method of treatment seems to be of greater value for the cases predominantly catatonic and schizophrenic than those predominantly paranoid in symptoms. I hope that the figures which I am able to present will be rather impressive and that the formation of similar organizations elsewhere will be encouraged.

Dr. Gregory Zilboorg (*White Plains, New York*).—I think this is the first encounter between Dr. Sullivan and myself on the floor of the American Psychiatric Association, but in various other meetings we have had many pleasant opportunities to thresh out certain differences which I believe are more superficial than actual.

The fundamental contentions of Dr. Sullivan's paper could be briefly summarized as follows:

First, the schizophrenic presents no special difficulties as regards transference reactions. I think that this point at least, made by himself, will make it possible for him to agree that the psychoanalytic technique which I have used in schizophrenics is probably workable since it led me to the same conclusions.

Second, the point of view of fixation borrowed from the general theory of neuroses is not entirely justified in our work with schizophrenics, for the schizophrenic process presents a number of definite clinical features, the origin of which is not dependent upon any definite fixation; hence the essential features of our therapy in schizophrenia are not so much the release from the point of fixation as the reconstruction of the whole personality. So far so good. However, certain contentions of Dr. Sullivan's paper ought to be approached with at least some doubt. On the basis of my clinical experience I feel compelled to believe that one is not justified in viewing the problem of technique too casually; this technique permits us to enter into the deepest layers of the human personality and should not be discarded with that ease which permits Dr. Sullivan to say: "Send them to an analyst who is psychiatrically trained but who is not too orthodox with regard to psychoanalysis." My contention is: send the patient to an analyst who is very well trained but beware of the analyst who has had poor psychiatric training. The great difficulty of the situation lies in the fact that the psychiatrist looks with suspicion at the analyst because he knows no analysis, while the analyst is just as suspicious of the psychiatrist because the analyst knows no psychiatry. This attitude, covered with a mask of mutual admiration at public meetings, is based on the deep unconscious feeling: "I know something that thou dost not comprehend." This attitude does very little for the progress of therapy in general and that of therapy of schizophrenias in particular.

Dr. Sullivan's emphasis on the socialization of the personality of the schizophrenic is of extreme importance, and I believe that the so-called socio-psychiatric methods are those which are covered by the term "reality testing" which to me is a part of every scientific psychoanalysis of a schizophrenic. That is the reason why I consider Dr. Sullivan's method nothing more than a series of preliminary measures which do not reach deep enough.

The remark that the paranoid schizophrenic is much better off than a healthy individual cannot obviously be taken seriously. Any psychotic prefers his psychosis to being well; otherwise he would not have embarked upon a psychotic path. If this were to serve as an impulse for and criterion of our therapeutic measures, we should refuse to treat a manic because he is so much happier than when he was well.

I have already talked more than I should have, and said less than I wanted to. I shall therefore conclude by emphasizing that in psychiatry, as in medicine, we cannot and should not concentrate on treating symptoms rather than diseases; that the subjective alleviation of symptoms, particularly in schizophrenics, is of no therapeutic significance; and that social recovery is not a recovery in the real sense of the word, since a patient may make a complete social recovery and continue to remain psychotic.

CHAIRMAN BRILL.—I would like to have this discussion continued, but I regret very much that we have not much time. As Chairman, I will use my prerogative to say a few words about the subject. I have been interested in this problem from the beginning of my existence as a psychiatrist, and I have treated schizophrenics psychotherapeutically, I might say analytically, for a long time. In fact, I have in mind patients who were treated by me psychoanalytically 18 or 19 years ago. When I reported here some of these cases about two years ago, I entitled my paper "Psychotherapy of Schizophrenia" because I did not use *lege artis* analyses because I found that I had to change my analytic technique to suit my cases. The reason I did not use such definite terms as were given here by the speakers is because I really do not believe that we have reached the stage of definite formulations. One thing I am sure of, and that is that by using as much of psychoanalysis as the patient can digest and by resorting to the techniques mentioned by both speakers, modifying them to suit the occasion, I have been able to accomplish results. I did not do exactly what Dr. Sullivan recommends. Thus, some of my greatest successes have been with female patients. Nor have I done everything that Dr. Zilboorg describes. But, listening to them, I do know that I have done everything that they recommend and have deviated as much as they did to suit the particular patients.

The patients I have in mind I did not have to send to any hospital. They were all cared for at home. With such cases I had the best results.

What impressed me in Dr. Sullivan's paper is the hopefulness that it inspires. It is very pleasant to hear such papers and such discussions as were given by Dr. Zilboorg and the others. The therapeutic future of schizophrenia looks quite hopeful.

I know perfectly well there are many others who would like to discuss, but owing to the late hour, I regret that I have to ask Dr. Sullivan to close the discussion.

DR. SULLIVAN.—Many important things have come up in the discussion. I can only express my gratitude to Dr. Silverberg for the report on what has been going on at Sheppard, and take this opportunity of emphasizing again the great prognostic importance of *insidious onset* where the individual has very gradually gotten eccentric and become far different from his previous personality, before conspicuous phenomena pointed to his being psychotic. That patient, so far as I know, is in a very bad way, and not apt to profit from the sort of effort I have been talking about.

The urgency of the early socialization is one of the points I am most anxious to carry over to you. Every disappointment the patient undergoes is another obstacle to his recovery.

As to the possible institutional results, there Dr. Silverberg and Dr. Zilboorg were superficially at difference; Dr. Silverberg remarked that the social recovery, which is accomplished in this process, is a definite growth in personality, and Dr. Zilboorg made the statement, which may have been the result of limitations on his time, that social recovery does not mean any sort of recovery. It seems beyond argument that there is an improvement in personality if one changes from obvious psychosis to a considerable measure of ability to live in one's environment. The fact that the patient can be carried to the point where he knows how to keep out of trouble is at least economically and pragmatically useful. It seems a century or two too early for enforcing perfection in this one field of human welfare work.

I have heard a good deal about the "choice of psychosis" and the difficulty of "curing" schizophrenics because they were "so much better off" in the psychosis than were they previously. I think that this interpretation is only one of several possible interpretations; I have seen a good many schizophrenics, and it does seem to me that they have passed from the frying pan into a very active fire by becoming schizophrenic. I do not think we are laying a sound foundation for therapeutics by holding that the patient prefers being psychotic to being well. That this is a superficial statement of the view, I quite realize. It is fairly close, however, to the discoverable content of those who talk this way. If some profound truth is concealed in it, so much the worse for those who cannot express it more adequately—and for those who might profit from understanding it.

The paranoid maladjustment, by which others are found to blame for one's difficulties, does contribute a certain measure of self-respect, and these patients require that you will guarantee them more self-respect before they will give up their paranoid adaptation. That is apparently a difficult achievement, at least for me. That is what I meant when I said they had something much better than at least can be our first offers to them in socialization.

I am grateful to Dr. Brill for his comment. I do not regard the conceptions I am presenting as wholly revolutionary or original. I am most emphatically in accord with his remark on the feasibility of non-institutional care for early schizophrenics; a work to which I am now devoting myself. His comment supports my thesis; namely, that the general adoption of this orientation in the treatment of incipient schizophrenia and of all younger patients of acute onset— with the creation of convalescent camps and open institutions to which these patients can be sent—should be regarded neither as a hope of the distant future nor a particularly expensive procedure. It seems to me that this addition to the modern state hospital service will pay far larger dividends on the taxpayers' money, than does the current type of custodial care and accidental treatment of schizophrenics, and that it would give the youth of today something like a fair chance of surviving at least the first episode of schizophrenic disorder.

12

Commentary

SULLIVAN wrote the next paper as the entry for "Mental Disorders" in the *Encyclopaedia of the Social Sciences* (1933).[1] It contains a brief history of various approaches to mental disorder and constitutes a summing-up of Sullivan's own theoretic position and of his clinical work with schizophrenics up to that time. For example, he reports, on the basis of follow-up investigation, "80 percent social recovery" for his experimental group of schizophrenic patients at Sheppard. The drama of such clinical success cannot be adequately realized unless one examines some of the literature on dementia praecox in vogue at the time that Sullivan went to Sheppard, in 1923. For instance, I have before me a copy of William Alanson White's *Outlines of Psychiatry*, the eighth edition, revised for publication in 1921. This, then, represents the thinking in 1921, of one of the more advanced superintendents of a great mental hospital, St. Elizabeths in Washington, D.C. The word, "schizophrenia," appears only once in White's book; the chapter on "Dementia Precox" begins "Dementia precox is a psychosis essentially of the period of puberty and adolescence, characterized by a mental deterioration tending to progress, though frequently interrupted by remissions." Near the end of the chapter, White makes his most optimistic statement: "While it is customary to consider this disease as hopeless so far as being able to influence it by therapeutic measures is concerned still this pessimistic attitude does not seem wholly warranted even though, in those cases

[1] Sullivan wrote another article for the *Encyclopaedia*, the entry for "Psychiatry" [Vol. 12: 578–580; New York: Macmillan, 1934], which has not been included here.

296 SCHIZOPHRENIA AS A HUMAN PROCESS

that get better, we cannot define how much of the result has been due to the treatment." These were the words of an advanced clinician and superintendent in 1921. Twelve years later, Sullivan could report a dramatic change in that attitude—a change that both White and Smith Ely Jelliffe had encouraged but that had been largely implemented by Sullivan's work at Sheppard.

Mental Disorders[†]

MENTAL disorders, or diseases, are always defined by reference to an explicit or implicit formulation of personality which sets limits to the manifestations of human individuality. That which deviates from the norm thus created is regarded as aberrant and is considered genius or crime or mental disorder, depending upon a large number of secondary definitions which fix the individual's relations with the group.

Prenaturalistic views of human personality consider mental disorders as the results of manipulations of the victim by transcendental agencies, as for example, in the case of belief in demoniacal possession. Naturalistic interpretations may be classified into naive mechanistic doctrines, such as those which regard mental disorders as the results of medical diseases and attribute them to lesions in the nervous system, the endocrine glands, or in other organs of the body; and the more sophisticated biological doctrines, according to which mental disorders are more or less rigidly determined by the individual's genetic constitution or his environment or by a combination of both. Most psychological theories of mental disorder belong in these categories, for example, that of conditioned response behaviorism, the psychoanalytic doctrine of libido fixation and other dynamic explanations. Finally, anthropology views mental disorders as the result of unduly complicated interpersonal integrations arising from innately conditioned but culturally directed tendency systems.

† Reprinted from the *Encyclopaedia of the Social Sciences*, 10: 313–319; New York: Macmillan, 1933. [In the original, Sullivan gives an extensive bibliography on mental disorder, which has been omitted here.]

The mystical and magical approach to mental disorder survives in folk belief; it casts a shadow of awe and fear upon patients called insane, keeps many persons from approaching the confines of psychiatric hospitals, and greatly interferes with public enlightenment as to the nature of mental disorders. This attitude is fostered by clergymen and others who undertake the healing of mental patients, when not frankly by exorcism, at least by magical appeals to better nature and to will power. The medical approach predominates in modern psychiatry and has produced a considerable literature, much of which is controversial as to classifications, pathologies, and therapeutic measures. The medical ideal is to discover the disease entity, with its specific cause, course, and outcome. This method was followed in the case of dementia paralytica, a neurosyphilitic disease first clearly defined by Bayle in 1822. Kraepelin, who was greatly influenced by the medical ideal, in 1896 diagnosed approximately 28 percent of his cases as dementia paralytica. After the adoption of Wassermann's serological technique for detecting syphilis, he [Kraepelin] diagnosed as dementia paralytica only about 9 percent of his cases.

Destructive changes in the central nervous system are an invariable concomitant of dementia paralytica. This is not the case, however, with the functional mental disorders which are not associated with known changes in the body. A considerable variety of major functional mental disorders had been recognized before 1886. Kraepelin reduced these to three: dementia praecox, manic depressive psychosis, and a group which in 1893 he differentiated into paranoia and paraphrenia. In 1901, over 50 percent of the cases admitted to his clinic at Heidelberg were diagnosed as dementia praecox. Ten years later fewer than 20 percent of his cases were so diagnosed, indicating that this symptomatic prognostic classification was not completely successful even when applied by its creator. It has nevertheless had wide influence and has been adopted with but slight modification by most hospitals in the United States and Canada. A study made by the author of the diagnostic distribution of the patient population in sixty hospitals treating mental disorders shows that in 1929 slightly under 62 percent of 124,028 patients were classified according to the rubrics of the functional psychoses. The ratio of the total number of paranoid and dementia praecox cases to the total number of cases of manic depressive psychoses is 3.75 to 1; the ratios in different hospitals vary, however, from 49 to 1 to 1 to 2.5, and the percentage of the functional disorders varies from 48 to 98 percent of the total number of patients. As there are no determining factors which may explain these wide discrepancies other than the personal equations of psychiatrists, it must be concluded that the symptomatic prognostic classification does not yield results which can be utilized statistically.

Medical treatment of mental disorders has been extremely varied. Hydrotherapeutic, occupational therapeutic, pharmacological, organotherapeutic, and recreational methods have vied with surgical operations ranging from modified eviscerations to injections of sundry substances into the body. Elevations of temperature some degrees above that of the healthy body are more promptly fatal to the germ of syphilis than to the human tissues; this form of therapy has been useful therefore in the case of patients suffering from dementia paralytica. Enthusiasts are now extending its use to other mental disorders. Patients formerly chained in dungeons and flogged; not long since exsanguinated and purged; recently drugged, isolated, and restrained; still more recently treated for teeth and tonsil infections or given spinal injections of horse serum—may now receive treatment by infection with malaria or have their bodily temperature raised by electrical induction.

The psychiatric hypothesis which holds that most or all mental disorders are ordained in the germ plasm has been applied to functional disorders by von Verschuer, who found that thirty-one of thirty-four identical twins and only three out of eight fraternal twins suffered from dementia praecox, or schizophrenia; his data are equally impressive in the case of the manic-depressive psychosis. Since the hereditary equipment of identical twins may be presumed to be the same, any differentiation must be the result of environmental factors. For this reason studies of identical twins are relevant, while other studies of human heredity are of limited applicability to the problem of mental disorder. A hereditary neuropathic or psychopathic taint has often been held to be important as the determining factor in mental disorders; the comparative frequency of this taint in relatives of the nonpsychotic and the psychotic has been calculated to be approximately 70 to 77, while the frequency of severe mental disorder in a parent of a nonpsychotic person and in a parent of a psychotic person seems to be approximately 1 to 6. The influence of psychotic parents may, however, operate through their functioning as part of the early environment of the child rather than through heredity. The psychiatric practises which arise from the heredity doctrines are chiefly preventive—eugenic reform, segregation, and sterilization.

Environmental influence has been stressed particularly in the works of Freud, Jung, and Adolf Meyer and also in the attempts to explain mental disorders on the basis of the conditioned reflexology of Pavlov. Freud came to regard mental processes as essentially unconscious, to consider conscious mental processes merely as isolated acts although parts of the whole psychic entity, and to contend that sexual impulses play an insufficiently appreciated role in the causation of nervous and mental disorders and of normal behavior. He conceptualized a force in the mind which functions as a censor, and which excludes from consciousness and from any recognized influence upon action all tendencies which are uncongenial to it. The force of repression falls especially upon the sexual instincts, the frustration of which may lead to the development of neurosis, psychosis, or crime. This frustration generally involves a regression to points of libido fixation established in earlier life. Whether the conflict between the censor and instinct finds a healthy solution or leads to a neurotic inhibition of function depends upon the relative strength of the forces concerned. The first important conflict in the course of personality growth is the Oedipus complex, which arises in the child's relation to his parents; those destined to succumb to mental disorder fail habitually in their attempt to grapple with this problem. If the patient can effect a transference to the physician, it is generally possible to assist him by the method of free association and through the interpretation of dreams to overcome internal resistances and to do away with repressions, so that he may replace unconscious by conscious mental acts. In 1907, Jung amplified Freud's results in his report upon three years of psychoanalytically oriented experimental work and clinical observation on dementia praecox patients. He contended that dissociated complexes explained much that was meaningless and bizarre in the speech and behavior of such patients. In the United States, Smith Ely Jelliffe and William Alanson White identified themselves with this type of psychogenetic explanation, and it is chiefly through their influence that a rigid medical formalism has been avoided in American psychiatry.

Adolf Meyer as early as 1906 interpreted mental disorders as inadequate habits of dealing with the difficulties of life. In 1908 he defined mind as a "sufficiently organized living being in action and not a peculiar form of mind stuff" and emphasized the important fact that "mental activity is really best understood in its full meaning as the adaptation and adjustment of the individual as a whole, in contrast to the simple activity of single organs." He has devised a nomenclature for psychiatry which is the nearest approach to a basis for reliable statistics that has yet appeared.* Adopting *ergasia* as the best term for performance and behavior and psychobiologically integrated activity in general, including mentation, he has derived from it the following classification of reaction types: the anergastic disorders, or organic deficits as acquired defect reactions or dementias; the dysergastic or support disorders, represented by the deliria and hallucination disorders of infection, poison, and malnutrition; the parergastic and paranoic reactions, which are diffuse and general as in the schizophrenic, or circumscribed and systematized as in paranoia or in the paranoic, or paranoid, types; the thymergastic or affective reactions of excessive speeding up or of depression and slowing, without essential distortion; the merergastic or minor psychosis, with neurasthenic, anxiety, obsession, submersion, and epileptic groups of reactions; and the oligergastic states of defective development represented by idiocy, imbecility, and moron types.

Psychiatric theory has more recently been reoriented on the basis of an appreciation of the fact that the human organism is made up not only of parts of the physicochemical world but also of accessions acquired from the universe of culture. This ap-

[* This is one of the few places in Sullivan's writings where he has made any serious attempt to use Meyer's *ergasia* series of terms. H.S.P.]

proach recognizes that the person, psychobiologically conceived, maintains organization, communal existence, and functional activity in and within both the physicochemical and the superorganic cultural universe. The study of the life course of the individual becomes more intelligible when personality is conceived as the hypothetical entity which manifests itself in interpersonal relations, the latter including interactions with other people, real or fancied, primarily or mediately integrated into dynamic complexes; and with traditions, customs, inventions, and institutions produced by man. These interactions indicate that in a somewhat homogeneous culture complex there is a rather consistent course of growth of personality. Along with the elaboration of physicochemical factors, there is a progressive elaboration and differentiation of motives. These integrating tendencies are acquired from a steadily expanding series of culture surrogates, such as the mother, the family group, teachers, companions, chums, friends, love objects, enemies, employers, and colleagues. The motives manifest themselves in the integration of total situations or systems involving two or more people, real or fancied, and a variety of cultural elements. Within these motives are demands for certain activities, sometimes consciously formulated in terms of a goal, at other times devoid of any conscious formulation, in which case the activity is unnoted by the participants. Frequently the formulation is imperfect and is expressed in accidental, meaningless or mistaken activity or rationalized in plausible abstractions from common experience without much regard to the possibility of consensual validation. When the activity demanded by the system has been consummated, the motivation is replaced by another. Not infrequently, however, the activity is complicated by conflicting motives and their attendant processes of system integration; in such cases maladjustive or nonadjustive processes are observed.

The activities both of integrating and of resolving interpersonal situations as well as of dealing with the nonpersonified world may be envisaged as manifestations of a biological organism possessing instrumental receptor and effector organs, which constitute its zones of interaction with the environment. The characteristics of these zones are fixed primarily by the constitution which the particular organism has developed through heredity and nutrition. If the individual at birth is endowed with little possibility of growth of the higher nervous system, or if early injury arrests its growth or if there is some chemical deficiency in the food which delays or enfeebles the organization and functional activity of these tissues, what is commonly called mental deficiency results. A great part of the cultural heritage which would otherwise be available then remains irrelevant; it cannot be assimilated into the personality, which is correspondingly limited in its capacity for integration with people and with the materials of civilization. If the individual from birth through infancy and childhood is subjected by the mother and the family group to highly inconsistent inhibitory and facilitating experience (if the family group is psychotic or if the child is generally unwelcome), the individual is likely to show increasing deviation from consistent growth through adolescence. Unless he is extraordinarily fortunate in his school situation, it is probable that his deviation will be so great that he will not develop the tendencies characteristic of preadolescent and adolescent individuals, so that he will be what is commonly designated as a psychopathic personality, a nuisance within the social fabric, incapable of accommodation and cooperation and unequal to the task of restraining himself from immediate satisfactions. Thus while the mentally deficient are fundamentally handicapped by constitutional factors, psychopathic personalities are the products of experience; both are relatively incompetent in their relations with other people.

The symptomatic acts which are expressions of the mentally disordered are therefore most meaningful for psychiatry when their interpersonal contexts are known. They are otherwise psychological, physiological, or biophysical aspects of human processes, unilluminating in reference to the personality chiefly concerned. Formulations in terms of mental mechanisms, neurological and endocrinological entities, reflex arcs and somatic tension sets are too general and too partial to aid in the understanding of mental health or its absence. They apply in cases of crippled personalities suffering from dementia paralytica, which, since it is characterized by a specific chain of symptomatic events, can be diagnosed with a high degree of probability. But even the interpersonal activity of the patient in the early stages of this malady is explicable only when referred to his personal history. Psychiatric consideration of dementia paralytica becomes a matter chiefly for physiology only after the disease process has destroyed the tissues associated with human as contrasted with infrahuman behavior.

Almost all of the milder maladjustments which are evidenced in personal, domestic, and occupational inefficiencies of various types, some seemingly because of physical illness, others clearly mental and still others a combination of the two, arise from warp encountered in earlier stages of personality growth, often in turn the effect of mild mental disorder in one or more of the family group. Once established, some maladjustments are very difficult to remedy; among them, for example, is the obsessional state, in which morbid doubts, scruples, fears, or preoccupation with ritualistic activities and systems of thought are substituted for direct interpersonal adjustment, to the great detriment of useful living and to the extreme inconvenience of those who are in contact with the patient. The obsessed person may be described as one who has come to utilize gestures and words, cultural entities, in an unduly complex and individualistic fashion. The performances of the person who must continually clear his throat, emit grunts, or activate various expressive neuromuscular units in lieu of aggressively compelling the submission of others, or of the sexually deviated male who must parody feminine behavior in order to stimulate and frustrate the equivalent motivations in other men he encounters are comparable to compulsions to step on certain cracks in the pavement or to obfuscate every issue with superficially irrelevant or incomprehensible theorizations. The obsessional states probably surpass in their vicious cultural consequences the more immediately grave paranoid states, wherein motivations which conflict with early inhibitory training are projected by morbid sensitivity, suspicion, and delusions of persecution, to such effect that all blame is transferred out of the self-consciousness, which is correspondingly exalted and regarded as grandiosely good.

Besides the chronic fatigue and irritability of the neurasthenic and the compromises of the hysteric, these merergastic disorders include the milder grades of hypochondriasis, which is often a parergastic disorder, and the anxiety states. Anxiety, in the psychiatric sense, is morbid fear, a symptom experienced from irrational threats to the personality. While it is an important factor in the development of many, if not all, mental disorders, it makes up the symptomatology of one of them. In the anxiety states, the sufferer undergoes obscurely motivated attacks of fear; the symptoms may be attacks of palpitation, perspiration, trembling, intestinal disturbance, or indigestion. If the disorder is severe and the attacks recur frequently, or more or less continuously, there may appear physical disorders which are often regarded as medical diseases.

The disastrous social consequences of mental disorders are of inestimable significance. The victims of parergastic (schizophrenic, dementia praecox) disorders alone filled in 1930 more than one half of the 438,000 hospital beds in the United States and comprise one fifth of the annual admittances; 70 percent are between twenty and forty years old when they enter the hospital, where many of them remain under care until they die. The per capita incidence of parergastic disorders in the United States does not appear to differ as between Negroes and whites; they are found among immigrant as well as native white and Mongoloid stock. Statistics are available as to the frequency of these disorders only in European-American countries. . . .*

The proportion of hospital patients suffering from the gravest disorders varies not only from country to country but in different sections of the same state. In general it is higher in urban than in rural communities, and in wealthier than in poorer sections. There is no basis for an accurate estimate of the number of people partially disabled by milder disorders, but there is every reason to believe that in Europe and the United States there are many more such victims than are receiving institutional care.

The treatment that has been developed from environmentalistic and from psychobiological psychiatry comprises immediate and mediate procedures. The former are based on direct contact

[* A table on "Institutions for the Mentally Disordered in Twenty-Six Countries," compiled from reports of the International Health Organization of the League of Nations, has been deleted at this point. H.S.P.]

with the psychiatrist, as in the case of the psychoanalytic, psychocathartic, and psychosynthetic techniques, the latter on the utilization of psychiatrically supervised personal environments. The immediate methods are often unavailable to the sufferer largely because of the time required and expense entailed; while, except in child guidance work and some work with delinquents, such as that by Aichhorn, the mediate techniques are in the stage of empirical application or scientific exploration. A significant experiment in this direction has been reported from one of the endowed hospitals.* Acute parergastic patients who had undergone rapid development of the psychosis were placed in a situation in which they were encouraged to renew efforts at adjustment with others and in which they were as little discouraged and rebuffed as was consistent with their bodily safety. Besides each other, they encountered only a trained personnel consciously integrated toward encouraging security in interpersonal relations. There are no reliable statistics as to the proportion of parergastic patients whose disorder was originally acute, but it is probably increasing and is perhaps now about one in three. Inasmuch as these disorders often appear in persons from fifteen to twenty-five years of age and fully as often among superior individuals as among those of inferior intelligence and ability, and since the recovery rate of those promptly hospitalized under ordinarily good care is probably less than 30 percent, this experimental achievement—80 percent social recovery—indicates tentatively that this method of treatment is efficacious. Social recovery here means, however, merely that the patient has regained the capacity to conduct his life without supervision; it does not mean that the underlying warp leading to the psychosis has been remedied completely but implies some degree of increased adaptability and is a prerequisite to more fundamental treatment. Some psychiatrists hold that by definition dementia praecox patients cannot recover; moreover another study in the same hospital suggests that parergastic phenomena of insidious rather than of acute onset are more serious. It is not therefore to be understood that a uniform high rate of improvement can be anticipated from the application of this sort of treatment to all parergastic patients, even if instituted

[* Here begins a summary of Sullivan's work at Sheppard. H.S.P.]

early.

The mediate, socio-psychiatric approach to the gravest disorders of adolescence employed in the experiment described above is the formulated application of long established therapeutic factors. Thus many adolescents are now saved from serious upheavals by the socializing influences of supervised recreational and educational activities such as those encountered in summer camps. A new type of therapy based on socialization programs within and outside of institutions should reduce the destruction of personality by parergastic disorders to a small part of the current figure and should go far toward alleviating the present burden of minor maladjustments.

13

Commentary

THE NEXT paper was part of a symposium on the relation of psychoanalysis to psychiatry, held by the American Psychiatric Association in 1934, in which A. A. Brill, Ross McC. Chapman, and Leland E. Hinsie also participated. The Association had just added a new Section on Psychoanalysis the year before; and the other members of the symposium presented material which was somewhat in the nature of a defense of psychoanalysis. Characteristically, Sullivan has examined the alternative hypothesis: Psychiatry adds something to psychoanalytic techniques and practice. He equates knowledge of psychiatry with experience in the mental hospital and notes that ". . . the good mental hospital offers opportunities for learning interpersonal reality such as most of us encounter elsewhere only in infancy."

Psychiatric Training as a Prerequisite to Psychoanalytic Practice†

THUS FAR in this symposium we have heard of the contributions from psychoanalysis to psychiatry. It is my privilege to point out something of the other current of exchange—something of that which psychiatry has to offer, and has given, to psychoanalysis. To cover this whole great topic in the minutes at my disposal would require very sketchy treatment, indeed, and I shall not even enumerate the points of prime importance in the relationship of general psychiatric theory and general mental hospital work to the growth of the important body of useful data that makes up current American psychoanalysis. Instead, I shall concentrate on the contribution of psychiatric training to the professional competence of the psychoanalyst, himself.

Any discussion of the importance of psychiatric experience in the training of the psychoanalyst must begin with a consideration of the factors that determine the choice of psychiatry and the subordinate choice of psychoanalysis as a life career. There are factors of a positive character operative here, and there are some negative ones. The role which the mental hospital may have in eliminating the influence of the negative factors that might appear

† Reprinted from *Amer. J. Psychiatry* (1934-35) 91: 1117-1126. Read at the ninetieth annual meeting of the American Psychiatric Association, Section on Psychoanalysis, New York City, May 28-June 1, 1934.

in psychoanalysts without this training cannot be overestimated in its bearing on the fate of one's patients. The mental hospital is a community characterized by a strong interest in human behavior and an alertness to personality characteristics. Some of the people who come to psychiatry make this choice of a route through life in part for reasons that promise little as to the welfare of their future patients. In the well-organized mental hospital, these young physicians themselves come under an intelligent, tolerant attention, a scrutiny by those skilled in observing human behavior and in clear thinking about the personality of the behaver, and receive constructive comments and friendly criticism that may encourage a change from the state in which they would perpetrate by neurotic mechanisms certain of their own character peculiarities upon the patients whom they treat—if in fact, these same influences do not cut short an unfortunate miscasting in the role of physician treating mental or personality difficulties. If the mental hospital did nothing else for the candidate for psychoanalysis but subject him to this scrutiny, appraisal, and advice, it would still be well justified as a prerequisite training for the practice of psychoanalysis.

The mental hospital validates one's choice of psychiatry and one's choice of psychoanalysis. Unfortunately, in this process there occur some events which give color to what I prefer to call the superstitions about the dangers of psychoanalysis. Textbooks and papers by psychiatrists whose acquaintance with psychoanalysis is far from adequate, and by analysts whose acquaintance with psychiatry leaves much to be desired, combine to perpetuate various beliefs to the effect that the application of psychoanalysis to the psychoses is dangerous, that it is destructive or at least detrimental to such patients. Undoubtedly, psychoses have been precipitated and beyond perchance social recoveries have been prevented by activities that might be called psychoanalysis, but which in fact are activities that have occurred because of improper utilization of the training functions of the mental hospital. . . .

If you will be tolerant, I must offer a simple statement as to the nature of the psychoanalytic process—not because psychoanalysis is so recondite to most of you, but because it will simplify my presentation if I say precisely what I mean. Psychoanalysis for the purpose of this presentation is the psychoanalysis properly derivative from the work of Sigmund Freud. It is made up of three classes of processes.

The first great class is that to which we may refer as processes of free association, of more or less freely verbalized reverie processes that appear in the psychoanalytic situation. It is easy for anyone to learn the formula, "Say every little thing that comes to your mind, that you notice in your consciousness." It is even probable that any of us might at times derive benefit from carrying out such a procedure in the presence of some good friend. By this I mean that everyone is apt to have in his reverie some manifestations of his life situation that he is ignoring or excluding from alert attention to the detriment of his successful adjustment in the situations through which he is progressing. This type of superficial expansion of one's clear awareness of self is, however, but a very small part of that which psychoanalysis has to offer to its patients.

The second great class of processes may be called interpretation. It is the participation by the psychoanalyst in the psychoanalytic situation that comes about on the basis of his skill, insight, and experience, in contradistinction to his role and general personal characteristics. He offers timely interpretation of obscure phenomena that are appearing in the life of the patient, including the psychoanalysis. At best, interpreting the activity—including the speech—of another person can never be perfect; and the correctness of one's interpretation of another's acts can vary from vast improbability to very high probability. In dealing with people who are fairly well able to deal with life as they find it, a good deal of misinterpretation is tolerable and approximately harmless. In dealing with people, however, whose margin of adjustive safety is greatly reduced, whose living is precarious or has failed, misinterpretation—interpretations of low probability—imposes an additional burden that may have very serious consequences. Interpretation, however, cannot be avoided; the psychoanalyst must offer timely interpretations because otherwise the stream of reverie processes remains superficial, and the reconstruction of the personality and the obliteration of maladjustive processes cannot be accomplished. In other words, psychoanalysis, primarily dependent on the free-association method of observing consciousness discovered by Freud, utilizes it therapeutically to remedy obscure aspects of the patient's living through the influencing of the associational stream by wise and timely interventions, called interpretations. Well-digested experience that has grown into insight as to one's relationship to one's past is obviously necessary if one is to offer sound and helpful interpretations to another.

The third great class of processes which go to make up the psychoanalytic situation, however, surpass in significance and in subtlety all other aspects of the interpretation of the data produced by free fantasy. Freud has referred to this third class as the transference phenomena. By transference the patient manifests interpersonal processes that open the gates of memory sealed by dissociations, reorients his experience, and facilitates the development of arrested or distorted systems of motives so that he moves forward toward the conditions of adult personality organization. The handling of the transference in psychoanalysis has been discussed since the very first paper by Freud. And yet anything like a definitive statement about transference situations, transference processes, and the handling of transference must await the completion of investigations that will take many years. I speak to you today solely because it has been my privilege to apply the psychoanalytic technique to schizophrenic patients and to others showing schizoid or detached personality organization. From this work, I have learned certain facts about transference relationships which otherwise would certainly have escaped me, and on this basis have come to insist on adequate psychiatric experience as a prerequisite to the practice of psychoanalytic therapy.

When I first submitted myself to some 75 hours of psychoanalysis, as psychoanalysis existed in the winter of 1916–17, I developed a conviction that I understood transference processes enough to work with them. Fortunately for me, however, I came to have [the experience of working] with schizophrenics. As the years pass, I have come more and more to understand the events that characterized the earlier part of my research into schizophrenic processes.

Schizophrenics differ from other types of patients in that their motivation is peculiarly integrated so that they undergo with extraordinary ease reactivations of emotional configurations that are seldom observed in other types of people—from which unpleasant experiences they come to protect themselves by "distance," indifference, and "apathy." Let me talk about them for a moment. If one is dealing with an hysteric, one anticipates in the course of a successful psychoanalysis the reappearance of some very early emotional configurations; but one begins at the level of one's fellow man in ordinary life. One talks first of more or less adult relationships, as they are manifested. And one works gradually back to the earlier configurations in a manner that is fairly smooth, and fairly easy to follow. On the other hand, when one has at last, by the skill of one's preliminary work, actually entered into relationships of intimacy with a schizophrenic, one passes suddenly from the realm of ordinary people, from the types of relationship that one recognizes among one's fellows from school years onward, into a type of interpersonal situation that can actually be referred only to the relationships that characterize the first three years of life. Abruptly, often without warning, one finds oneself integrated by powerful motives of the type of hatred and primitive love and others for which our language is lacking in terms.

Schizophrenics are the people with whom one must never make a serious mistake. These patients have learned long before they appear for treatment that there is no one in the wide world who can be trusted to value and to love one. They have developed a certain timelessness in these negative convictions and often wait quite patiently for the physician to prove that he is not trustworthy, either. His mistake accomplishes his classification with the other ones who have failed to appreciate and to love the patient; from thenceforth there is no increase in intimacy with the patient—seldom any chance to undo the damage one has done. It is for this reason that psychoanalytic work with schizophrenic patients teaches one a great humility as to formulation and to interpretation, a great caution as to determining what may really be meaningful in the life of another, and gives one the subtle simplicity, if you will permit this locution, which is indispensable in dealing with a great section of one's fellows—all those shy and detached people the number of whom perhaps increases from generation to generation, whose achievements under favorable circumstances clearly entitle them to proper treatment.

It is extremely difficult to learn about psychoanalysis from the direct comparison of the results achieved by different psychoanalysts. Psychoneurotic patients are able to compensate for great numbers of mistakes on the part of analysts—even sometimes surviving and tolerating amazingly blind behavior on the part of the physician. I can present to you only some comments on my personal experience, somewhat confirmed by the work of the few of my colleagues with whose patients and whose personality I am somewhat familiar. As I say, in the years after the [First World] War it seemed to me that I was acquainted with psychoanalysis. Some spectacular failures with schizophrenic women impressed upon me that I was suffering what we call a scotoma—or better a field of scotomata. In other words, I was doing things of which I had no awareness, in situations that I did not comprehend to a satisfactory degree. After more than a decade, and with the experience of intensive research, I went on to some 300-odd hours further of personal psychoanalysis, and a great deal that I had undergone in the years before took on new meaning. It is on the basis of this training and the experience of more than 10,000 patient-hours, hours spent with patients in psychoanalytic situations, that I have accumulated the insight and the humility which is the basis for the views I am now laying before you.

The meaning of the free associational material—the formulations that the psychoanalyst can offer to assist the patient—in the last analysis come entirely from the interpersonal relationship which the physician participates in and permits the patient to integrate with him. There is nothing else in the activity of man that approximates the complexity and subtlety of the psychoanalytic situation. No one can know all about this type of relationship as it exists today, and it is unthinkable that anyone can delineate the psychoanalytic situations that will be integrated with people in the future. Culture grows, and the human personality is an expanding series. Techniques of therapy must grow in the same manner. None the less, admitting that this work is an unending quest, in which the best of us must at times prove opaque or inattentive or incapable of grasping a sufficient number of factors, one still can point out certain failures which are or should become unpardonable in psychoanalytic practice. I refer here to failures of the psychoanalyst to recognize the transference processes, the shifting emotional relationships which spring up in his work with each individual patient. Any blindness in this field produces great stresses in the personality undergoing psychoanalysis, can lead to serious disorders of behavior and in fact to the appearance of more ominous symptoms than those preceding the attempt at psychoanalysis. Just as you, before you had acquired some of the wealth of the Greek and the Latin languages for creating terminologies, could have read medical books without much profit, so also in psychoanalysis until one has learned the signals, the signs and the symptoms of transference manifestations, by successes and failures, by tedious trials and errors, one knows nothing of what is really psychoanalysis—something which is talked about a great deal, but is understood only after a long apprenticeship.

The experience of the student physician in the mental hospital is indispensable to his safety as a practitioner, at least among character disorders, detached personalities, schizoid types, and the like. I do not generalize this further because of lack of experience. But going to a mental hospital and living and working there for a time is not by any manner of means the experience which I have in mind. Under extraordinarily favorable circumstances, I have seen something of the development of a number of young physicians. From these data and from consideration of the deficiencies in my own education, I have come to the following conclusions: It is perfectly possible to spend a year or a lifetime on the staff of a mental hospital without having detected anything of any profound significance about interpersonal relations, about transference phenomena, or anything else peculiarly useful in preparing one for the practice of psychoanalysis. Clearly, one must be supervised in one's work with mental patients, one's activities must be directed, and the type of activity engaged in must be suited to one's expanding capacity. But before I develop this aspect of my views, let me summarize what I conceive that the mental hospital has to offer.

In the first place, the good mental hospital offers opportunities for learning interpersonal reality such as most of us encounter elsewhere only in infancy. Secondly, it leads many young physicians who are overzealous of helping patients into what we call flippantly "transference jams," into interpersonal relationships involving a patient which are so complicated and so stressful that even though they may embarrass the patient gravely, they also— if there is any sort of competent supervision—embarrass the young physician and lead him to inquire into his deficiencies. How often these so-called transference jams have led promising young men to undergo a personal psychoanalysis is by no means sufficiently publicized. It is certainly a very important function, even if rather expensive to the patients concerned, that the mental hospital performs in teaching these young physicians that it requires knowledge to help a person in trouble. Before I proceed to my last point as to the opportunities provided by the mental hospital, let me touch upon a particularly favorable outcome of the transference jam. While it might be ideal that one be really competent before one undertakes the healing of the sick, all of you know that the nature of things prohibits such an ideal. While it might be ideal to have only highly competent psychiatrists and psychoanalysts dealing with the mentally ill, I need not stress reality in this connection. The combination of a personal psychoanalysis with one's work with patients in the mental hospital has certain singular advantages which I believe are not shared by psychoanalysis under other circumstances. There is a very real danger that any psychoanalyst will perpetuate in his analysands many or all of the limitations of his own analysis—and analyst. This is the reason that we are so insistent that psychoanalytic training shall include a good deal of work under supervision by others than the training psychoanalyst. Now, people who are suffering mental disorders have so serious a diminution of their capacity to adjust to mistakes and to tolerate conceit and limitations on the part of their therapist that they provide a unique opportunity to discover that one has been analyzed, or is being analyzed, to suit some psychoanalyst, and not in order to attain maximum integration of personality and maximum insight. In other words, psychotic and subpsychotic patients respond vividly to the psychoanalyst's scotomata, or blind spots, and demonstrate his incompetence with remarkable precision.

Finally, the mental hospital provides the young physician with an opportunity to learn something which is most vital to the welfare of his future patients. He learns what a neurotic choice of patients amounts to; and what a sound choice of patients is, for him. Young psychiatrists show interest in sundry patients, and a competent psychopathologist can in each case say why, if he has data enough; but in general it comes about that where there is very little insight, the choice of patients with whom to work is sometimes incredibly bad, foredoomed regardless of effort. The training in the mental hospital, coupled with one's own psychoanalysis, clarifies these neurotic drives to interest oneself in the very people one cannot work with because of an overlapping problem.

Let me take up now the content of adequate mental hospital experience. The purposes of working in the mental hospital as a preliminary to the practice of psychoanalysis amounts in a sentence to this: It is a vast augmentation of alertness. This augmentation cannot be expected to happen as a concomitant of mere existence among the mentally ill. I am convinced that methodic steps amounting to intensive supervision of the potential psychoanalyst from the very day of his entrance to the mental hospital service is urgently necessary. On the one hand, it requires a good deal of supervision to bring any young physician's ideas of what he is doing into harmony with what the patients and perhaps their relatives who come in contact with him think about it. From these two streams of data, with a great deal of help from someone who is aware of personality processes, there can be a slow growth in the objectivity of the young physician's behavior, a slow expansion of his field of conscious awareness, in contradistinction to unconscious mischief, regrettable misunderstandings, and the like. In the second place, there is an unremitting necessity for intensive criticism and clinical demonstrations. I personally favor heartily the requirement that the young physician make many written statements as to his view of this and that.

Suave, quick-minded people often conceal in their spoken comments serious misapprehensions that they entertain. Once their views are recorded, deficiencies in their formulations are readily pointed out. Intensive criticism of all clinical histories, notes of interviews, reports of events concerning patients, coupled with some clinical demonstrations of how things really are done and of what has significance in the relationship of a competent psychiatrist and his patient, would vastly abbreviate the staggering amount of time it takes the average interne to find a clue to the nature of psychiatric therapy. I have said often that it takes 18 months residence in a good mental hospital to provide the average psychiatric interne with some notion of what psychiatry and psychiatric patients are. This would not be the case were the supervision adequate. Moreover, adequate supervision would remedy immediately one grave development that now involves many young physicians who enter the psychiatric field. I refer here to the damnable business of learning how to "get away with it" without really knowing what is going on, or caring—no asset to any psychiatrist or psychoanalyst. Supervision cannot begin too soon in the mental hospital. Without it, only the most exceptional person secures reasonable returns on the time and effort he spends.

With excellent supervision, on the other hand, so great is the teaching value of intensive therapeutic work with psychotic patients either in periods of remission or (when one has become competent) during active aggravation, that this should be required in the education of every psychoanalyst who by accident or design is to deal with detached and schizoid patients, character disorders, and similar serious problems.

14

Commentary

AN EXCERPT from the unpublished book manuscript, *Personal Psychopathology*, is presented as the final paper in this book. The fact that the manuscript as a whole has not yet been published, after a span of twenty-five years, is a subject for some speculation among Sullivan's colleagues and students. Much of the writing is simpler and more communicative than most of Sullivan's prose before and after. Certainly many of Sullivan's colleagues—Patrick Mullahy and Harold Lasswell, for instance [1]—consider this manuscript a major contribution. At one time, Sullivan actually made a tentative arrangement with a publishing house for publication, but the manuscript was then withdrawn—in part, at the insistence of an overzealous colleague who predicted that publication might be "regretted" by Sullivan at a later date as representing a premature statement of his theory. At any rate, Sullivan put it aside for further revision, although it had already gone through several, and the press of life did not allow him to return to it; new ideas and new tasks intervened. In a competitive society, friends and colleagues of the productively creative person sometimes set standards of perfection that, in the light of perspective over time, seem harsh and regrettable. The following excerpt will give the reader an opportunity to judge for himself.

The style of this excerpt shows the influence of the then current literary climate of the United States generally and, interestingly enough, of Baltimore in particular. Sullivan's satirical use of capital letters for social institutions of doubtful worth—such as Criminal Justice and the Established Elite—is reminiscent of the *Smart Set*

[1] Personal communication.

319

under the editorship (1914–1924) of the Baltimore Sage, H. L. Mencken, and of George Jean Nathan. Echoes of this same general climate are, of course, found in Sinclair Lewis' *Main Street* (1920) and *Babbitt* (1922). For the interested reader, Mark Schorer's new biography of Sinclair Lewis,[2] which contains a sweeping study of this whole period in American letters and culture, will lend perspective to Sullivan's work as reported in this book.

[2] Mark Schorer, *Sinclair Lewis: An American Life;* New York: McGraw-Hill, 1961.

Cultural Stress and
Adolescent Crisis†

HISTORICALLY, psychiatry has been a field peculiarly afflicted by bad thinking and premature hypothetic formulation. Of many reasons for this, I will touch upon two. The facts of mental illness have often been seen through the aberrating medium of patho-physiological preconceptions—brain pathology and the like, endocrine disorders being perhaps the most recent. And the physician has been carried into the recondite field of mind without training in the technologies suiting him to his enterprise, and with training tending definitely to disqualify him for perceiving the data on which he should base his conclusions. Especially in the field of the schizophrenic phenomena, there has been a pandemic of formulating on limited if not actually irrelevant basic data, with singularly bad hypotheses, some of the most vicious features of which have been incorporated into persisting psychiatric astigmatisms.

Now therefore, being about to take up discussion of the origin of schizophrenic processes, I find myself not alone confronted by entrenched erroneous conceptions supported by many adherents, but also embarrassed by the fact that I, too, have a formu-

† From Chapter VII, entitled "Male Adolescence," in *Personal Psychopathology*, unpublished book manuscript, written between 1929 and 1933. [The title of the excerpt has been supplied by me, although the ideas and words are from the text. H.S.P.]

lation—a premature formulation, beyond doubt.[1] It seems to me that there is evident a certain course of sequents and consequents that make up the reality of this type of personality disaster; and I wish now to present some of the facts, as I see them, on the nature of anteceding conflicts from which many—perhaps 'predisposed'—adolescents progress into this very grave form of mental disorder.

There was admitted, one day, to the most disturbed ward of the hospital a nineteen-year-old patient. He was brought to the hospital in a patrol wagon, in the custody of several police and attendants. I was told that he had become disorderly in his home the preceding evening, and had broken some windows. That morning, he had been seen by a neurologist and diagnosed as a case of dementia praecox, paranoid type. I saw him a few minutes after he had reached the ward—he was engaged in arguing with a group of attendants as to whether he should be disrobed and put to bed. When I entered the situation, he assumed a distinctly hostile, superior, and somewhat sardonic attitude toward me. After some formalities I reduced the number of people present to himself and me, and touched upon several points of his life history with him. The result of our fifteen-minute talk is in many ways expressive of the points that I wish to discuss.

He said that he must, if we wished to help him, immediately be sent home to his father—that he would have been all right had it not been for two vile characters who had been in the house last night, and that he would not have known what they were plotting if it were not for his acquaintance with the language of the underworld. He went on to say that everything was

[1] While some several thousand of my fellows have flowed through the field of my attention, only some two hundred of them, seemingly fruitful sources of information, have been made the subjects of approximately scientific study. In all humility, I must relate that it is on the data of some seventy-five patients suffering undoubtedly schizophrenic processes, and a hundred and fifty persons in whom the outcropping of schizophrenic processes seemed more than ordinarily probable—on such few data from this field of incalculable vastness I have proceeded to a formulation. How diligently I have sought for negative instances destructive to my formulation, I am scarcely the one to judge. The controls to be derived from comparative studies—the consideration of adolescence and adolescent mental disorder in cultures other than ours—have not been available to me.

all right until two months ago, when, through the carelessness of one of 'those people,' he had learned of the plot. He remarked that these people, who by their carelessness had permitted him to stumble upon something of importance, had arranged a fight between him and another young man at Miami Beach, but that he had been fortunate enough to defeat the youngster—adding that a young man like himself had no chance. "They wouldn't give a fellow like me a chance." I asked him what he meant by saying a fellow like him—what it was that he felt distinguished him from most people—and he did not produce anything of importance. I reiterated that he had said they wouldn't give a fellow like him a chance, adding that I could not see wherein he was very different from most nineteen-year-olds; that if anything, he seemed to have some things in his favor—and he said something which indicated that he more or less agreed. The long and short of it seemed to be that there was nothing peculiarly remarkable excepting that he had stumbled upon this profoundly significant information. I remarked that quite often adolescents who were far from satisfied with themselves came to believe that they had discovered something of the utmost importance. He said he knew what was meant by adolescence—that he understood that the term meant the period after puberty. I said to him, "Yes: the period in which one discovers sex and attempts to do something with it." He looked interested. I might add that in the course of these few remarks he had lost most of the antagonistic mask and signs of poorly concealed fear. We went on from there by my remarking that I supposed, as seemed always to be the case with people of his age who were brought to a mental hospital, that there was some difficulty confronting him in the field of sex, whereupon he said, "No, I have never been interested in anything but women." I said, "Oh, is that so?" He said, "Yes." I said, "Well, have you had sexual relations?" He said, "Yes, but only with women." I said, "Is it that you wish to emphasize to me that you have not had homosexual affairs?" He said, "Never— I hate it." I said, "Well, then you have come in contact with it?" He said, "Oh yes, in my theatre work I have seen a great deal of it, but I have never had anything to do with it. Whenever anyone approached me in that way I have loathed it because it was so . . . ," pausing, "so unnatural and so dirty." I said, "Well, I suppose you have had some actual experience with it, though, have you not?" He replied, "Never—only with women. Whenever a person has approached me that way I have—loathed it—I have had a strong impulse to hit him in the face. I wanted to knock him down." I said, "Well—I would interpret such a feeling as reflecting a pretty strong interest in it on your part"; by this time I seemed to be talking more or less to myself, thereby providing him with a way of absorbing the intelligence without too strong an urge for impressing me. He said nothing about it; showed no signs of particular distress. He had settled himself in bed, free from any conspicuous tensions. I added some general comments on the social situation created by one's admission as a patient into a mental hospital, on the character of misunderstandings, illusions, and delusions that young schizophrenics are prone to develop in such a situation, and on my hope that he would cling to the belief that he was in the hands of friends and well-meaning, however stupid, people. Having received some measure of assurance from him as to the last point, I took my departure.[2]

It is difficult to avoid a conclusion from a long series of data similar in character to that of this patient. This young man is typical of a large proportion of my patients in acute schizophrenic disorders, in that, as soon as the topic of sex is introduced, he finds himself called upon to protest as to the normality of his sexual interests. He projects upon me, in response to my neutral remark to the effect that all adolescents have somewhat of a problem in the matter of sex, his own suspicion that his sexual interest focuses on members of his own sex. He finds himself suspected of homoerotic interests as soon as the topic of sex appears in the conversation. His activity in resolution of this situation,

[2] While I deem it irrelevant to this presentation, I am constrained to present three additional facts concerning this patient. Firstly, nothing of the procedure of being brought to the hospital, or admitted thereto, or in the events immediately preliminary to my interview with him, had any reasonable implication of knowledge or belief that he might be entertaining homoerotic interests. Secondly, he *had actually*, by clumsy and doubtlessly only vaguely conscious arrangement, secured himself the active attention of an homosexually inclined boy, some months before, and had engaged in behavior showing distinct homoerotic interests on his part. Thirdly, the patient has continued in a severe schizophrenic condition for over two years.

his over-stressing of normal direction of sexual interest, expresses the conflict which he cannot escape—namely, the knowledge that his sexual tendencies include other than women as objects, and the opposing ethical appraisal of this condition as bad, wrong, and shameful, and destructive to the regard of others.

To illustrate the other important group of problems also culminating in acute schizophrenic illnesses, I will present in outline the case of another patient, this one a six-foot-three youth of eighteen. This young man came in the custody of two attendants from a general hospital at which he had been under observation because of suspected *encephalitis lethargica* ('sleeping sickness'). I saw him immediately on admission, finding him very morose and forbidding in his attitude. He was quite willing to state that he was sick, but "of course" there was not any reason for his being sent to a mental hospital, as nothing ailed his mind. His trouble was not of the mind but of the belly; his bowels didn't work, and things were not any longer all there in his belly. It was not difficult to learn that this state had come about by his wearing himself out masturbating. He had masturbated so long and so much that things inside were worn out, gone. I remarked, "In other words, you masturbated until you could no longer have the ejaculation?" He said very simply that this was the case, adding that on the occasion on which he had found that he was "through," could not bring himself to orgasm, a change had come over him. He said that thereafter he had gone into the kitchen, eaten his dinner, and then sat around staring at his mother and making noises with his mouth. These annoyed her, and they had sent him to a hospital. As a matter of fact, the family had been so disconcerted by his peculiar behavior and threatening attitude that they had called in a neurologist. This patient proved quite amenable to treatment and made a rather prompt social recovery.[3] He was not permitted to collaborate in intensive study of the underlying problems, and relapsed into a quite paranoid episode after about a year at large. When returned

[3] The conception of *social recovery* is one used in mental hospital practice to refer to the reintegration of personality to the degree that permits of conventional behavior in the hospital situation, without known remedy of the underlying problems.

to the hospital, he again recovered—this time with the acquisition of some considerable insight—and remained comfortably employed for some three years. I then saw him on one occasion. He consulted me because he was growing tense and somewhat apprehensive because the woman (considerably his senior) with whom he was having sexual intercourse was urging him to marry her. Our conversation aided him in becoming satisfied with his decision to go slow in taking this step, and the discomfort diminished.

This young man had at one stage of his illness a phenomenon of great importance in many early schizophrenic disorders—namely, a dream of frankly incestuous content. It is not uncommon for those progressing into these grave disturbances to encounter in sleep or other states of reduced consciousness, profoundly disturbing outcroppings of sexual desire for the mother. They dream of having intercourse with her, of being on the verge of it, of palpating her genitals, or something similar. I have known patients to make violent efforts at suicide by immediate reason of the recurrence of such a dream. One is apt to find that the sexual dreams and fantasies that these preschizophrenic youths have been experiencing for months or years before the acute disturbance, have pertained to an *unidentified* representative of the other sex. The paradigm is the dream of sexual intercourse with a woman whose body is clearly revealed, but whose face is not at all clear. Or intercourse is had with "some girl," perhaps seemingly a different one in each dream—although often the girl is continually a stranger, and one poorly remarked as to recognizable characteristics. From what has already been said regarding the obstruction of growth of sexual tendencies by too intimate a linkage with the mother, it might be suspected that these quasi-heterosexual dreams are not all that they seem. We learn that they may mark a course that culminates in a schizophrenic illness, in which there is intense conflict over homoerotic interests; and they are not uncommon in individuals presently to adopt maladjustive homosexual habits. In fact, it is not uncommon for the dream-life to show a gradual or abrupt change from intercouse with unidentified women to sexual relations with someone who turns out to be, if not in fact clearly of the same sex as that of the dreamer, at least a sexually confused, perhaps hermaphroditic, individual.

From my material, in which negative instances are conspicuously absent, I am forced to the conclusion that schizophrenic illnesses in the male are intimately related as a sequent to unfortunate prolongation of the attachment of the son and the mother. That schizophrenic disorders are but one of the possible outcomes of persisting immature attitudes subtending the mother and son relationship must be evident. The failure of growth of heterosexual interests, with persistence of autoerotic or homoerotic interests in adolescence, is the general formula. The factors that determine a schizophrenic outcome may be clarified by a discussion on the one hand of the situations to which I shall refer as homosexual cravings and acute masturbation conflict—often immediate precursors of grave psychosis—and of the various homoerotic and autoerotic procedures, on the other.

By the term *homosexual cravings*, I refer not to homoerotic interest, nor to desire for homosexual activity, but to a very disturbing form of conflict arising from vague to clear consciousness of a desire to engage in the genital stimulation of other persons of the same sex, when the self is in violent opposition to this tendency. Homosexual cravings may appear very insidiously in a personality unaware of homoerotic interests, or very dramatically in one morbidly certain of heteroerotic interests. Thus, an adolescent of the graphically isolated type may quite unwittingly arrange opportunities for sexual activity with another of the same sex, and become aware of the meaning of the situation only when it succeeds *or* fails. In the latter case, the frustration is so acute that he cannot longer remain unmindful of his wish, and conflict immediately appears. In the former, the shock of finding himself cooperative is the initial phenomenon of conflict. In the defensively heterosexual individual, the last mentioned denouement may occur, or the subversive desire may gain expression in remembered dreams or in behavior in states of reduced consciousness—*e.g.*, alcoholic intoxication, or light sleep. In any case, the appearance within awareness of the homoerotic interest stirs such violent self-reproach that a dissociation or a vigorous defensive process results. If the self is able to dissociate the abhorrent system, the personality continues thereafter to be in grave danger of panic with succeeding schizophrenia, unless the sexual tensions are being drained off by some collateral procedure such as frequent masturbation or more or less definitely autosexual intercourse with women. Moreover, under cover of the dissociation, experience in any case continues to be integrated into the dissociated system, and its partition of energy in the personality to grow.

After the appearance of homosexual cravings, the individual finds himself much distracted, with reduced "power of concentration" owing to interference with his other interests, and corresponding impairment of efficiency in his routine life. The sexual tendencies, whether still accessible to awareness or existing in complete dissociation from the self-consciousness, tend to integrate interpersonal situations in which the abhorrent behavior might occur, and create relevance and strong (positive or negative) interest in suitable people and their views and behavior in keeping with the tendencies. The opposing tendencies within the self tend to integrate situations and to determine relevance and interest in sexually unattractive people and in personal acts and utterances strongly opposed to homosexual procedures. Both sorts of situations tend to be integrated, with more or less complete blocking of satisfaction to either group of tendencies. The accumulation of sexual or other erotic tension increases the power of the related tendencies, and an accidental encounter with a person particularly suitable for the sexual behavior generally precipitates an acute disturbance. Not uncommonly this denouement is facilitated by the subject-individual's preternatural naiveté, by which he is led to attempting the integration of an interpersonal situation favorable to the self—to the dissociating system opposed to the erotic strivings—with a person equally conflictful or defensive towards complementary sexual desires. In either case, it is but a matter of time and the flow of events until the victim finds himself being swept towards an abhorrent consummation. If panic does not supervene, a grave defensive process such as the paranoid state may now appear, or the individual may adopt a course of occasional lapses into the contemned satisfactions, with remorse or increasing desperation, thereafter.

It might be thought that the outcropping of homosexual cravings could occur only in those without experience in sexual behavior with others of their own sex. It would seem that all those who had passed through the gang sexuality would be insured from these grave eventualities. There are, however, important exceptions to these generalizations. The preadolescent who is estopped from the growth of heteroerotic interests, and who is engaged in frank homosexual performances, comes ultimately to the time when most of his one-time partners have outgrown his type of interest. He now experiences instead of the social sanction of his behavior—which disintegrated or dissociated any earlier inhibitions he brought from the juvenile era—a slowly increasing influx of unfavorable reflections from the other boys. He may continue the sexual and other erotic satisfaction by associating himself with younger boys and progress along the line of a more or less maladjusted homosexual life. If he is an otherwise rather well-developed personality, and is fortunate, he may secure himself a homosexual mate of appropriate status and work out a satisfactory mode of life. But many such boys encounter crisis situations in which a sexual integration leads to great embarrassment, with the appearance in consciousness of a tendency opposed to the homoerotic gratification, that has been growing up to this time in a state of dissociation. And others find themselves in situations in which affectional ties of great importance to the self are increasingly jeopardized by manifestations of the homosexual tendencies. In either case, the sex-condemnatory system may gain expression in some state of reduced consciousness— for example, in a very impressive dream. There may come a night in the course of which the boy awakens in terror from a dream in which a Voice has uttered a warning, couched usually in general ethical terms, that puts an end to comfortable sexual behavior. These sudden reintegrations of tendencies opposed to homosexual activity in turn set up the situation of homosexual cravings, with consequences similar to those above indicated. That the outcome in these individuals who have had earlier overt experience is somewhat less ominous than is the case in its absence is not only theoretically to be expected, but actually the case both in the paranoid developments and in those who undergo schizophrenic disorders.[4]

In those who have grown past puberty without any direct contact with mutual genital interests, one often finds a dissociation of some of the erotic tendencies, usually including the sexual. There is apt to be delayed pubescence in these boys, and their personality warp is often of the type that culminates in homoerotic interests. The primitive genital phobia may have been an important factor in their deviation, or there may have been dissociation of the genital (phobic) or other erotic tendencies in late childhood or the juvenile era. One may learn, for example, of an instance when the boy, as a juvenile, reported to one of his parents some sexually motivated behavior of an older boy, some vulgarism heard or seen around school, or some precocious experimentation, with a reception of the data so painful that the related interest was excluded from the self.[5] As the sexual tensions increase, there come nocturnal emissions with or without remembered dreams, and an involuntary reactivation and interest in data previously acquired and currently available as to sexual matters. There may be consideration of "trying masturbation to see what it is really like," and other conscious preoccupations

[4] Some considerable number of these people, on the appearance of the *craving* situation, adopt a modified course of interpersonal relations, discontinuing all overt homosexual acts and becoming mildly paranoid towards all members of the same sex, carry on a vigorous (juvenile) social life with women, and often finally marry a daughter-equivalent, with whom there is sufficient potency to insure offspring—a very gratifying demonstration of virility.

[5] Perhaps an example will point towards the important dynamic summation and cancellation arising from sentiments and stereotypes concerned in this sort of ethical learning. A boy a little over five years of age for the first time observed his father's penis, semi-erect, and hastened to the mother and maiden (maternal) aunt with the report that "Daddy has a great big dickey, and it's made of wood." The information proved extremely disconcerting to the auditors, and his interest in other people's penes was dissociated. Within six months, however, he, in company of some men, witnessed coitus of a bull and a cow, and reported this interesting event to the self-same audience, with a notably different reception. The aunt's reaction of shocked virtue proved amusing to the mother, who refused to be chagrined. The juvenile then prehended several personal facts, including the unwisdom of discussing such events with women. The dissociation was lifted, it now being necessary merely to suppress behavior (including speech) about such things when in the women's company.

with sexual topics—even discussions, when started by another boy. But actual behavior is delayed, on various pretexts, and enough unwillingness displayed to discourage opportunities for mutual performances. When finally autosexual behavior begins, there is much self-condemnation, and efforts to augment the "will-power" against it. Not only does this fail, but the boy generally experiences incidents in which he finds himself remarkably free from conflict and self-reproach in satisfying the sexual tendencies. In retrospect he is disconcerted at realizing how "depraved" he can be in states of sexual excitement. He may suffer great self-reproach and make extreme efforts to lift himself from the degradation, seeking aid from the church or the family doctor. Spartan habits of life may be adopted. Physical exertion may become the only serious matter in life.[6] The diet may be modified. Sleep may be interfered with. Everything is done to insure the sexually-inhibitory system within the self from dissociation or suppression by incidents of sexual excitement, with the ensuing appalling abandon to sexual sin. A stream of evil consequences comes to attach to the sexual acts, aiding thereby the suppression of the system. "Weakness," loss of mental ability, aches and pains here and there, but especially in the region of the spinal cord—everything to the proverbial growth of hair in the palms of the hands—come to serve the self in the contest with sexuality. The traditions of damage by masturbation exist widespread in the medical profession, the clergy, and among parents. Masturbation is alleged to lead to enfeeblement of the body and of the mind, to "insanity," and to physical disease. The troubled adolescent who seeks help in overcoming sexual impulses can always find someone to supply these lurid details.[7] His

[6] One of these boys—who became pubescent at the age of seventeen and a half years—remarked to me, after his fourth schizophrenic episode before the age of twenty, that he thought some of the boys "expressed themselves in athletics" (his chosen course), while others, the unfortunate minority for some reason unable to use this method, "expressed themselves in sex."

[7] The student should appreciate that there is a considerable part of the population in which there has been no great problem in handling masturbation, for the good reason that it did not occur to anybody that the individuals concerned might have such a problem; thus there was no particular puritanic interference with their lives, and they progressed from masturbation to more satisfying sexual performances without any stress. This is the normal

failure in control of the sexual impulses then brings increasing results.

The boy who has been led to expect some determinate evil consequence from masturbation, but who cannot control the impulse to the extent of suppressing the behavior, progresses into a sad state. Under cover of what appearance of complacency he is able to muster, he seeks in every personal contact the feared confirmation of the damage he believes to be ensuing. His chagrin at being the victim of his own penis increases, and his self-respect is so gravely reduced that he grows more and more subject to embarrassment. Blushing, shiftiness of gaze, even sudden impediments of speech, contribute to his humiliation. Social cooperation becomes most painful to him and he tends to seclude himself, or to develop screen-activities more or less unwittingly directed to the distraction of attention from his extreme self-contempt. His awareness is often occupied with pessimistic sexual reveries, and these tend often to focus in some part of the somatic schematization of the self. If he has been caused to anticipate mental enfeeblement, he is apt to evolve not alone symptoms to be explained as the effects of preoccupation, but also aches and pains in the head and neck. The inability to "concentrate" in routine work and the incapacity to integrate a satisfactory sleep-situation combine to produce chronic fatigue, and the picture of so-called neurasthenia appears.[8] If he has been led to anticipate bodily evils perhaps from the loss of semen, these tend to be represented

course of events in dogs, horses, apes, and men who are not suffering too much from unfortunate social intervention. Many of these more fortunate people later encounter the traditions in common speech, in smoking car discussion of sexual topics, and the like. They are prone to develop secondary convictions about masturbation based in part on their own superiority and in part on actual facts, and come to regard and to talk about it as childish. Their influence, however, is relatively innocuous unless they chance to be psychiatrists or doting uncles, and has little to do with the path of destruction that ensues from chronic masturbation. Sometimes, however, the patient—or the nephew—who 'knows' that his continued masturbation is enfeebling his body, being pooh-poohed by these well-meaning ones who have "put away childish things," thus acquires a new conviction of evil in the form of a belief that he is interfering with his masturbation.

[8] The meaning of this chronic fatigue and the neurasthenic picture will become more clear after the discussion of Sleep, in Chapter IX [not included here].

nuisances may be adopted, and the youth from thenceforth strives increasingly to bolster his self-respect by vanquishing the singular difficulties that he encounters in getting the right things to eat—becoming a burden to himself and everyone else who gives him a meal, additional to the misfortune implied in being important chiefly as a person who has diminished gastric capacity.[9]

This hypochondriacal interference with bodily function is especially apt to focus in the genital apparatus itself. The pessimistic reverie centers on the offending organ and a variety of urological and genitourinary symptoms appear. These may be anything from rumination on the discovery of hitherto unnoted anatomical peculiarities—such as the customary discrepancy in size of the two divisions of the scrotum—to delusion formations and hallucinated symptoms amounting to schizophrenia. Frequently, the overattention to the genitals begins in an unimpressive manner, and the boy is treated by his advisor as merely uninformed. He is told that nothing is the matter with him, that he is perfectly normal. This does not help in solving his masturbation conflict, and he either seeks a new advisor or develops more symptoms with which to harass the first. Not infrequently he secures some treatment, even if it is only a suspensory bandage—the wearing of which makes consciousness of the genitals even more acute. Occasionally, he is given intensive treatment for something or other allegedly physically wrong with him. He may undergo an operation for the repair of a perhaps authentic varicocele, or of a patulous inguinal ring. He may be urethroscoped or even cystoscoped—an experience not immediately to be forgotten. It may be found that his verumontanum is congested, and deep urethral instillations may be made. And his prostate may

[9] The pylorus seems generally to mark in the somatic schematization of the self, the end of the *upper part* of the alimentary tract. The oral erotic type of personality, usually unwittingly, "draws the line" in symptom formation at this point. He is pre-eminently the victim of "diseases"—and their "treatment"—of the mouth, nose and throat, and stomach. He contributes much to the specialties of dentistry, rhinology, and laryngology—including tonsil-removing—, and gastroenterology. He may involve the lungs or the heart as an extension, but he seldom gets below the stomach—excepting he proceed directly to the genital tract—excepting *to screen* more or less clearly prehended oral desires.

in his gloomy ruminations, and a hypochondriacal state may supervene. The coenaesthesia, the influx of sentience arising in the viscera, that forms an important element in the backgrounding of personal reality, is affected. Attention swings gradually to particular items in this flow of sentience, and the interest fixed in the region concerned begins to disturb the somatic functional activity. Phenomena which should continue to be of the character of local physiological action are elevated into focal consciousness, and made part of the total integration, subject to influence from situational factors that should normally have no connection with them. The somatic unity is strangely disturbed so that the stomach, for example, may be required in addition to its activity in dealing with part of our physico-chemical food intake, to function in some relation to a quite different universe of communal existence—viz., the symbolic-social and cultural. It is integrated more or less specifically (as symbolically schematized) into situations in which not foodstuffs but perceived and fancied aspects of interpersonal situations are concerned. It is stimulated and inhibited in relation to the digestion of social contexts. The gastric secretion of hydrochloric acid tends now to be excessive and wholly unutilized in the depraved "digestion." The hyperacidity gives rise to symptoms from irritation of the already hyperaesthetic nerve-endings, and the coenaesthetic influx becomes peculiarly rich in the very data that has been made prepotent. The musculature of the stomach tends to become hypertonic, and spasm of the pylorus is added to the sources of discomfort and gloomy rumination. Pain, burning sensations, excessive and often peculiar appetite, epigastric distress before or after eating, "heartburn," anorexia, and even vomiting—all these confirm the sufferer in the conviction of bodily ruin. A vicious circle is established, with increasing detachment of the sufferer from more externally conditioned events, and an increasing partition of energy to fantasy processes. The doctor to whom this boy is sent may or may not discover the "functional" nature of the trouble. If he does not, a gastric ulcer is suspected and perhaps "discovered." If he does, he is apt to have little to offer the patient, and often prescribes antacids, and other more or less active drugs—with novel increments to the difficulty. Or dietary be examined, to the extent of massage—quite a destructive experience, especially if any excess of erogeny attaches to the anal region. Or again, his complaints of *night losses,* or *losses at stool,* or *a drop that follows urination,* or of *peculiar sensations* in the scrotum, groin, or perineum—any or all of these may be diagnosed as "sexual neurasthenia"—and everything from electrical claptrap and 'violet rays,' to firm counsel to buck up, forget it, or get himself a woman, is prescribed in its treatment. If he is extraordinarily unfortunate, he consults a quack "specialist for men," and from thenceforth is treated for money only, with liberal cultivation of new symptoms, so that he can always be "refeed" [i.e., charged further fees] whenever he seems to have more money. In any case, it is rather certain that he has *not* presented to his advisor an understandable account of his trouble, for the excellent reason that he does not have full access to the data concerned.[10] And in any case, he will follow one of three courses: a progression to grave mental disorder; a settled hypochondriacal state, itself a rather serious mental disorder; [11] or a marked improvement when an all too frequently quite accidental event of interpersonal relations starts him towards a more adjustive solution of his sexual problem.

Many youths in the grip of severe conflict between the sexual drives and tendencies opposed to masturbation never establish a situation of mutual confidence with another person. Some of them attempt it, and find themselves in so anomalous a position

[10] It would be a great mistake to assume from these comments that *all* "functional" (*i.e.,* nonorganic) genitourinary complaints of adolescents are concomitants of masturbation conflict. The fundamental thesis of this presentation emphasizes that *no phenomenon of total activity can be stripped of its personal embodiment and translated directly into causative factors.* There are no personality phenomena that always mean a particular thing. It is true that these hypochondriacal complaints centering in the genitals *often* arise as sequents in a conflict over masturbation. They *occasionally* arise from quite different sexual sources. They *may* arise in the course of an apparently normal heterosexual life.

[11] The more or less stable hypochondriacal sexual maladjustments that contribute so much to the income of quacks and the like may be closely related to defense reactions by projection of blame. We encounter many individuals who progress from hypochondriasis to paranoid state, and some who show a sort of alternation of the two states to such effect that they are chronically either paranoid *or* hypochondriac.

that they give up hope of securing assistance. Thus, the boys in high or preparatory school may be given a lecture on sex hygiene, with the suggestion that all those who wish may confer with the professor in private. Unless the lecturer has created an impression of most extraordinary sympathy, the really harassed pupils go nowhere near him. Not uncommonly, however, some of the more intelligent pupils do seek him out and attempt to convey to him their formulation of the problem. All too often they have the attitude of "knowing it all," of dispensing pearls of wisdom to the ignorant. A boy who has, for reasons susceptible of discovery, come to suppose that erections of his penis constitute that which is called masturbation, then "learns" a body of confusions that adds quite remarkably to his troubles—without the helpful advisor having any suspicion that they have been discussing barely related topics in using a common term. Or the boy finds that the advisor's thirst for intimate data repels him, and despite the best of intentions, claims problems that have little reality and avoids any frankness. Or yet again, he plunges desperately into confidences that are for discoverable reason intensely interesting to the advisor, only to meet rebuff and upbraiding, to be bathed in ethical whey that nourishes the conflict, or to find that his confidant's interest is expended as soon as the spicy details are exhausted and that the interview is being terminated with banal assurances and some haste to get on to the next boy.[12] The expectation that a youth who is suffering a severe masturbation conflict will be so facile at confidence as to be intelligently frank in the initial interview with a stranger is at best rather fantastic —while the optimism that leads a counselor to give advice in a situation thus uncertainly adumbrated is but another demonstration of the low regard in which personality is held by that great majority who have not enough personal insight to know that problems of living transcend matters of gossip or preaching.

In the adolescents who manifest these genital hypochondriases, we often encounter the so-called *castration fear* or anxiety. By

[12] We are not concerned here with the well-organized teaching of sex information in the grammar school. The feasibility of this highly desirable instruction has already been demonstrated. Also, the unwisdom of abbreviated and poorly managed courses of this kind is well known to the psychopathologist.

this term, we refer to a particular component of personality that has arisen from some more or less specific experience sequence in childhood or early in the juvenile era. It may be that a parent or someone else in authority over the child has enforced his disapproval of genital manipulation by a direct threat to the effect that if the behavior is continued, the penis will be cut off—perhaps pointing the threat by exhibiting the instrument to be used; *e.g.*, a pair of scissors. Or it may be that some intercurrent misfortune is coincident with a situation in which the child is enjoying the forbidden pleasure, and the two become confluent. Thus, an attack of earache coming on after the child has retired and engaged in some genital stimulation, *known to be severely disapproved* (sinful) may have the effect of a punishment for the sin, and become dynamically as effective as a direct threat of amputation of the penis. Finally, a stream of unfortunate events may become associated with the genital pleasure, and lead the child on some occasion to wish that the offending member did not exist. This thought, however, represents a complex fantasy of change in the somatic representations of the self, and usually one that the child has been taught to regard as also "sinful." It brings with it threats of evil that would flow from the "remedy." There is now a secondary conflict, and confusion of the self-integration, with fear of a magical tendency of the injury to occur as punishment for the prohibited genital manipulation.[13] If any of these influences add to the self enough energy to dissociate the then relatively feeble impulses making for genital stimulation, there is apt to be no recrudescence of the problem until preadolescence. In the meanwhile, the memorial elements of the actual events are overlaid with the details of life, and, in common with all reflections to the self that have given pain, tend to fail of ready recall—in fact, frequently to exist in the repressed quasi-mythological condition. When now in adolescence the

---

[13] These rather obscure processes, as they are revealed in individual personalities, are closely related to the category next preceding—in turn related to the direct threat of "castrating," *i.e.*, amputating the penis. The religious culture built into the personality is the link from act to fear. It is another manifestation of the effect of inculcating the doctrines of crime and punishment, sin and penitential act, from which comes the generalization of the need for punishment.

genital sexuality makes appearance and conflict supervenes, these
earlier relatively inaccessible deviations may manifest in the service of the opposing tendencies as an undue fear of evil consequences to flow from masturbatory or other sexual behavior, and
a deepening hypochondriasis.[14]

An occasional outcome of all these sorts of adolescent conflict
is *suicide*. Besides the self-destruction that may terminate the
graver mental disorders, there also occur instances in which the
act is not preceded by serious disorder of social behavior. Some
adolescents are so baffled in their attempt to subjugate the interest
in autoerotic satisfactions that they destroy themselves almost as
if in revenge on the offending part of the somatic equipment. The
paralysis of interest in others and in future possibilities of the
self has progressed in them to the point that life has become
colorless and wholly unattractive. Their deaths may therefore
be classed as quasi-rational, in contradistinction to those of the
depressed and the schizophrenic youth. The probability of self-
destruction is always rather high in the course of the manic-
depressive depression—particularly in the stage of convalescence.[15]
Deaths resulting from personal acts in the course of schizophrenic
disorders are often the result of misadventure. The sufferer ends

[14] The conception of castration fear has been overgeneralized, as have
those of compensation, sublimation, and the defense reactions. The enthusiasts for this interpretation reason somewhat as follows: the penis is all-
important; therefore, any reverse or reduction in self-esteem, leads to a feeling of castration, and all the non-pleasant emotions are but manifestations of
"the castration complex," or castration fear, anxiety, etc. I do not wish to
minimize the importance of the penis as a factor in personality: a medium-
sized man with a small penis is generally very different in his attitude to
others, from a medium-sized man with a large penis—everything else being
equal. But the notion that the penis can be equated to or made to exceed in
importance anything or everything else in the male personality is absurd.
The interpreting of any derogatory or aggressive behavior as castrative does
not seem to be particularly illuminating. In fact, all this sort of universalizing
"reasoning" reminds one of the "henid" of Weininger, or the grammatic
definition reported in one of the "Boner" series: all sentences are either
abstract *or cement*.
[15] The greater number of suicides at all ages is to be referred to this
disorder. Deep depression in a personality characterized by more or less
cyclic mood swings should always indicate great care in this particular,
to be redoubled as the patient improves and seems to be fairly near his
average state. A great many of these patients have destroyed themselves in
the course of the first "visit" home from the mental hospital.

his life quite incidentally to some fantastic procedure for the remedy of his distress: to be reborn, to protect others from some delusional contamination, to save the world, to demonstrate omnipotence, and the like. Psychopathic and other badly warped adolescents sometimes "use" the threat of suicide as a tool for insuring attention from others, and occasionally die as a result of "accidental" misjudgment—too great a dose of poison, too long a delay in calling for help, and so forth. These latter, in particular, manifest the tendency that is called the wish for death.[16] This complex motivation that manifests superficially as a desire for death, or even in facilitation of self-destructive impulses, is of far from a unitary source. *Passim*, the disturbances of the somatic schematization connected with this motivation tend frequently to concentrate about the head in the form of recurrent headaches, migraine, and neuralgias.

Consideration of suicide takes us to the contemplation of religious interpretations of the observed growth of personality by the long-circuiting of tendency-systems. *Hope*, which we may define as the integration in a total situation of more or less probable but contingent factors subsisting in the future, carries many people through severe disappointments and states of temporary thwarting to belated success or old age without despair. The religious cultures which have sprung up from time to time have included formulae in this connection, very frequently offering, as matter for integration in one's current situation, factors not of a mere earthly future but of a transcendental Future Life, to be experienced only after this one is finished—often to be gained only by approval of the priestly caste. These doctrines have

---

[16] Freud, in *Beyond the Pleasure Principle*, and in his subsequent writings, has developed a conception of "death instincts" that are universally distributed in people, and opposed to the "life instincts." This is part of the so-called metapsychological formulation, the philosophy of Freud. Like all other philosophies, it is insusceptible of rigorous demonstration, and may be considered to be valid for its formulator and some others of related life experience. I do not recommend its wide adoption. The student is certain to have difficulty enough preventing premature crystallizations of his own opinions in some universalizations of terms. For a discussion of the wish for death, see, for example, Ernest E. Hadley, "Vertigo and the Death Wish," *J. Nervous and Mental Disease* (1927) 65:131–148; and perhaps *ibid.*, "Presidential Address of the Washington Psychopathological Association," *Psychoanalytic Rev.* (1928) 15:384–392.

served to render the prehended real *rational*, and have been a great boon to those who live by the exploitation of the socially underprivileged, who are taught to seek their reward for unhappy compliance here, in the shimmering expanses of the Other World. Unfortunately, whenever man power has come to be valuable to the Elite, there has had to be added to these doctrines a restraint calculated to overcome a certain urgency of the particularly thwarted about reaching the realms of bliss.[17] Interest in the Future State comes easily to the denizens of any social order of extreme inequality of opportunity, if the greater number have no means for prehending the real inequalities of personal abilities and opportunities, or have no means of communicating these prehensions from one to another. When, however, the adaptive culture available to the most unfortunate caste has grown to the point at which many of its denizens become aware of these individual variations in personal ability and in the opportunities provided, then, if the social fabric is to be preserved in its grossly discriminative state by dependence on a Future State and related dogmata, some universal tendency system that cannot be entirely restrained has to be legislated out of bounds. The underprivileged then obviously fail to live up to the rules, and are open to censure and punishment. Merely secular law can scarcely serve in this connection, for the more enlightened masses at least vaguely surmise that secular authority vests in their collective submission. The law that disqualifies a part of human nature must therefore be transcendentally sanctioned; it must be an addition to the mores, as such inculcated into most people within the family-group; and it must be wholly exterior to the social criticism that begins in the juvenile era. The tendency systems

---

[17] Saint Augustine, I believe, made it against the rules in the Western culture for one to hasten his translation from this vale of woes. Psychopathologically considered, suicide, while always anti-biological, was rational and pseudo adjustive up to the time of this religious enactment (dogma). It would be interesting to trace the cultural processes that fixed the time at which Western Europeans were required thus to forego the privilege of expediting their receipt of the Heavenly reward. Now that the religious culture is deliquescing and the Hereafter is losing value along with the other dogmata, current adolescent suicides are not at all in the class of the pre-Augustinian flights to eternal bliss, and must be regarded as irrational and nonadjustive.

that have been subjected to this dogmatic thwarting in our culture are numerous, but by far the most powerful of them is that manifesting in sexual behavior.[18]

The adolescent of bygone generations often came promptly to be "religious." He accepted the entrenched regulations of life perforce. One could not but interpret one's own peculiarities as Satanic—good reason for seeking to learn the rules by which to live through the years in this cruel world accumulating as much merit as might be towards the blessed future. Sexual asceticism was the greatest good, and both organized and informal opportunities for its achievement were provided. Once one had turned from the lure of the flesh, one could live quietly in a considerable measure of sanctified intimacy with a group of kindred souls. Or one could take to a dignified paranoid state and go about a slow "psychical castration." If schizophrenic phenomena appeared, this did not necessarily disable one: quite a few opportunities for utilizing this eccentricity were provided in the business of evangelism. Moreover, one might, if needs be, found an eccentric religion and often secure the necessary disciples. If there was some skidding on the slippery path to superhuman chastity and other fantastic virtues, these could be charged off as temporary gains in the losing battle waged against the good by the Evil One. The sweet odor of sanctity could best be appreciated in the ecstasy of repentance for Sin. The noble rhetoric of those whose duty it was "to be cruel to be kind" was so powerful that a multitude of little prophets interpreted the Almighty Ones to their followers, without uncertainty as to the accuracy or completeness of their information. Sex without issue was Sin. And as

---

[18] I would not wish to be interpreted as holding that the structure of the mores has arisen by *deliberate acts* of theocrats or others aware of the dynamics with which they operate. Far from it; the mores have arisen as the implemented fantasies of religious leaders, generally highly rationalized in the faiths that they professed. These fantasies, being those of people of more or less related cultural backgrounds, have been acceptable to the followers—if the latter did not *know better*—i.e., have culture actually adaptive to life in the particulars concerned. That those fantasies have functioned to promote achievement, and to work extreme cruelty, are alike beside the point. The day is still far beyond the scope of the writer's imagination when there will be no mores, no religious culture, but only adaptive ways of doing things.

sex is inescapable in youth, issue was abundant; and the wheels of the growing industries, and the guns of the growing States, and the coffers of the budding capitalists, turned them.

The Renaissance, the rapid growth of physical sciences and technologies, and the dissemination of literateness, were some of the factors that hastened the flowering of the religions of nationalism that had been growing parasitically on the religions of the Other Worlds. Education in mundane things, even today in its infancy, nonetheless accomplished some realization of secondary group relationships. It interlocked in this effect with the rapidly expanding systems of transportation and communication. Concentrations of population in urban centers functioned to accelerate the dissolution of many superstitions of various primary groups. The ascetic ideal grew increasingly absurd, and the ideal of the brotherhood of man moved off even further beyond the horizon. Disillusionment became the spirit of the times. Superstitions that had at least the virtue of wide acceptance were destroyed in wholesale. The claptrap of statecraft was offered in their place. But the nationalist theocrats were puny specimens in contrast with the great of old who manifested but ephemeral glory here, in their tedious proconsulate for the Transcendental Ones. It became increasingly difficult to conceal from the now verbal masses the shallow and shortsighted self-seeking of most representatives of the State. The ministration to the common weal was observed very frequently to lead to personal profit. Even the mighty rhetoric, automatic acceptance of which seems all too human, was degraded in political bickerings for preferment—the successful achievement of which often led to so immediate a profit-taking that it violated public decorum. Money— now regarded by some psychoanalysts as a transubstantiation of the infant's meconium—and Power—similarly regarded as the castration of the father—became the matters of importance. The Western culture had progressed into late childhood, and the adolescent must look to earthly preferments instead of treasures in Heaven. The socialization of men, the collaboration of compeers, the integration of enduring and benevolent intimacies—for these even the religious culture was becoming tenuous. Those who could find their way through the jungle along the footpaths adaptive to money or power might fare passing well. But those who turned aside from these pursuits and sought a fairly human life risked their necks amid eldritch wonders of crumbling faiths matted together with a swiftly growing fungus of laws and short-lived institutions exuded by antisocial statesmen in the protection of special privilege. Individualism and National Independence were the watchwords. The Great War taught many adolescents the futility of the new religions of individualism and nationalism, even as it gave birth to a rival to the growing international faith, capitalism, in the shape of the communistic dogmata. The theocrats of the two have ever since waged war under warrant of the noble rhetoric, to which not alone the most underprivileged, but most of the Elite, still attend devoutly.[19]

At the level of least social privilege where hunger, squalor, pariah-hood, abysmal ignorance, and often disease, combine to emphasize the consciousness of utter inferiority, there are born some infants who embody exceptional abilities. Some of these not only survive but come to adolescence. If their personalities are not already so warped that they might well be dead, or accident has not lifted them somewhat above their expectations, these youths generally find themselves confronted with the alternatives of grave mental disorder or crime. Compulsory education and the less estimable of the public prints equip them to rebel against their apparent fate. Their intelligence and experience dissipate notions of preferment in Church, State, scientific or learned pursuits. They readily discover that in commerce or industry

---

[19] The panic of 1929 and the slough that followed it pointed to something so radically wrong in all that had gone before, that the religious culture of the Western World at the time of this writing survives almost wholly by human inertia and the necessity to fill the gaps in our grasp on life. The Chief Executive and other exalted American theocrats counsel patience while the "economic pendulum" slowly swings back to "American normalcy" —allegedly a *natural* cyclic phenomenon—while striving with might and main to *do something* that will give their creeds new "face" by temporarily extricating the people from their misery. Some little lasting good will doubtless come out of the political expediency, but it is to be hoped by the thoughtful that something more than emergency patchwork will take place. Encouragement may be found in the increasingly vocal dissatisfaction of a few of the great industrial leaders. When the most privileged in our world of money and power perceive the inadequacy of our current religions, fundamental remedies should be near.

they can "get ahead" only by patiently accommodating themselves for an indefinite but certainly long period to the pattern of the moron. They readily infer that there is no ultimate necessity for the extreme hardships that they encounter—that in fact these inequalities that deny them any opportunity to enjoy the exercise of their abilities are ordained by nothing more august than a group of men in the stupidly selfish exercise of power. If they express their grievances by merely verbal behavior, they come promptly to discover that one's voice does not carry if one has neither money nor power. And if they act more directly, they violate the all-pervading web of laws, and are apt to find that they have forfeited even the little security the State grants to "the least of its subjects." Never sympathetic towards the myth of Justice, such a one has long since learned that even the Established Elite must sometimes resort to the highest courts to protect their rights and privileges. It seems also that status or money are often needed to energize even the first cogs of this machinery of protection, so God-like in its leisurely indifference and arbitrariness, so punily human in many of its personifications. At the same time, such a one is taught that there is nothing to insure one from being seized upon by this machinery of Criminal Justice. This is a part of evil chance that inheres in one's lack of status. It is quite impossible to live within the letter of the Law, which no one any longer knows in its entirety and which everyone is by definition made to know. And there are generally instances to be observed of *highly selective*, mean, partisan, and criminal interventions of this machinery to wreak unmerited hardship on some unfortunate compeers. Aware that one cannot without fortunate accident "earn" enough by legitimate activity to "pay" those whose income derives from providing a roof over one's head, heat in cold weather, and food, it is not strange that the underprivileged adolescent of superior ability often chooses to be exploited by organized crime. Here he finds opportunity for the competitive pursuit of status, for he is at last opposed to compeers in the established order. Here he can fraternize intimately with some kindred souls. And even the sexual tendencies may often be dealt with somewhat more satisfactorily than was the case before he embarked on his "career." [20]

Crime, generally definable as the wilful violation of any law that is alleged to protect the public, assumes the proportions of a special problem in relation to adolescence. According to the archaic dogmata from which one Law proceeds, a person grows from irresponsible infancy to some point at which he achieves free will, knowledge of all the laws, the capacity to intend public damage, the ability to know and judge the nature and consequences of one's acts, and an exquisite discrimination as to the difference between right and wrong. Before this marvelous point has been achieved, one cannot *intend* an act to the extent required for the perpetration of most full-fledged crimes. But all citizens achieve this point at one and the same particular *chronological* age, excepting one be "insane," "mentally incompetent," or "of unsound mind." As the student may surmise, the psychobiologist has a certain difficulty in this field; he cannot find anything but dogma in the entity, free will; he is certain that only a small proportion of the citizens are capable of learning the more coherent of the laws, much less the vast body of statutes and similar ordinances that are in fact the Law; he has not previously granted much importance to the business of "intending" within awareness; he has come to view almost all intentions as good rationalizations that seemed chiefly to obscure from the self all that might be judged unworthy in the effective motivation of one's behavior and thought.[21]

[20] A chapter entitled "The Working of Welfare" [not included here] survived the fourth revision of this book. Its elimination should not endanger the thesis that the personal embodiments of law and other alleged welfare institutions with whom people enter into primary (direct) relationships mean more to most of the denizens of the culture than do the more abstract entities that these agents more or less imperfectly make manifest. As long as the personnel of law enforcement and other welfare work is recruited without regard for the nuclear fact that these agents should *work primarily in the extraordinarily difficult field of interpersonal relations, for benevolent ends,* the excogitation of laws and philanthropies will be somewhat futile. Once more than merely verbal acknowledgement of this nuclear fact has been achieved, the problem of training this personnel for its function may receive some measure of the attention that it warrants. . . .

[21] At this point one may well notice that the criminal law finds it con-

The psychobiologist, by arduous self-searching, comparative studies, and inferences from phenomena that have seemed to occur while he slept, has come to some insight into the "nature" and purpose of some of his own actions in emotionally toned interpersonal situations, to such effect that he is able to predict the consequences that might flow from them. When he turns to the general public—and particularly to the underprivileged sections of it—the *assumption* of this difficult achievement is glaringly ridiculous. Obviously "the nature and consequences of one's acts" must be something quite different from insight into one's motivation in a total situation. . . . The psychobiologist has been trained to suspect common sense when it passes beyond the field of sensory observation, and to scrutinize the presuppositions on which supposed observations are made by intelligent individuals. He may recall with faint amusement some of the notable "observations" made by students of the Watsonian Behaviorism, when it was young. And, finally, he has come to believe that the discrimination of "right" and "wrong" by anyone is generally nothing more than the manifestation of their training in infancy and childhood, as it has survived the later stages of personality growth, and remains effective in the superego aspects of the personality. For that matter, he recalls many instances from his study of personalities, in which evil has been wrought without violating any law. And if he has worked with prisoners, he knows other instances when crime was committed without any evil having been done anyone. His respect for the jurist who works good with this incredible implement of the Law is therefore very great. His expectations regarding the "consequences" to a personality from becoming involved in the criminal law, cannot but be guarded. And, if he has been called to assist in the enforcement of the law, as an expert witness in the trial of someone accused of a crime, he may well extend his pessimism as to "consequences" of a criminal "act" to include all those who are concerned with the legal proc-

---

venient in some cases to *presume* the criminal intention. The wisdom beyond Solomon that each juror manifests in judging these matters of intention is all the more spectacular in that *negligence* (to have the proper good intentions?) may in some cases establish the occurrence of crime, rather than accident—*e.g.*, reckless driving of an automobile. And negligence, too, may be presumed, under some statutes.

esses arising from it—including the public present as visitors in court or as readers of the more sensational newspapers.

The young science of psychobiology and the somewhat older science of biology alike teach the impossibility of securing data susceptible of consensual validation by the study of an *act* torn from its situational context—including the acting organism. The act is of indefinable scope and meaning when it is abstracted from its place in reality, and made the subject of cogitation, as an entity. When, therefore, the State in its business of promoting and protecting the common weal, deals with the acts of certain people without regard for the persons concerned or the cultural and other factors potent in the growth and manifestation of any and all personalities, when it neglects to teach parents the content of each year's crop of legislation, produced by the uninformed and irresponsible representatives of its people in legislature assembled, when it prosecutes and convicts people for violating laws created after they have passed out of the eras of formal instruction, when it functions in its law enforcement through persons largely without training in the rudiments of human nature—awarding to all sorts of prevailing superstitions and prejudices a like place in the administration of justice: under these circumstances, the psychopathologist can scarcely be filled with enthusiasm even for the "remedies" of "treatment" in place of punishment for criminals, of psychiatric commissions to "advise" the courts, of "examination and recommendations in regard to disposition" of all persons convicted of felonies, and the like. To him, it then would seem that there is not very much hope left for those caught up in the web of the criminal law—or in the business of its practical enforcement—for it is a fantastic structure like the world of a mistrained juvenile who seeks to solve social situations by threatening to black the eye of his compeer if not given his own way about everything, regardless of anyone or anything. To succeed for long in this rudimentary method of social control, one would have to be ubiquitous and omnipotent, unthinking, and wholly ruthless. While many agents of the State may secretly aspire to these qualifications, it is probably impossible to turn back the stream of human progress so far that any people will crystallize such an attitude as their State. And, if it happened, this apotheosis of arbitrary social control would scarcely waste its substance and encumber itself with an intricate web of verbally expressed Laws, the administration of which had to find its way through a maze of purely verbal behavior, past and present, the *current meaning* of which had finally to be judged by some weary thinkers sitting on a Supreme Court to adjudicate the more vigorously contested disputes.[22]

History shows that the State has come more and more to discover the spread of damage beyond the persons directly concerned in injurious activities, to the public, at large. This is the general formulation by which it establishes the criminal nature of certain "acts." The next step should follow the even more cogent consideration of the spread of causation beyond the persons most directly concerned in the criminal or other injurious behavior, to the culture itself, and the surfaces of stress between its patterns and the personalities of its denizens. The prohibitive-retaliative character of the Law; the pastoral and agrarian, intolerant mythology underlying our way of law-making and its tawdry enforcement; the particularistic vindictiveness of people trained to regard themselves as autonomous entities having "rights" in their own name; and the entrenched *laissez faire* of those who enjoy privilege—these are some of the more formidable difficulties that must be overcome in remedying these aspects of social control. The profligate abandon to exploitation, accidental utilization, or wholly useless wastage, of the human values now within our power to identify seems, however, to be the most fundamental defect of our culture, from which flows most of our other evils. As long as the individual fruits of human evolution are so worth-

---

[22] This discussion should include considerations of the civil law as distinguished from the criminal, of the doctrine of *torts*, personal injuries as opposed to public injuries (crimes), and of the gradually evolving proceedings in *equity*, now fairly widespread in juvenile and domestic relations courts. In courts of equity and in some courts of criminal justice, an effort is made to deal with meaningful situations, rather than with mythological states of universal equality, etc. I would be remiss, indeed, did I not take occasion to acknowledge the wisdom shown by some of our judges, all the more estimable because of the difficulties which the State (its politicians), the sensation-mongers, and the legitimately evil-doing (therefore very conservative) class, combine to place in the way of enlightened judicial initiative.

less that they can all be thrown into the same bin to rot or keep whole, as chance dictates, it can scarcely matter if some good human material is ground up in the machinery of Law. By the time one now becomes politically significant, he has generally worn himself down to the point at which his formula, his trick of making a living, seems to be about the last thing that he can learn. If it is scrapped by the appearance of a better formula, he may find himself impoverished and his family reduced to want, without hope. It is all "up to" him; life is all a competition, if not a conflict, in which tears are not wasted on the loser. In such a society, we can scarcely expect that the conservation of exceptional human abilities and their untrammeled nurture will become a function of the State.[23]

Whatever his place in the social fabric, the adolescent can scarcely fail to discover in his seeking of a way of life that the satisfaction of some of his tendencies is anything but a simple matter. Mores, Law, economic pressures, population concentration and mobility, intercommunication, disintegrative criticism, privilege, privation—above all, the total disintegration of the stable world for which his parents trained him—combine to impress on him the incomprehensibility of life as it goes on around him. He becomes afraid. Moreover, as he seeks to rid himself of fear, he discovers that everyone is afraid, excepting only the stupid. Three paths open before him. His personality organization and his opportunity determine the course that he shall try. He may be able to postpone the plunge, seeking the relative security of the university and the pursuit of knowledge, perhaps having recourse to compensatory dynamics in reducing the stress that he experiences. But this is no panacea, for he now embodies tendencies that cannot be discharged in this way. Maladjustments of severe degree are frequent—psychoneuroses, anxiety states, even major psychoses—among those to whom the Higher Education is prin-

---

[23] The wolf-pack ideal and references to the profligacy of Nature are not to be condemned, if they are not mixed with a damnable "compassion" that preserves a vast body of people from death, without giving them any justification for life. Once a culture outgrows the "struggle for existence" with infra-human opponents, it doubtless comes to the internecine competitive stage. We seem to be ready to quit this struggle for individual acquisitions for a stage of collaboration in the assembly of enduring values.

cipally a delay in meeting life. He may, particularly if he is enabled by a juvenile personality and the opportunity, adopt the ideal of respectability, and recast himself as rapidly as may be to compliance with the conventional hypocrisies and evasions of his class, making up for the loss of self-esteem by overvaluing material augmentations of his self, and draining off dangerous tensions by a surreptitious "double life," gambling, alcoholic overindulgences, or the pursuit of other excitements that are only partly frustrating—all of which dwarf his potentialities to the level of a solid citizen and fix him in the pattern of late adolescence for life. Or he may identify himself directly or secondarily with a kindred group that lives in some degree of disharmony with the prevailing majority, often somewhat stealthily, coming frequently to waste his youth and energy in misdirected revolt against fantastically exaggerated opposition, in pursuit of poorly judged goals, or in the overzealous nurture of illusion based on misapprehension of what he seeks. It used to be that generally the adolescent came finally to "settle down"—an expression all the better in that the process was often a regressive disintegration of interest from the adolescent state. The "settling" process has grown quite uncertain, of late, and many factors suggest that there will be no return to the good old days.

The lack of culture adaptive to the sexual tendencies, in particular, has been accentuated recently by the changed role of woman as wife and as member of the family-group (mother). The blanket of secrecy and shame that has covered the field of sexual behavior has always functioned to work evil, both by ingraining vicious attitudes to sex and in concealing remediable disharmonies in marriage. Now the difficulties of married life are greatly augmented, for only a part of the depraved attitudes to sex have been dissipated, and the new factors of personal prestige, intersex conflict, economic interdependence, political franchise, etc., combine with the continuing sexual inhibitions to augment marital maladjustments very greatly. Warped adolescents therefore abound, while the Law and the economic *laissez faire* combine to make it ever more difficult for any adolescents to satisfy their sexual tendencies without violation of the mores and the criminal law. The proportion in each generation who must turn aside from the traditional pattern of marriage and the home must grow rapidly, while the number who are estopped by personality warp from any approximation to the heterosexual pattern becomes larger and larger. It appears that the current situation implies an almost geometrically increasing stress between individuals and this part of the social fabric, with outcome in mental disorder or crime. Since it is the ubiquitous and very powerful sexual tendencies that are concerned, it would seem that some intelligence might well be applied to the revision of our culture, if we are to continue to call ourselves civilized, much less to function as a mighty influence in world affairs. . . .

Name Index

* First names have been omitted from entries so marked, since text did not furnish sufficient clue to the positive identity of the author.

Subject Index

† Sullivan's major writings from 1924 through 1935 are marked in this fashion and form a complete bibliography (exclusive of book reviews, brief notes, and so on) for that period.